CLAY LORD

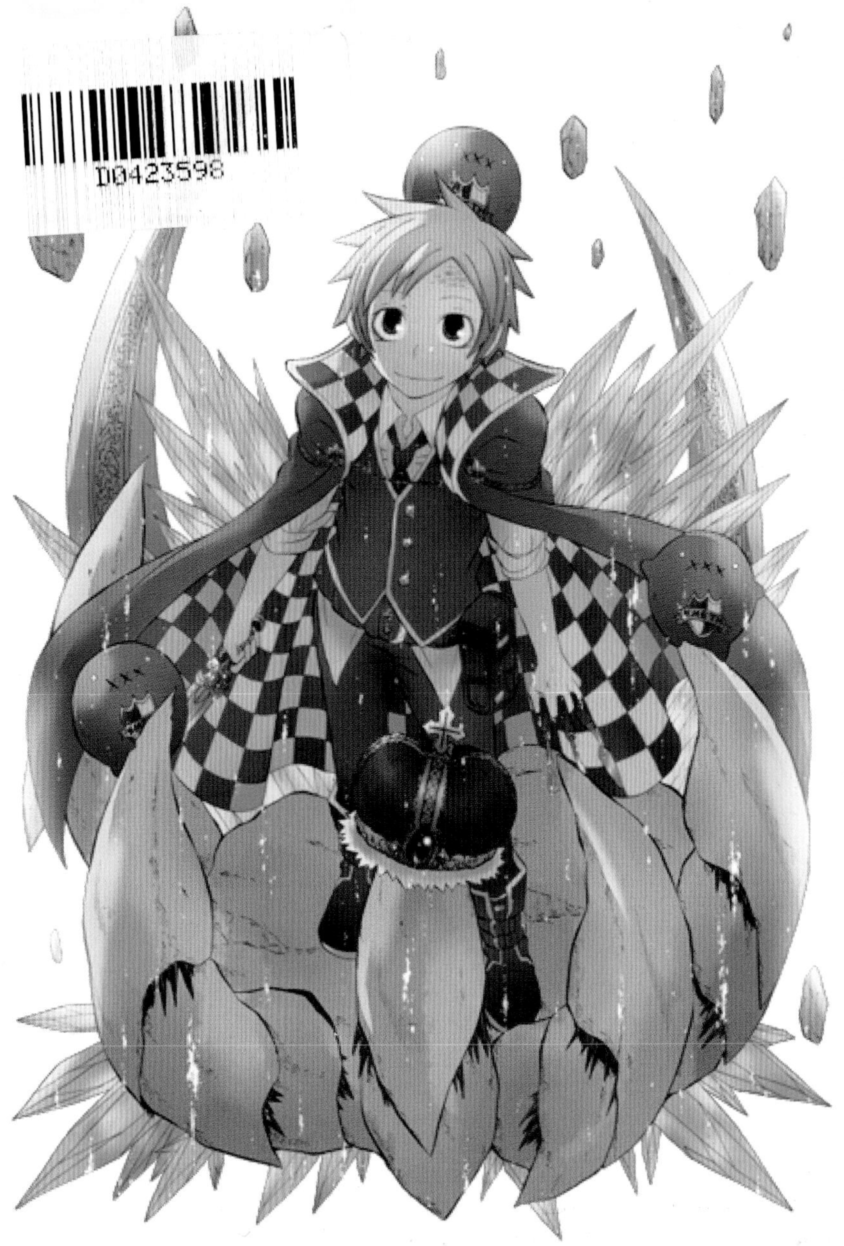

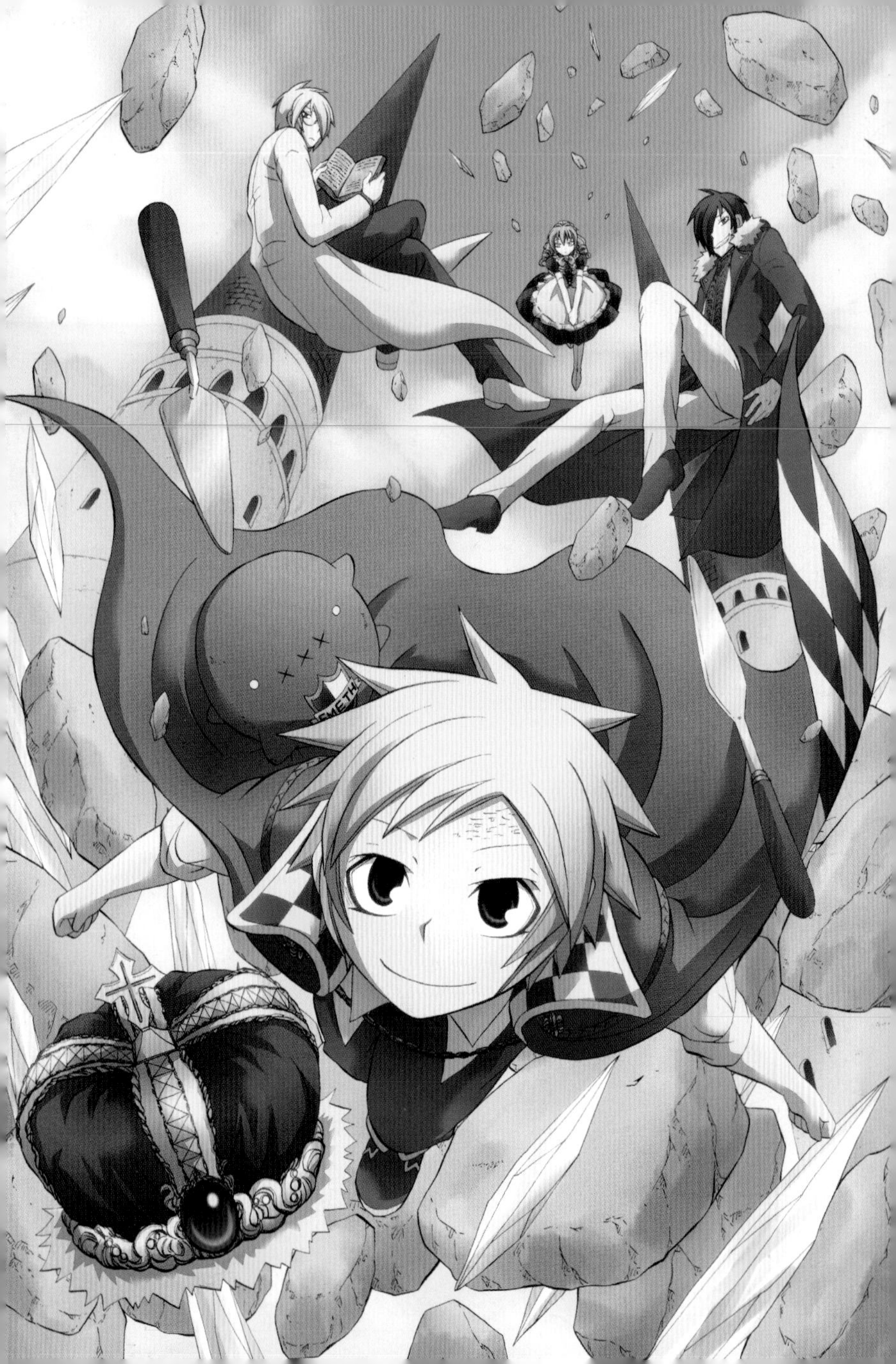

CLAY LORD

MASTER of GOLEMS

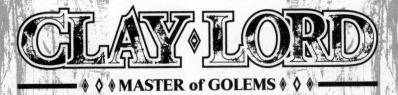

1

Jun Suzumoto

SEVEN SEAS ENTERTAINMENT PRESENTS

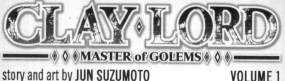

CLAY LORD

MASTER of GOLEMS

story and art by **JUN SUZUMOTO** **VOLUME 1**

TRANSLATION
Jill Morita

ADAPTATION
Patrick King

LETTERING AND LAYOUT
Alexandra Gunawan

LOGO DESIGN
Lissa Pattillo

COVER DESIGN
Nicky Lim

PROOFREADER
Lee Otter

MANAGING EDITOR
Adam Arnold

PUBLISHER
Jason DeAngelis

CLAY LORD: MASTER OF GOLEMS VOL. 1

First published in Japan in 2013 by ICHIJINSHA Inc., Tokyo.
English translation rights arranged with ICHIJINSHA Inc., Tokyo, Japan.

ISBN: 978-1-626921-49-8

Printed in Canada

First Printing: April 2015

10 9 8 7 6 5 4 3 2 1

FOLLOW US ONLINE: ***www.gomanga.com***

READING DIRECTIONS

This book reads from ***right to left***, Japanese style. If this is your first time reading manga, you start reading from the top right panel on each page and take it from there. If you get lost, just follow the numbered diagram here. It may seem backwards at first, but you'll get the hang of it! Have fun!!

1
2
3
4
5
6
7
8
9

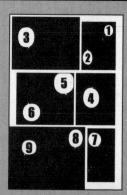

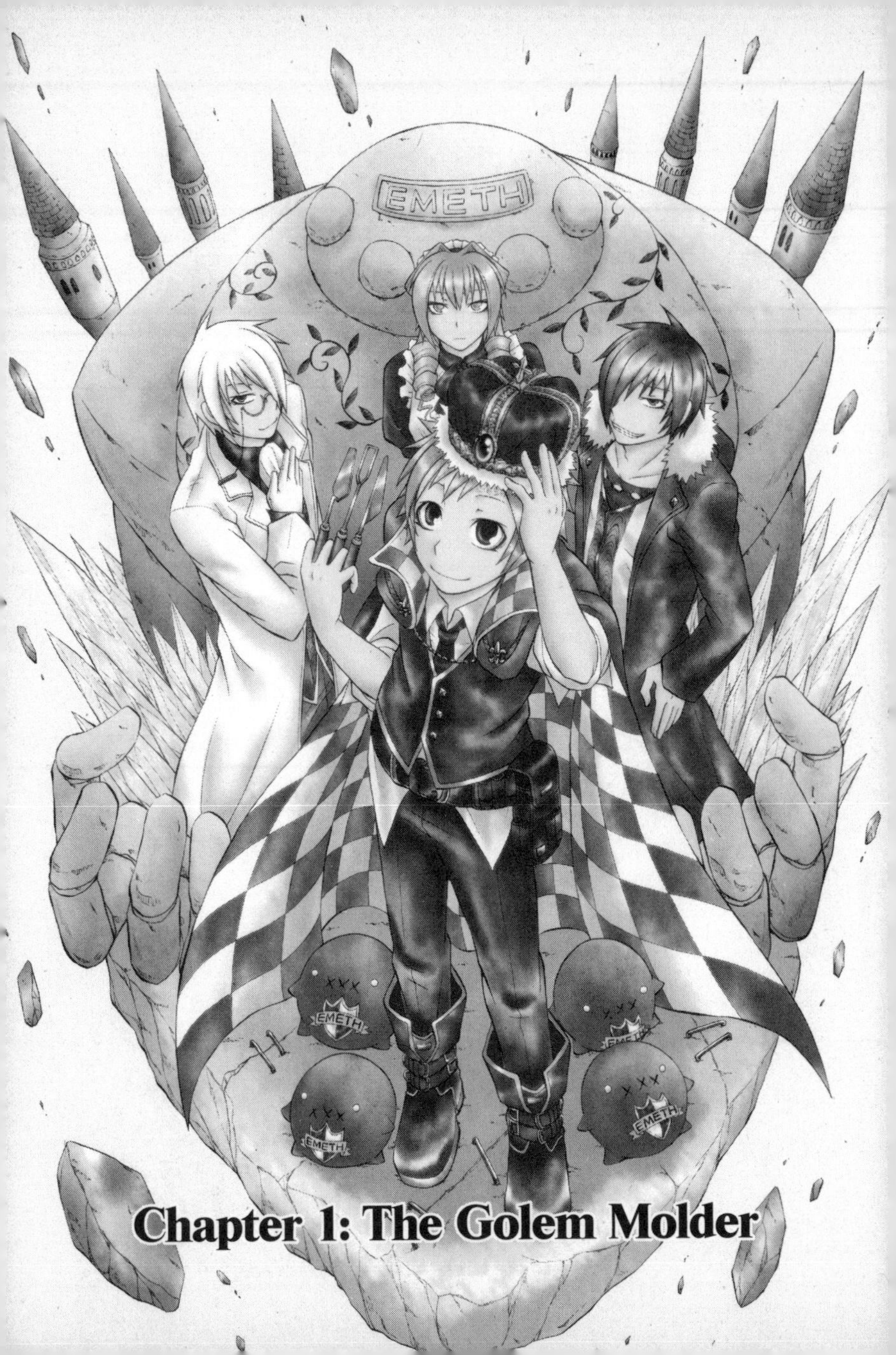
EMETH
EMETH
EMETH
EMETH
EMETH

Chapter 1: The Golem Molder

CLAY·LORD

◆ ◇ ◆ MASTER of GOLEMS ◆ ◇ ◆

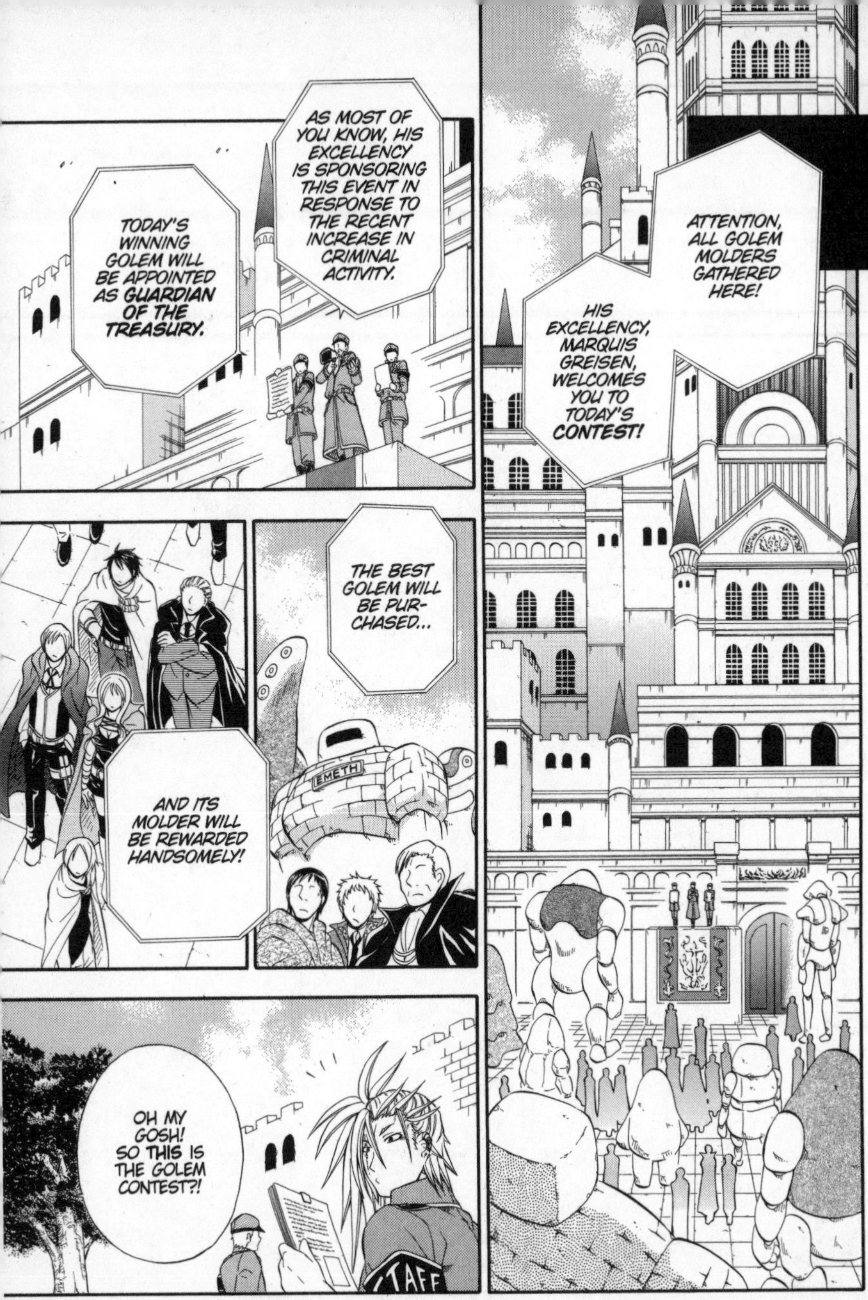
ATTENTION, ALL GOLEM MOLDERS GATHERED HERE!
HIS EXCELLENCY, MARQUIS GREISEN, WELCOMES YOU TO TODAY'S CONTEST!
AS MOST OF YOU KNOW, HIS EXCELLENCY IS SPONSORING THIS EVENT IN RESPONSE TO THE RECENT INCREASE IN CRIMINAL ACTIVITY.
TODAY'S WINNING GOLEM WILL BE APPOINTED AS GUARDIAN OF THE TREASURY.
THE BEST GOLEM WILL BE PURCHASED...
EMETH
AND ITS MOLDER WILL BE REWARDED HANDSOMELY!
OH MY GOSH! SO THIS IS THE GOLEM CONTEST?!

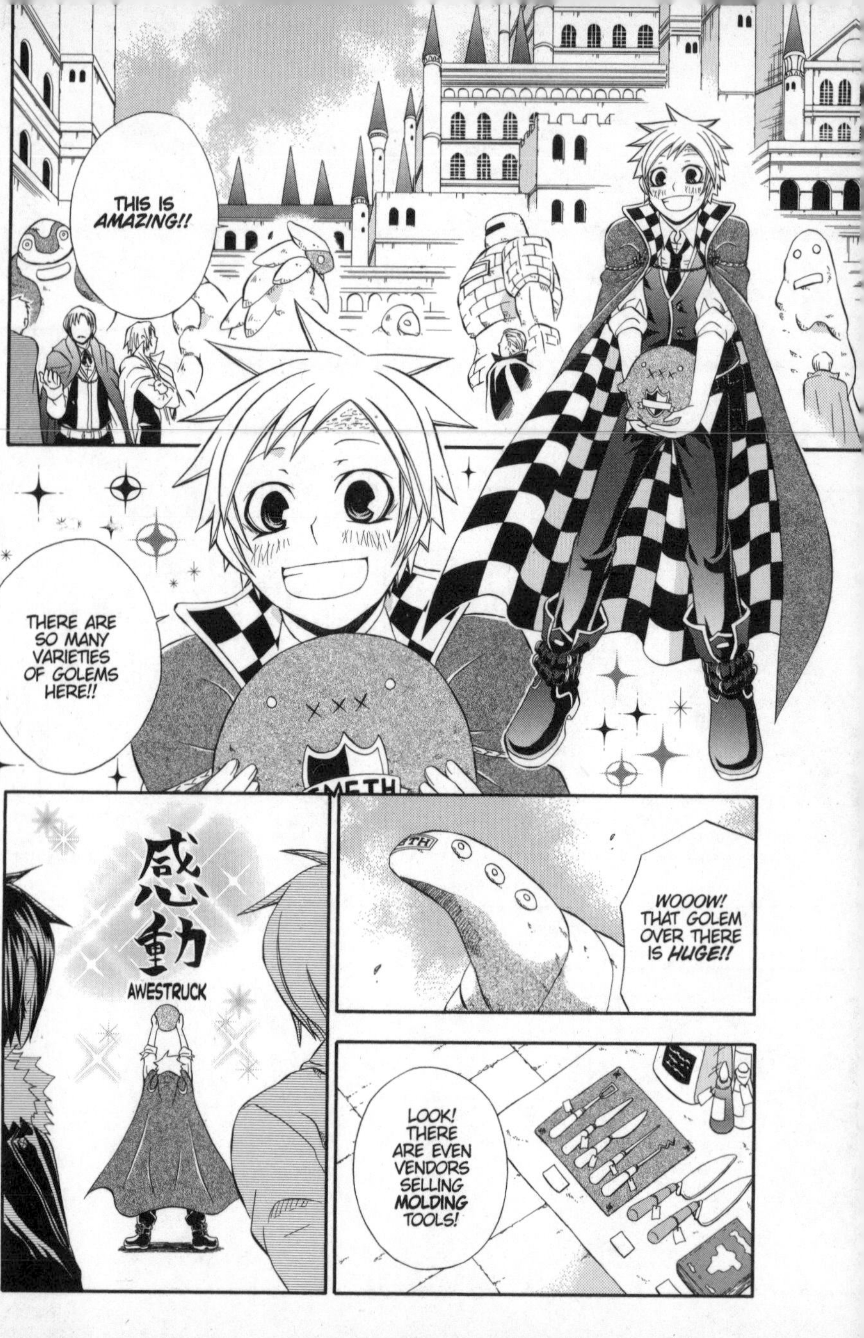
THIS IS AMAZING!!
THERE ARE SO MANY VARIETIES OF GOLEMS HERE!!
WOOOW! THAT GOLEM OVER THERE IS HUGE!!
LOOK! THERE ARE EVEN VENDORS SELLING MOLDING TOOLS!
感動
AWESTRUCK

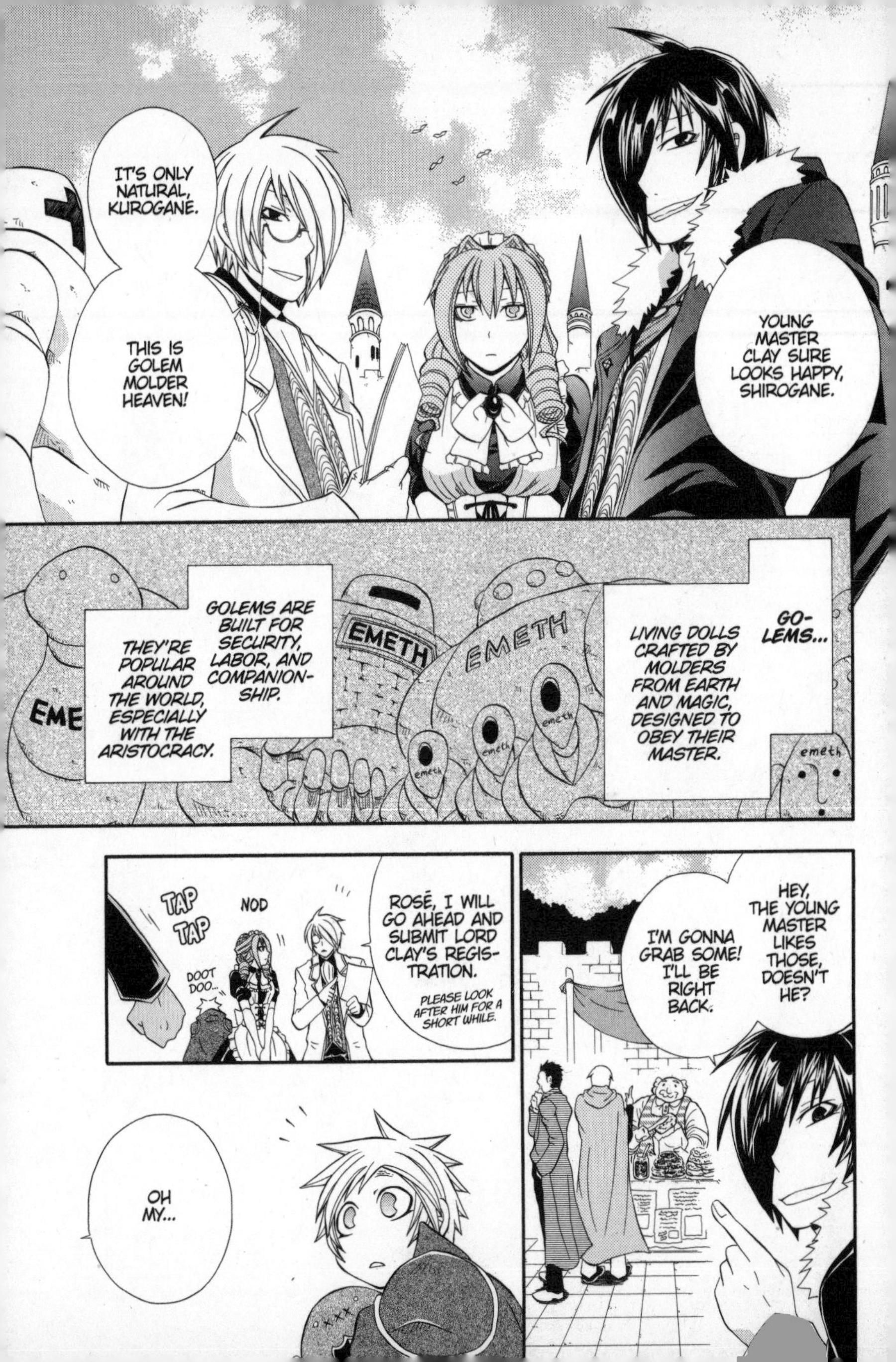
YOUNG MASTER CLAY SURE LOOKS HAPPY, SHIROGANE.
IT'S ONLY NATURAL, KUROGANE.
THIS IS GOLEM MOLDER HEAVEN!
GO-LEMS...
LIVING DOLLS CRAFTED BY MOLDERS FROM EARTH AND MAGIC, DESIGNED TO OBEY THEIR MASTER.
emeth
EMETH
EMETH
emeth
emeth
emeth
GOLEMS ARE BUILT FOR SECURITY, LABOR, AND COMPANION-SHIP.
THEY'RE POPULAR AROUND THE WORLD, ESPECIALLY WITH THE ARISTOCRACY.
EME
HEY, THE YOUNG MASTER LIKES THOSE, DOESN'T HE?
I'M GONNA GRAB SOME! I'LL BE RIGHT BACK.
ROSÉ, I WILL GO AHEAD AND SUBMIT LORD CLAY'S REGIS-TRATION.
PLEASE LOOK AFTER HIM FOR A SHORT WHILE.
NOD
TAP TAP
DOOT DOO...
OH MY...

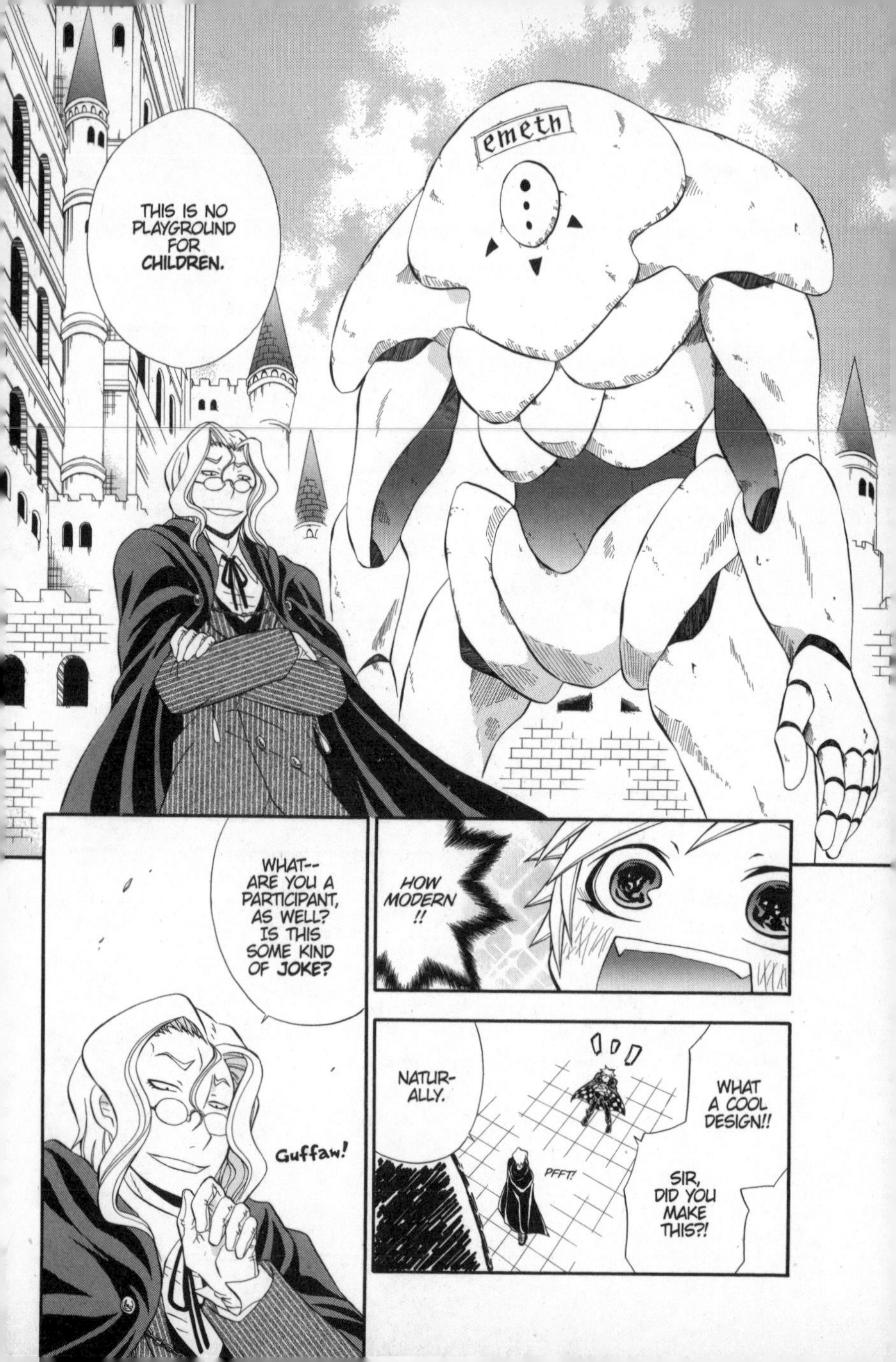
emeth
THIS IS NO PLAYGROUND FOR CHILDREN.
HOW MODERN!!
WHAT A COOL DESIGN!!
SIR, DID YOU MAKE THIS?!
NATUR-ALLY.
PFFT!
WHAT-- ARE YOU A PARTICIPANT, AS WELL? IS THIS SOME KIND OF JOKE?
Guffaw!

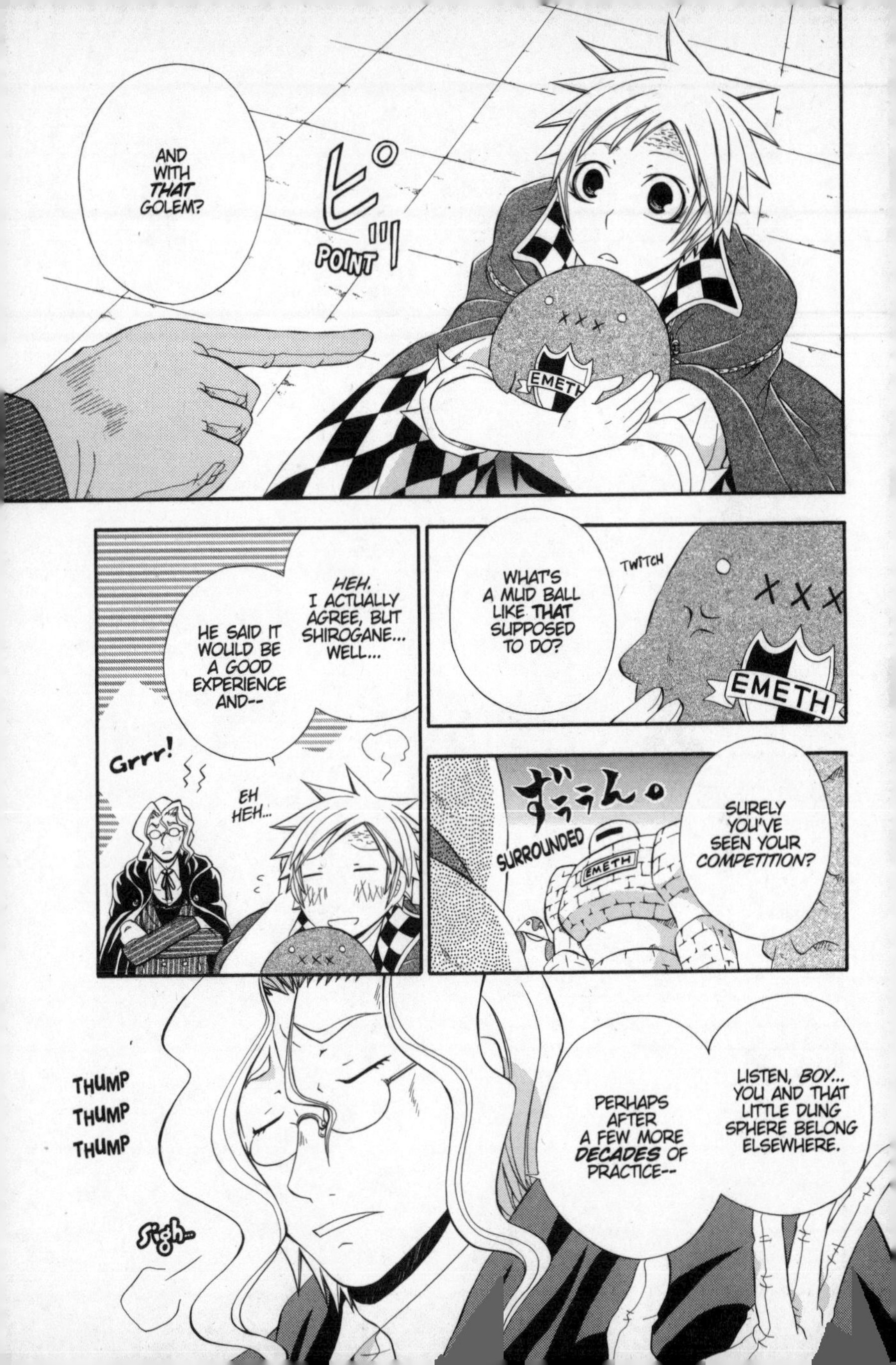
AND WITH THAT GOLEM?
ピッ
POINT
WHAT'S A MUD BALL LIKE THAT SUPPOSED TO DO?
TWITCH
HEH. I ACTUALLY AGREE, BUT SHIROGANE... WELL...
HE SAID IT WOULD BE A GOOD EXPERIENCE AND--
Grrr!
EH HEH...
SURELY YOU'VE SEEN YOUR COMPETITION?
ずううん
SURROUNDED
EMETH
LISTEN, BOY... YOU AND THAT LITTLE DUNG SPHERE BELONG ELSEWHERE.
PERHAPS AFTER A FEW MORE DECADES OF PRACTICE--
THUMP THUMP THUMP
Sigh...

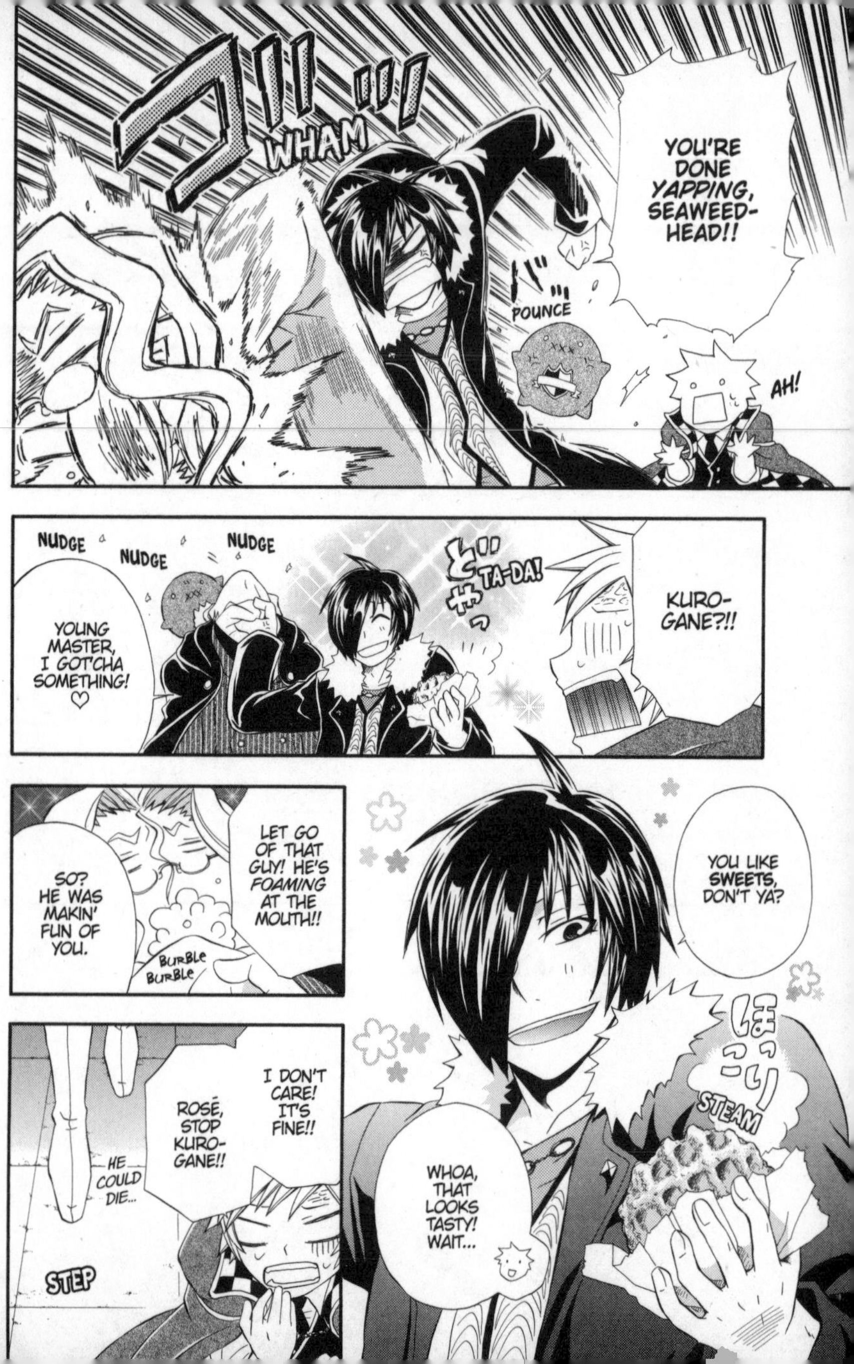
YOU'RE DONE YAPPING, SEAWEED-HEAD!!
WHAM
AH!
POUNCE
KURO-GANE?!!
TA-DA!
NUDGE
NUDGE
NUDGE
YOUNG MASTER, I GOT'CHA SOMETHING! ♡
YOU LIKE SWEETS, DON'T YA?
STEAM
WHOA, THAT LOOKS TASTY! WAIT...
LET GO OF THAT GUY! HE'S *FOAMING* AT THE MOUTH!!
SO? HE WAS MAKIN' FUN OF YOU.
BURBLE BURBLE
I DON'T CARE! IT'S FINE!!
ROSÉ, STOP KURO-GANE!!
HE COULD DIE...
STEP

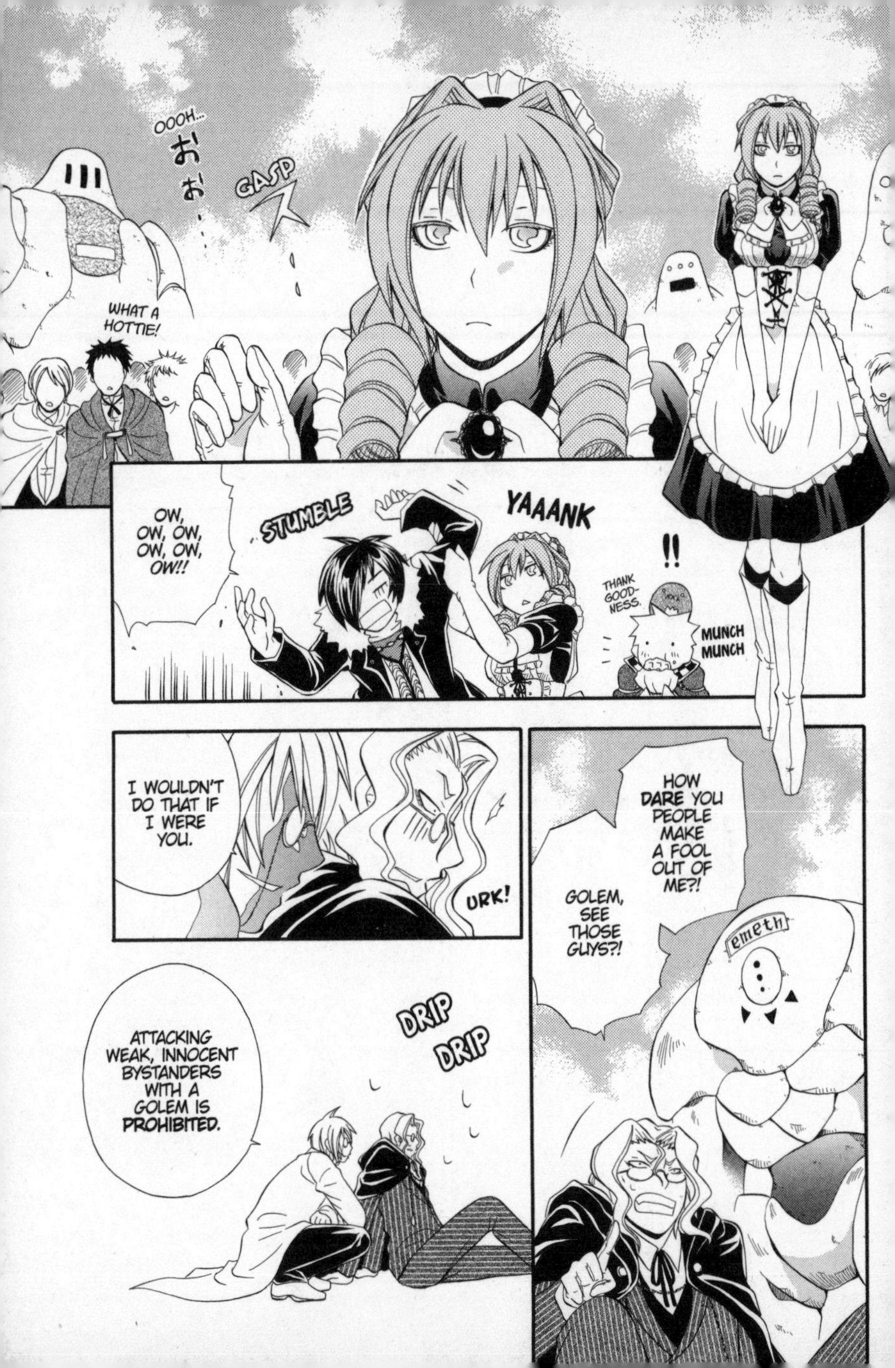
GASP
OOOH... おぉ!
WHAT A HOTTIE!
YAAANK
!!
THANK GOODNESS.
MUNCH MUNCH
STUMBLE
OW, OW, OW, OW, OW, OW!!
HOW DARE YOU PEOPLE MAKE A FOOL OUT OF ME?!
GOLEM, SEE THOSE GUYS?!
emeth
I WOULDN'T DO THAT IF I WERE YOU.
URK!
DRIP DRIP
ATTACKING WEAK, INNOCENT BYSTANDERS WITH A GOLEM IS PROHIBITED.

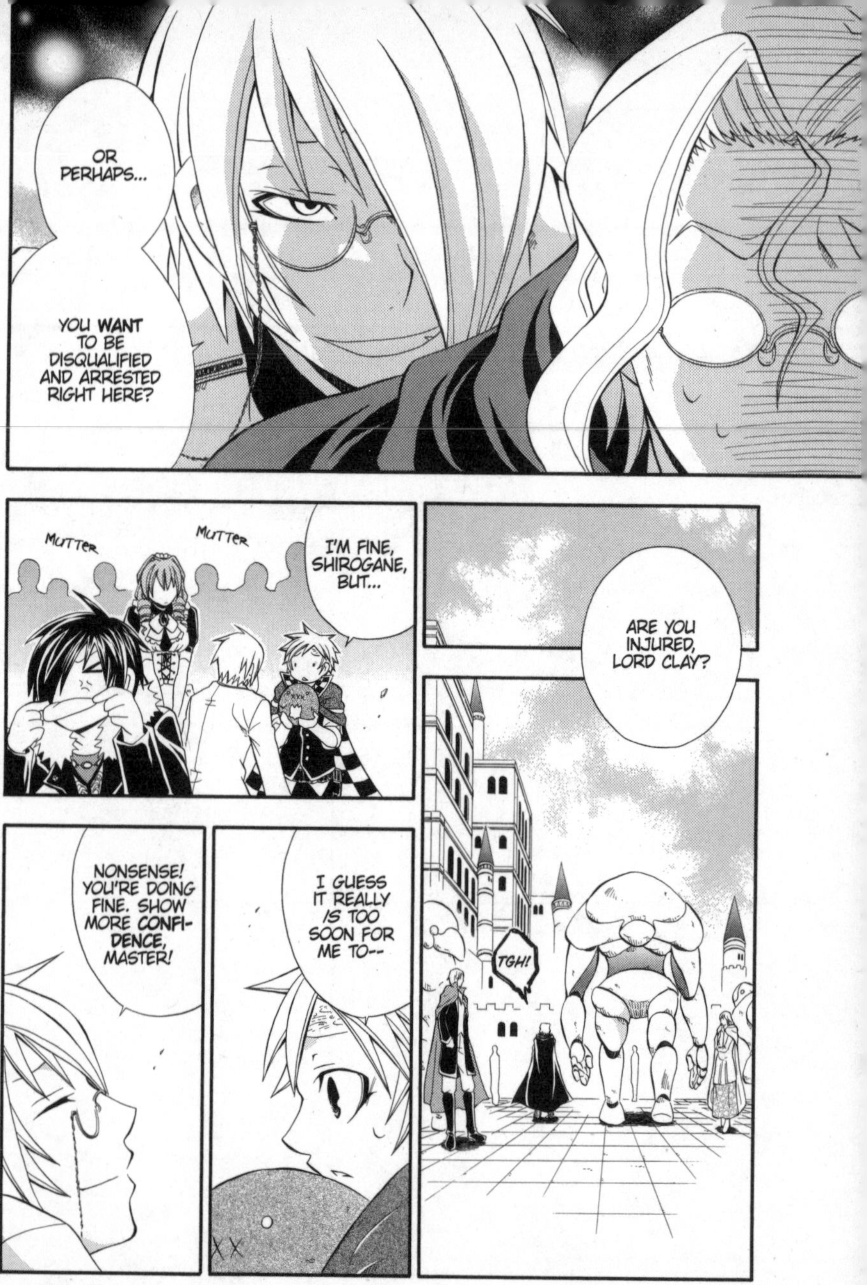
OR PERHAPS...
YOU WANT TO BE DISQUALIFIED AND ARRESTED RIGHT HERE?
ARE YOU INJURED, LORD CLAY?
MUTTER
MUTTER
I'M FINE, SHIROGANE, BUT...
TGH!
I GUESS IT REALLY IS TOO SOON FOR ME TO--
NONSENSE! YOU'RE DOING FINE. SHOW MORE CONFI-DENCE, MASTER!

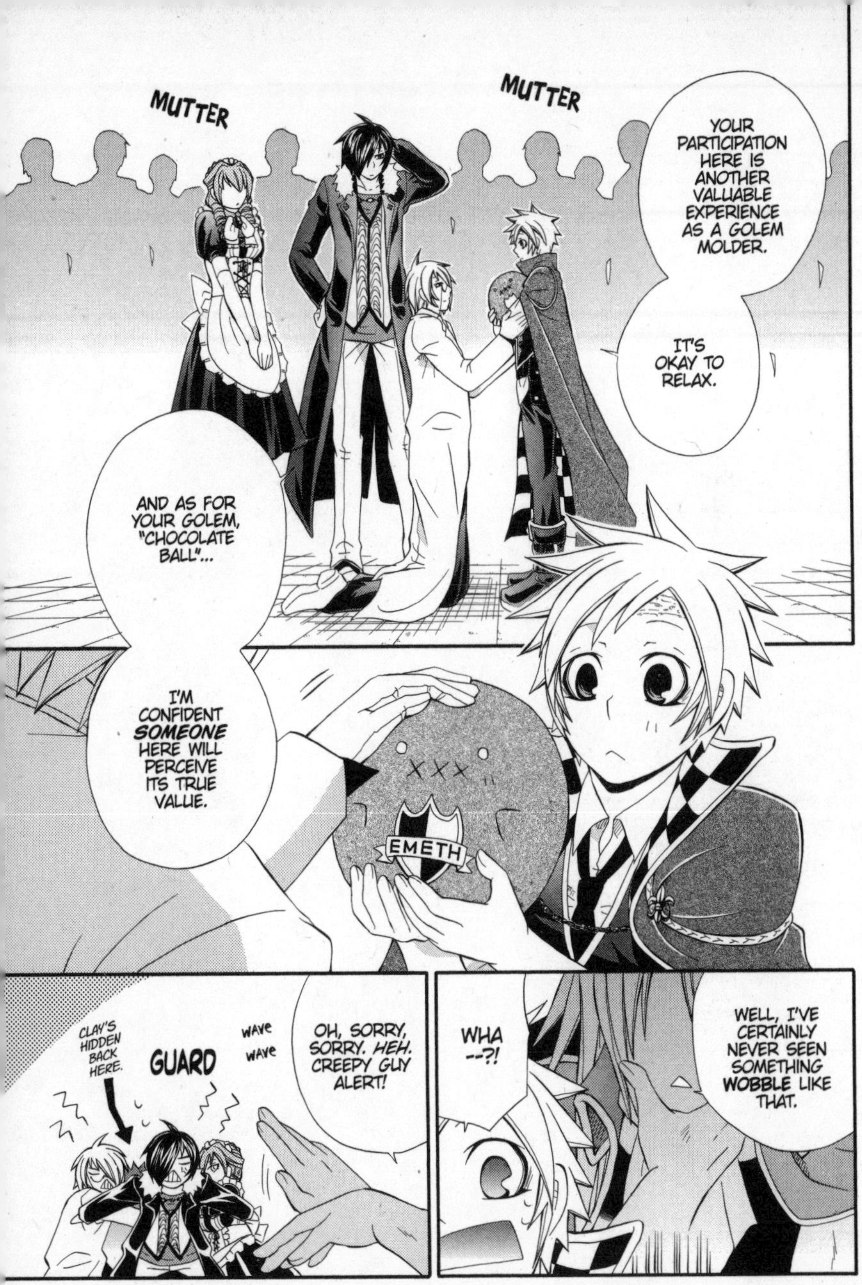
MUTTER
MUTTER
YOUR PARTICIPATION HERE IS ANOTHER VALUABLE EXPERIENCE AS A GOLEM MOLDER.
IT'S OKAY TO RELAX.
AND AS FOR YOUR GOLEM, "CHOCOLATE BALL"...
I'M CONFIDENT SOMEONE HERE WILL PERCEIVE ITS TRUE VALUE.
EMETH
WELL, I'VE CERTAINLY NEVER SEEN SOMETHING WOBBLE LIKE THAT.
WHA--?!
OH, SORRY, SORRY. HEH. CREEPY GUY ALERT!
wave wave
GUARD
CLAY'S HIDDEN BACK HERE.

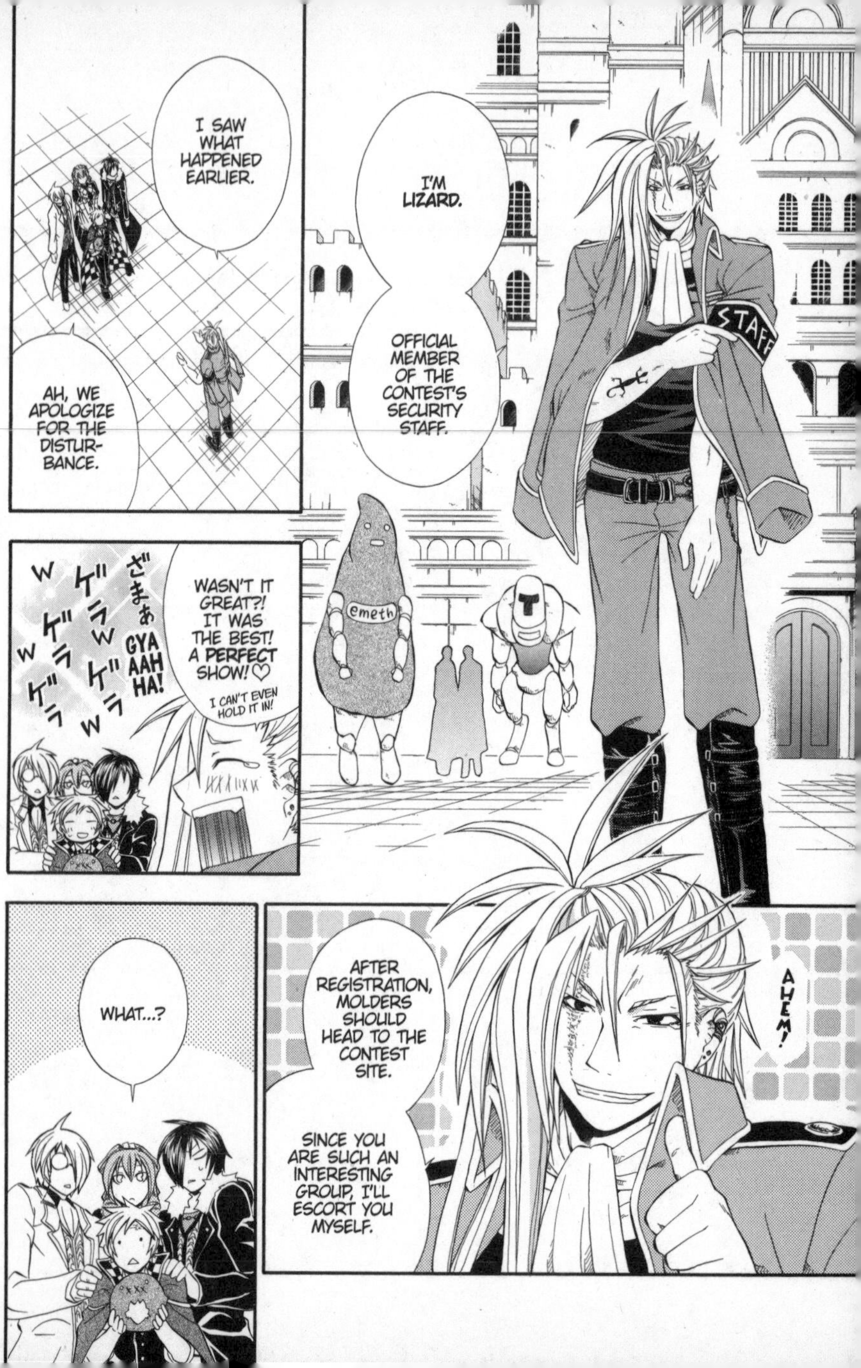
I'M LIZARD.
OFFICIAL MEMBER OF THE CONTEST'S SECURITY STAFF.
STAFF
emeth
I SAW WHAT HAPPENED EARLIER.
AH, WE APOLOGIZE FOR THE DISTURBANCE.
WASN'T IT GREAT?! IT WAS THE BEST! A PERFECT SHOW!♡
I CAN'T EVEN HOLD IT IN!
ざまぁ
GYAAAHHA!
ゲラ ゲラ ゲラ ゲラ
w w w w w
AFTER REGISTRATION, MOLDERS SHOULD HEAD TO THE CONTEST SITE.
AHEM!
SINCE YOU ARE SUCH AN INTERESTING GROUP, I'LL ESCORT YOU MYSELF.
WHAT...?

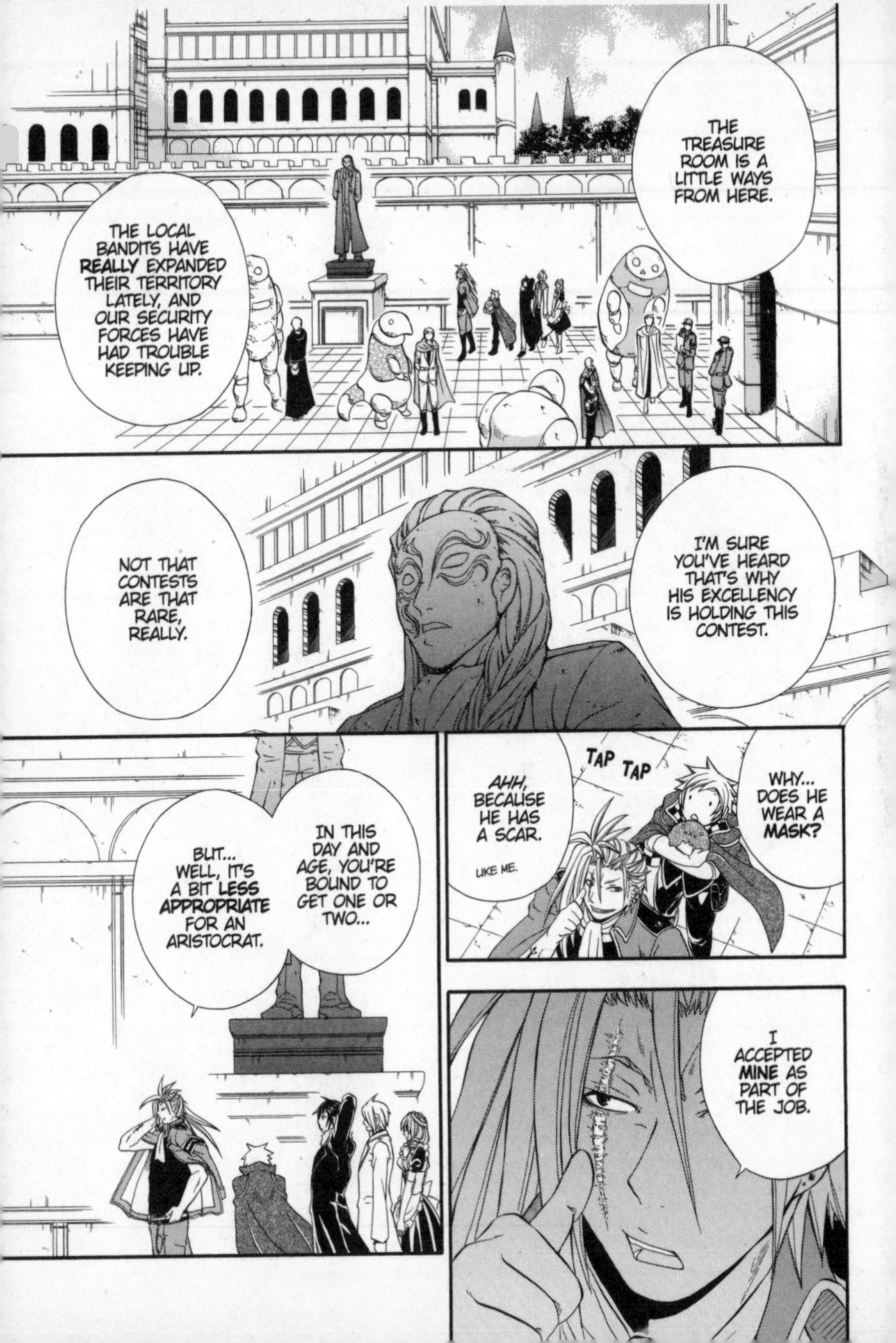

THE TREASURE ROOM IS A LITTLE WAYS FROM HERE.
THE LOCAL BANDITS HAVE **REALLY** EXPANDED THEIR TERRITORY LATELY, AND OUR SECURITY FORCES HAVE HAD TROUBLE KEEPING UP.
I'M SURE YOU'VE HEARD THAT'S WHY HIS EXCELLENCY IS HOLDING THIS CONTEST.
NOT THAT CONTESTS ARE THAT RARE, REALLY.
WHY... DOES HE WEAR A **MASK?**
TAP TAP
AHH, BECAUSE HE HAS A SCAR.
LIKE ME.
I ACCEPTED **MINE** AS PART OF THE JOB.
IN THIS DAY AND AGE, YOU'RE BOUND TO GET ONE OR TWO...
BUT... WELL, IT'S A BIT **LESS APPROPRIATE** FOR AN ARISTOCRAT.

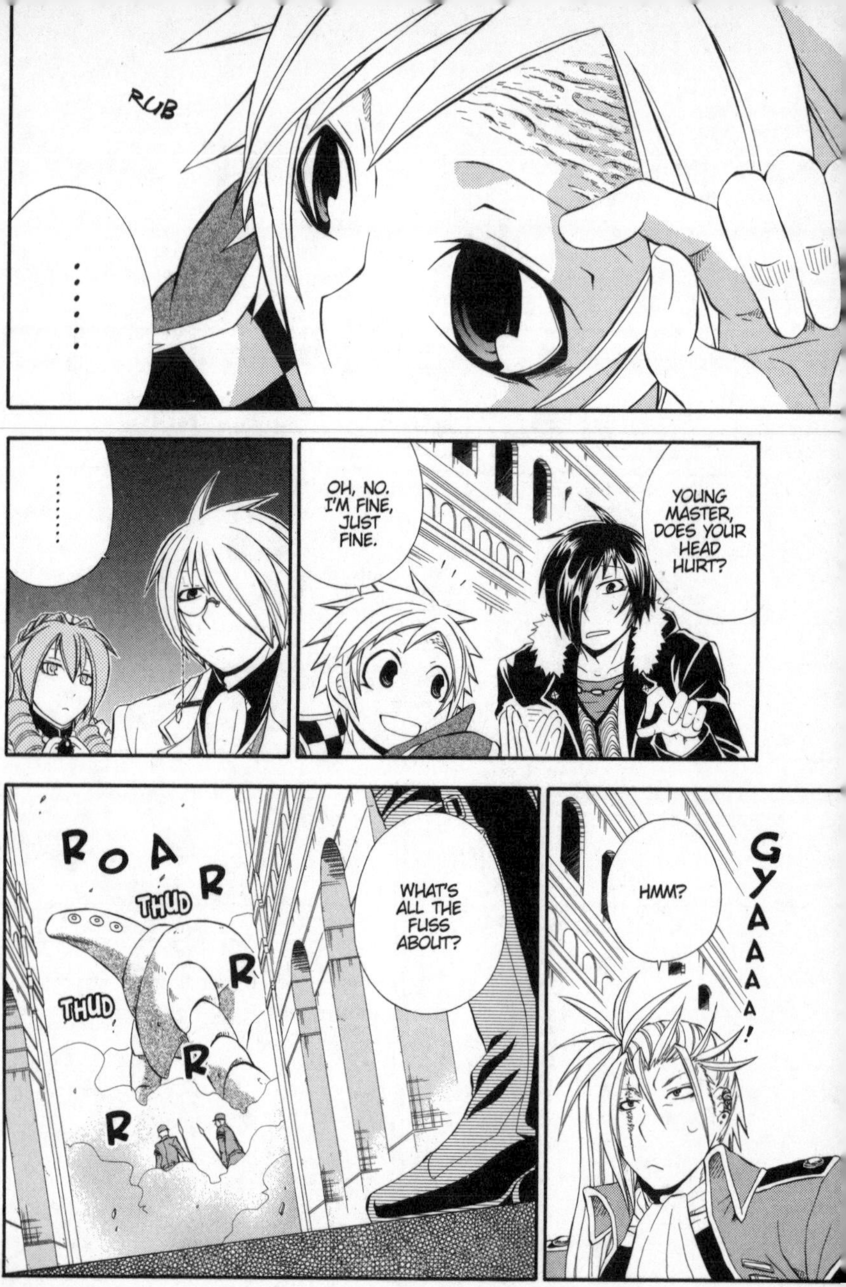
RUB
......
YOUNG MASTER, DOES YOUR HEAD HURT?
OH, NO. I'M FINE, JUST FINE.
......
GYAAAAA!
HMM?
WHAT'S ALL THE FUSS ABOUT?
ROARRRR
THUD
THUD

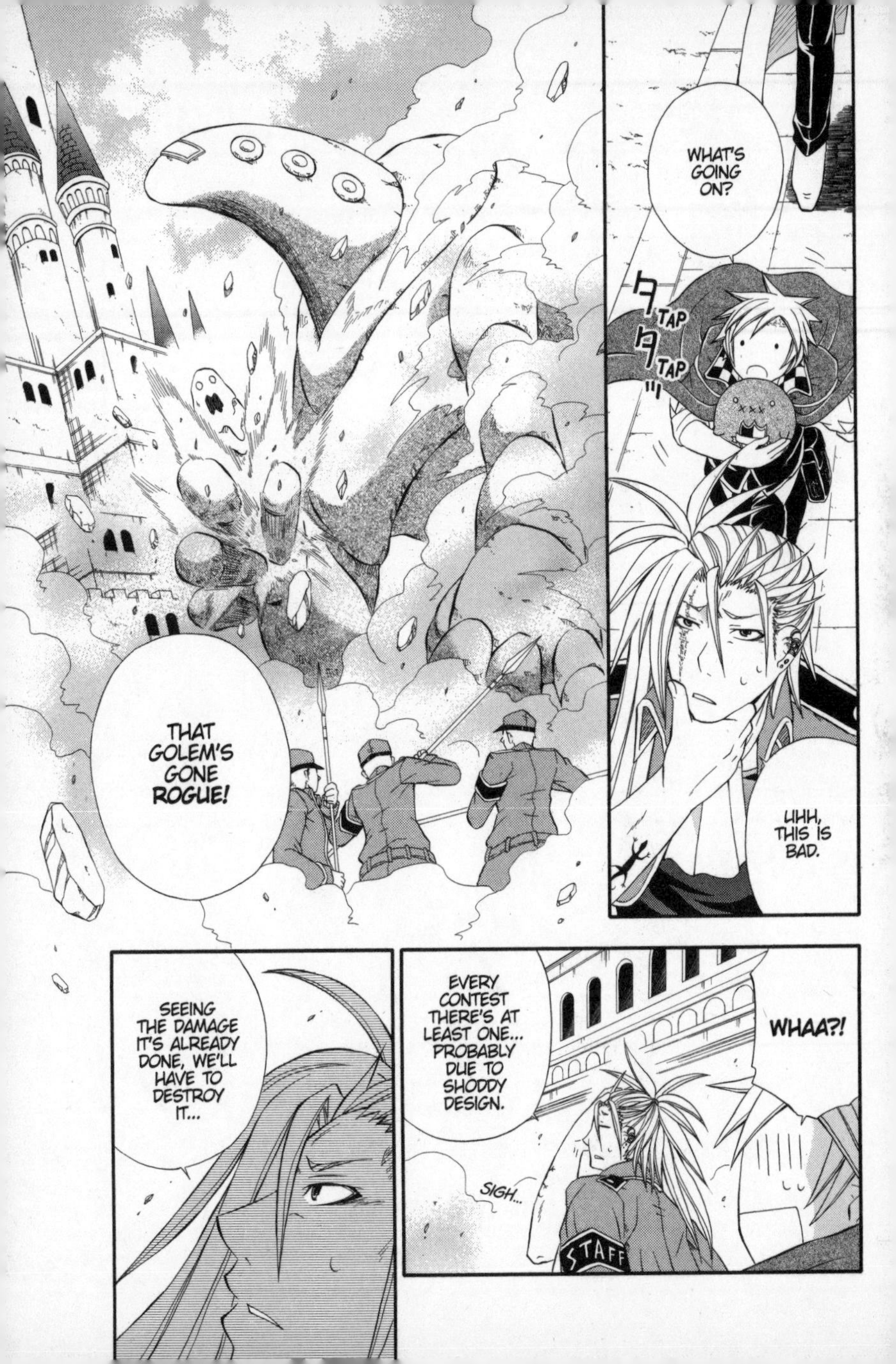
WHAT'S GOING ON?
TAP
TAP
UHH, THIS IS BAD.
THAT GOLEM'S GONE ROGUE!
WHAA?!
EVERY CONTEST THERE'S AT LEAST ONE... PROBABLY DUE TO SHODDY DESIGN.
SIGH...
STAFF
SEEING THE DAMAGE IT'S ALREADY DONE, WE'LL HAVE TO DESTROY IT...

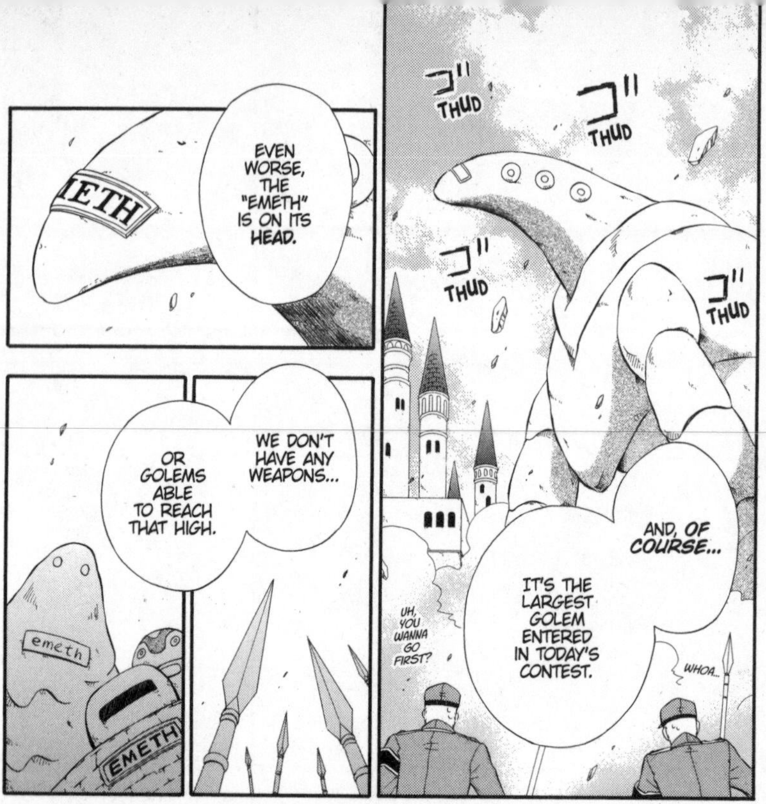

ゴ" THUD
ゴ" THUD
ゴ" THUD
ゴ" THUD
AND, OF COURSE...
IT'S THE LARGEST GOLEM ENTERED IN TODAY'S CONTEST.
WHOA...
UH, YOU WANNA GO FIRST?
EVEN WORSE, THE "EMETH" IS ON ITS HEAD.
METH
WE DON'T HAVE ANY WEAPONS...
OR GOLEMS ABLE TO REACH THAT HIGH.
emeth
EMETH

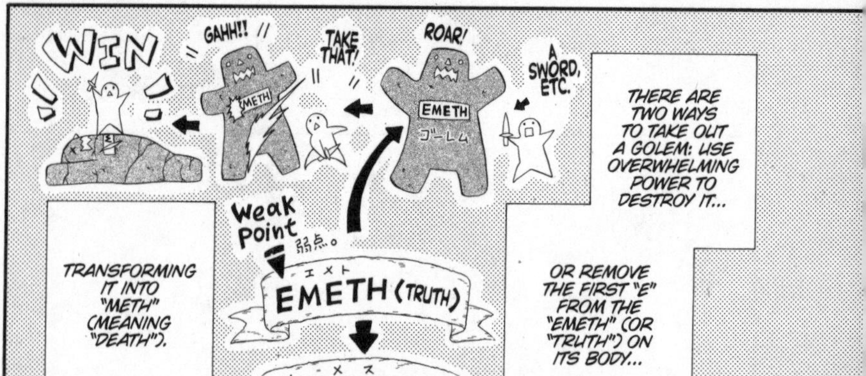

THERE ARE TWO WAYS TO TAKE OUT A GOLEM: USE OVERWHELMING POWER TO DESTROY IT...
A SWORD, ETC.
ROAR!
EMETH
ゴーレム
TAKE THAT!
GAHH!!
METH
WIN
OR REMOVE THE FIRST "E" FROM THE "EMETH" (OR "TRUTH") ON ITS BODY...
Weak Point 弱点。
エメト
EMETH (TRUTH)
メス
METH (DEATH)
TRANSFORMING IT INTO "METH" (MEANING "DEATH").

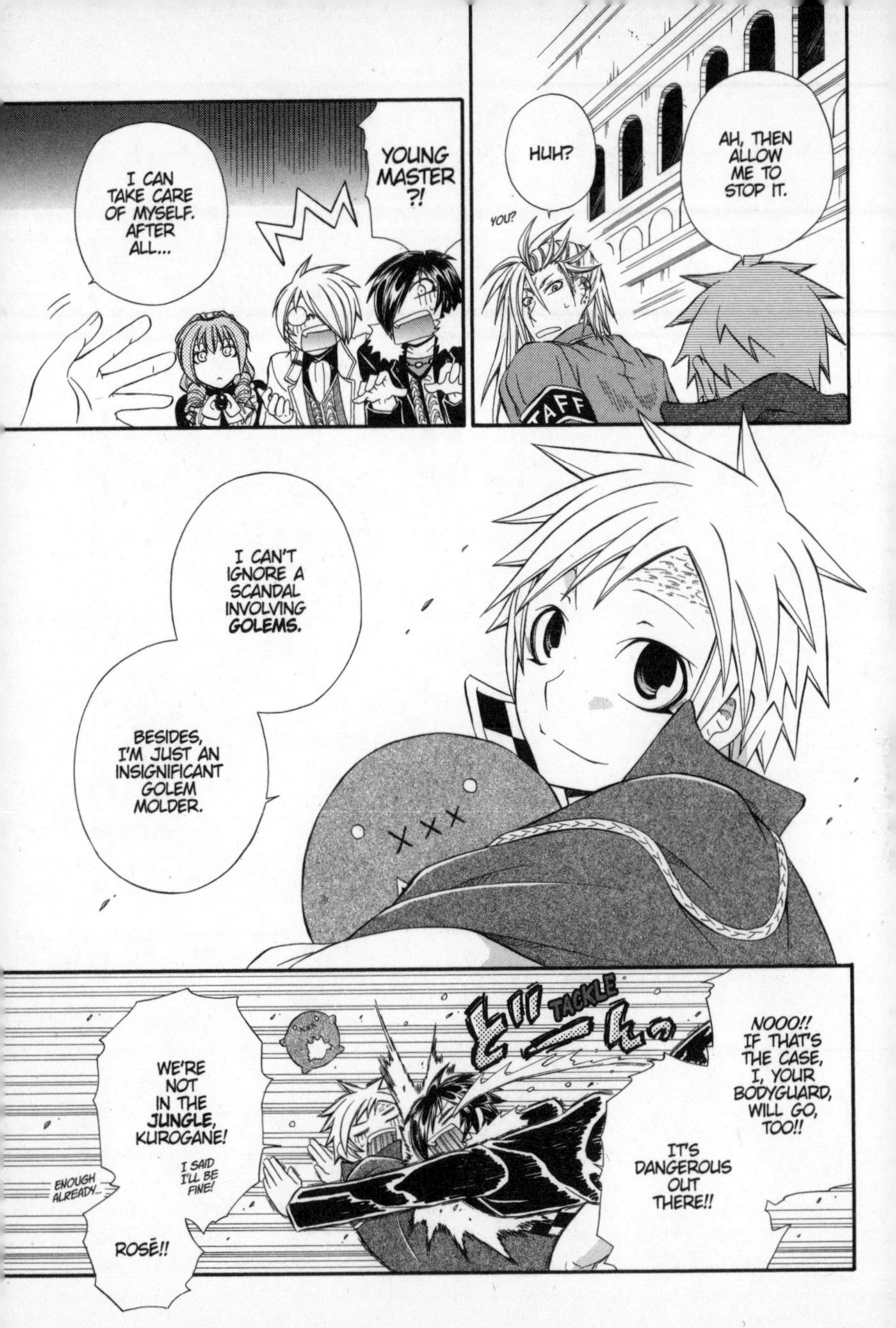
AH, THEN ALLOW ME TO STOP IT.
HUH?
YOU?
YOUNG MASTER ?!
I CAN TAKE CARE OF MYSELF. AFTER ALL...
I CAN'T IGNORE A SCANDAL INVOLVING GOLEMS.
BESIDES, I'M JUST AN INSIGNIFICANT GOLEM MOLDER.
NOOO!! IF THAT'S THE CASE, I, YOUR BODYGUARD, WILL GO, TOO!!
IT'S DANGEROUS OUT THERE!!
TACKLE
WE'RE NOT IN THE JUNGLE, KUROGANE!
I SAID I'LL BE FINE!
ENOUGH ALREADY...
ROSÉ!!

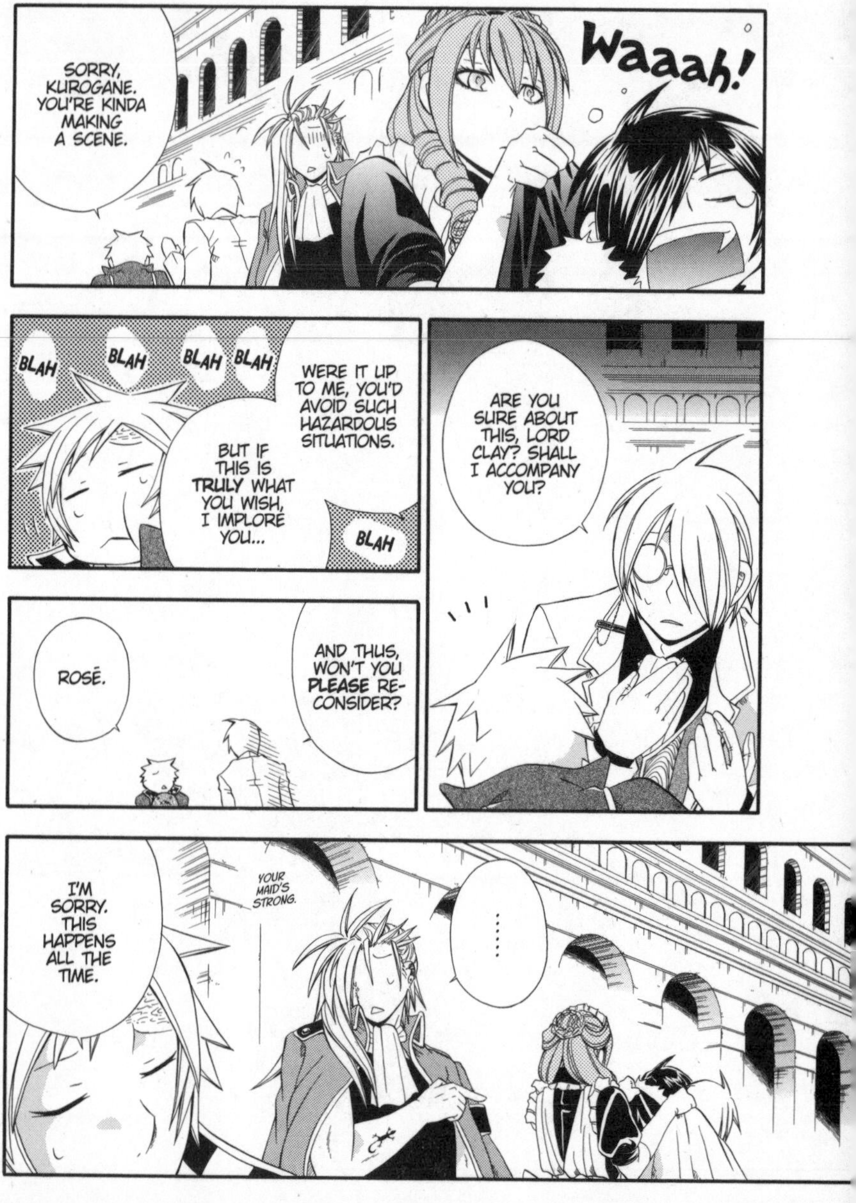
Waaaah!
SORRY, KUROGANE. YOU'RE KINDA MAKING A SCENE.
ARE YOU SURE ABOUT THIS, LORD CLAY? SHALL I ACCOMPANY YOU?
BLAH BLAH BLAH BLAH
WERE IT UP TO ME, YOU'D AVOID SUCH HAZARDOUS SITUATIONS.
BUT IF THIS IS TRULY WHAT YOU WISH, I IMPLORE YOU...
BLAH
AND THUS, WON'T YOU PLEASE RE-CONSIDER?
ROSÉ.
......
YOUR MAID'S STRONG.
I'M SORRY. THIS HAPPENS ALL THE TIME.

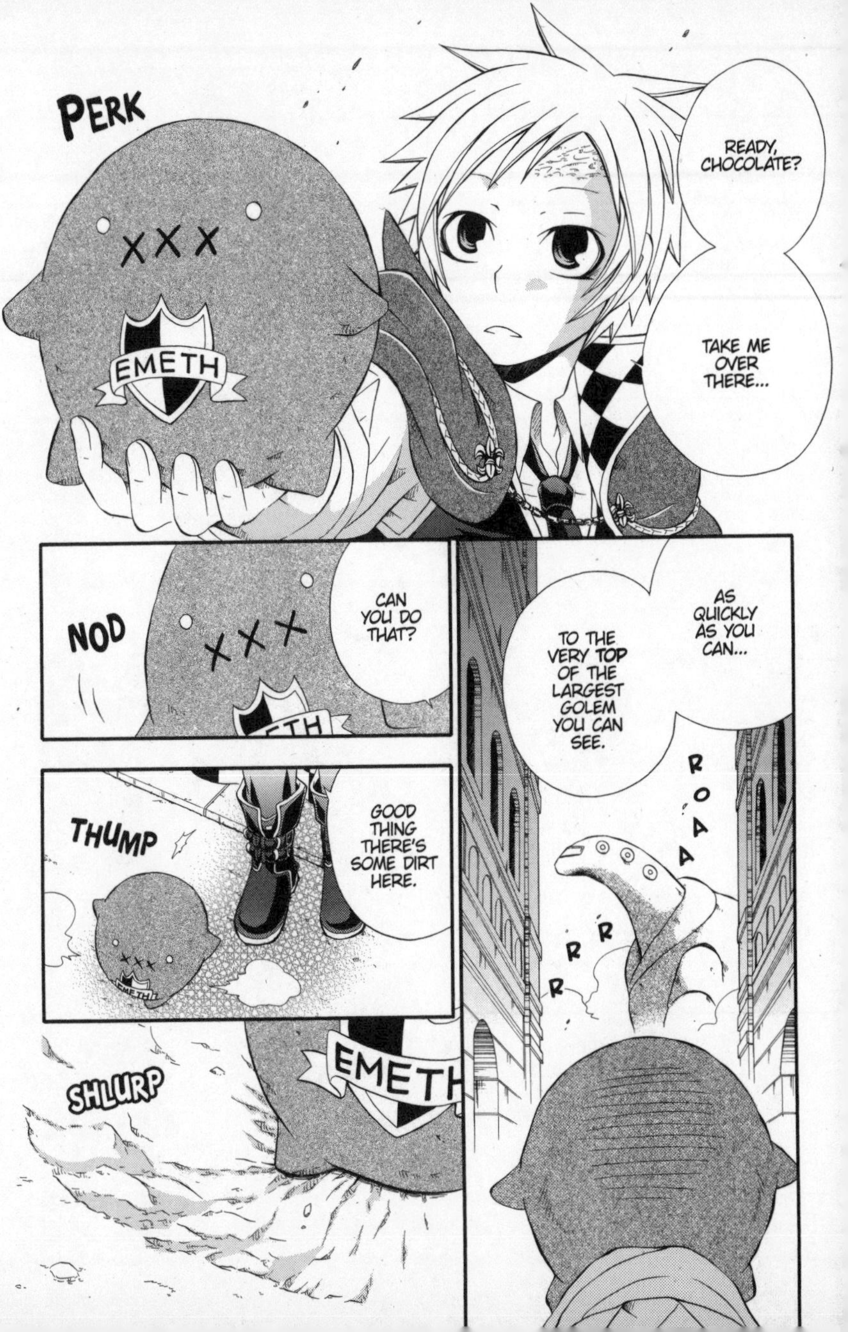
READY, CHOCOLATE?
TAKE ME OVER THERE...
PERK
AS QUICKLY AS YOU CAN...
TO THE VERY TOP OF THE LARGEST GOLEM YOU CAN SEE.
ROAA
RRR
CAN YOU DO THAT?
NOD
GOOD THING THERE'S SOME DIRT HERE.
THUMP
EMETH
SHLURP

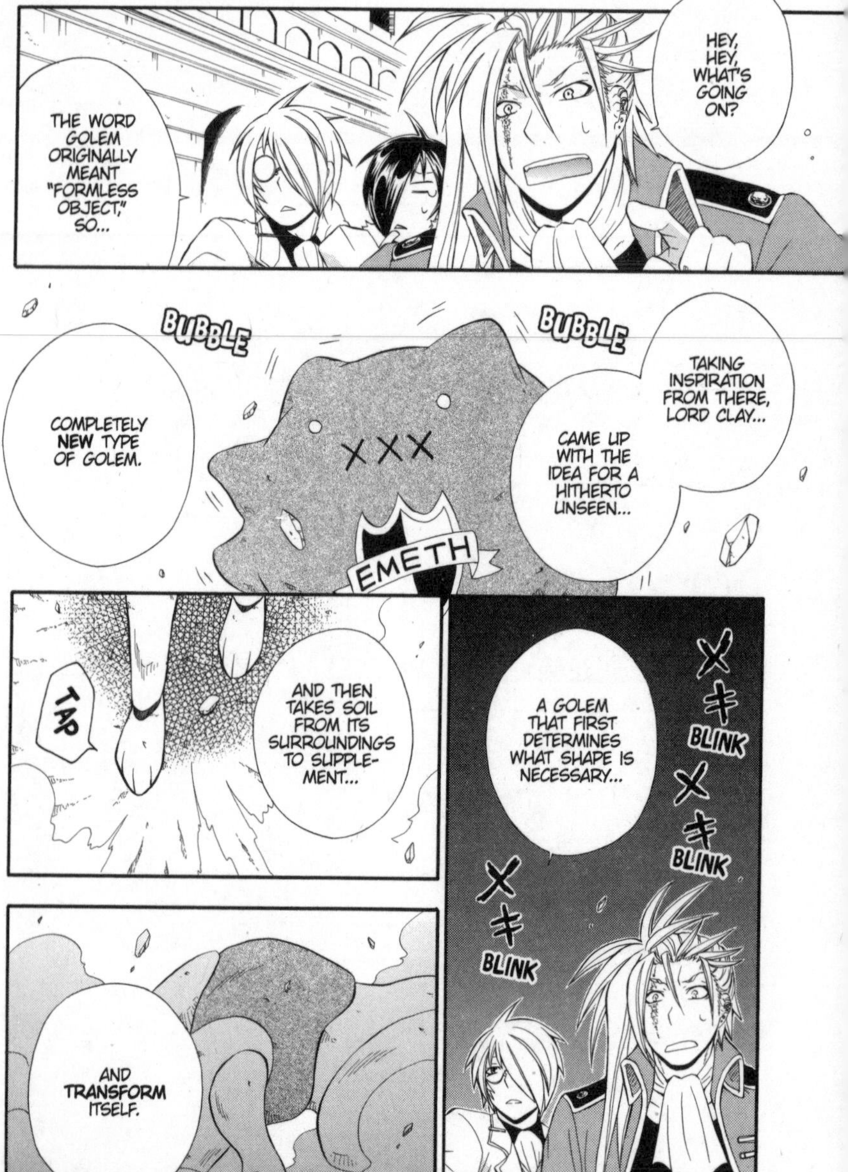
HEY, HEY, WHAT'S GOING ON?
THE WORD GOLEM ORIGINALLY MEANT "FORMLESS OBJECT," SO...
BUBBLE
TAKING INSPIRATION FROM THERE, LORD CLAY...
CAME UP WITH THE IDEA FOR A HITHERTO UNSEEN...
BUBBLE
COMPLETELY NEW TYPE OF GOLEM.
EMETH
BLINK
BLINK
BLINK
A GOLEM THAT FIRST DETERMINES WHAT SHAPE IS NECESSARY...
AND THEN TAKES SOIL FROM ITS SURROUNDINGS TO SUPPLE-MENT...
TAP
AND TRANSFORM ITSELF.

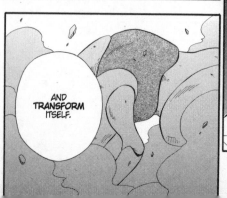

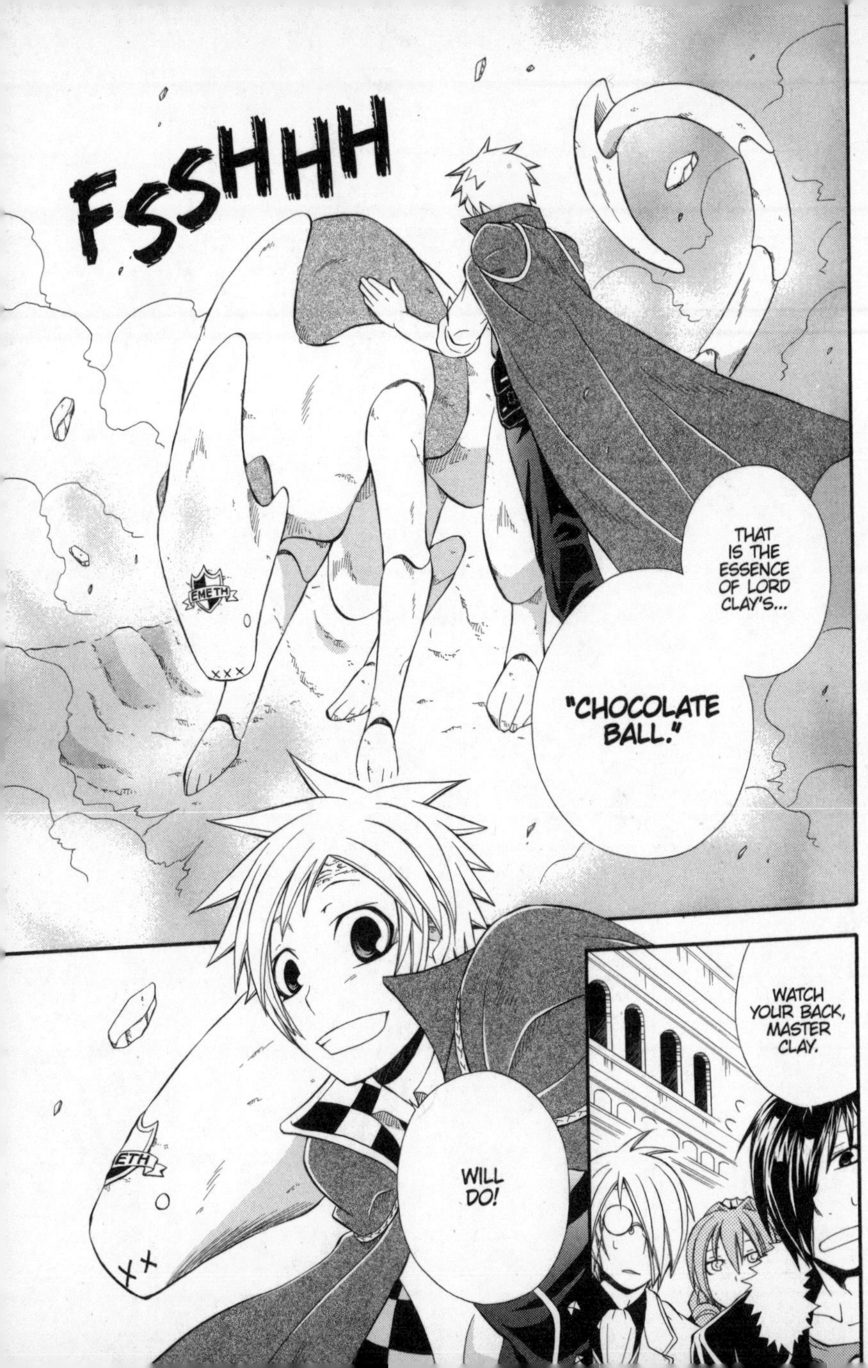
FSSHHH
THAT IS THE ESSENCE OF LORD CLAY'S...
"CHOCOLATE BALL."
WATCH YOUR BACK, MASTER CLAY.
WILL DO!

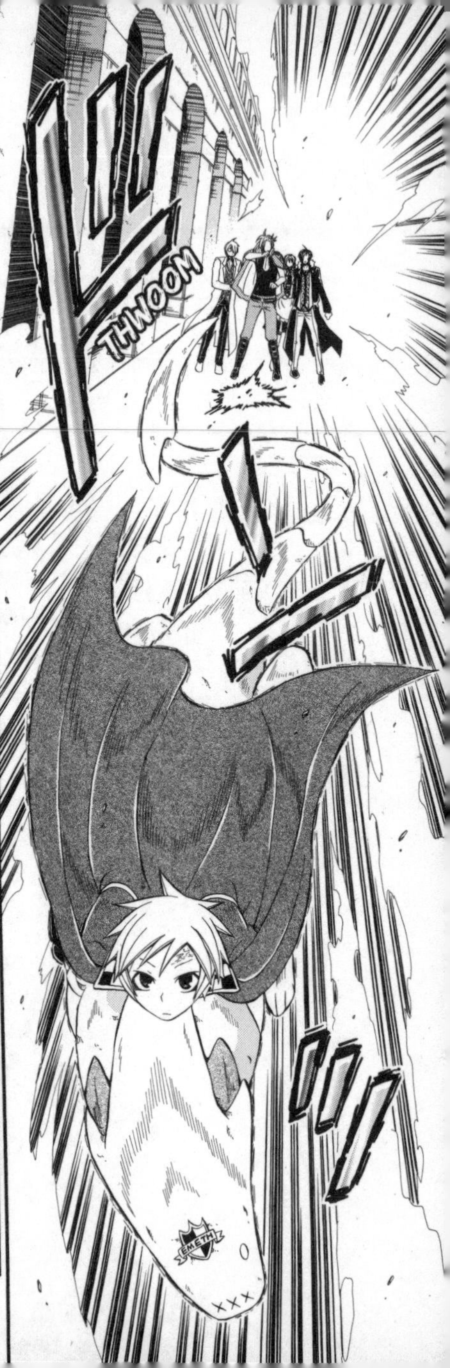
THWOOM
EMETH

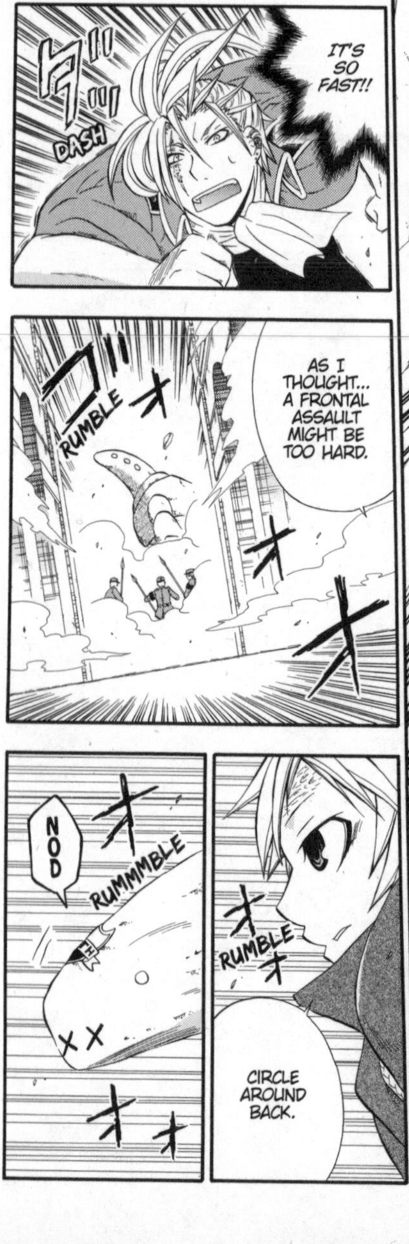
IT'S SO FAST!!
DASH
AS I THOUGHT... A FRONTAL ASSAULT MIGHT BE TOO HARD.
RUMBLE
RUMBLE
CIRCLE AROUND BACK.
NOD
RUMMMBLE

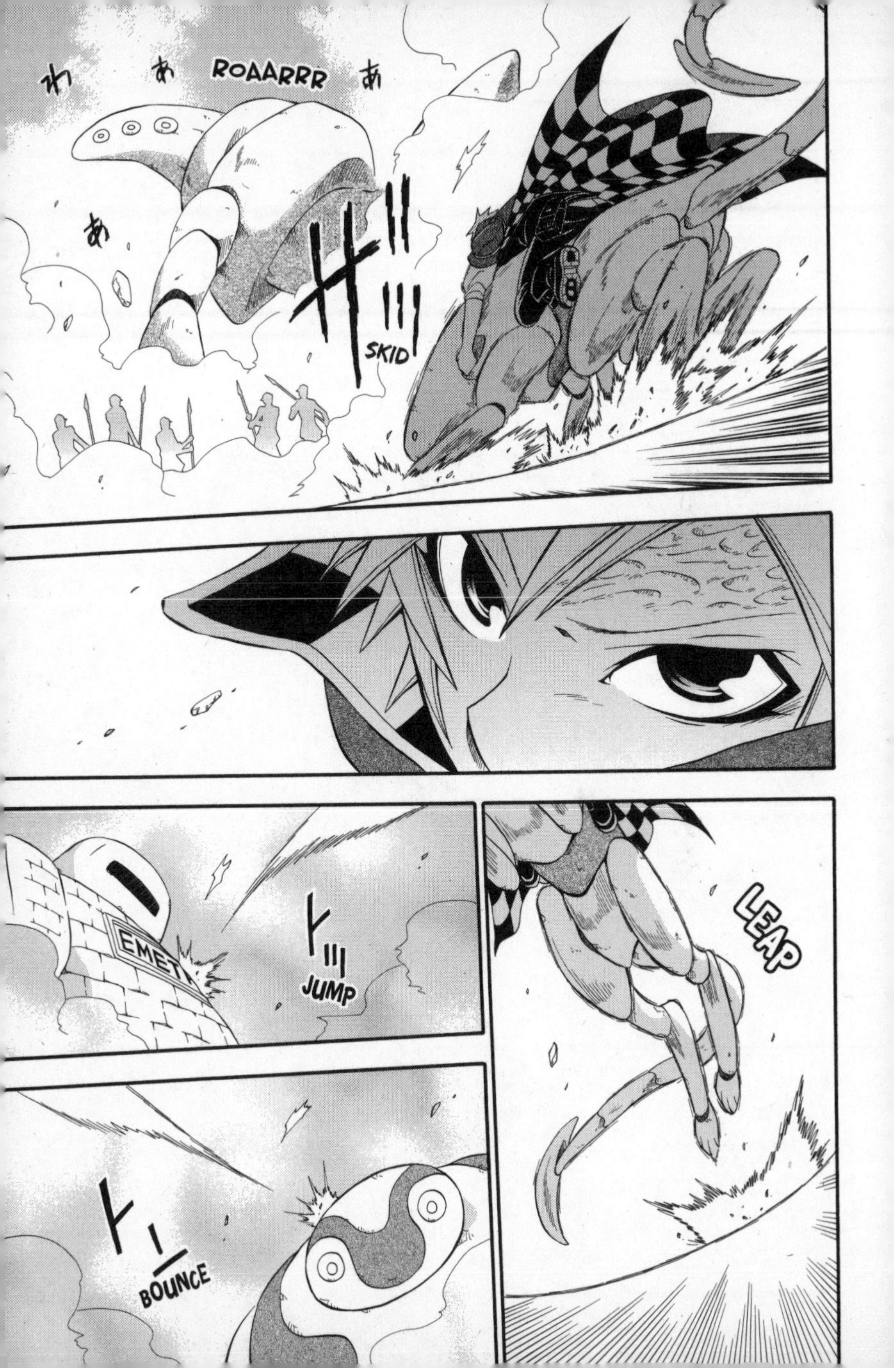
わ あ ROAARRR あ
あ
SKID
LEAP
JUMP
BOUNCE

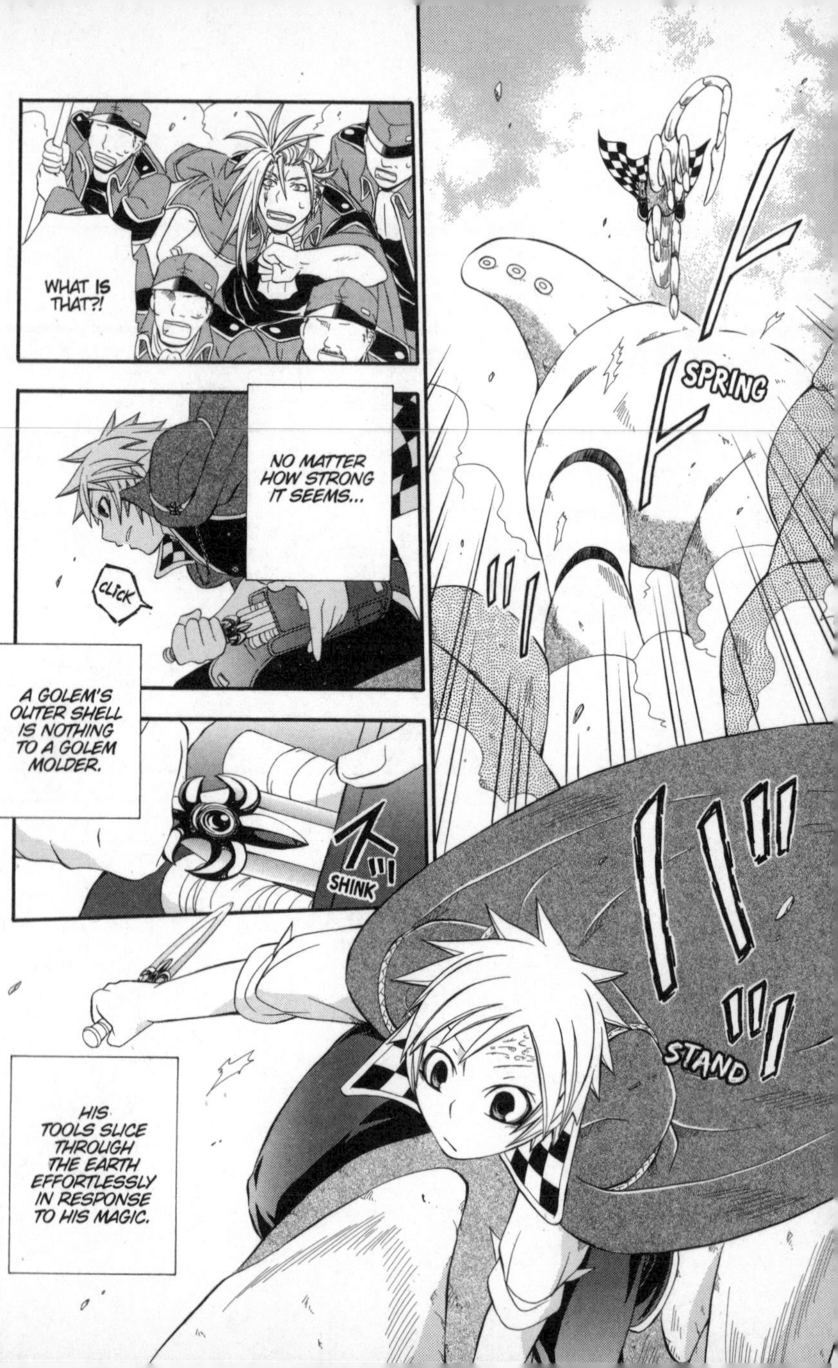
SPRING
WHAT IS THAT?!
NO MATTER HOW STRONG IT SEEMS...
CLICK
A GOLEM'S OUTER SHELL IS NOTHING TO A GOLEM MOLDER.
SHINK
HIS TOOLS SLICE THROUGH THE EARTH EFFORTLESSLY IN RESPONSE TO HIS MAGIC.
STAND

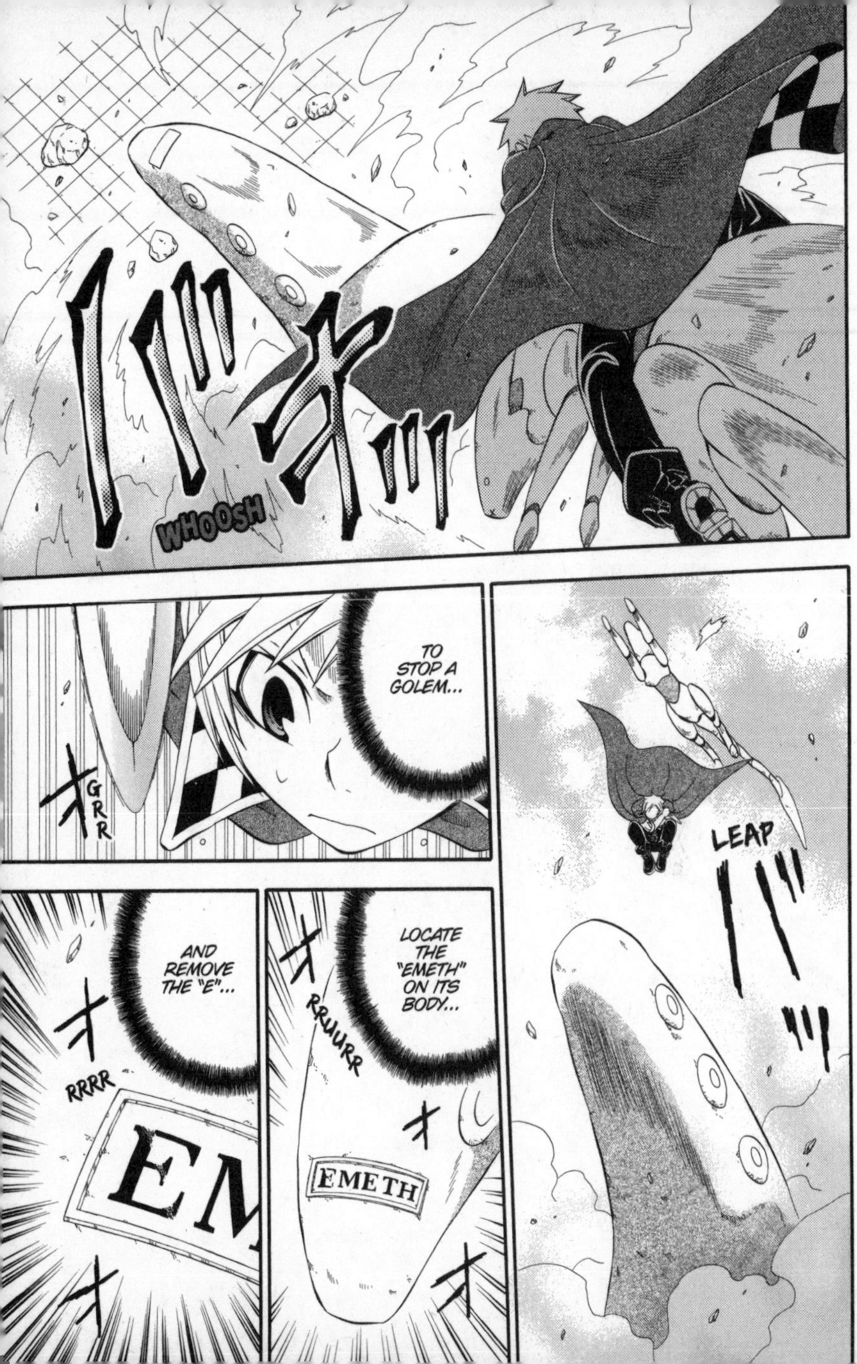
WHOOSH
LEAP
TO STOP A GOLEM...
GRR
LOCATE THE "EMETH" ON ITS BODY...
RRUUURR
EMETH
AND REMOVE THE "E"...
RRRR
EM

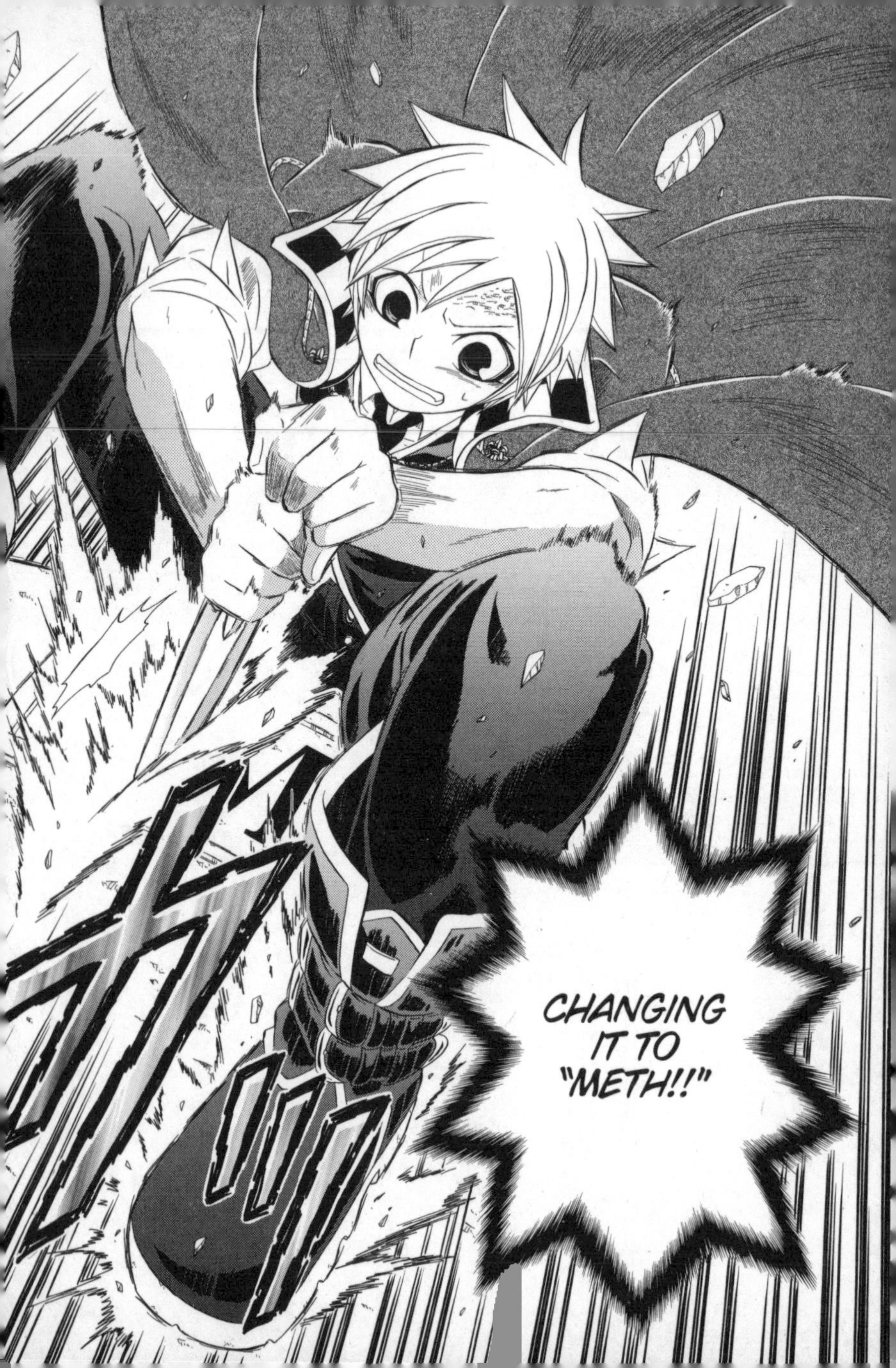
CHANGING IT TO "METH!!"

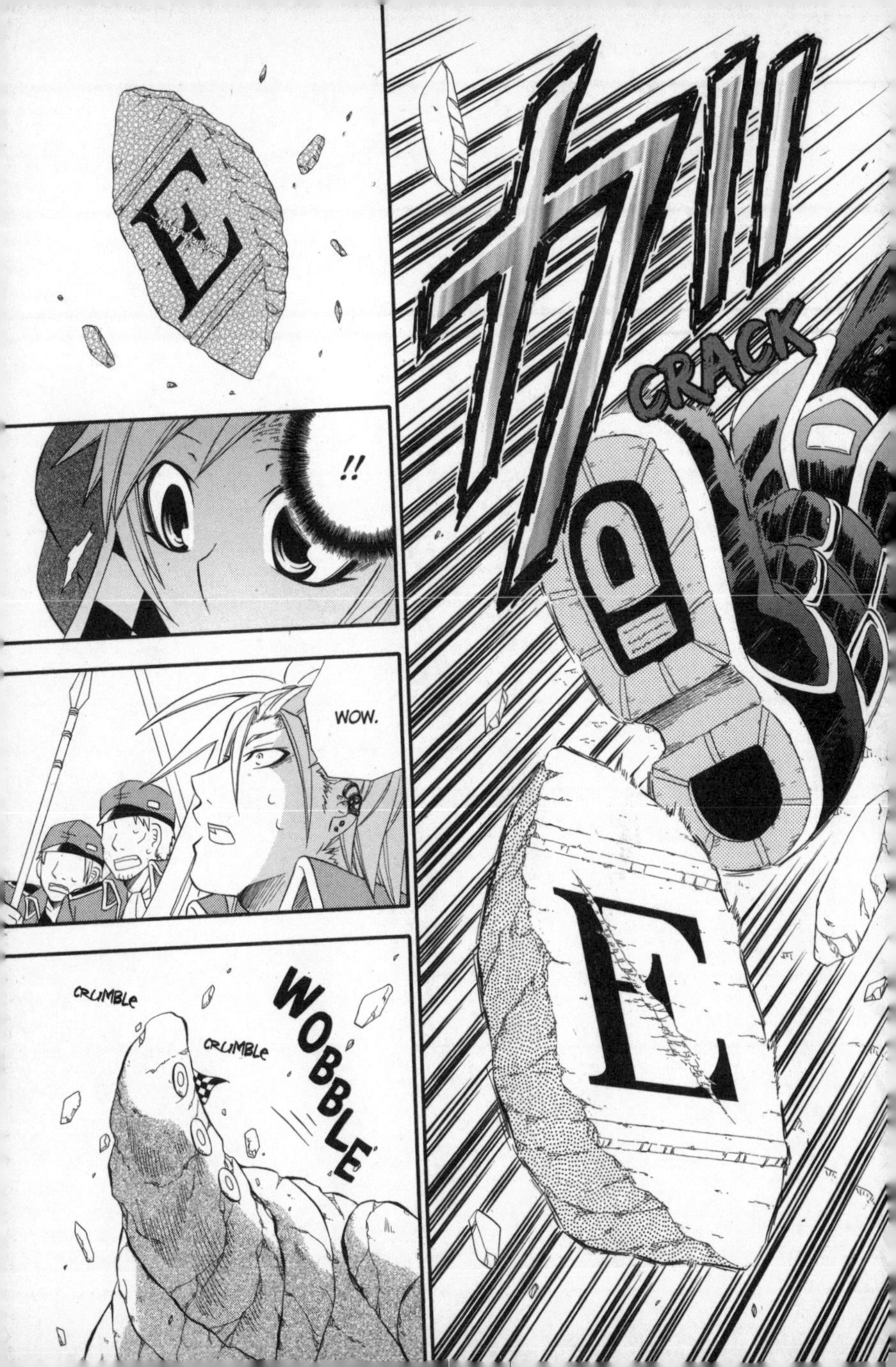
CRACK
!!
WOW.
WOBBLE
CRUMBLE
CRUMBLE

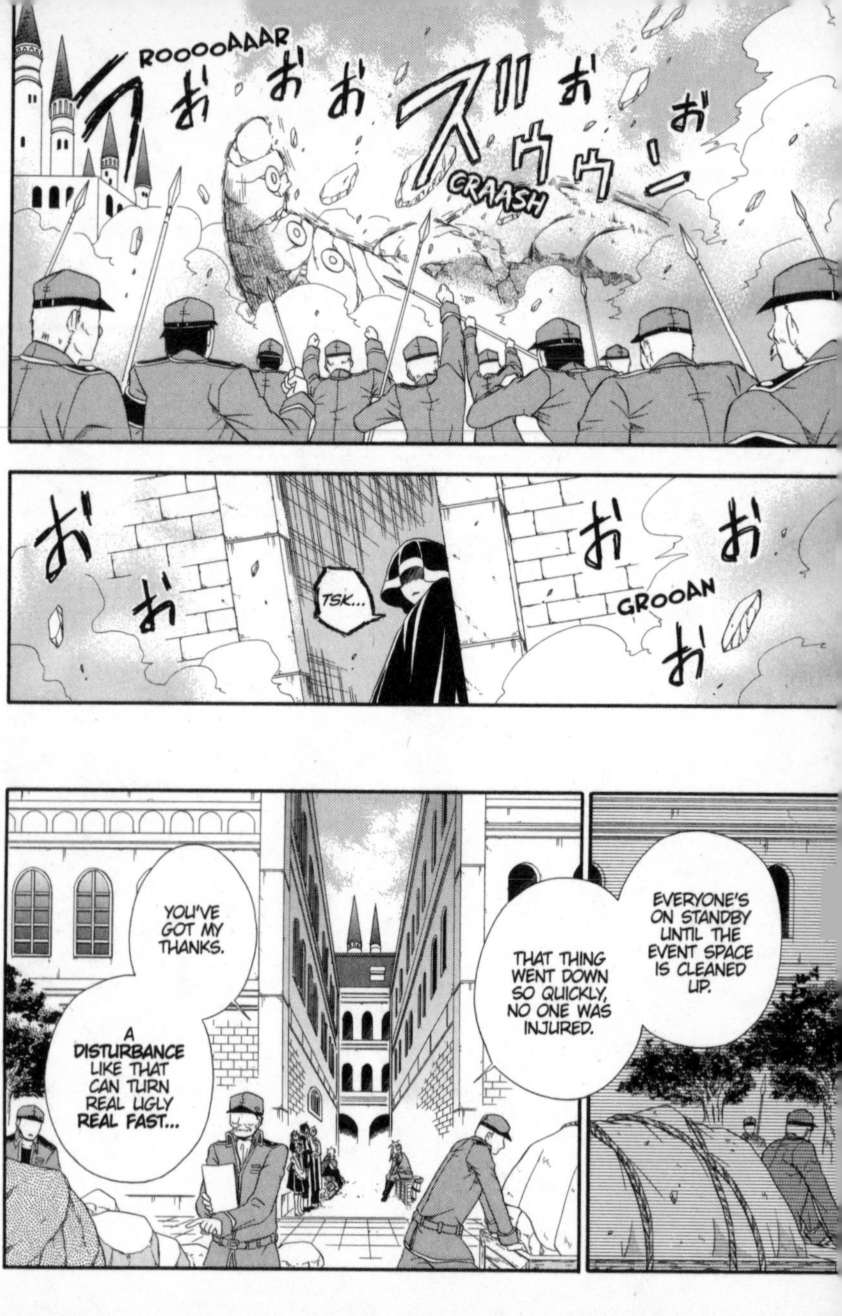
ROOOOAAAR
CRAASH
TSK...
GROOAN
EVERYONE'S ON STANDBY UNTIL THE EVENT SPACE IS CLEANED UP.
THAT THING WENT DOWN SO QUICKLY, NO ONE WAS INJURED.
YOU'VE GOT MY THANKS.
A DISTURBANCE LIKE THAT CAN TURN REAL UGLY REAL FAST...

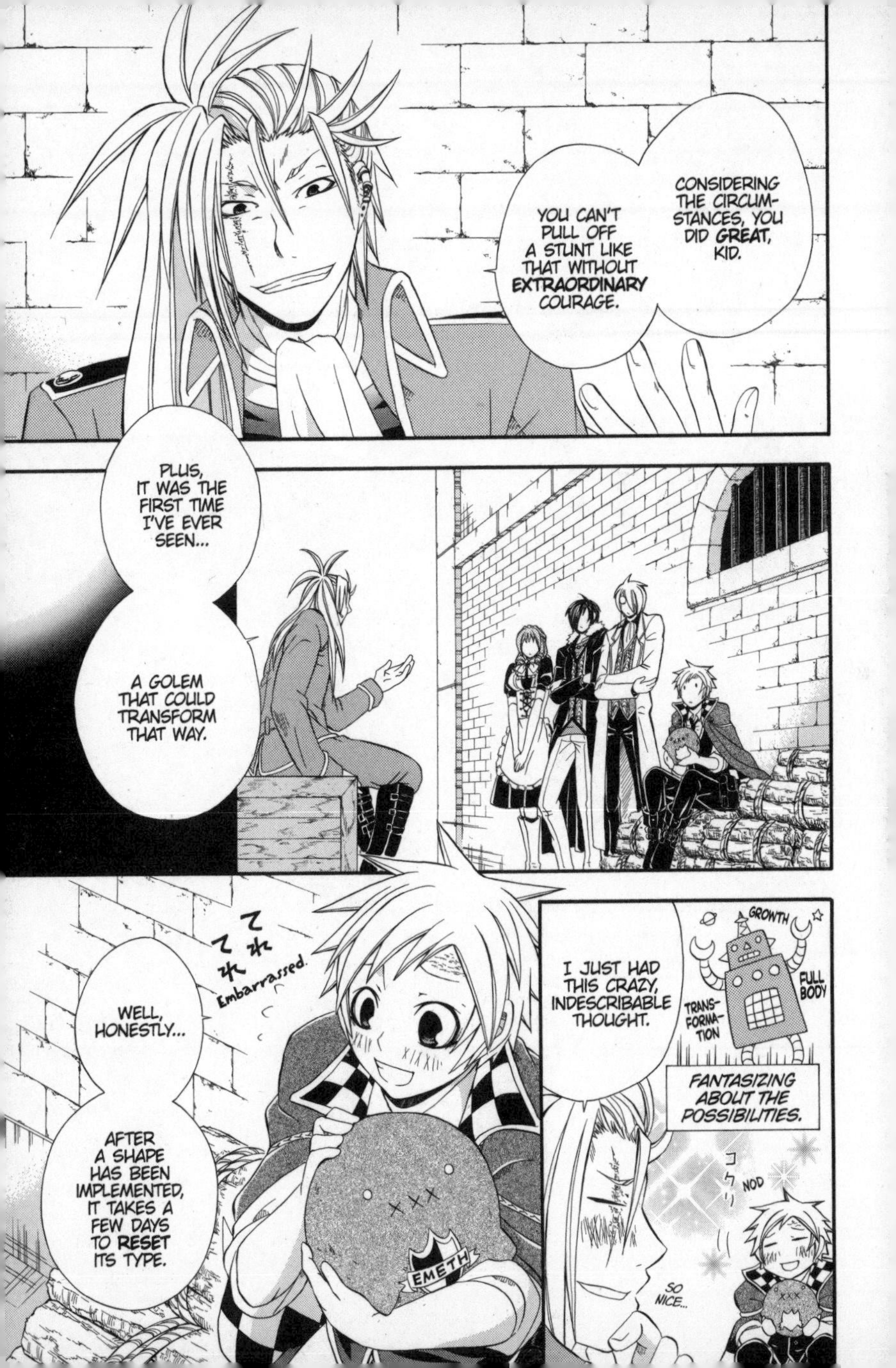
CONSIDERING THE CIRCUM-STANCES, YOU DID GREAT, KID.
YOU CAN'T PULL OFF A STUNT LIKE THAT WITHOUT EXTRAORDINARY COURAGE.
PLUS, IT WAS THE FIRST TIME I'VE EVER SEEN...
A GOLEM THAT COULD TRANSFORM THAT WAY.
I JUST HAD THIS CRAZY, INDESCRIBABLE THOUGHT.
GROWTH
FULL BODY
TRANS-FORMA-TION
FANTASIZING ABOUT THE POSSIBILITIES.
NOD
SO NICE...
Embarrassed
WELL, HONESTLY...
AFTER A SHAPE HAS BEEN IMPLEMENTED, IT TAKES A FEW DAYS TO RESET ITS TYPE.
EMETH

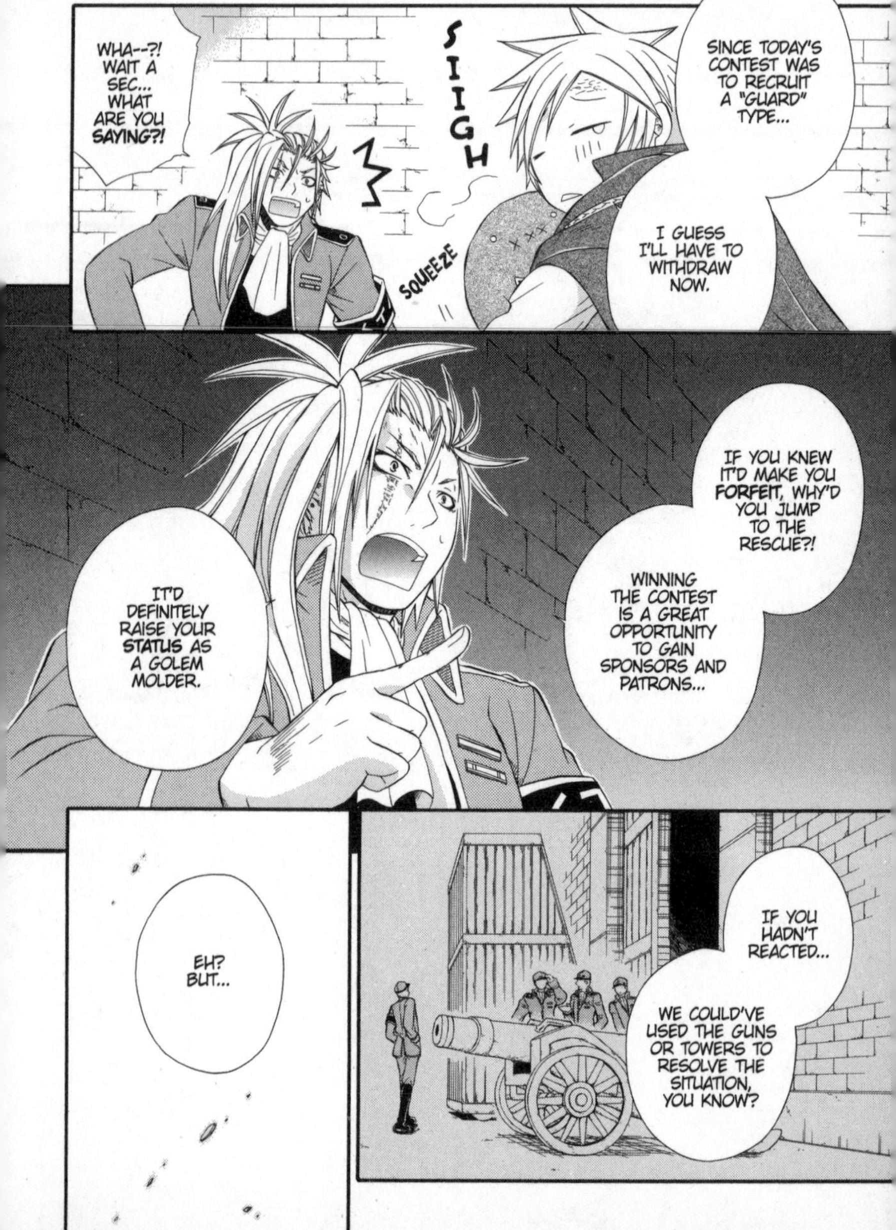
SINCE TODAY'S CONTEST WAS TO RECRUIT A "GUARD" TYPE...
SIIGH
I GUESS I'LL HAVE TO WITHDRAW NOW.
SQUEEZE
WHA--?! WAIT A SEC... WHAT ARE YOU SAYING?!
IF YOU KNEW IT'D MAKE YOU FORFEIT, WHY'D YOU JUMP TO THE RESCUE?!
WINNING THE CONTEST IS A GREAT OPPORTUNITY TO GAIN SPONSORS AND PATRONS...
IT'D DEFINITELY RAISE YOUR STATUS AS A GOLEM MOLDER.
IF YOU HADN'T REACTED...
WE COULD'VE USED THE GUNS OR TOWERS TO RESOLVE THE SITUATION, YOU KNOW?
EH? BUT...

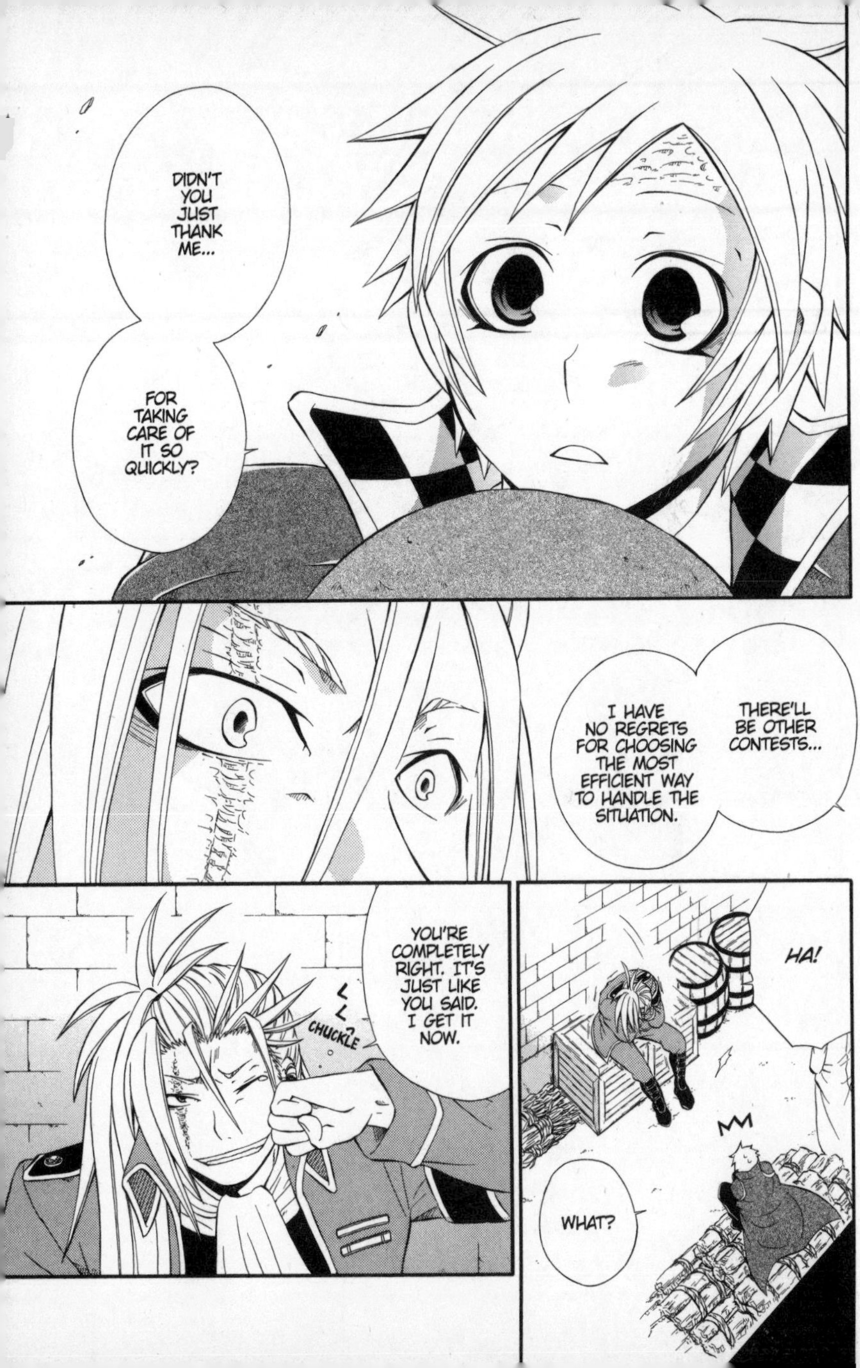
DIDN'T YOU JUST THANK ME...
FOR TAKING CARE OF IT SO QUICKLY?
THERE'LL BE OTHER CONTESTS...
I HAVE NO REGRETS FOR CHOOSING THE MOST EFFICIENT WAY TO HANDLE THE SITUATION.
HA!
WHAT?
YOU'RE COMPLETELY RIGHT. IT'S JUST LIKE YOU SAID. I GET IT NOW.
CHUCKLE

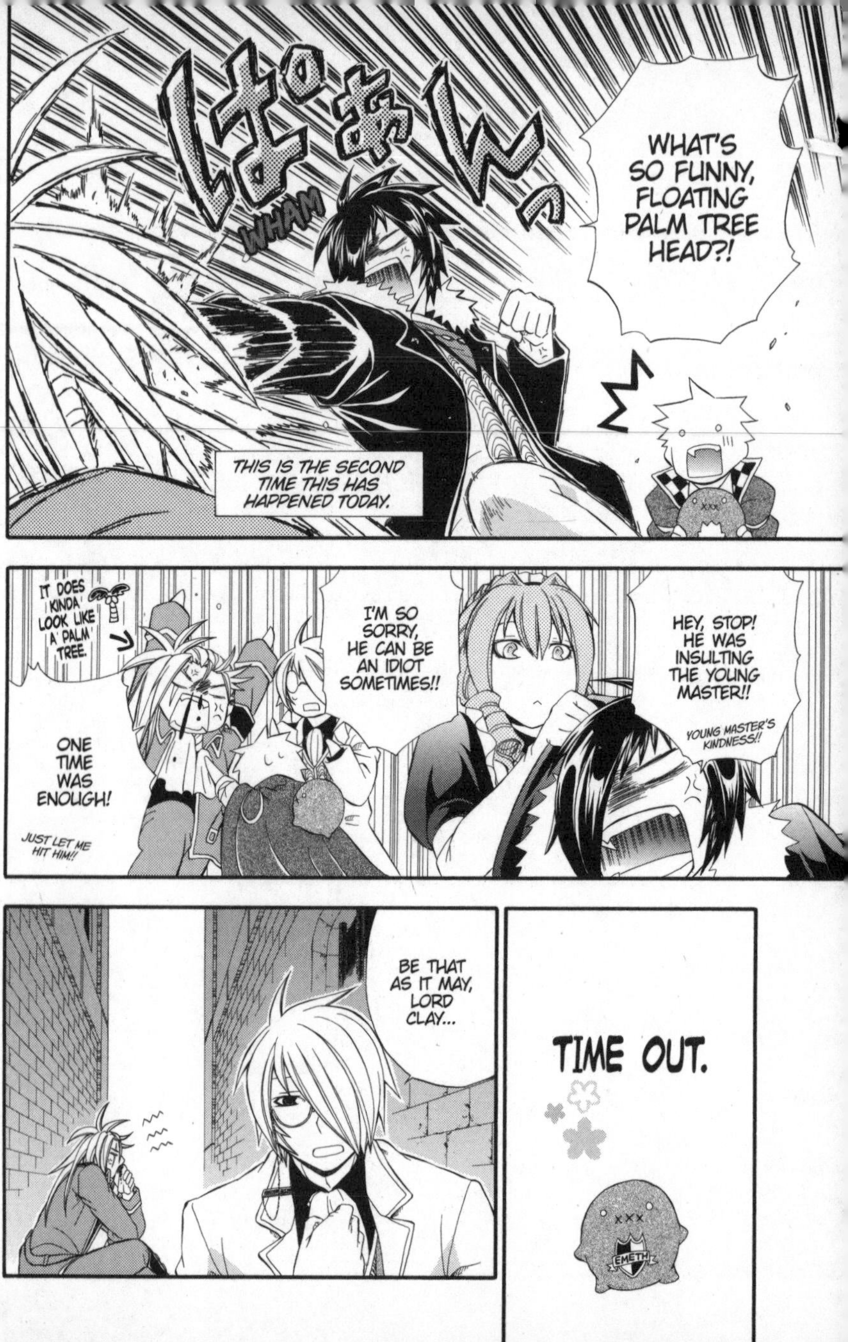
WHAT'S SO FUNNY, FLOATING PALM TREE HEAD?!
WHAM
THIS IS THE SECOND TIME THIS HAS HAPPENED TODAY.
HEY, STOP! HE WAS INSULTING THE YOUNG MASTER!!
YOUNG MASTER'S KINDNESS!!
I'M SO SORRY, HE CAN BE AN IDIOT SOMETIMES!!
IT DOES KINDA LOOK LIKE A PALM TREE.
ONE TIME WAS ENOUGH!
JUST LET ME HIT HIM!!
TIME OUT.
EMETH
BE THAT AS IT MAY, LORD CLAY...

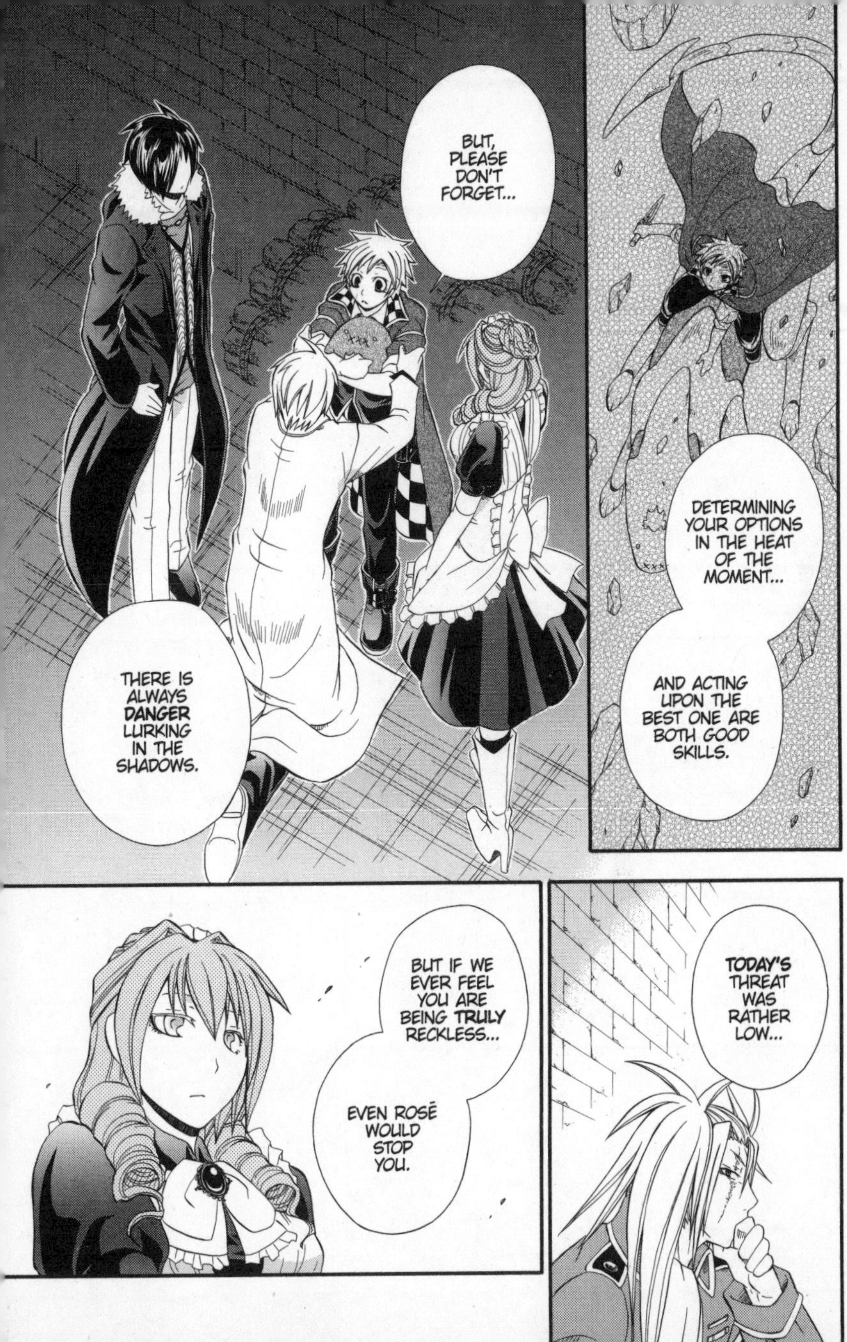
DETERMINING YOUR OPTIONS IN THE HEAT OF THE MOMENT...
AND ACTING UPON THE BEST ONE ARE BOTH GOOD SKILLS.
BUT, PLEASE DON'T FORGET...
THERE IS ALWAYS DANGER LURKING IN THE SHADOWS.
TODAY'S THREAT WAS RATHER LOW...
BUT IF WE EVER FEEL YOU ARE BEING TRULY RECKLESS...
EVEN ROSÉ WOULD STOP YOU.

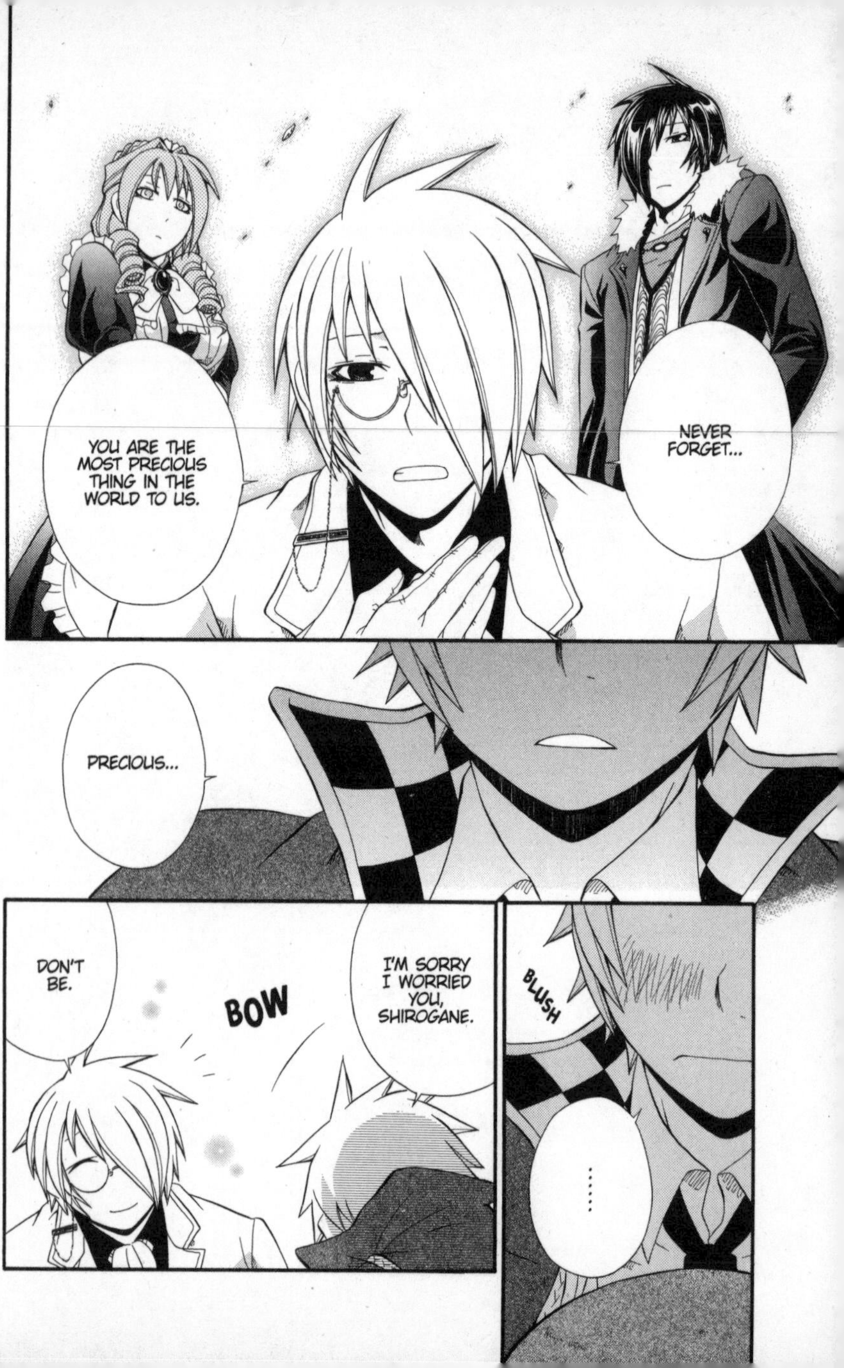
NEVER FORGET...
YOU ARE THE MOST PRECIOUS THING IN THE WORLD TO US.
PRECIOUS...
BLUSH
......
I'M SORRY I WORRIED YOU, SHIROGANE.
BOW
DON'T BE.

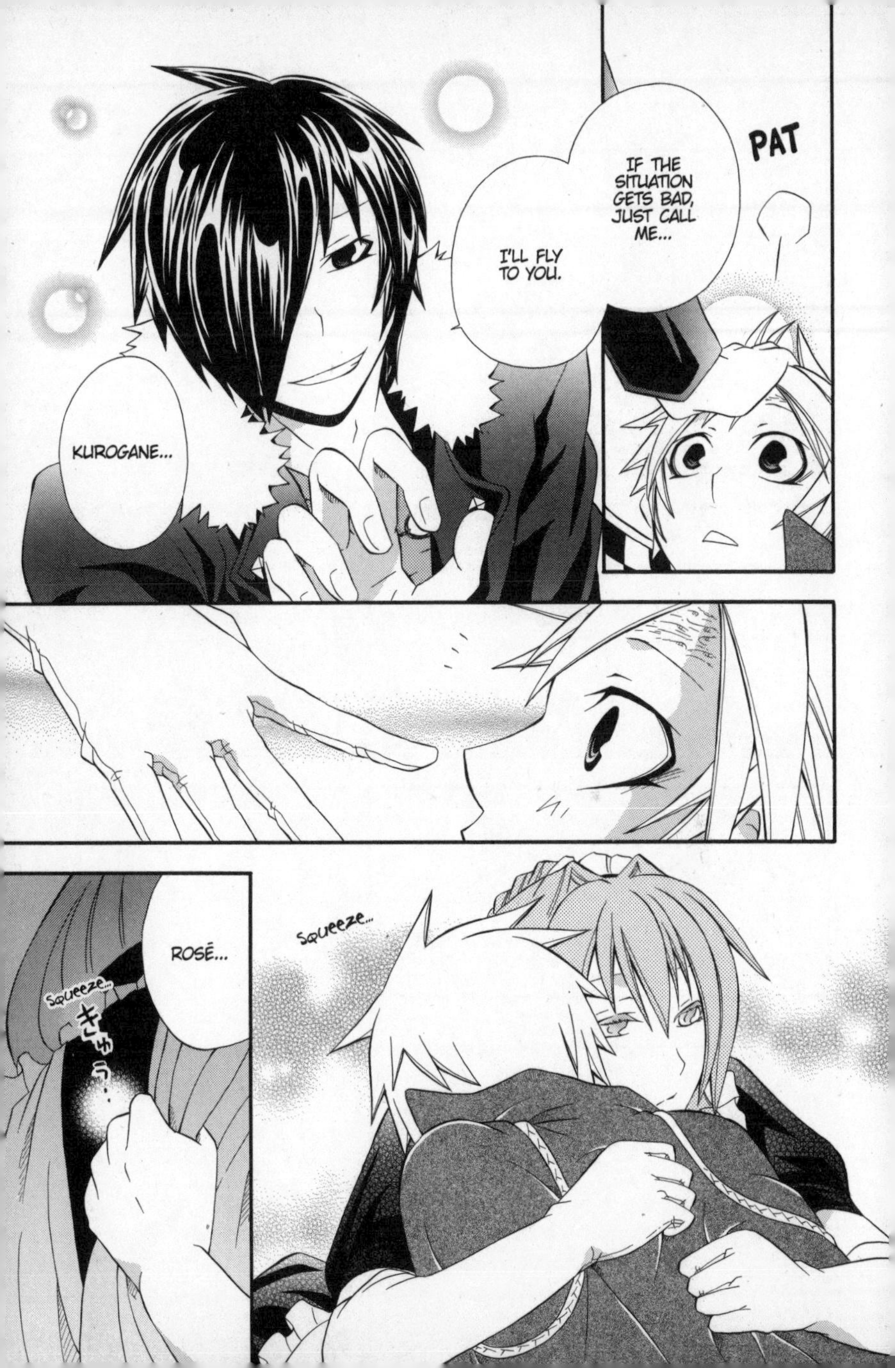
PAT
IF THE SITUATION GETS BAD, JUST CALL ME...
I'LL FLY TO YOU.
KUROGANE...
Squeeze...
ROSÉ...
Squeeze...
きゅう…

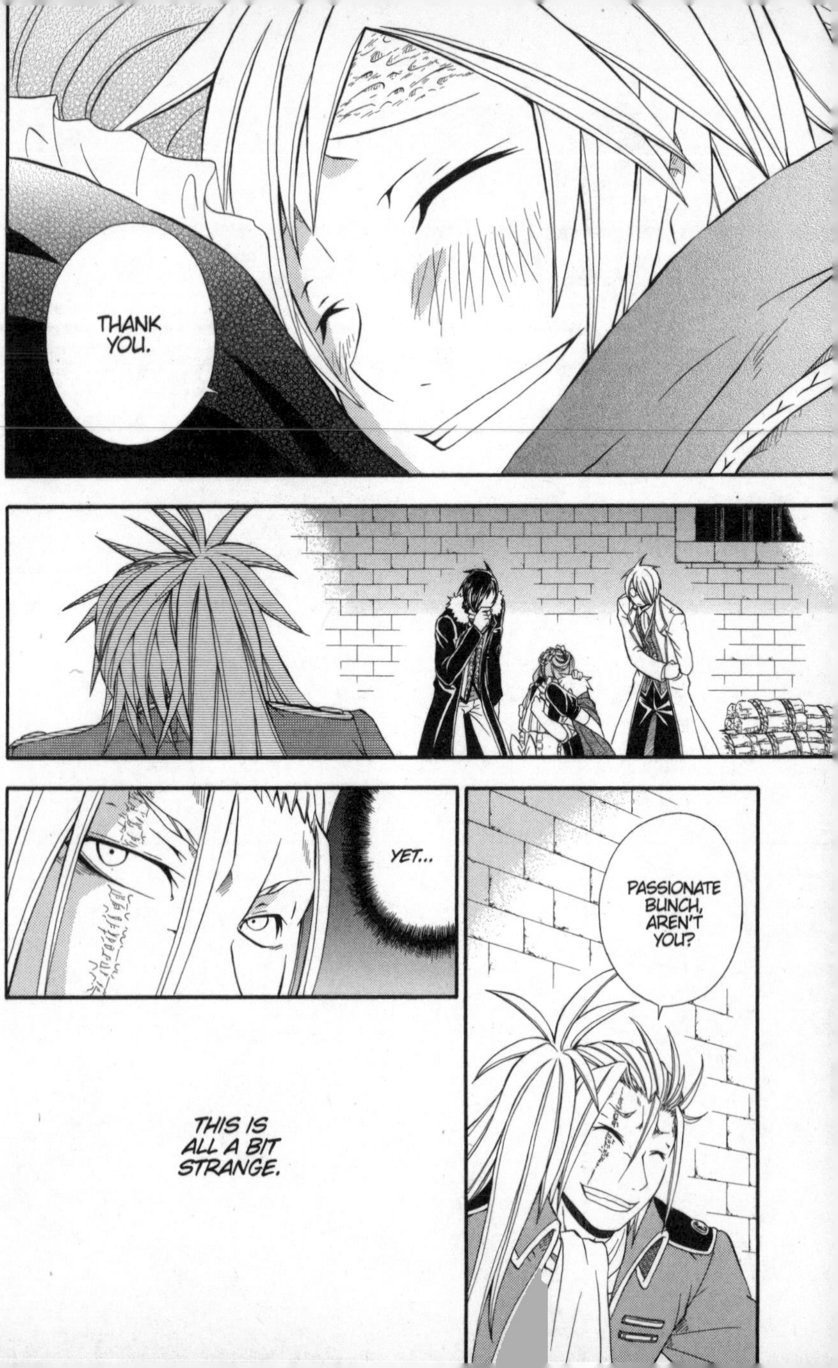
THANK YOU.
PASSIONATE BUNCH, AREN'T YOU?
YET...
THIS IS ALL A BIT STRANGE.

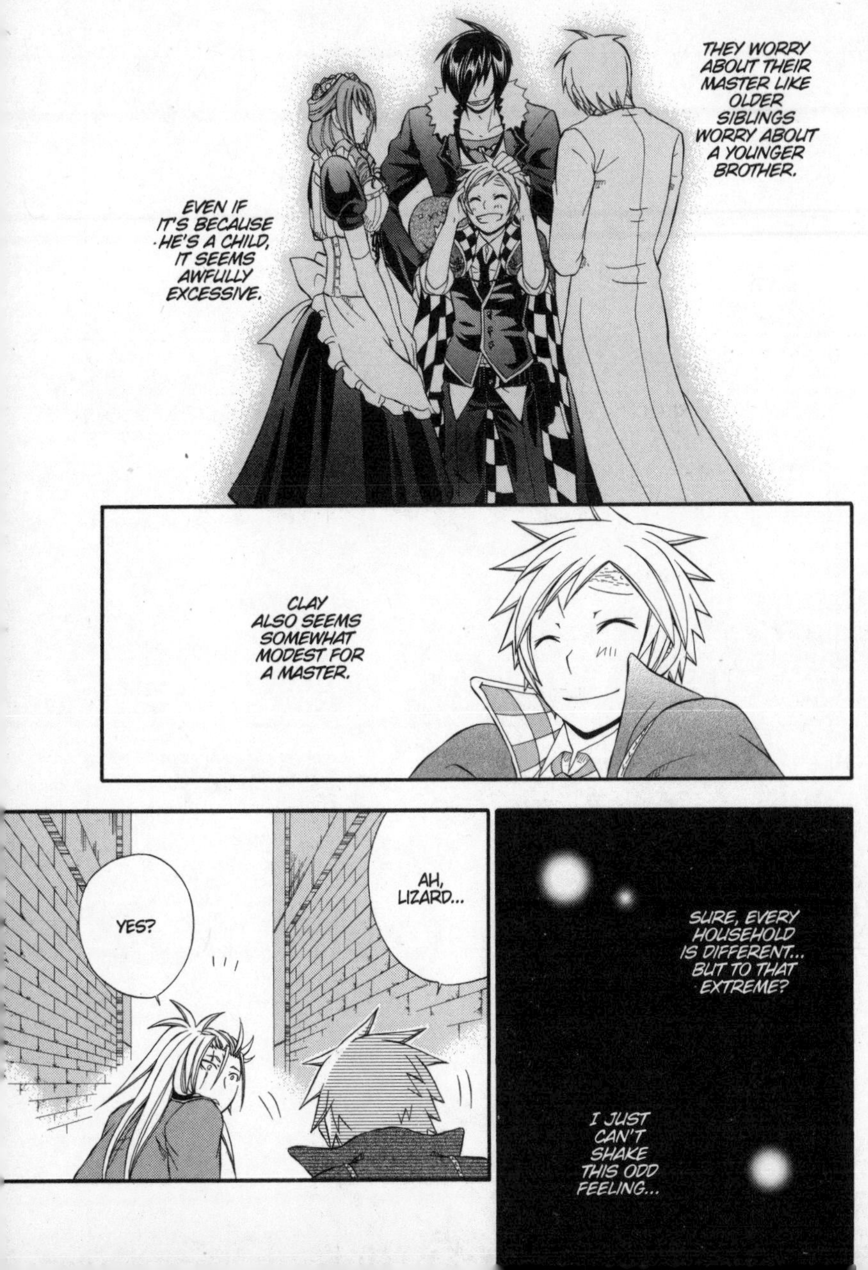
THEY WORRY ABOUT THEIR MASTER LIKE OLDER SIBLINGS WORRY ABOUT A YOUNGER BROTHER.
EVEN IF IT'S BECAUSE HE'S A CHILD, IT SEEMS AWFULLY EXCESSIVE.
CLAY ALSO SEEMS SOMEWHAT MODEST FOR A MASTER.
SURE, EVERY HOUSEHOLD IS DIFFERENT... BUT TO THAT EXTREME?
I JUST CAN'T SHAKE THIS ODD FEELING...
AH, LIZARD...
YES?

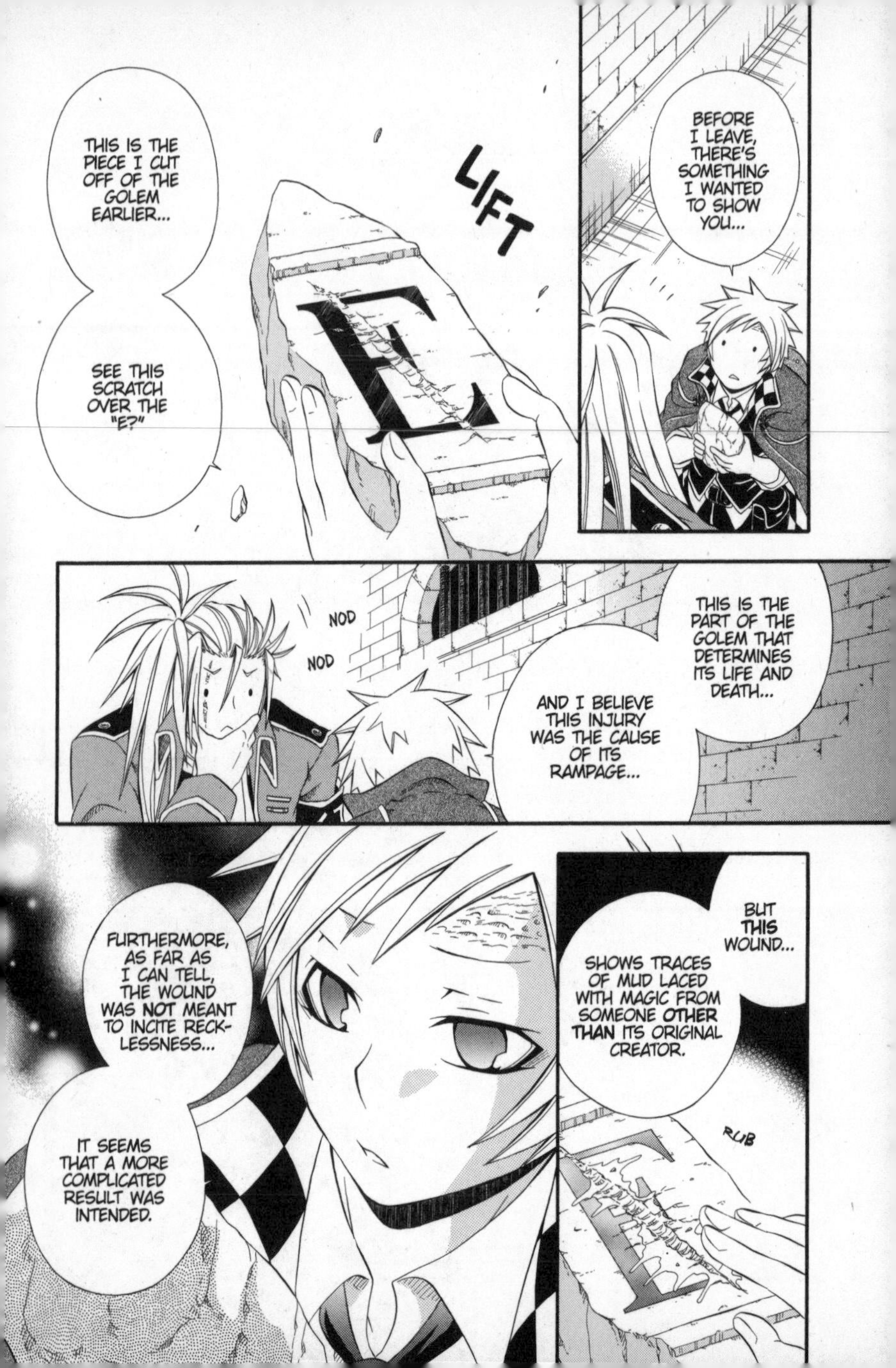
BEFORE I LEAVE, THERE'S SOMETHING I WANTED TO SHOW YOU...
LIFT
THIS IS THE PIECE I CUT OFF OF THE GOLEM EARLIER...
SEE THIS SCRATCH OVER THE "E?"
THIS IS THE PART OF THE GOLEM THAT DETERMINES ITS LIFE AND DEATH...
AND I BELIEVE THIS INJURY WAS THE CAUSE OF ITS RAMPAGE...
NOD
NOD
BUT THIS WOUND...
SHOWS TRACES OF MUD LACED WITH MAGIC FROM SOMEONE OTHER THAN ITS ORIGINAL CREATOR.
RUB
FURTHERMORE, AS FAR AS I CAN TELL, THE WOUND WAS NOT MEANT TO INCITE RECK-LESSNESS...
IT SEEMS THAT A MORE COMPLICATED RESULT WAS INTENDED.

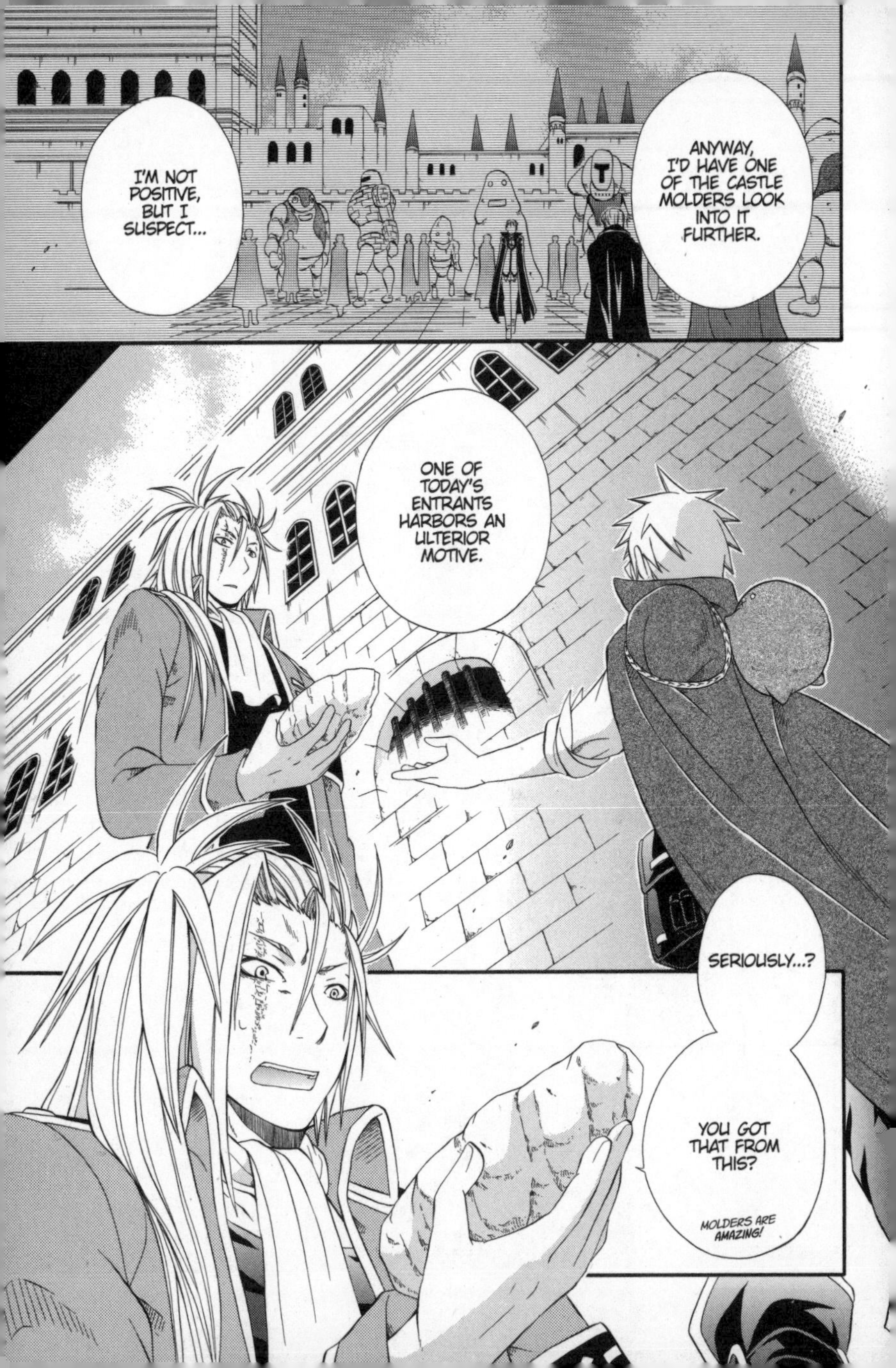
ANYWAY, I'D HAVE ONE OF THE CASTLE MOLDERS LOOK INTO IT FURTHER.
I'M NOT POSITIVE, BUT I SUSPECT...
ONE OF TODAY'S ENTRANTS HARBORS AN ULTERIOR MOTIVE.
SERIOUSLY...?
YOU GOT THAT FROM THIS?
MOLDERS ARE AMAZING!

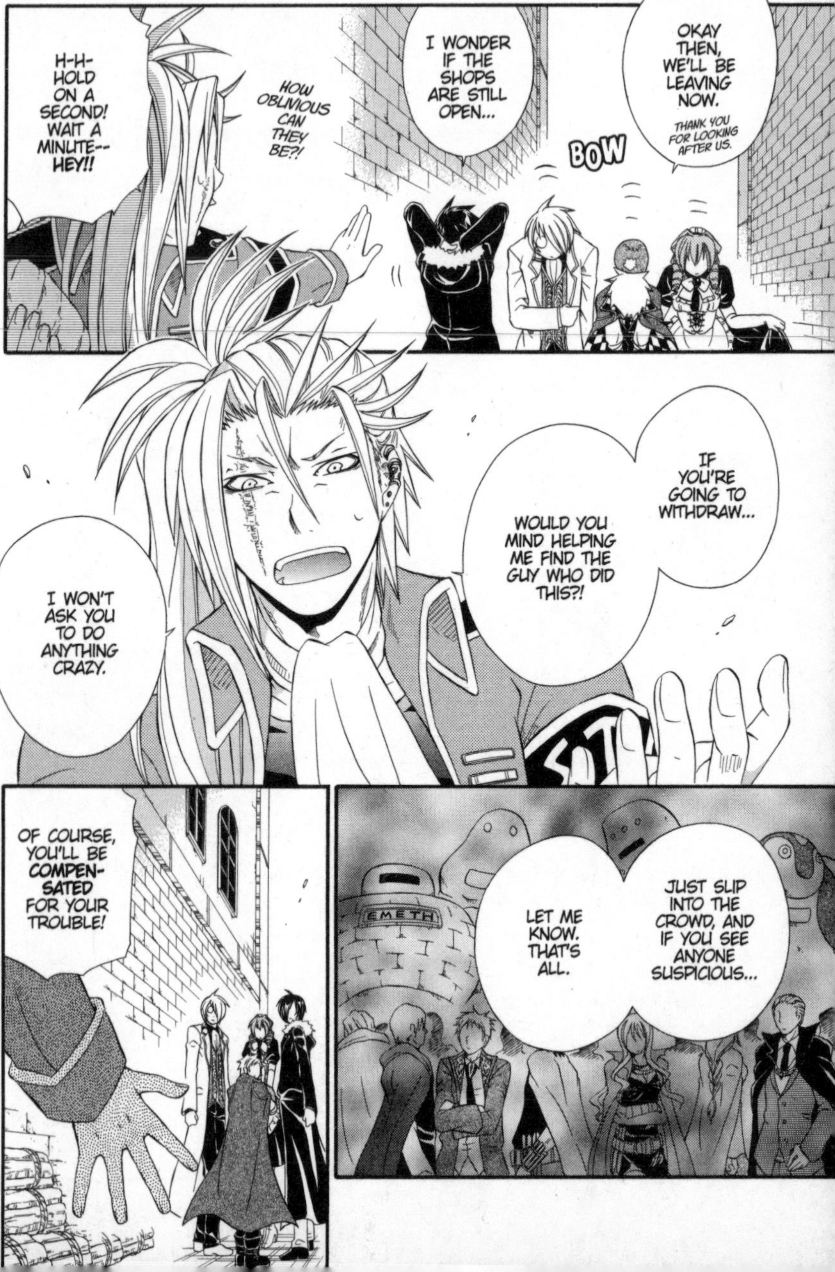
OKAY THEN, WE'LL BE LEAVING NOW.
THANK YOU FOR LOOKING AFTER US.
BOW
I WONDER IF THE SHOPS ARE STILL OPEN...
HOW OBLIVIOUS CAN THEY BE?!
H-H-HOLD ON A SECOND! WAIT A MINUTE--HEY!!
IF YOU'RE GOING TO WITHDRAW...
WOULD YOU MIND HELPING ME FIND THE GUY WHO DID THIS?!
I WON'T ASK YOU TO DO ANYTHING CRAZY.
JUST SLIP INTO THE CROWD, AND IF YOU SEE ANYONE SUSPICIOUS...
LET ME KNOW. THAT'S ALL.
EMETH
OF COURSE, YOU'LL BE COMPEN-SATED FOR YOUR TROUBLE!

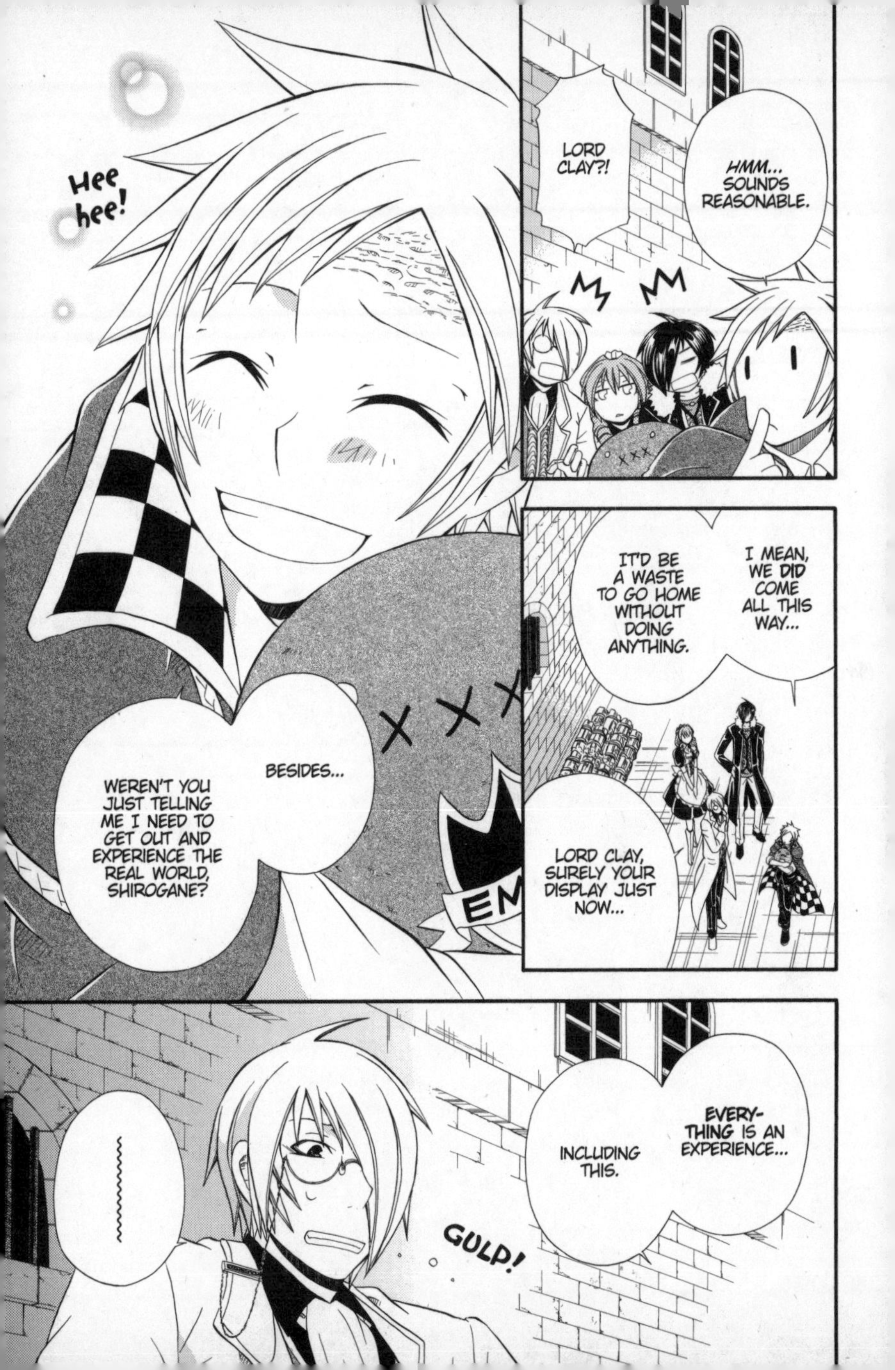
HMM... SOUNDS REASONABLE.
LORD CLAY?!
I MEAN, WE DID COME ALL THIS WAY...
IT'D BE A WASTE TO GO HOME WITHOUT DOING ANYTHING.
LORD CLAY, SURELY YOUR DISPLAY JUST NOW...
Hee hee!
BESIDES...
WEREN'T YOU JUST TELLING ME I NEED TO GET OUT AND EXPERIENCE THE REAL WORLD, SHIROGANE?
EVERY-THING IS AN EXPERIENCE...
INCLUDING THIS.
GULP!

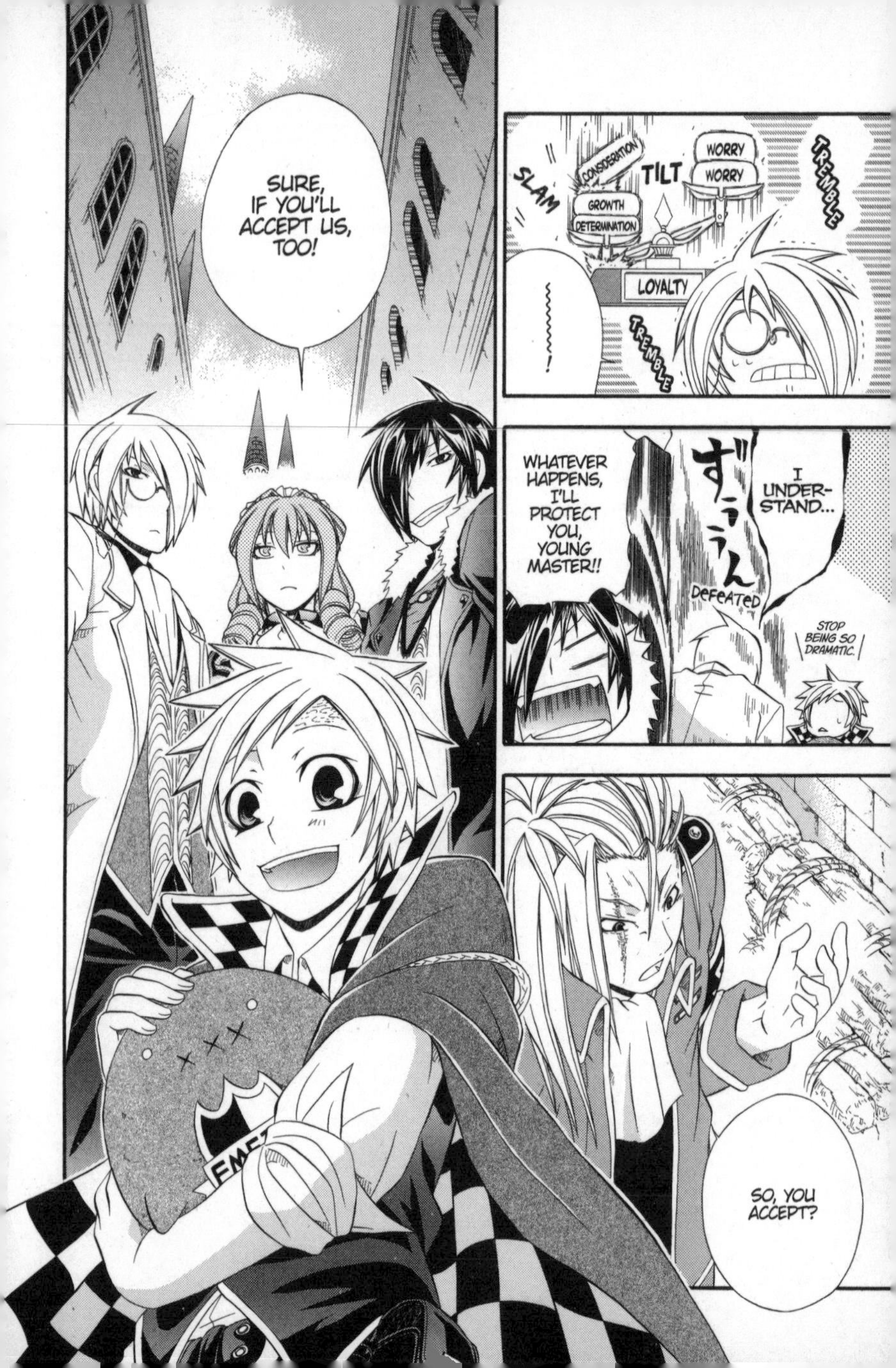
TREMBLE
WORRY
WORRY
TILT
CONSIDERATION
SLAM
GROWTH
DETERMINATION
LOYALTY
TREMBLE
~~~~~!
I UNDER-STAND...
ずううん
DEFEATED
WHATEVER HAPPENS, I'LL PROTECT YOU, YOUNG MASTER!!
STOP BEING SO DRAMATIC.
SO, YOU ACCEPT?
SURE, IF YOU'LL ACCEPT US, TOO!
~~~~~

Chapter 2: The Three Servants

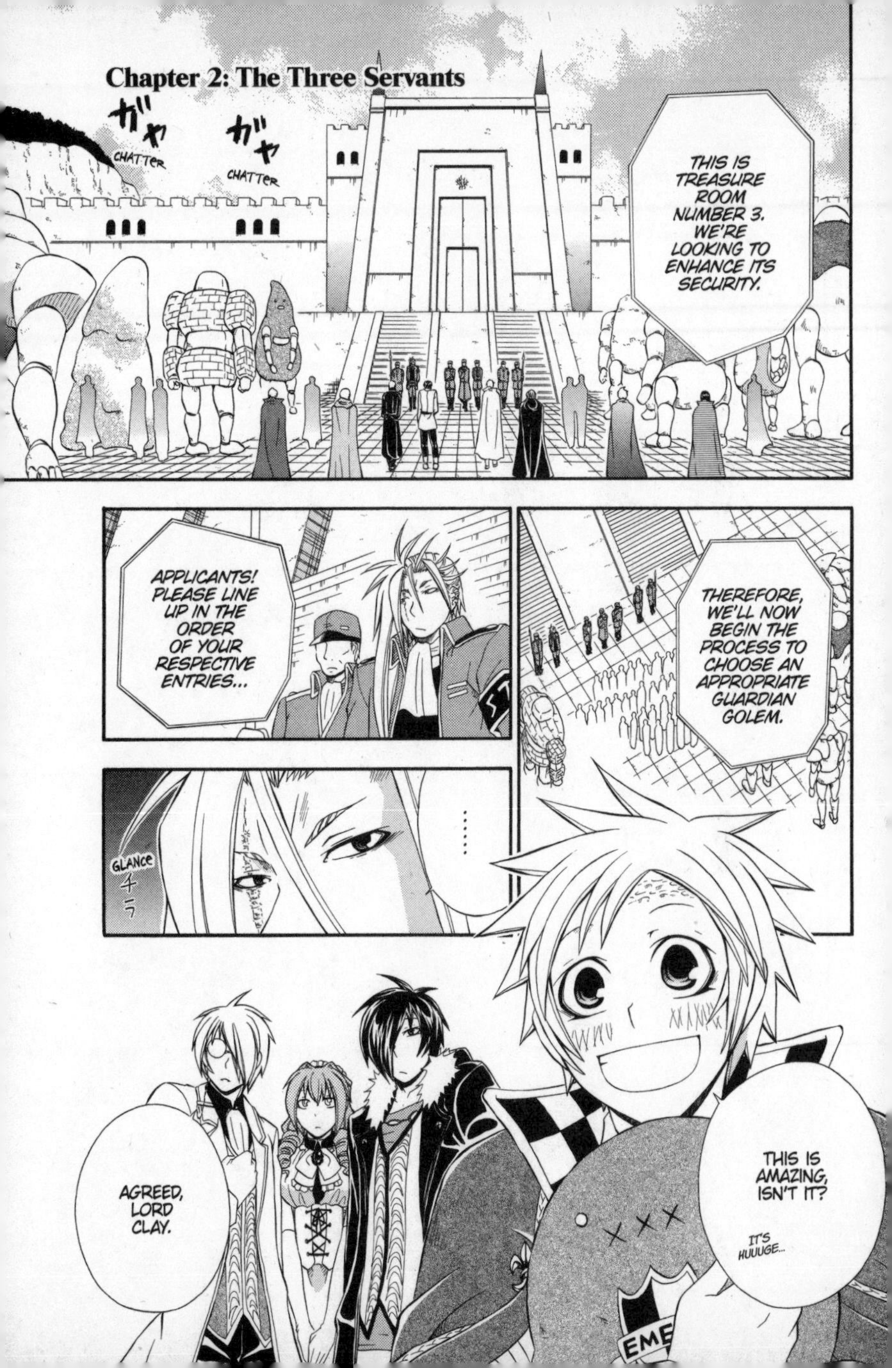
ガヤ
CHATTER
ガヤ
CHATTER
THIS IS TREASURE ROOM NUMBER 3. WE'RE LOOKING TO ENHANCE ITS SECURITY.
THEREFORE, WE'LL NOW BEGIN THE PROCESS TO CHOOSE AN APPROPRIATE GUARDIAN GOLEM.
APPLICANTS! PLEASE LINE UP IN THE ORDER OF YOUR RESPECTIVE ENTRIES...
......
GLANCE
チラ
THIS IS AMAZING, ISN'T IT?
IT'S HUUUGE...
AGREED, LORD CLAY.

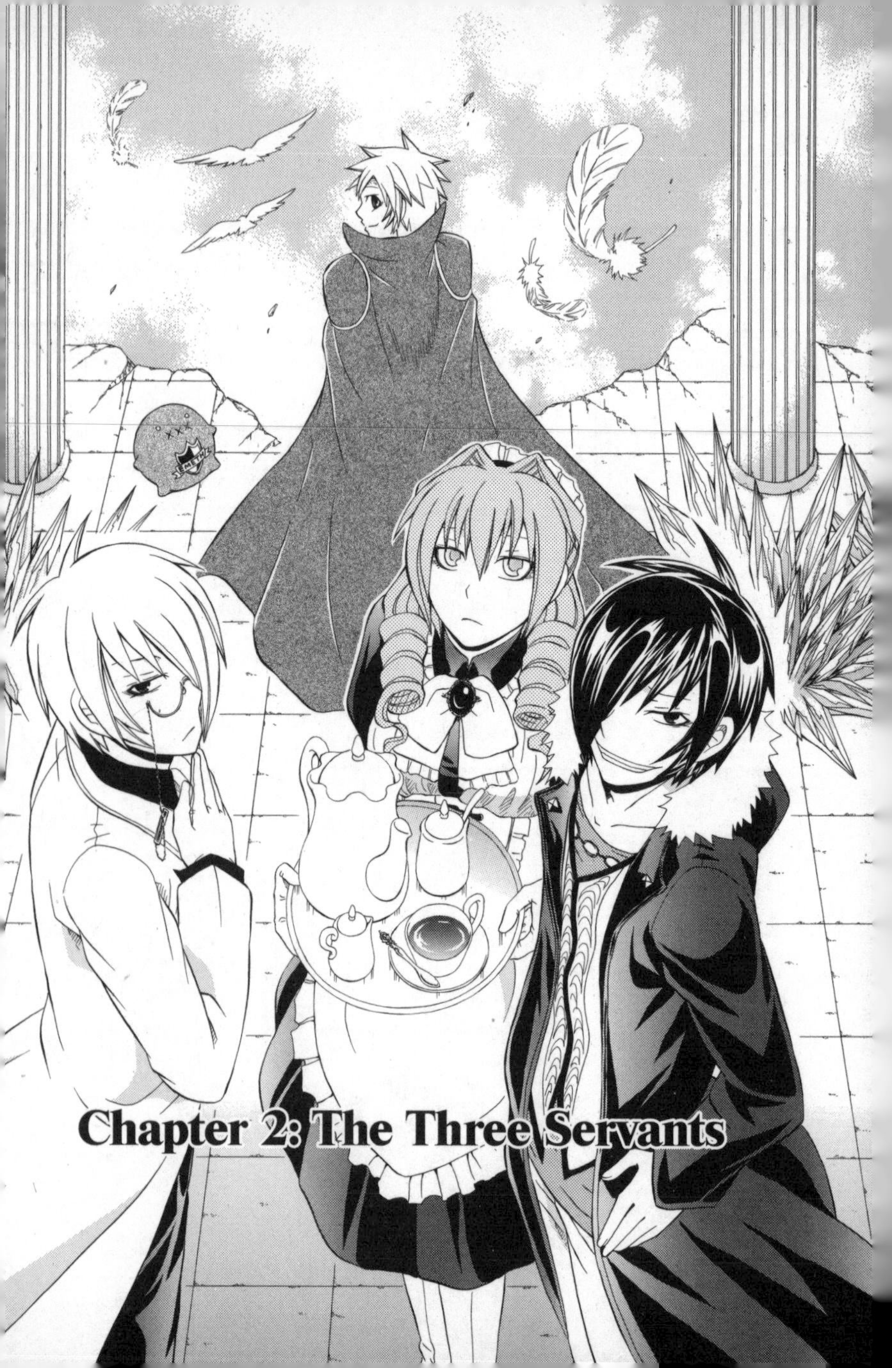

Chapter 2: The Three Servants

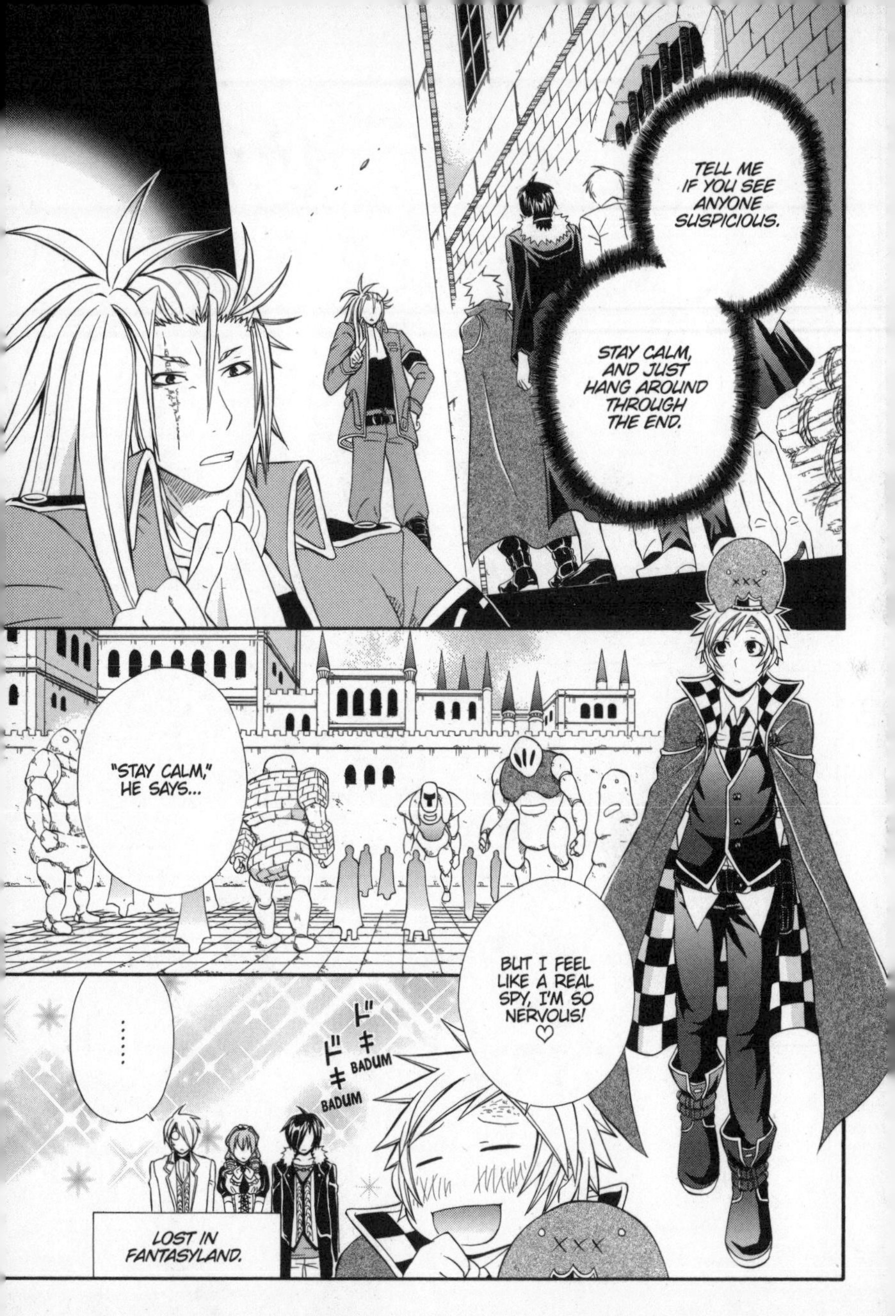
TELL ME IF YOU SEE ANYONE SUSPICIOUS.
STAY CALM, AND JUST HANG AROUND THROUGH THE END.
"STAY CALM," HE SAYS...
BUT I FEEL LIKE A REAL SPY, I'M SO NERVOUS! ♡
ドキ ドキ
BADUM BADUM
......
LOST IN FANTASYLAND.

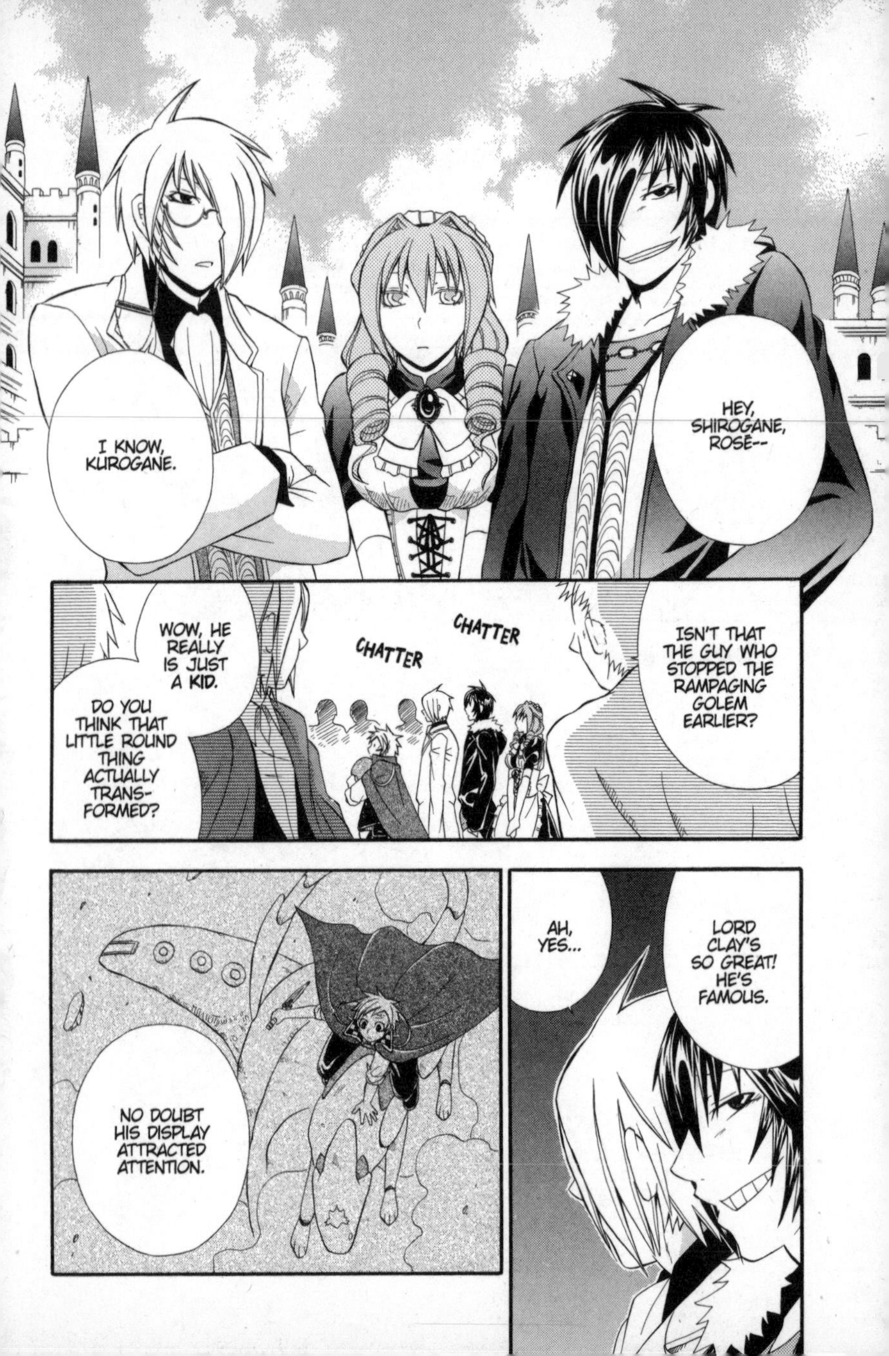
HEY, SHIROGANE, ROSE--
I KNOW, KUROGANE.
ISN'T THAT THE GUY WHO STOPPED THE RAMPAGING GOLEM EARLIER?
CHATTER
CHATTER
WOW, HE REALLY IS JUST A KID.
DO YOU THINK THAT LITTLE ROUND THING ACTUALLY TRANS-FORMED?
LORD CLAY'S SO GREAT! HE'S FAMOUS.
AH, YES...
NO DOUBT HIS DISPLAY ATTRACTED ATTENTION.

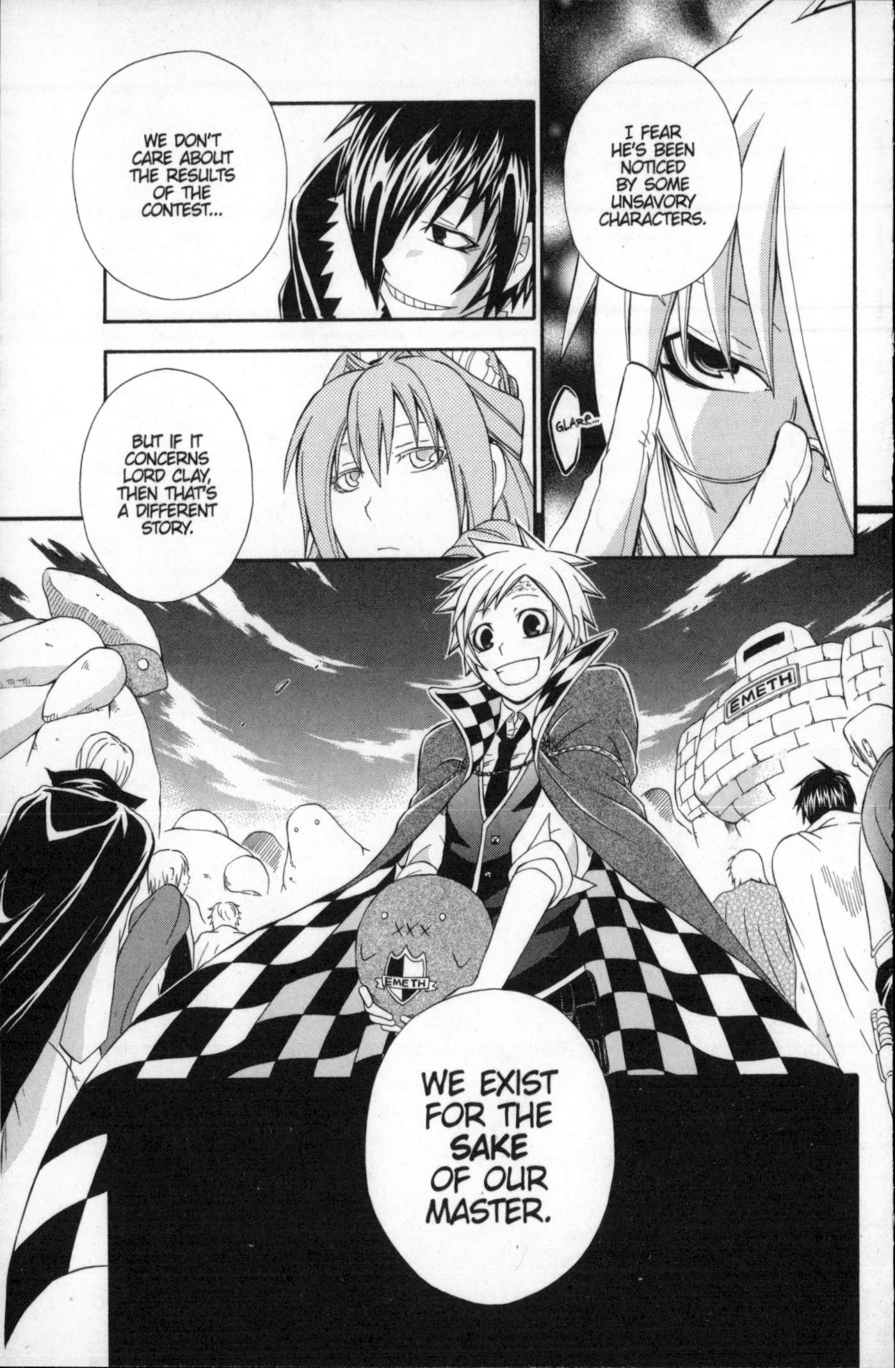
I FEAR HE'S BEEN NOTICED BY SOME UNSAVORY CHARACTERS.
GLARE...
WE DON'T CARE ABOUT THE RESULTS OF THE CONTEST...
BUT IF IT CONCERNS LORD CLAY, THEN THAT'S A DIFFERENT STORY.
EMETH
EMETH
WE EXIST FOR THE SAKE OF OUR MASTER.

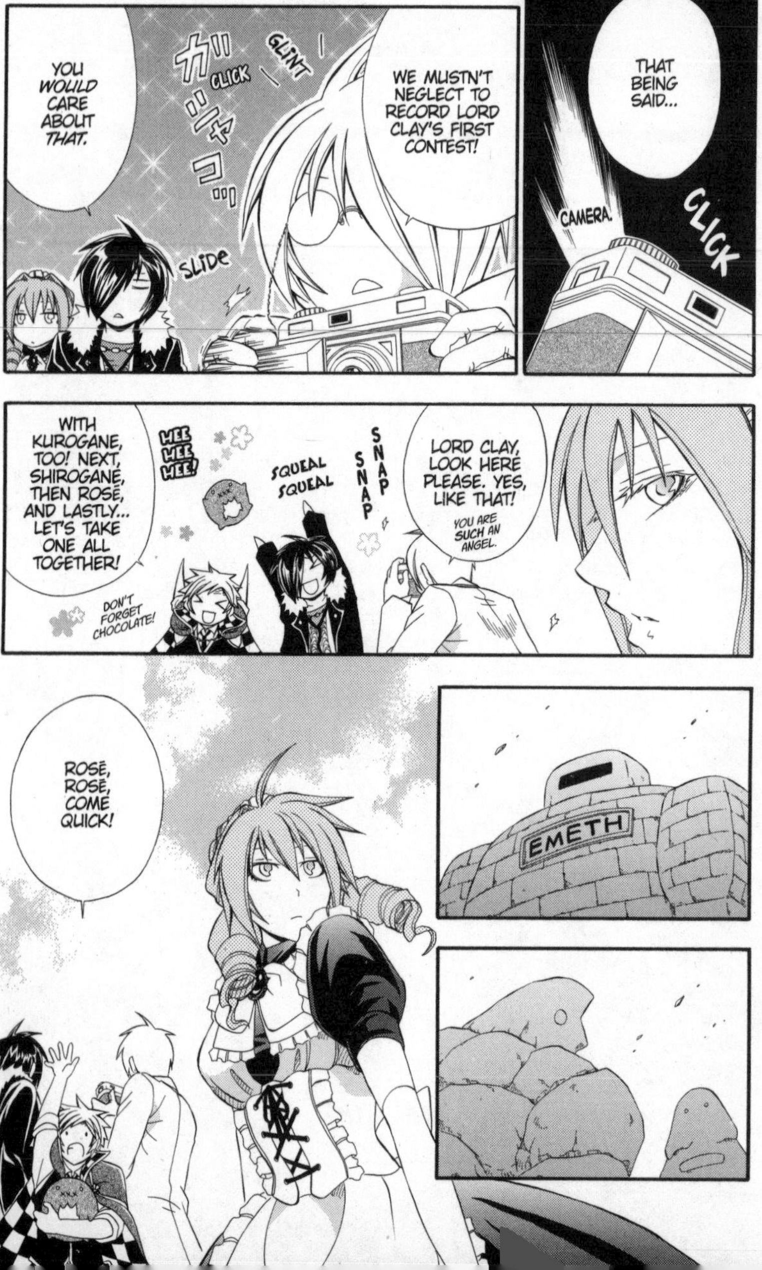
THAT BEING SAID...
CAMERA.
CLICK
WE MUSTN'T NEGLECT TO RECORD LORD CLAY'S FIRST CONTEST!
GLINT
CLICK
SLIDE
YOU WOULD CARE ABOUT THAT.
LORD CLAY, LOOK HERE PLEASE. YES, LIKE THAT!
YOU ARE SUCH AN ANGEL.
SNAP SNAP
SQUEAL SQUEAL
HEE HEE HEE!
WITH KUROGANE, TOO! NEXT, SHIROGANE, THEN ROSE, AND LASTLY... LET'S TAKE ONE ALL TOGETHER!
DON'T FORGET CHOCOLATE!
EMETH
ROSE, ROSE, COME QUICK!

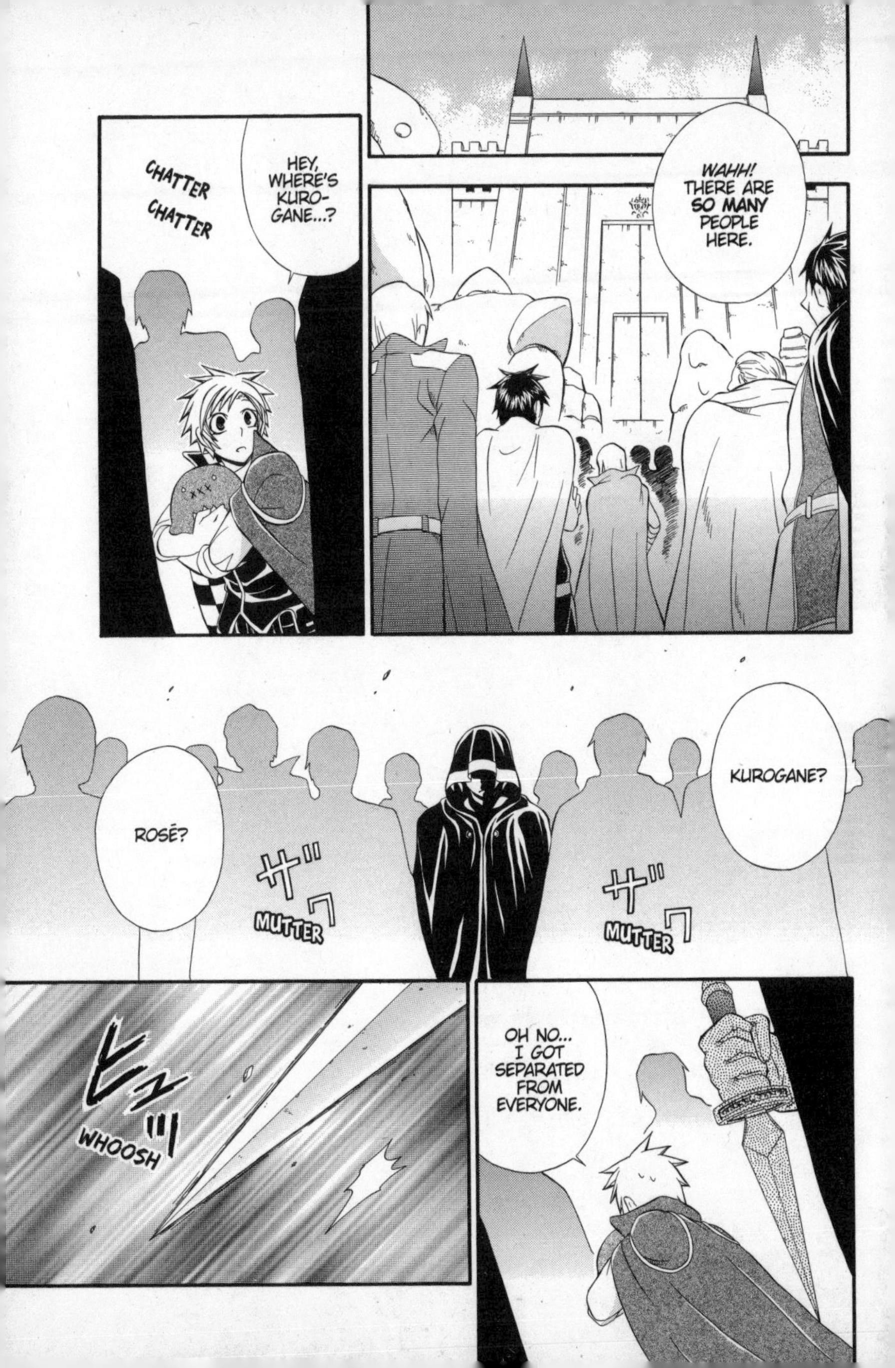
WAHH! THERE ARE SO MANY PEOPLE HERE.
HEY, WHERE'S KURO-GANE...?
CHATTER CHATTER
KUROGANE?
ザワッ
MUTTER
ザワッ
MUTTER
ROSÉ?
OH NO... I GOT SEPARATED FROM EVERYONE.
ヒュッ
WHOOSH

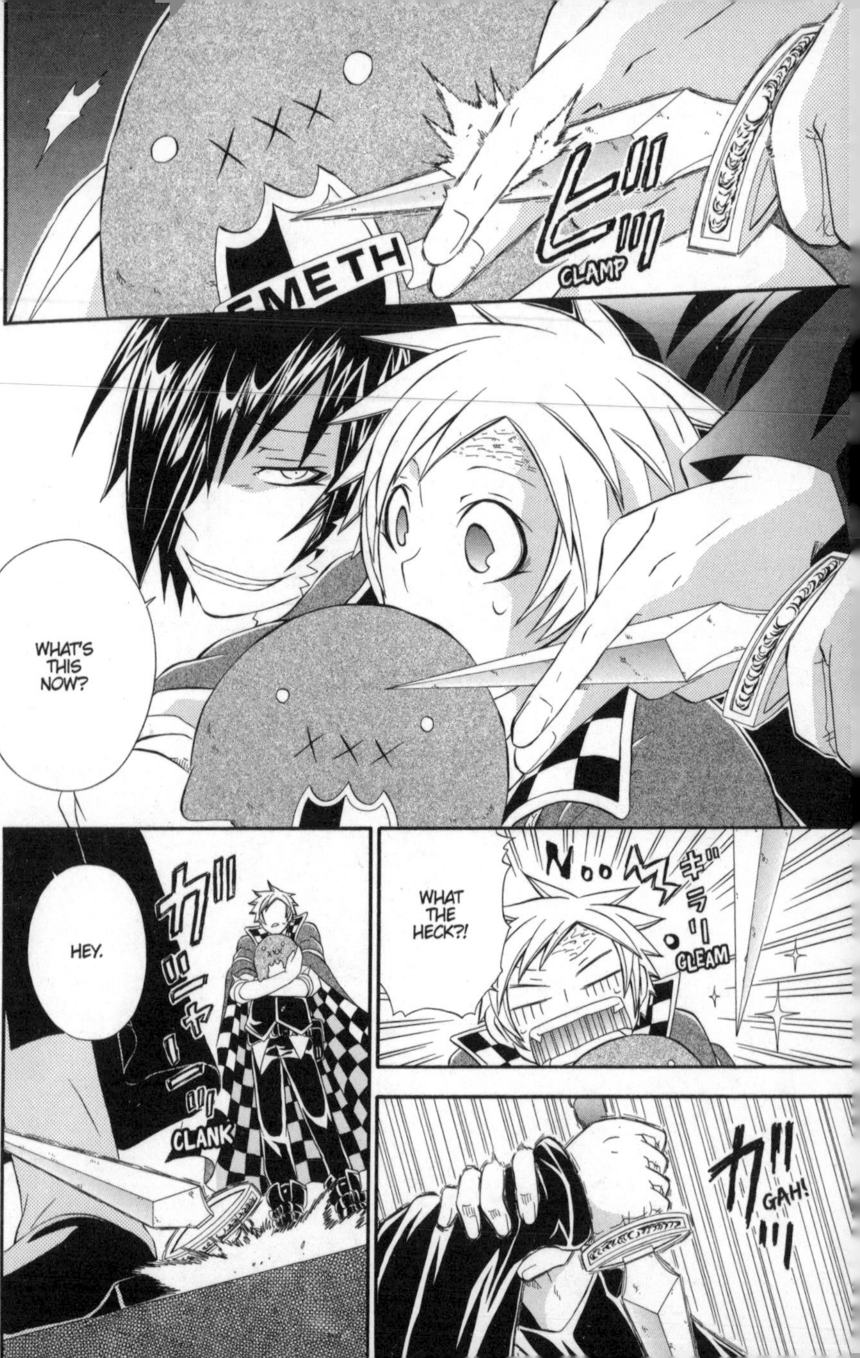
EMETH
CLAMP
WHAT'S THIS NOW?
WHAT THE HECK?!
Noo
GLEAM
GAH!
HEY.
CLANK

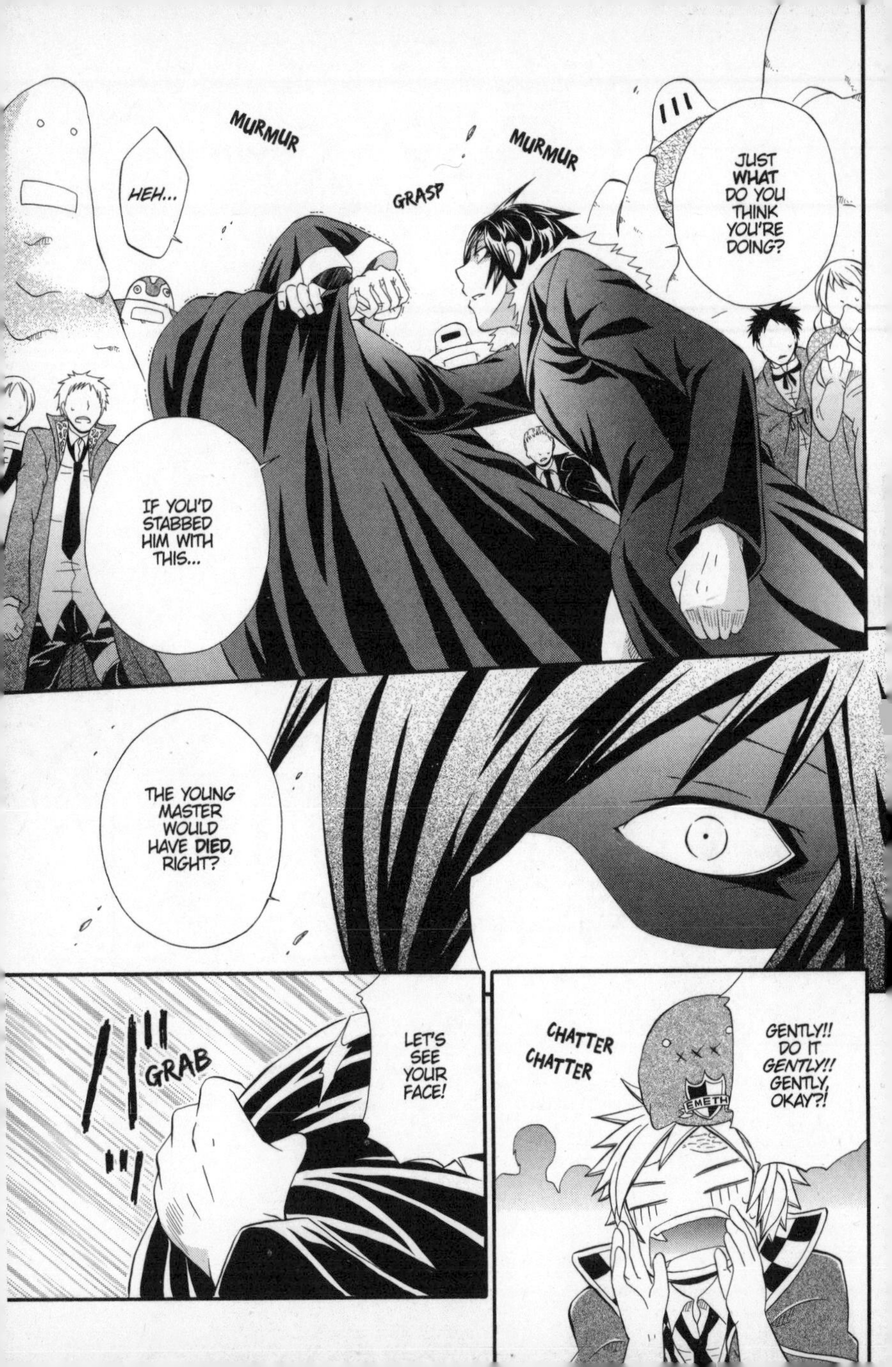
JUST WHAT DO YOU THINK YOU'RE DOING?
MURMUR
GRASP
MURMUR
HEH...
IF YOU'D STABBED HIM WITH THIS...
THE YOUNG MASTER WOULD HAVE DIED, RIGHT?
CHATTER CHATTER
GENTLY!! DO IT GENTLY!! GENTLY, OKAY?!
EMETH
LET'S SEE YOUR FACE!
GRAB

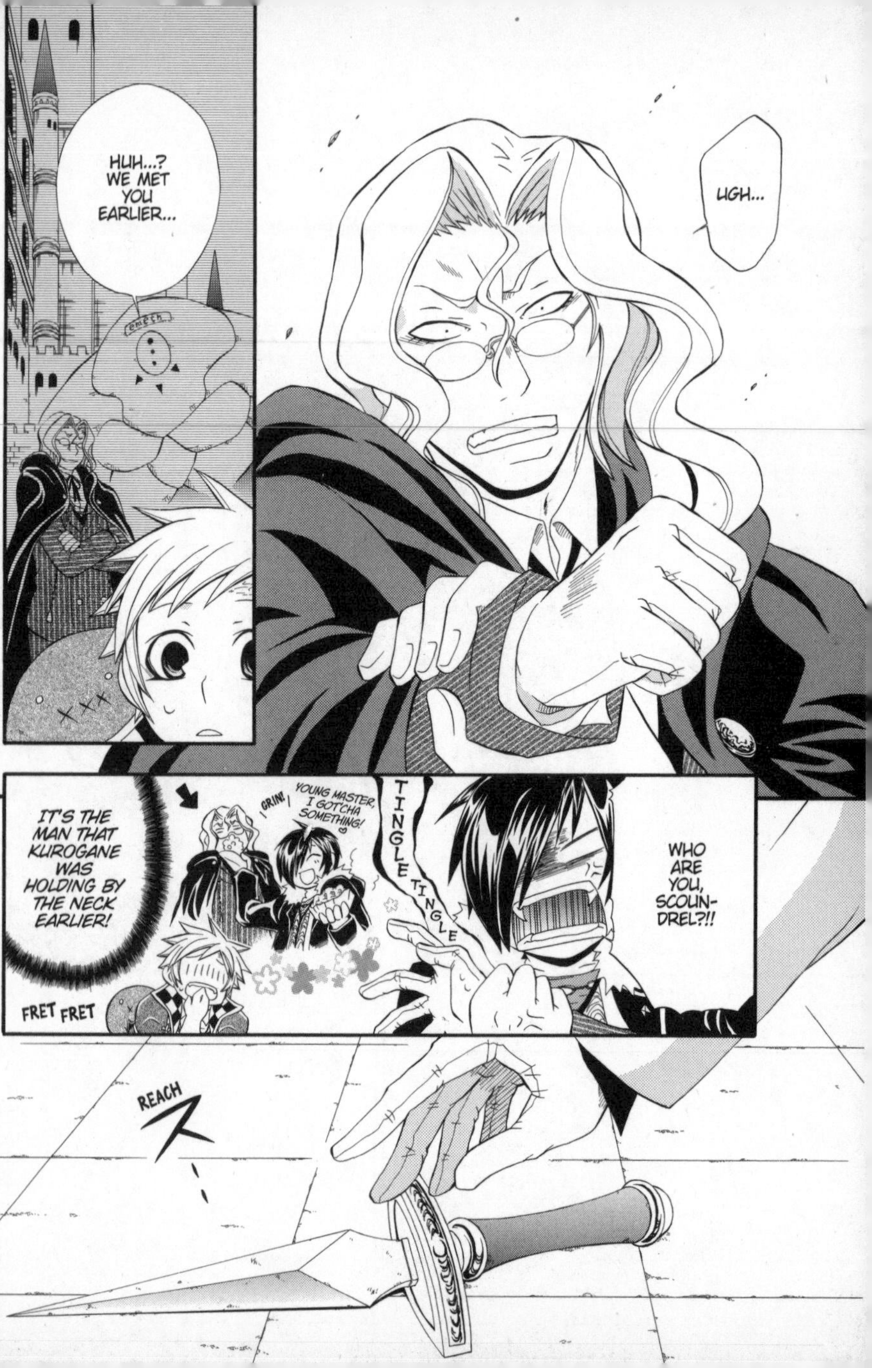
UGH...
HUH...? WE MET YOU EARLIER...
emeth
WHO ARE YOU, SCOUN-DREL?!!
TINGLE TINGLE
YOUNG MASTER, I GOTCHA SOMETHING!
GRIN!
IT'S THE MAN THAT KUROGANE WAS HOLDING BY THE NECK EARLIER!
FRET FRET
REACH

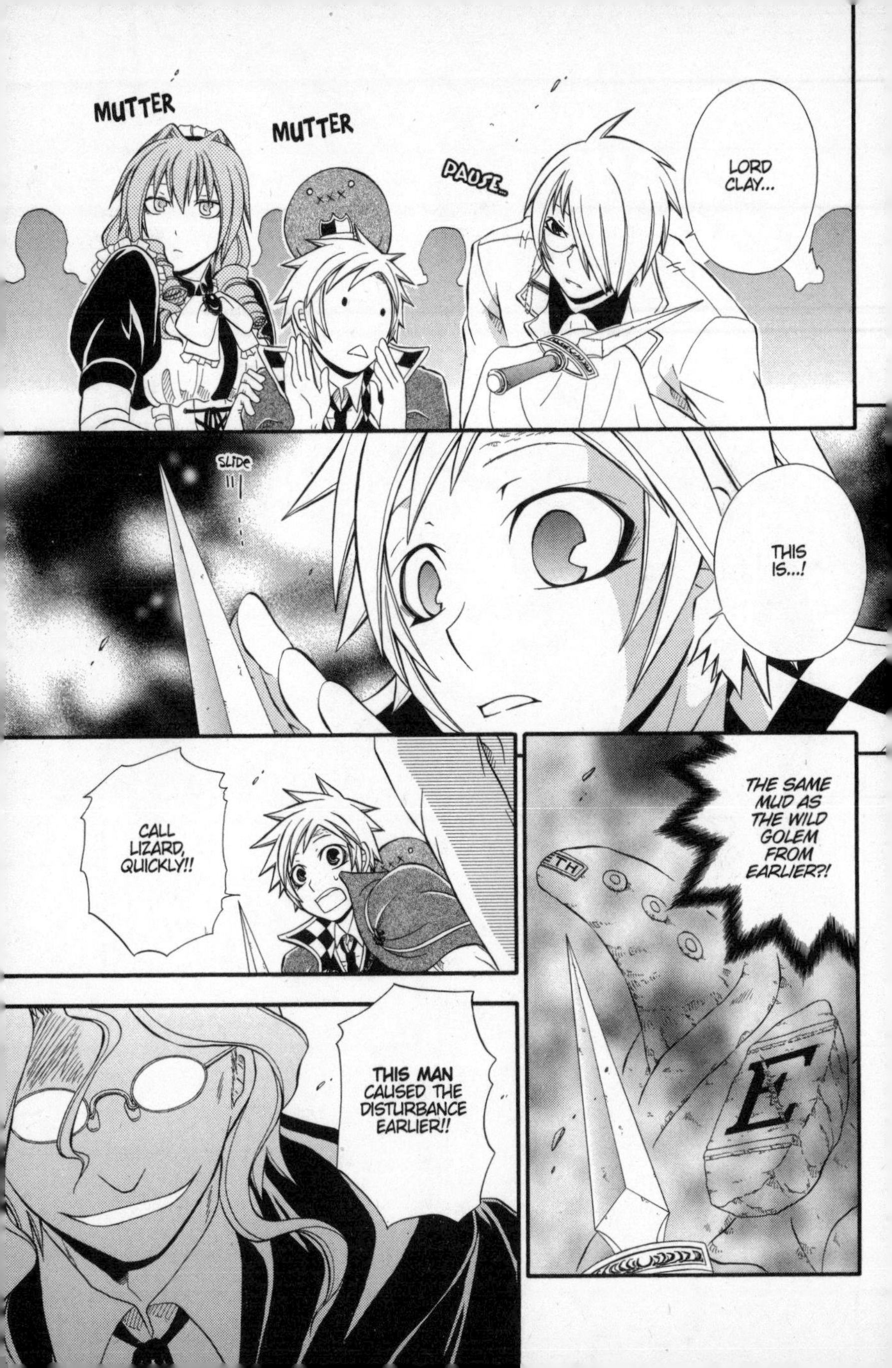
LORD CLAY...
PAUSE...
MUTTER
MUTTER
THIS IS...!
SLIDE
THE SAME MUD AS THE WILD GOLEM FROM EARLIER?!
CALL LIZARD, QUICKLY!!
THIS MAN CAUSED THE DISTURBANCE EARLIER!!

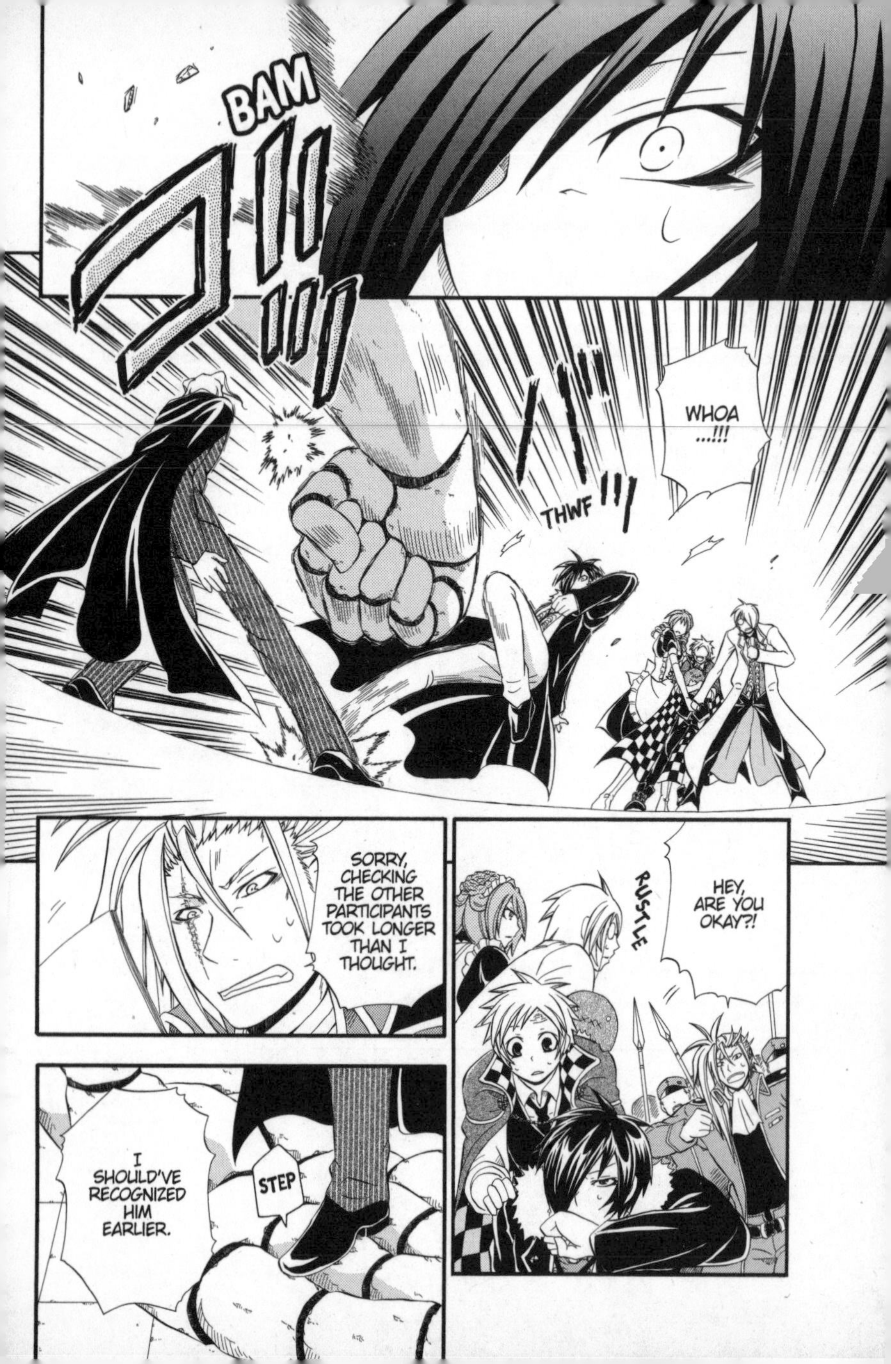
BAM
WHOA ...!!!
THWF
HEY, ARE YOU OKAY?!
RUSTLE
SORRY, CHECKING THE OTHER PARTICIPANTS TOOK LONGER THAN I THOUGHT.
STEP
I SHOULD'VE RECOGNIZED HIM EARLIER.

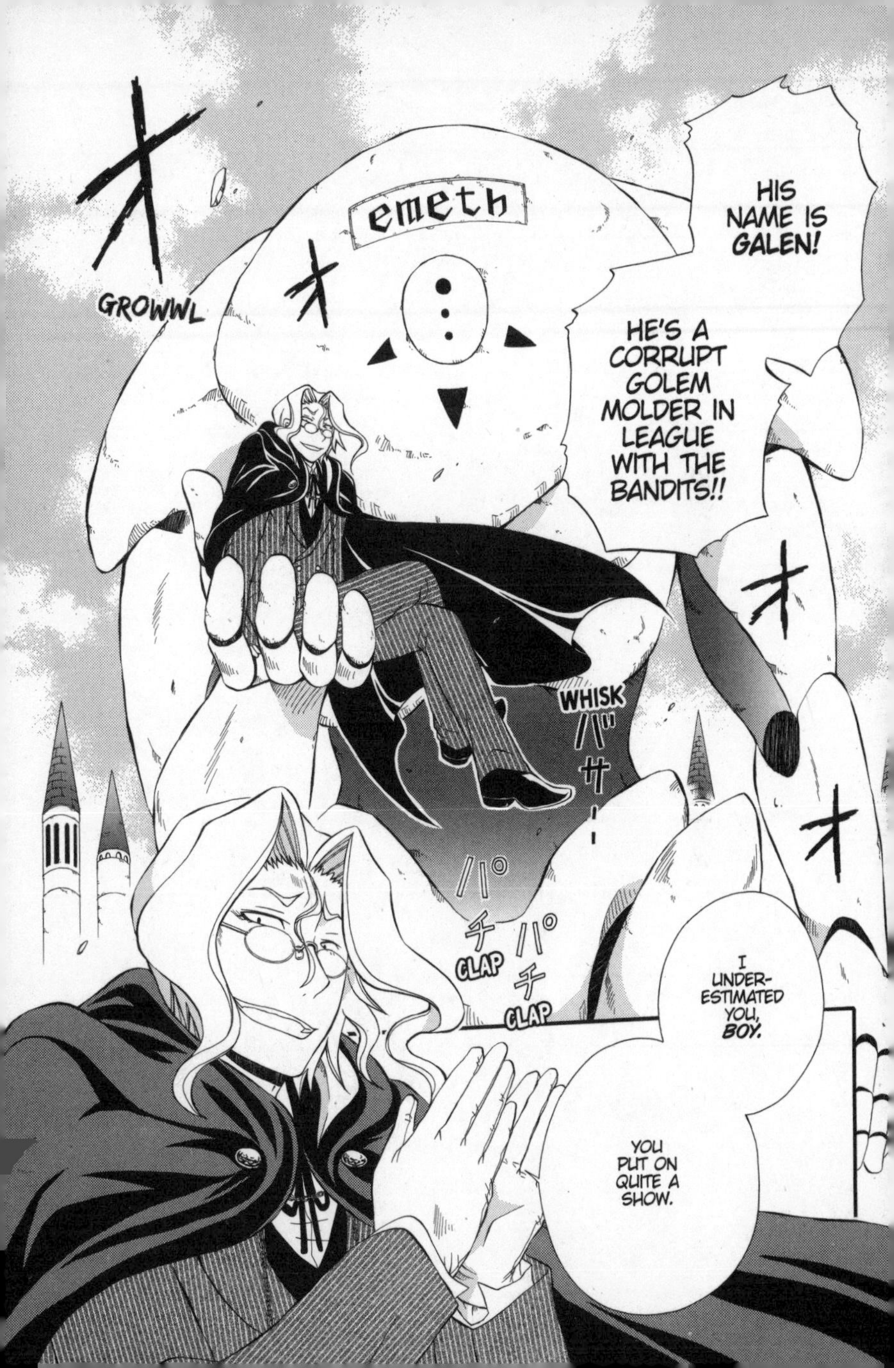
HIS NAME IS GALEN!
HE'S A CORRUPT GOLEM MOLDER IN LEAGUE WITH THE BANDITS!!
emeth
GROWWL
WHISK
バサー
パチ CLAP
パチ CLAP
I UNDER-ESTIMATED YOU, *BOY.*
YOU PUT ON QUITE A SHOW.

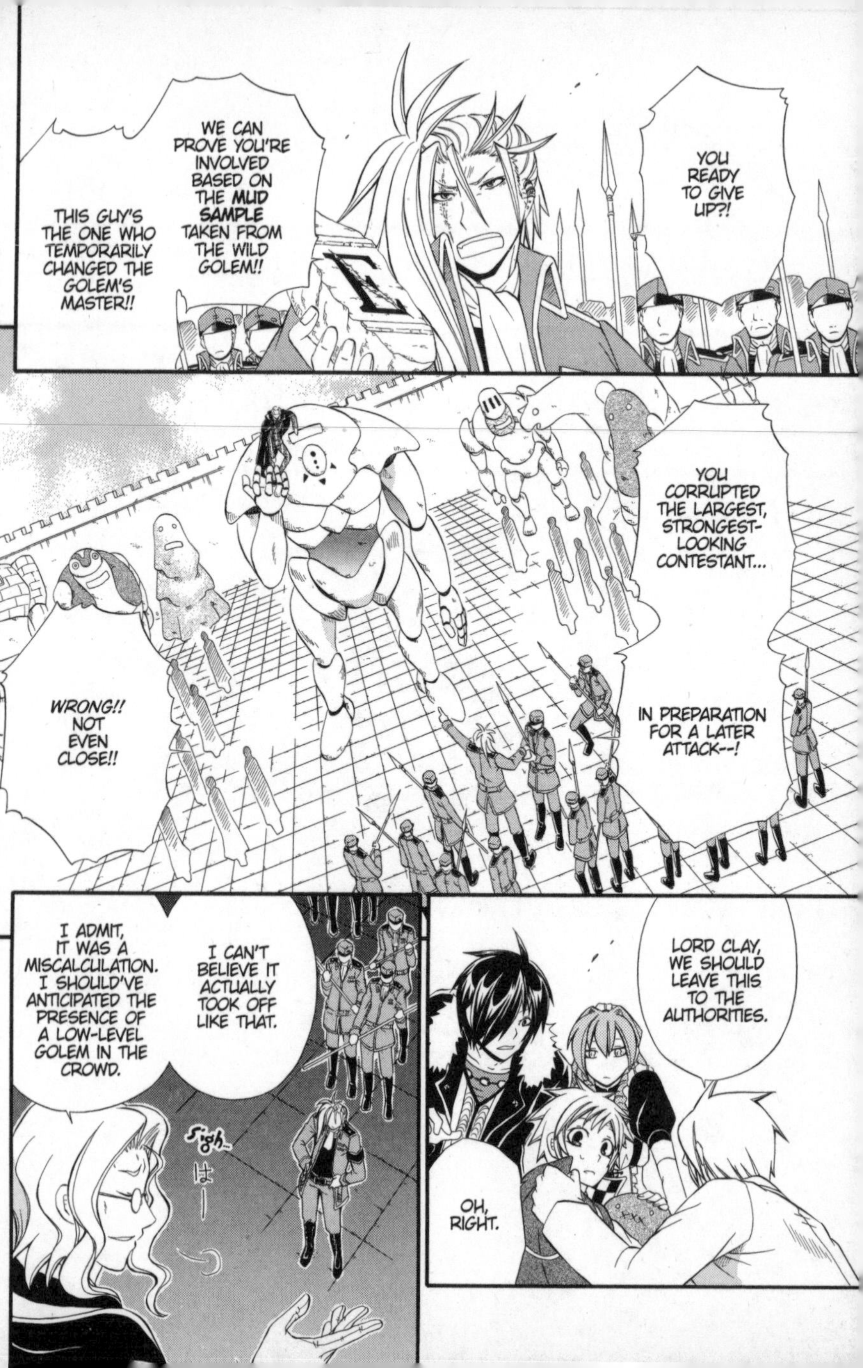

YOU READY TO GIVE UP?!
WE CAN PROVE YOU'RE INVOLVED BASED ON THE MUD SAMPLE TAKEN FROM THE WILD GOLEM!!
THIS GUY'S THE ONE WHO TEMPORARILY CHANGED THE GOLEM'S MASTER!!
YOU CORRUPTED THE LARGEST, STRONGEST-LOOKING CONTESTANT...
IN PREPARATION FOR A LATER ATTACK--!
WRONG!! NOT EVEN CLOSE!!
LORD CLAY, WE SHOULD LEAVE THIS TO THE AUTHORITIES.
OH, RIGHT.
I CAN'T BELIEVE IT ACTUALLY TOOK OFF LIKE THAT.
I ADMIT, IT WAS A MISCALCULATION. I SHOULD'VE ANTICIPATED THE PRESENCE OF A LOW-LEVEL GOLEM IN THE CROWD.
Sigh

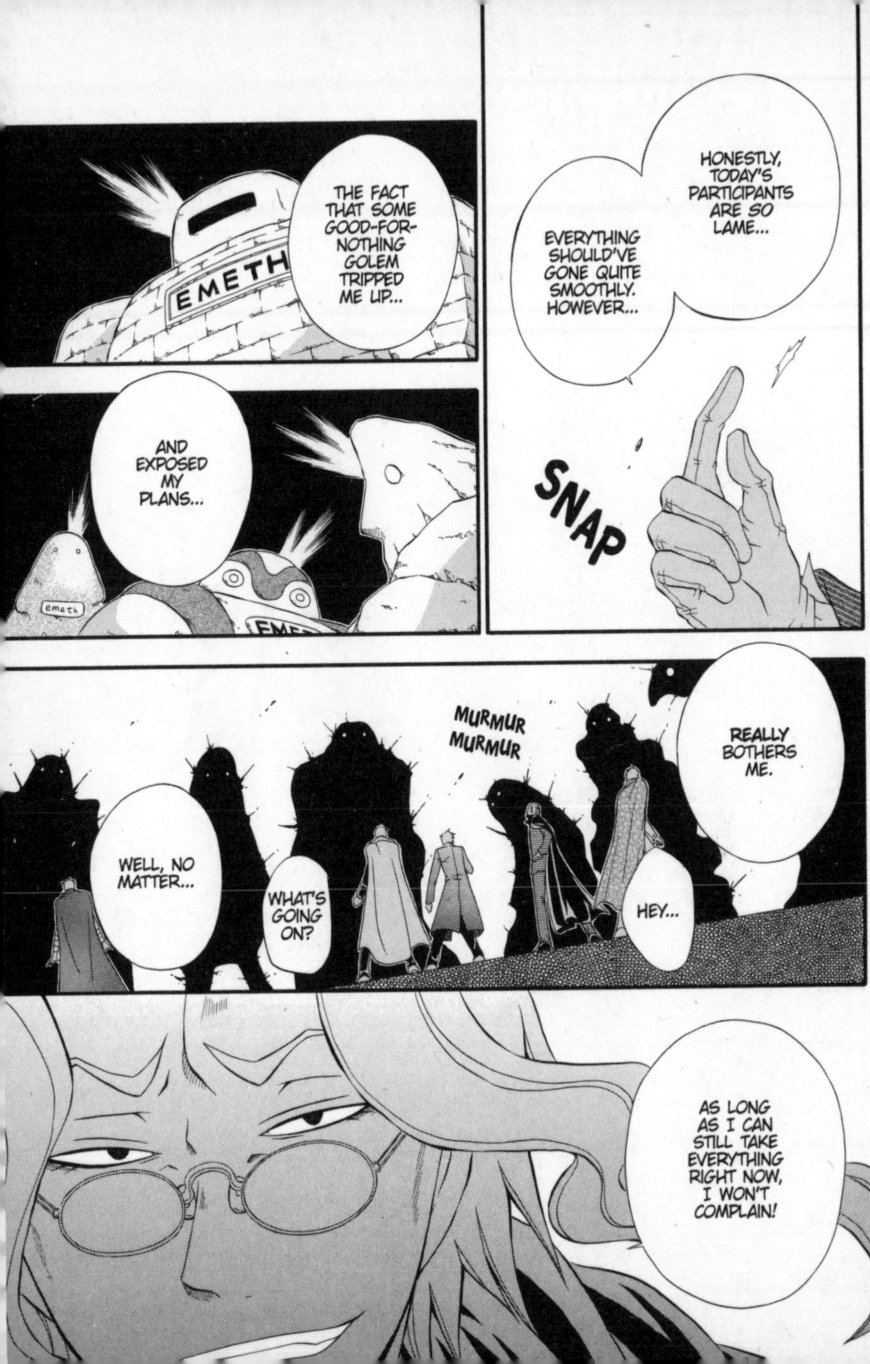
HONESTLY, TODAY'S PARTICIPANTS ARE SO LAME...
EVERYTHING SHOULD'VE GONE QUITE SMOOTHLY. HOWEVER...
SNAP
THE FACT THAT SOME GOOD-FOR-NOTHING GOLEM TRIPPED ME UP...
EMETH
AND EXPOSED MY PLANS...
emeth
REALLY BOTHERS ME.
MURMUR MURMUR
HEY...
WHAT'S GOING ON?
WELL, NO MATTER...
AS LONG AS I CAN STILL TAKE EVERYTHING RIGHT NOW, I WON'T COMPLAIN!

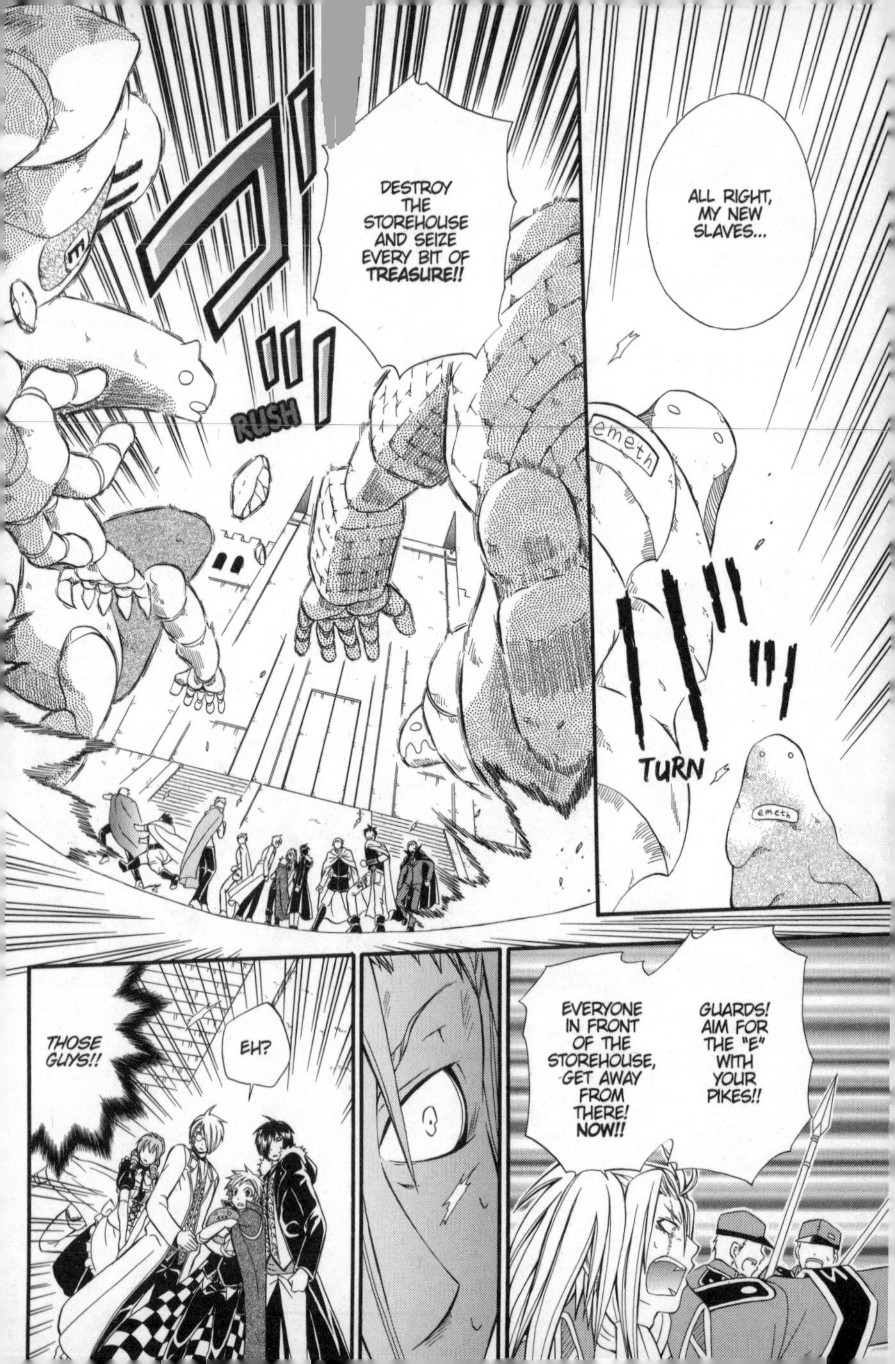
ALL RIGHT, MY NEW SLAVES...
TURN
DESTROY THE STOREHOUSE AND SEIZE EVERY BIT OF TREASURE!!
RUSH
GUARDS! AIM FOR THE "E" WITH YOUR PIKES!!
EVERYONE IN FRONT OF THE STOREHOUSE, GET AWAY FROM THERE! NOW!!
EH?
THOSE GUYS!!

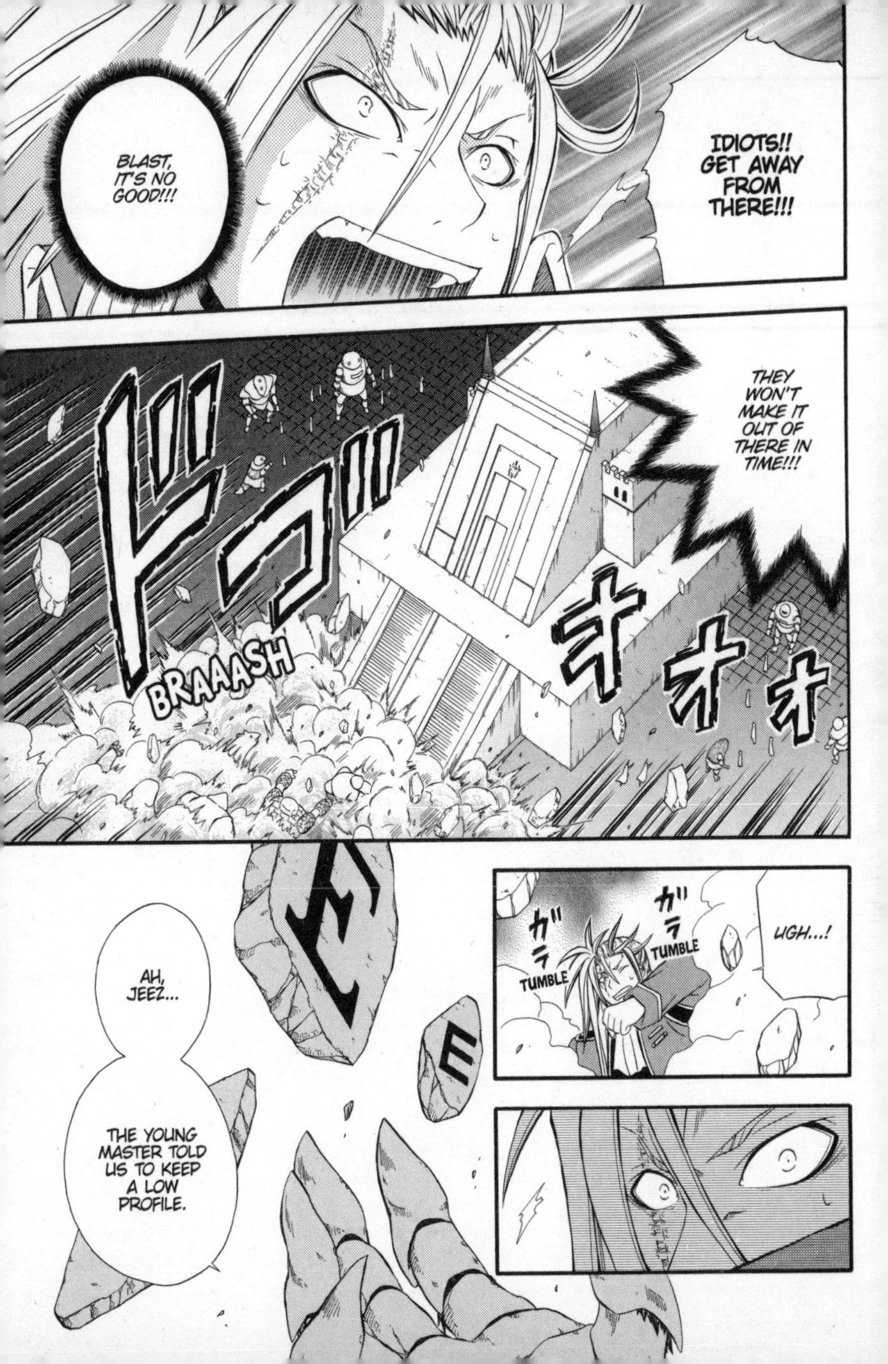
IDIOTS!! GET AWAY FROM THERE!!!
BLAST, IT'S NO GOOD!!!
THEY WON'T MAKE IT OUT OF THERE IN TIME!!!
ドゴオォォ
BRAAASH
UGH...!
ガラ
TUMBLE
ガラ
TUMBLE
AH, JEEZ...
THE YOUNG MASTER TOLD US TO KEEP A LOW PROFILE.

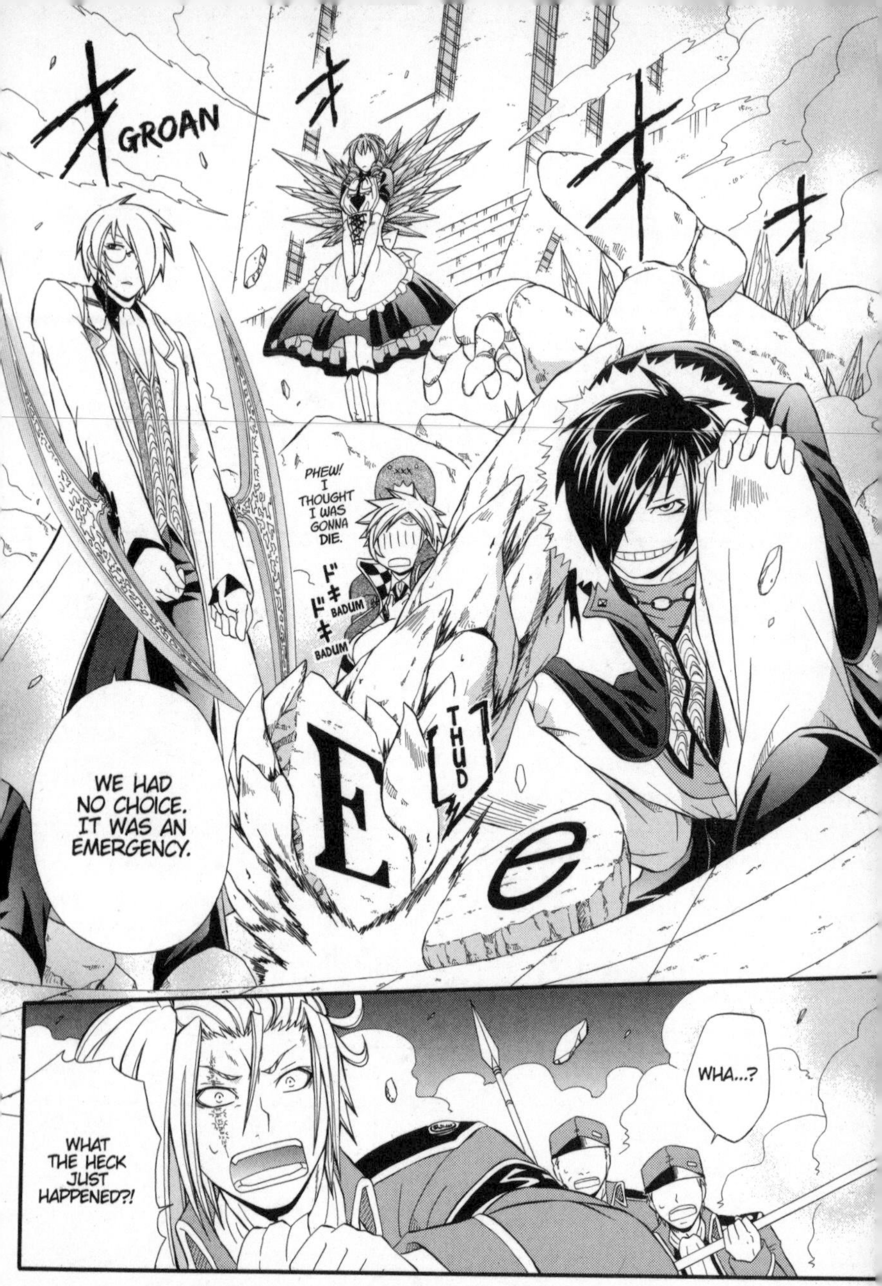
オオオオ
GROAN
PHEW! I THOUGHT I WAS GONNA DIE.
ドキドキ
BADUM BADUM
THUD
WE HAD NO CHOICE. IT WAS AN EMERGENCY.
WHA...?
WHAT THE HECK JUST HAPPENED?!

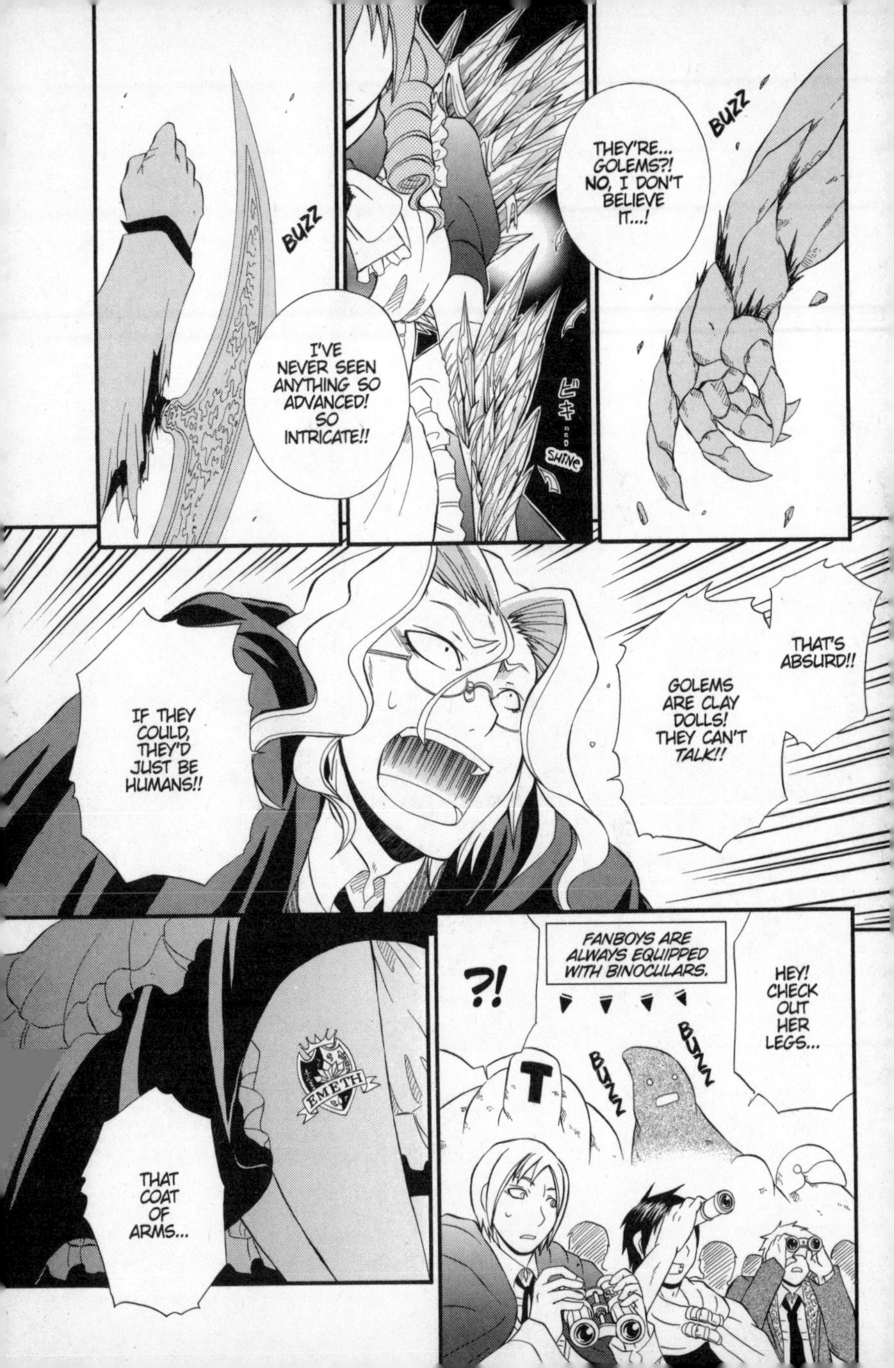

BUZZ
THEY'RE... GOLEMS?! NO, I DON'T BELIEVE IT...!
ビキ...
SHINE
I'VE NEVER SEEN ANYTHING SO ADVANCED! SO INTRICATE!!
BUZZ
THAT'S ABSURD!!
GOLEMS ARE CLAY DOLLS! THEY CAN'T *TALK*!!
IF THEY COULD, THEY'D JUST BE HUMANS!!
HEY! CHECK OUT HER LEGS...
FANBOYS ARE ALWAYS EQUIPPED WITH BINOCULARS.
?!
BUZZ
BUZZ
T
EMETH
THAT COAT OF ARMS...

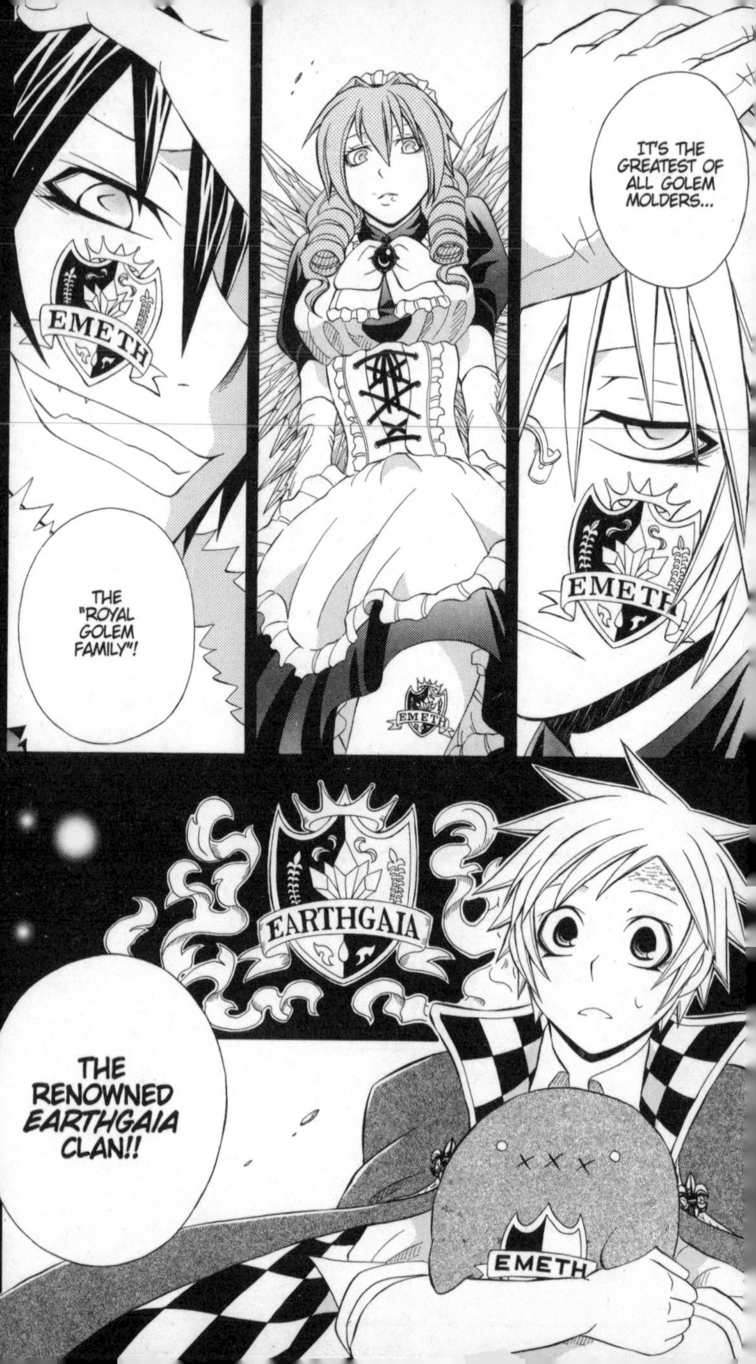
IT'S THE GREATEST OF ALL GOLEM MOLDERS...
EMETH
EMETH
EMETH
THE "ROYAL GOLEM FAMILY"!
EARTHGAIA
THE RENOWNED *EARTHGAIA* CLAN!!
EMETH

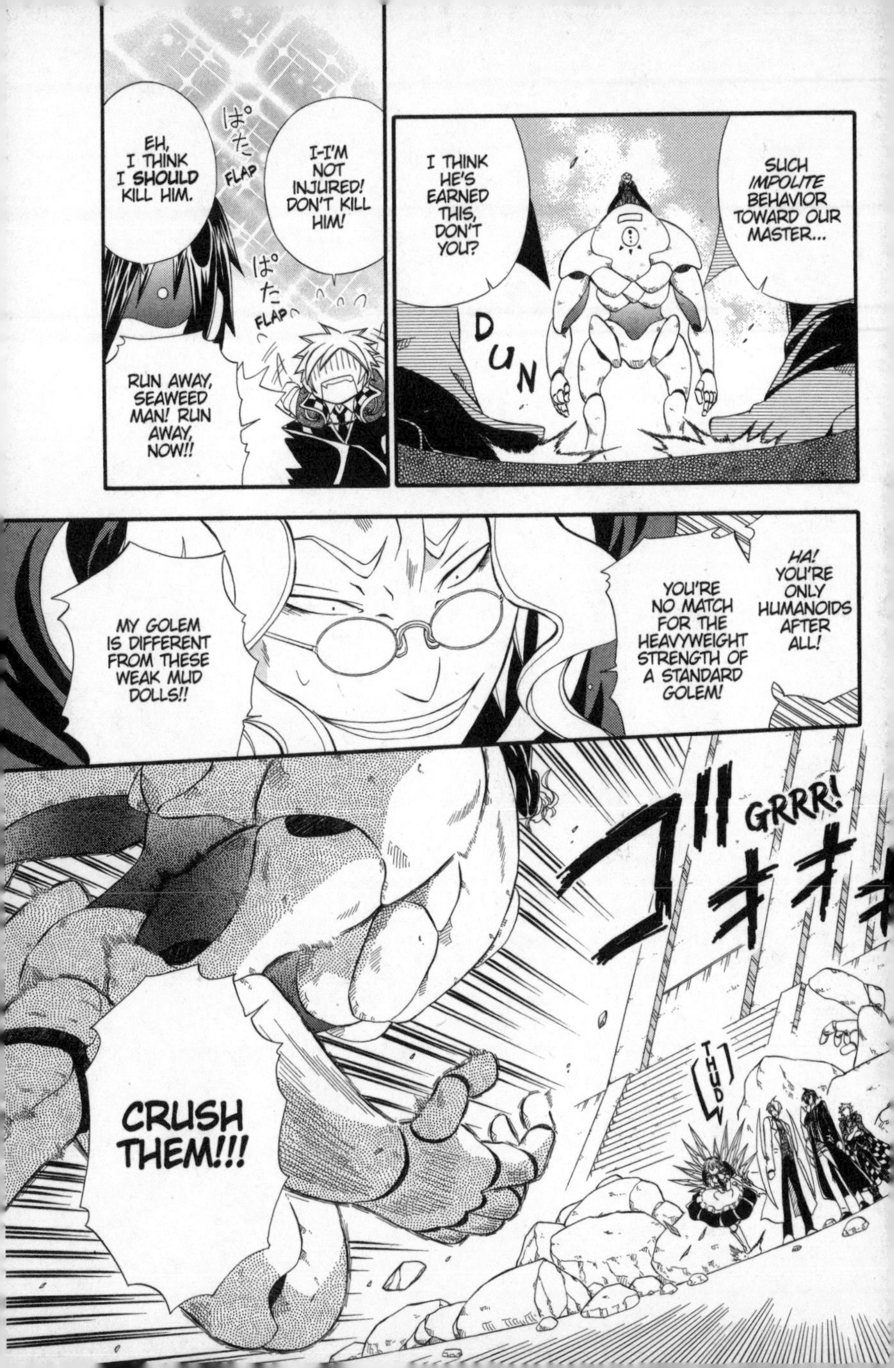
SUCH IMPOLITE BEHAVIOR TOWARD OUR MASTER...
I THINK HE'S EARNED THIS, DON'T YOU?
DUN
I-I'M NOT INJURED! DON'T KILL HIM!
ぱた FLAP
ぱた FLAP
EH, I THINK I SHOULD KILL HIM.
RUN AWAY, SEAWEED MAN! RUN AWAY, NOW!!
HA! YOU'RE ONLY HUMANOIDS AFTER ALL!
YOU'RE NO MATCH FOR THE HEAVYWEIGHT STRENGTH OF A STANDARD GOLEM!
MY GOLEM IS DIFFERENT FROM THESE WEAK MUD DOLLS!!
ゴオオオ GRRR!
THUD
CRUSH THEM!!!

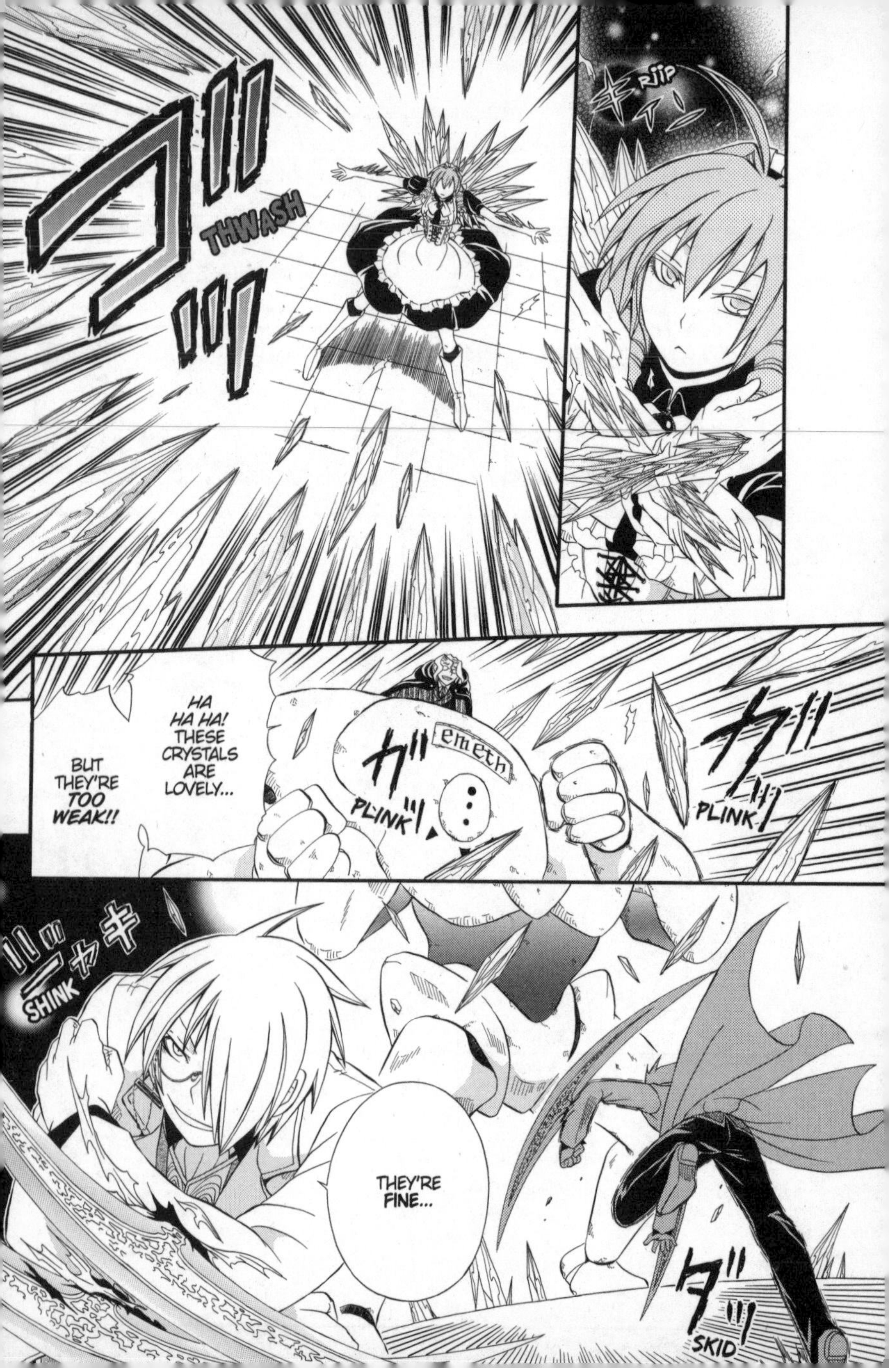
RIIP
THWASH
PLINK
emeth
PLINK
HA HA HA! THESE CRYSTALS ARE LOVELY...
BUT THEY'RE *TOO WEAK!!*
SHINK
THEY'RE FINE...
SKID

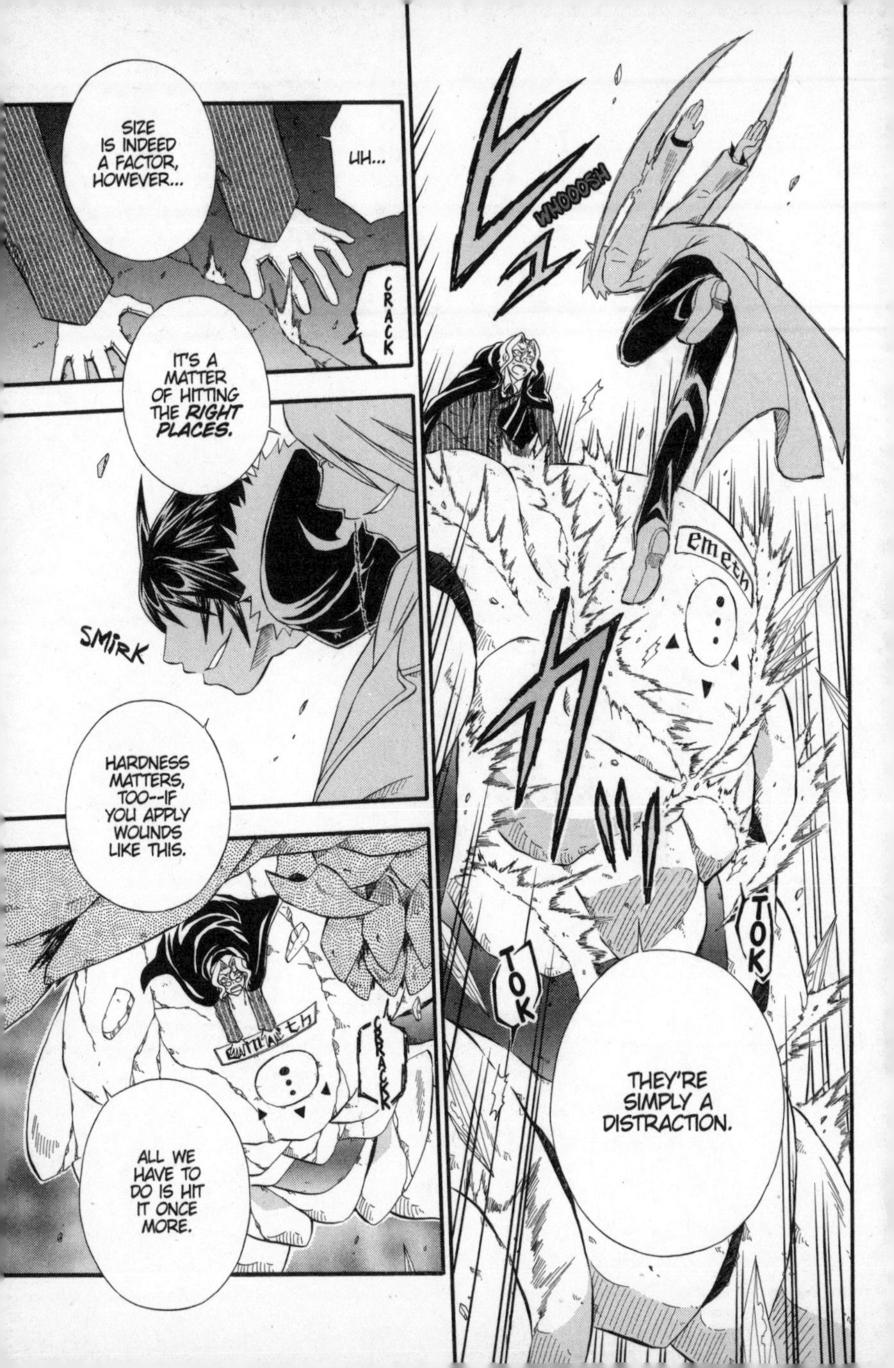
WHOOOSH
emeth
TOK
TOK
THEY'RE SIMPLY A DISTRACTION.
SIZE IS INDEED A FACTOR, HOWEVER...
UH...
CRACK
IT'S A MATTER OF HITTING THE *RIGHT PLACES.*
SMIRK
HARDNESS MATTERS, TOO--IF YOU APPLY WOUNDS LIKE THIS.
CRACK
ALL WE HAVE TO DO IS HIT IT ONCE MORE.

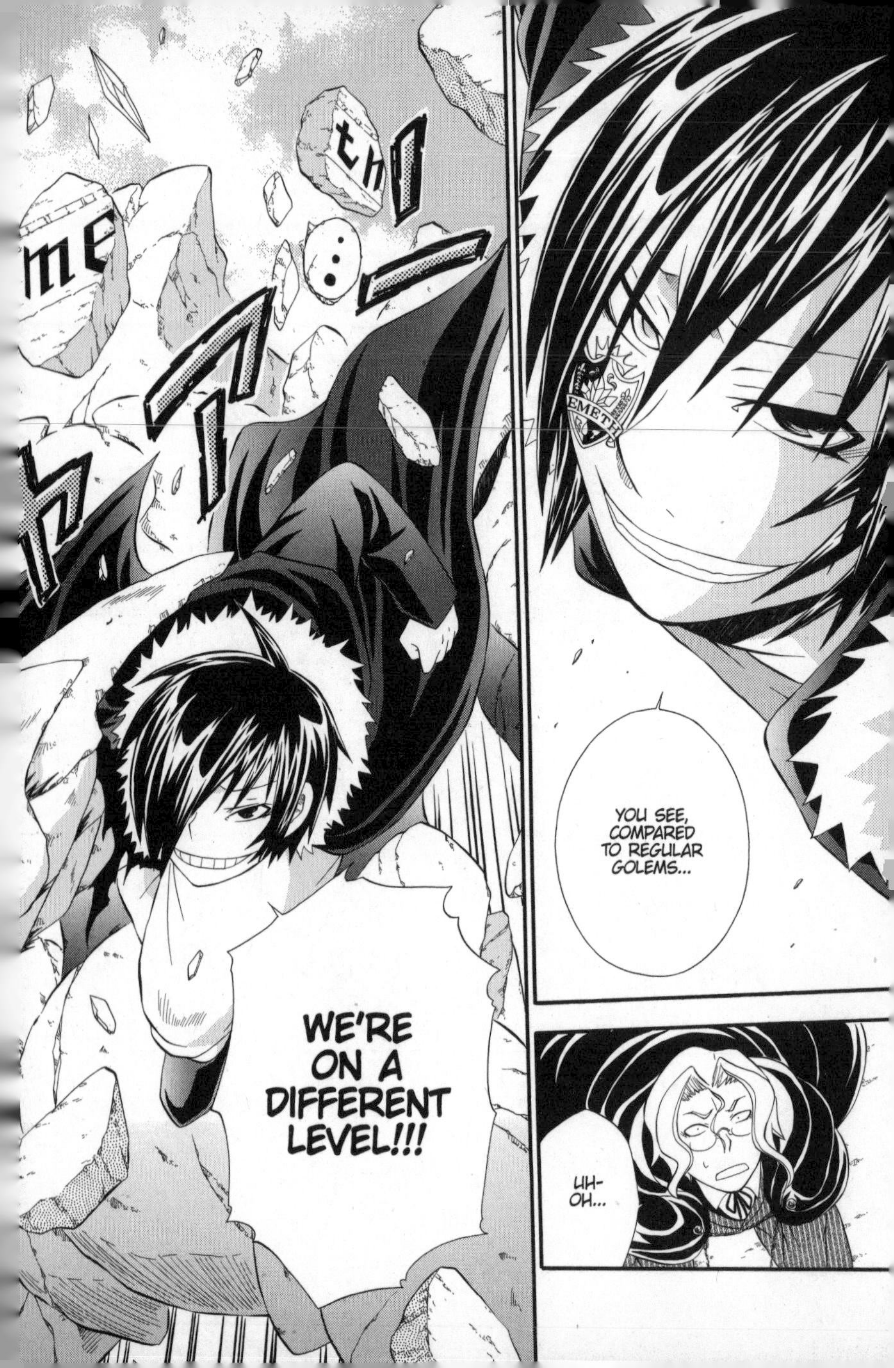
EMETH
YOU SEE, COMPARED TO REGULAR GOLEMS...
UH-OH...
WE'RE ON A DIFFERENT LEVEL!!!

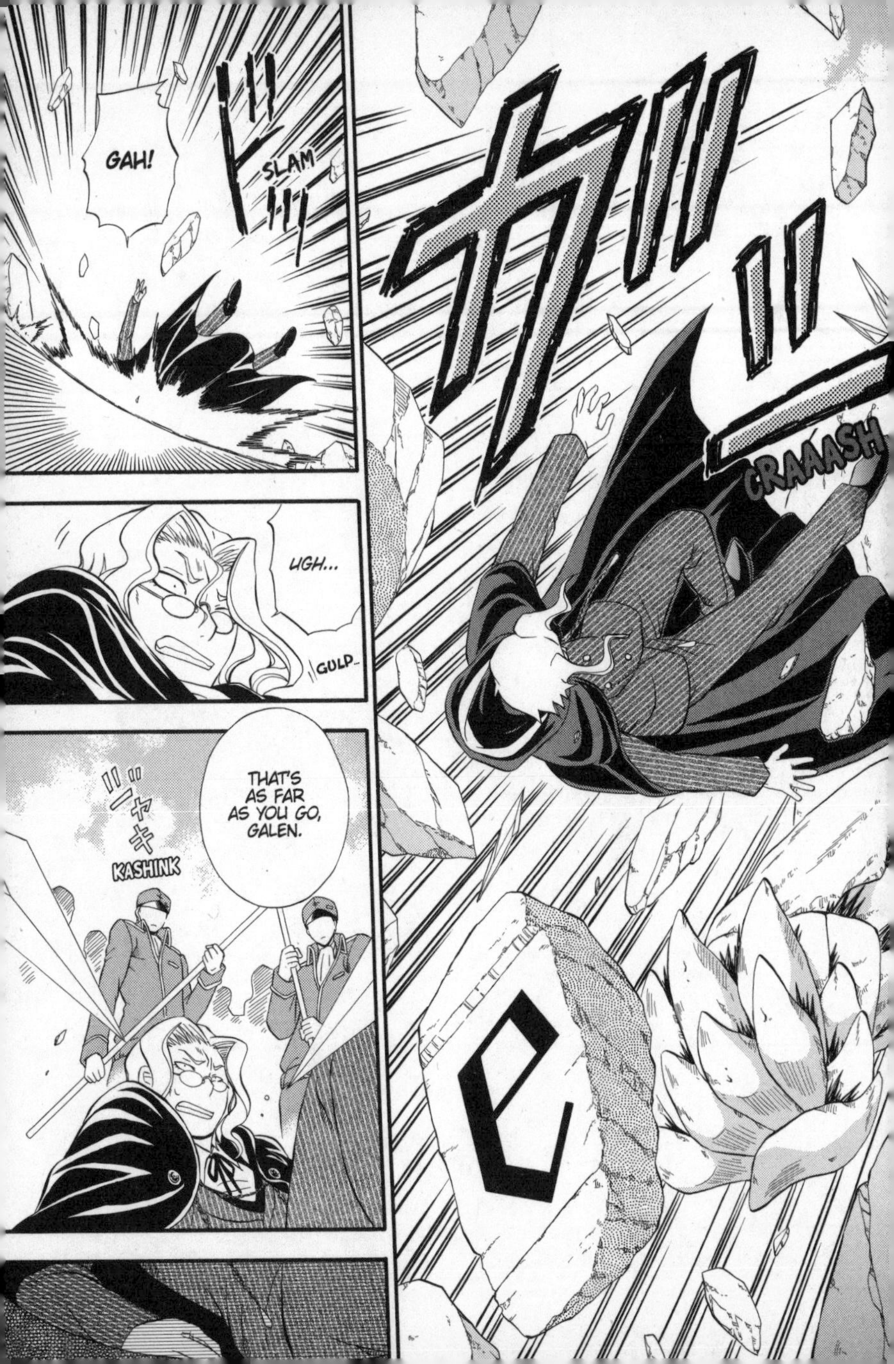
CRAAASH
GAH!
SLAM
UGH...
GULP
THAT'S AS FAR AS YOU GO, GALEN.
KASHINK

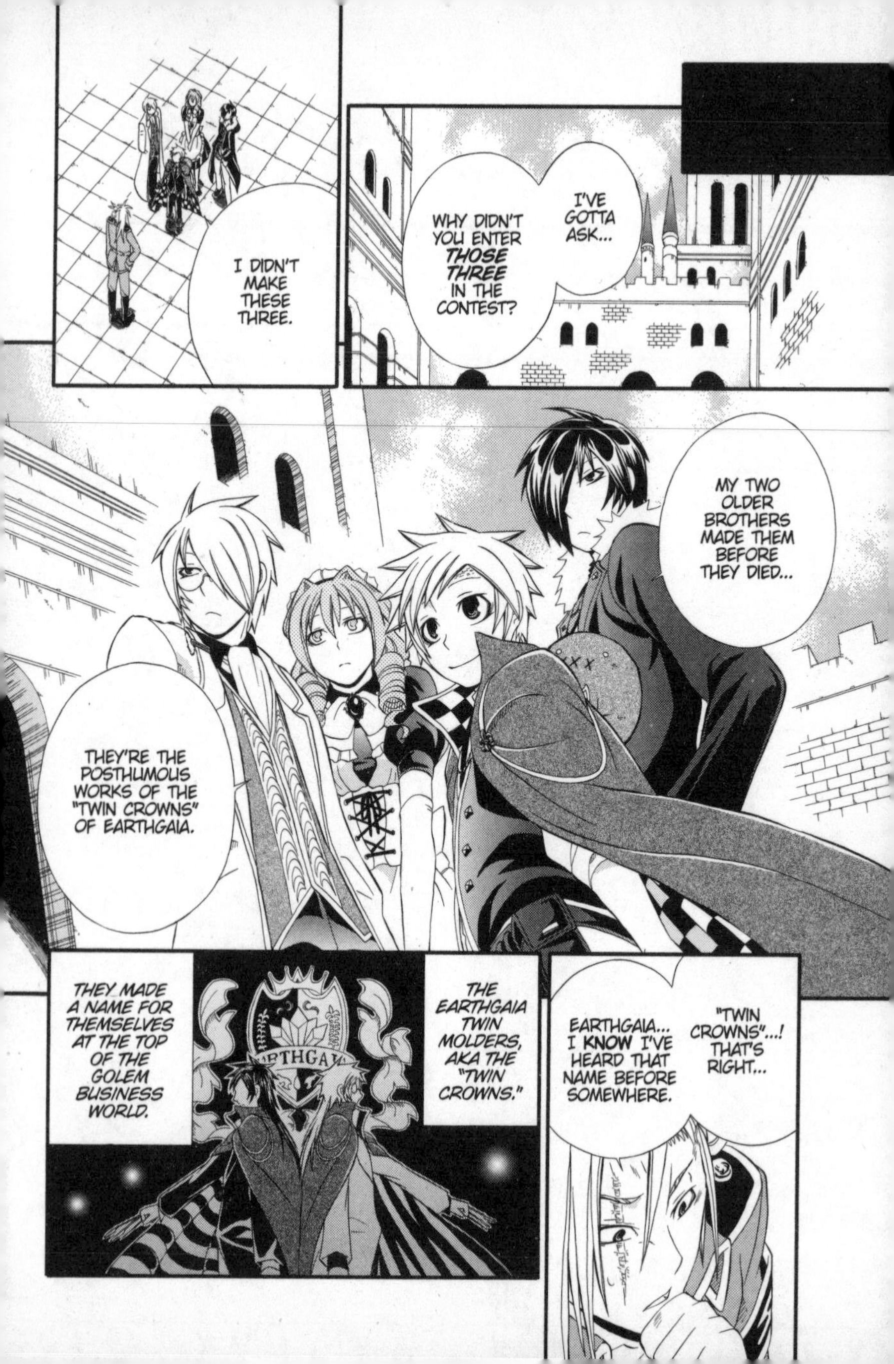
I'VE GOTTA ASK...
WHY DIDN'T YOU ENTER *THOSE THREE* IN THE CONTEST?
I DIDN'T MAKE THESE THREE.
MY TWO OLDER BROTHERS MADE THEM BEFORE THEY DIED...
THEY'RE THE POSTHUMOUS WORKS OF THE "TWIN CROWNS" OF EARTHGAIA.
EARTHGAIA... I **KNOW** I'VE HEARD THAT NAME BEFORE SOMEWHERE.
"TWIN CROWNS"...! THAT'S RIGHT...
THE EARTHGAIA TWIN MOLDERS, AKA THE "TWIN CROWNS."
THEY MADE A NAME FOR THEMSELVES AT THE TOP OF THE GOLEM BUSINESS WORLD.

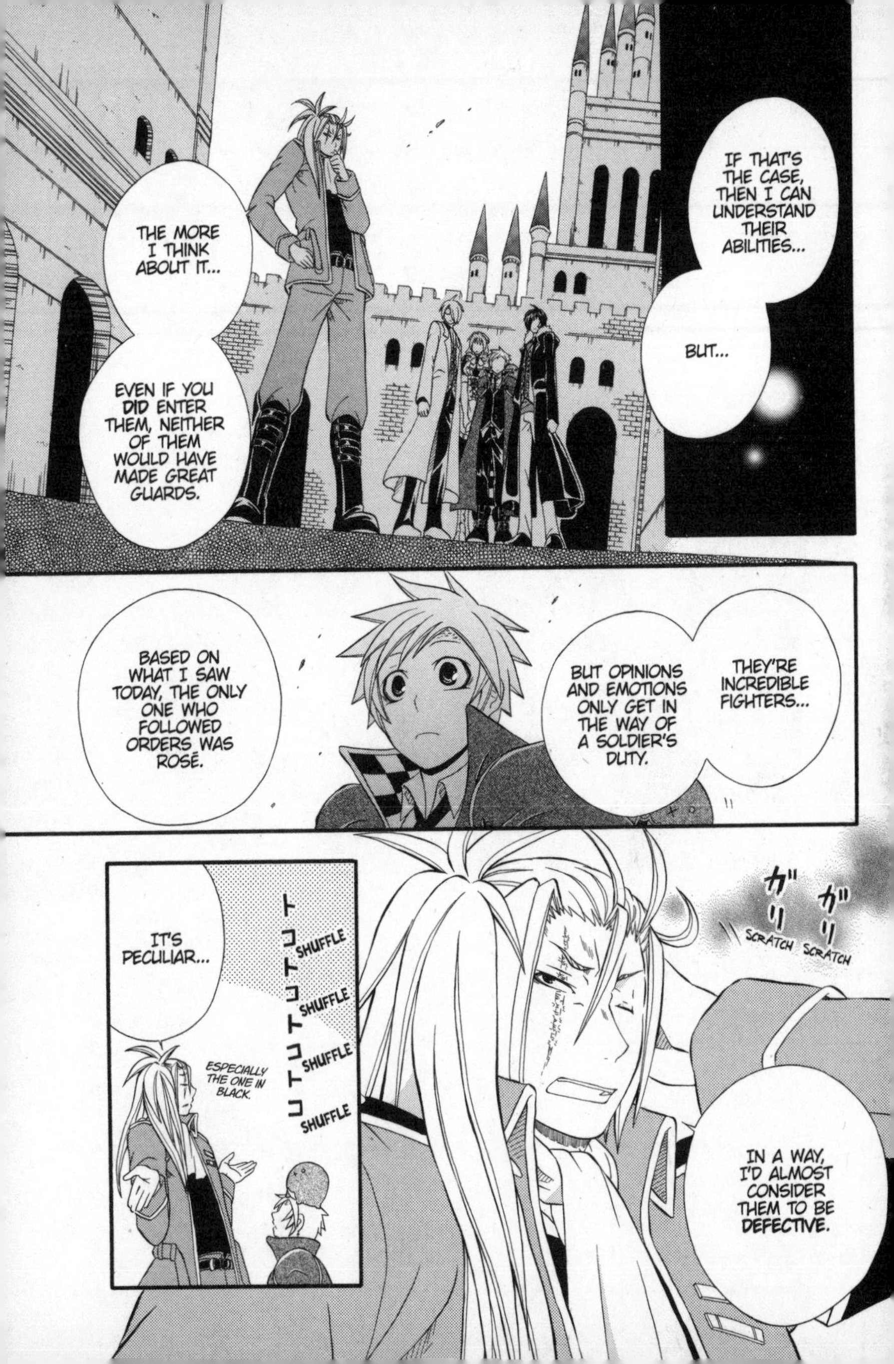
IF THAT'S THE CASE, THEN I CAN UNDERSTAND THEIR ABILITIES...
BUT...
THE MORE I THINK ABOUT IT...
EVEN IF YOU DID ENTER THEM, NEITHER OF THEM WOULD HAVE MADE GREAT GUARDS.
THEY'RE INCREDIBLE FIGHTERS...
BUT OPINIONS AND EMOTIONS ONLY GET IN THE WAY OF A SOLDIER'S DUTY.
BASED ON WHAT I SAW TODAY, THE ONLY ONE WHO FOLLOWED ORDERS WAS ROSÉ.
!!
ガリ ガリ
SCRATCH SCRATCH
IN A WAY, I'D ALMOST CONSIDER THEM TO BE DEFECTIVE.
IT'S PECULIAR...
SHUFFLE SHUFFLE SHUFFLE SHUFFLE
ESPECIALLY THE ONE IN BLACK.

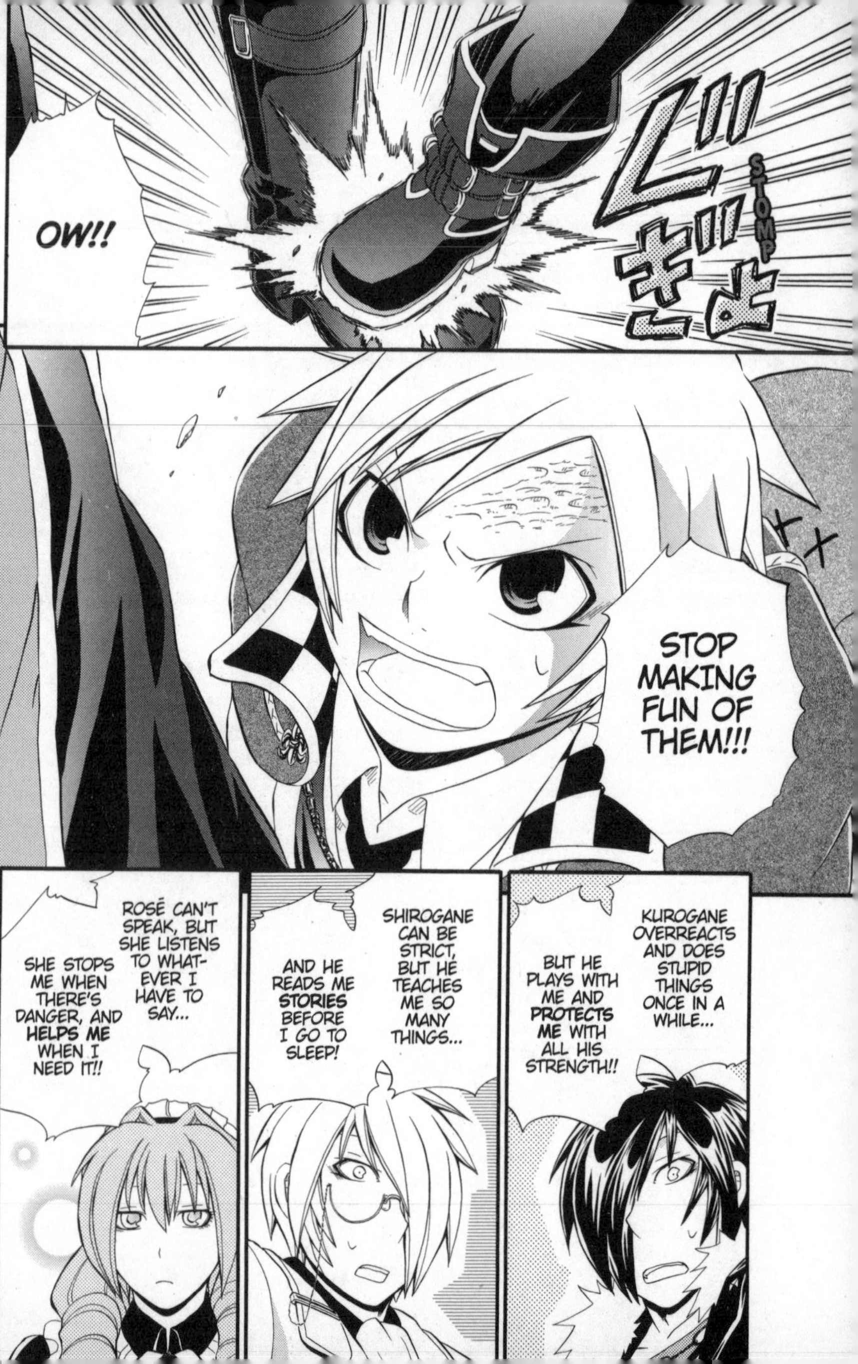
STOMP
OW!!
STOP MAKING FUN OF THEM!!!
KUROGANE OVERREACTS AND DOES STUPID THINGS ONCE IN A WHILE...
BUT HE PLAYS WITH ME AND PROTECTS ME WITH ALL HIS STRENGTH!!
SHIROGANE CAN BE STRICT, BUT HE TEACHES ME SO MANY THINGS...
AND HE READS ME STORIES BEFORE I GO TO SLEEP!
ROSÉ CAN'T SPEAK, BUT SHE LISTENS TO WHATEVER I HAVE TO SAY...
SHE STOPS ME WHEN THERE'S DANGER, AND HELPS ME WHEN I NEED IT!!

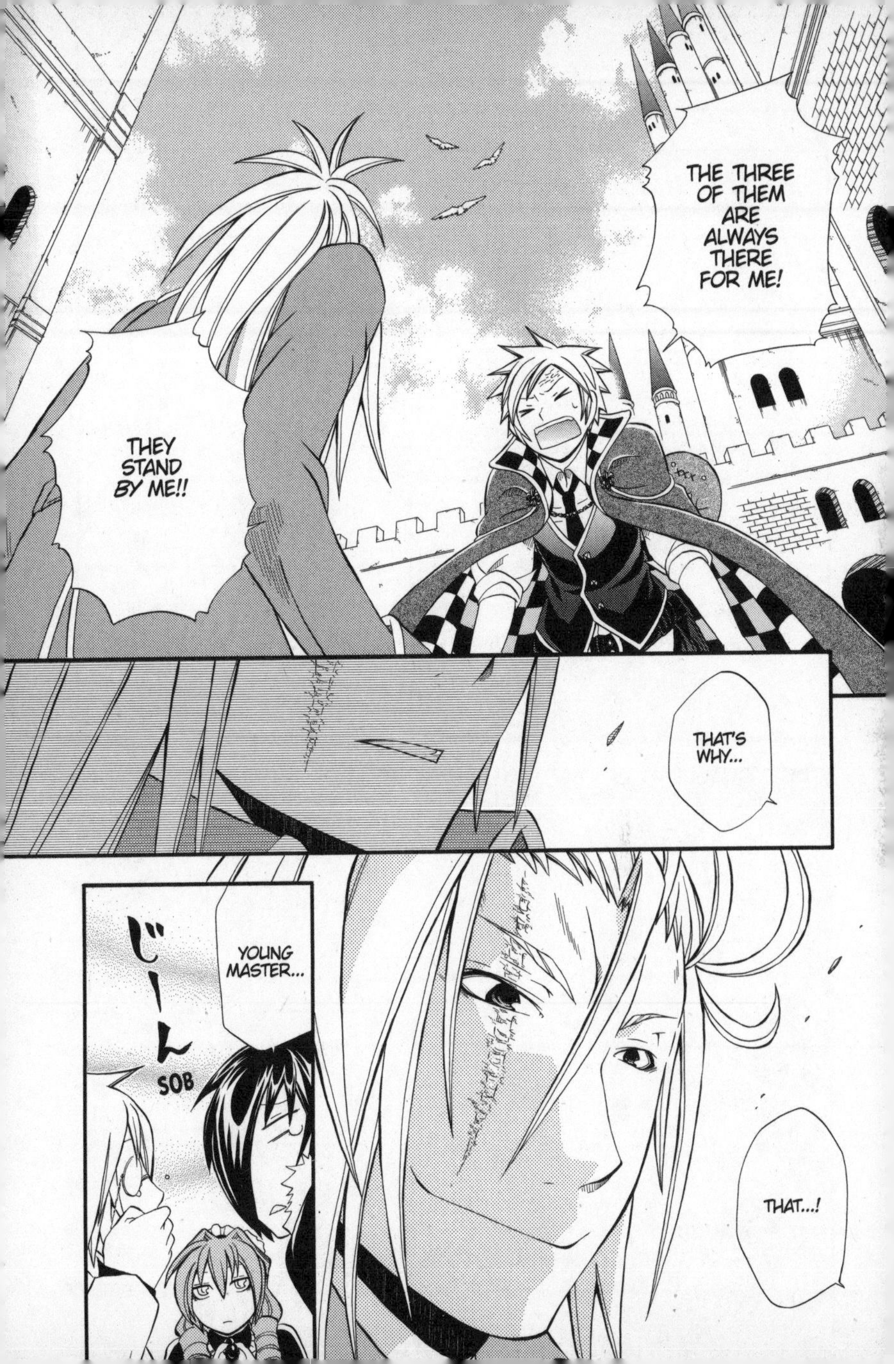
THE THREE OF THEM ARE ALWAYS THERE FOR ME!
THEY STAND BY ME!!
THAT'S WHY...
THAT...!
YOUNG MASTER...
じーん
SOB

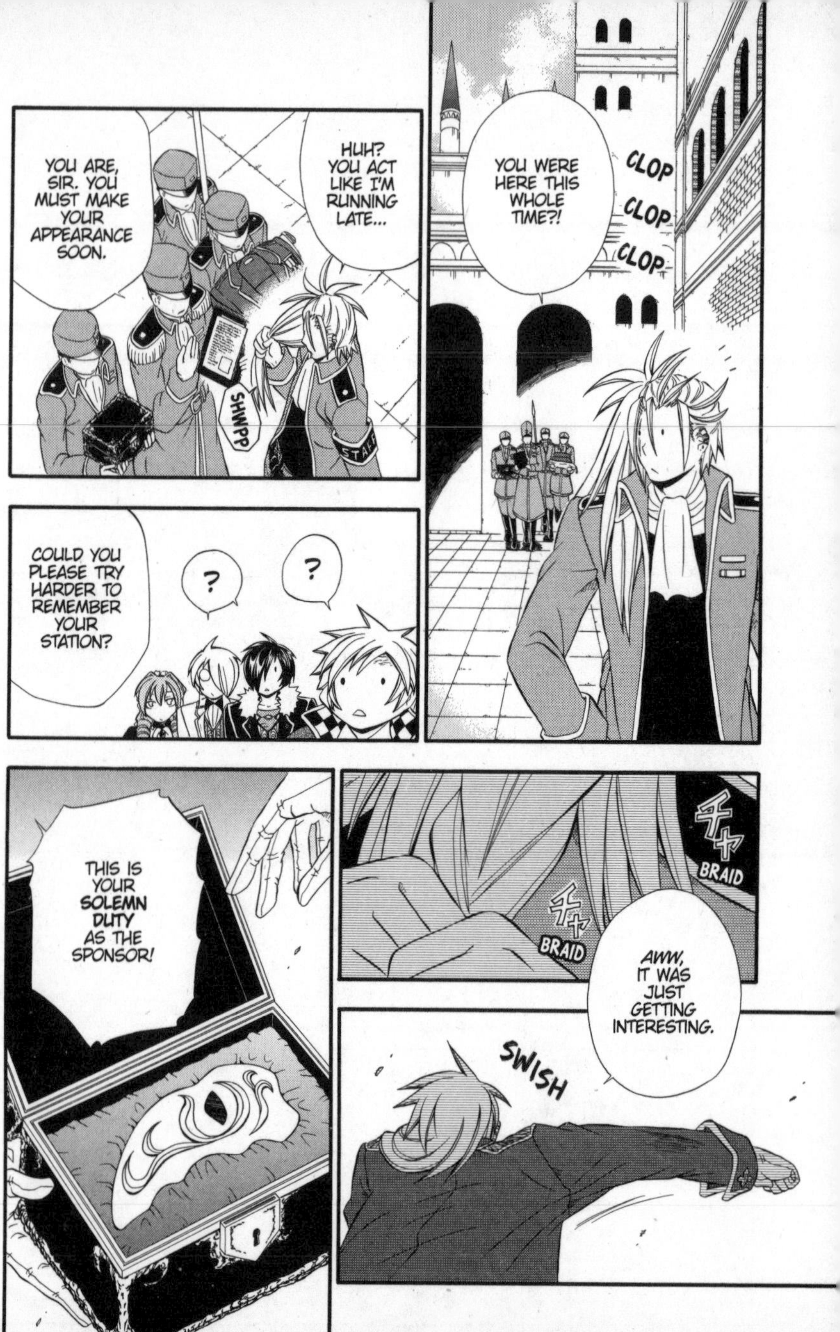

YOU WERE HERE THIS WHOLE TIME?!
CLOP
CLOP
CLOP
HUH? YOU ACT LIKE I'M RUNNING LATE...
YOU ARE, SIR. YOU MUST MAKE YOUR APPEARANCE SOON.
SHWPP
?
?
COULD YOU PLEASE TRY HARDER TO REMEMBER YOUR STATION?
チャ
BRAID
チャ
BRAID
AWW, IT WAS JUST GETTING INTERESTING.
SWISH
THIS IS YOUR SOLEMN DUTY AS THE SPONSOR!

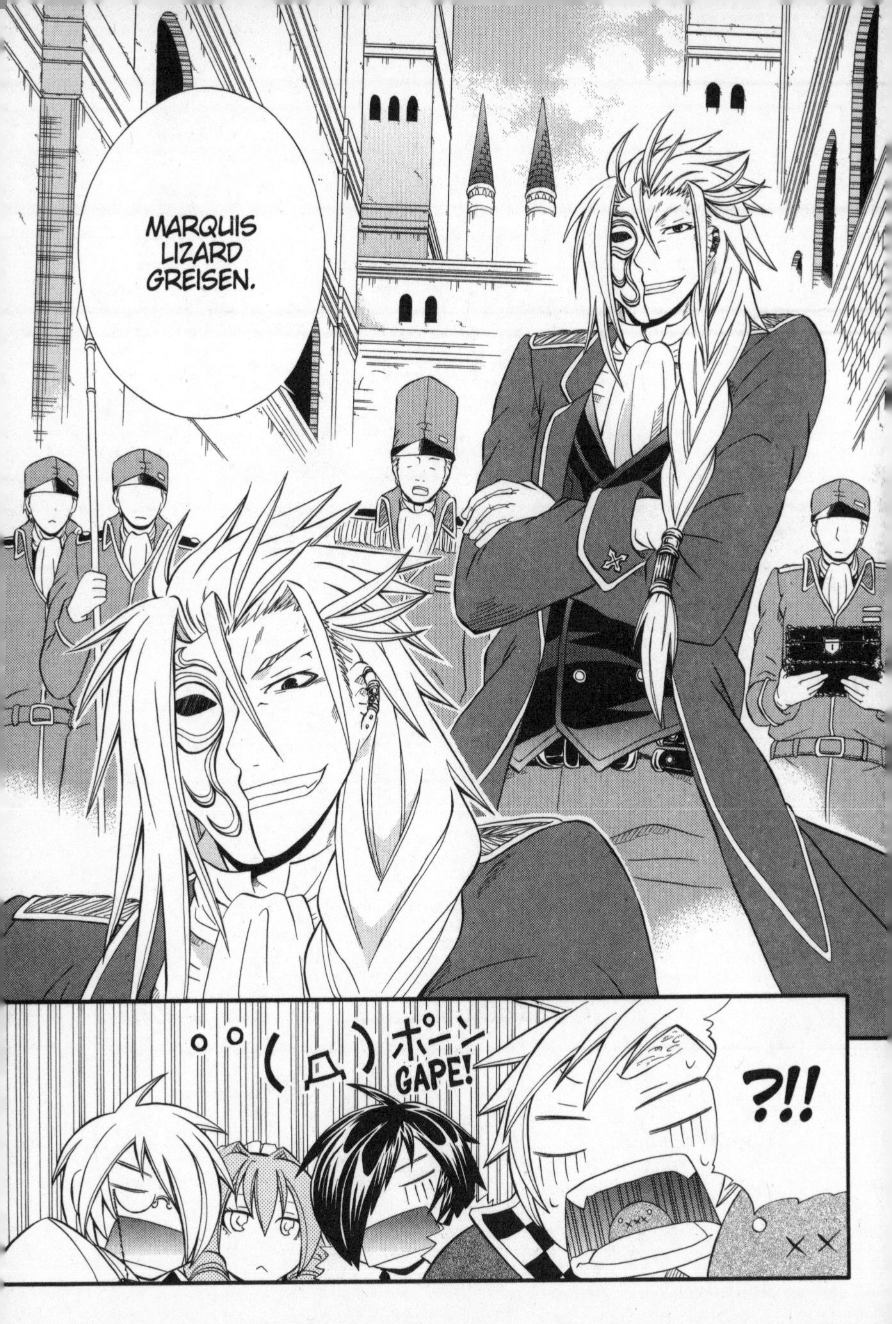
MARQUIS LIZARD GREISEN.
°° (口) ポーン
GAPE!
?!!

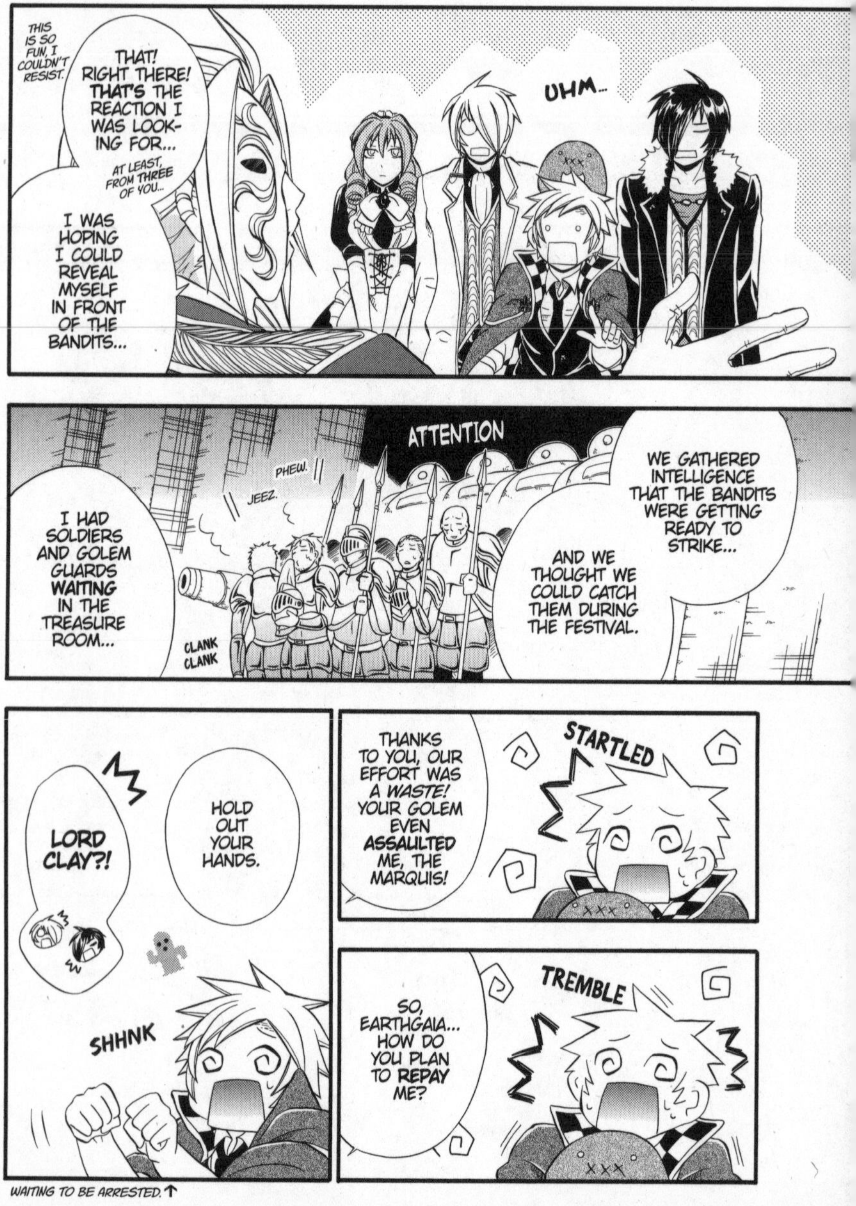
UHM...
THAT! RIGHT THERE! THAT'S THE REACTION I WAS LOOKING FOR...
THIS IS SO FUN, I COULDN'T RESIST.
AT LEAST, FROM THREE OF YOU...
I WAS HOPING I COULD REVEAL MYSELF IN FRONT OF THE BANDITS...
WE GATHERED INTELLIGENCE THAT THE BANDITS WERE GETTING READY TO STRIKE...
AND WE THOUGHT WE COULD CATCH THEM DURING THE FESTIVAL.
ATTENTION
PHEW.
JEEZ.
I HAD SOLDIERS AND GOLEM GUARDS WAITING IN THE TREASURE ROOM...
CLANK CLANK
STARTLED
THANKS TO YOU, OUR EFFORT WAS A WASTE! YOUR GOLEM EVEN ASSAULTED ME, THE MARQUIS!
TREMBLE
SO, EARTHGAIA... HOW DO YOU PLAN TO REPAY ME?
HOLD OUT YOUR HANDS.
LORD CLAY?!
SHHNK
WAITING TO BE ARRESTED.↑

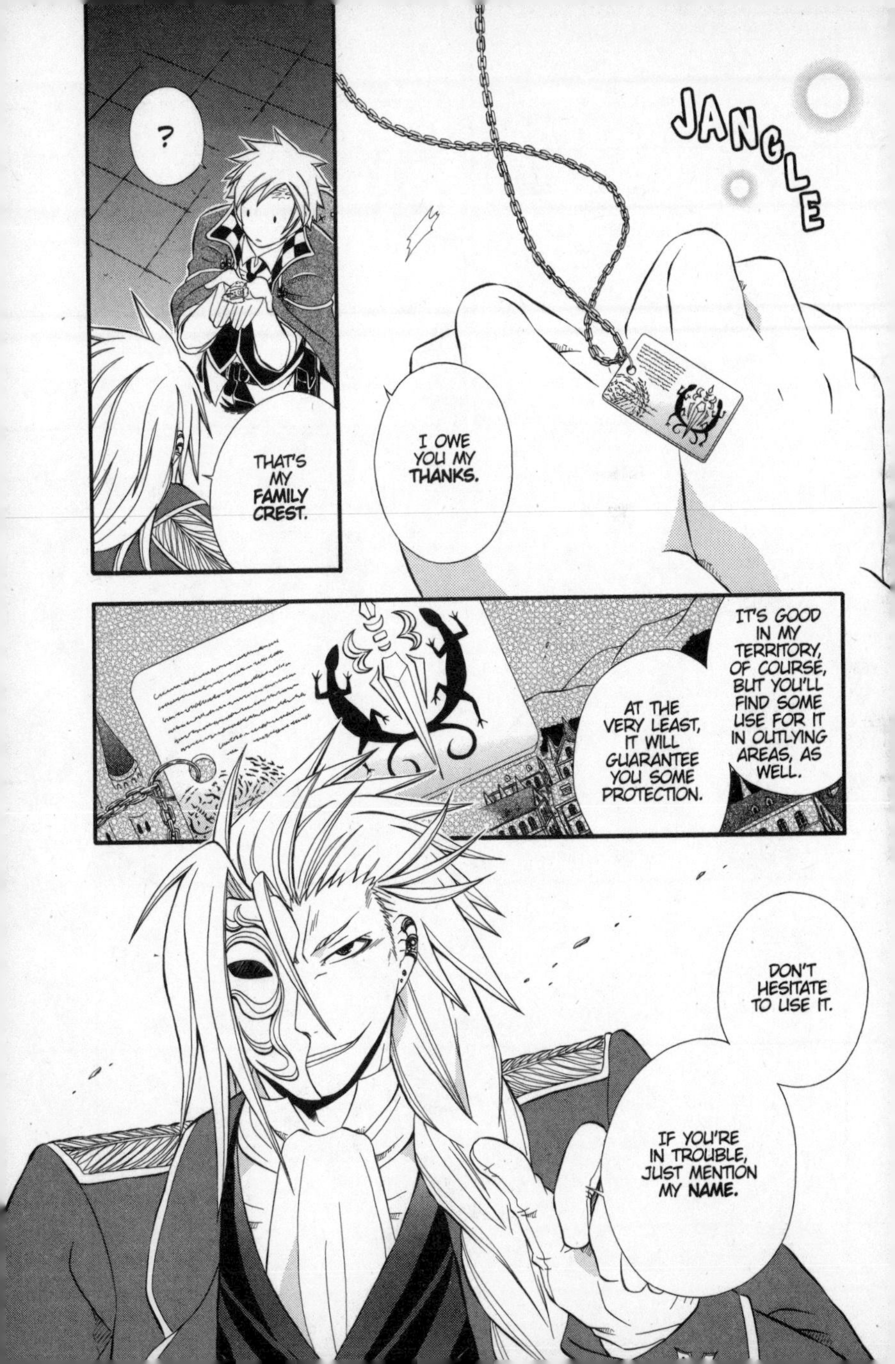
JANGLE
I OWE YOU MY THANKS.
?
THAT'S MY FAMILY CREST.
IT'S GOOD IN MY TERRITORY, OF COURSE, BUT YOU'LL FIND SOME USE FOR IT IN OUTLYING AREAS, AS WELL.
AT THE VERY LEAST, IT WILL GUARANTEE YOU SOME PROTECTION.
DON'T HESITATE TO USE IT.
IF YOU'RE IN TROUBLE, JUST MENTION MY NAME.

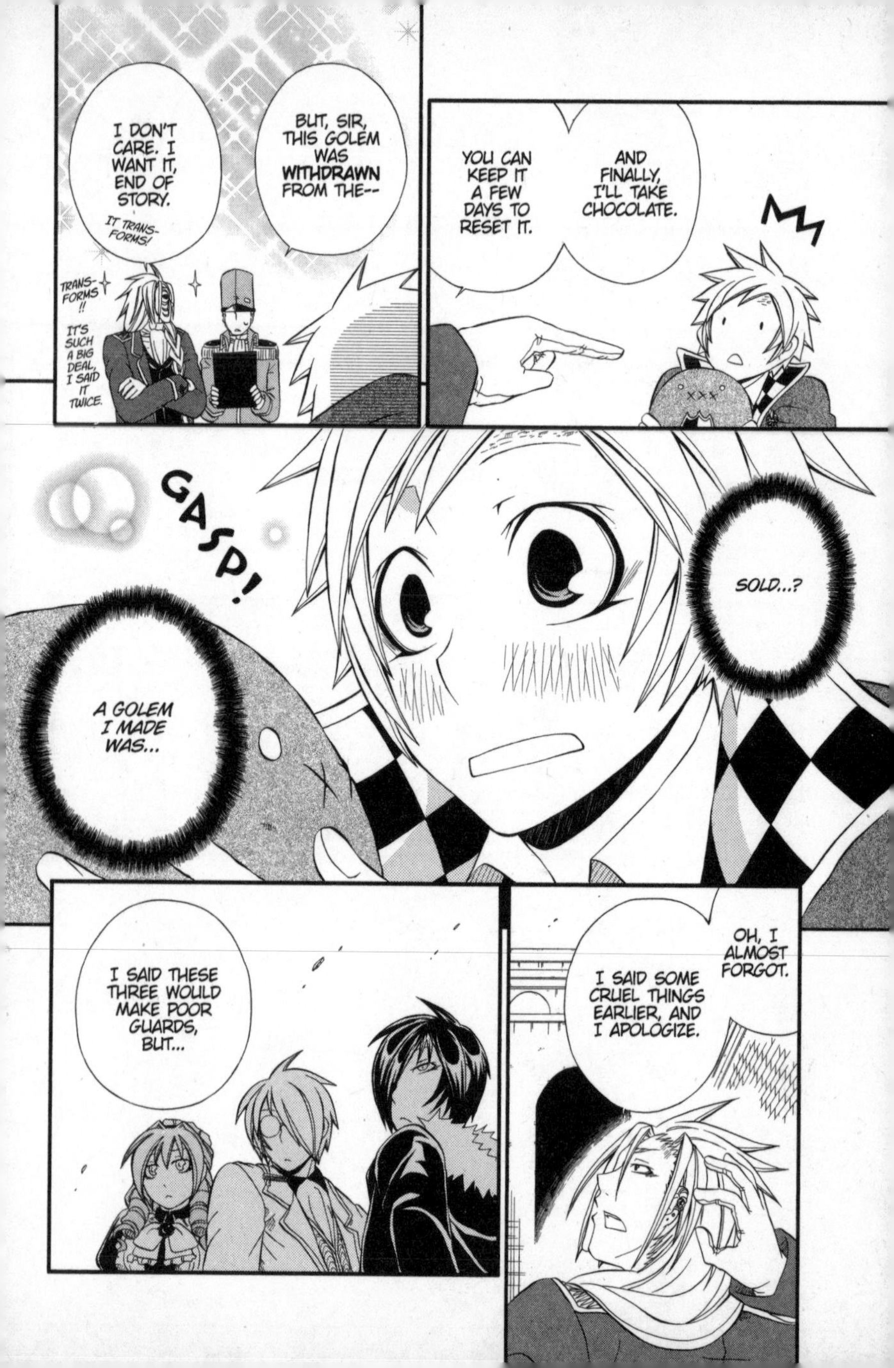
AND FINALLY, I'LL TAKE CHOCOLATE.
YOU CAN KEEP IT A FEW DAYS TO RESET IT.
BUT, SIR, THIS GOLEM WAS WITHDRAWN FROM THE--
I DON'T CARE. I WANT IT, END OF STORY.
IT TRANSFORMS!
TRANSFORMS!!
IT'S SUCH A BIG DEAL, I SAID IT TWICE.
GASP!
SOLD...?
A GOLEM I MADE WAS...
OH, I ALMOST FORGOT.
I SAID SOME CRUEL THINGS EARLIER, AND I APOLOGIZE.
I SAID THESE THREE WOULD MAKE POOR GUARDS, BUT...

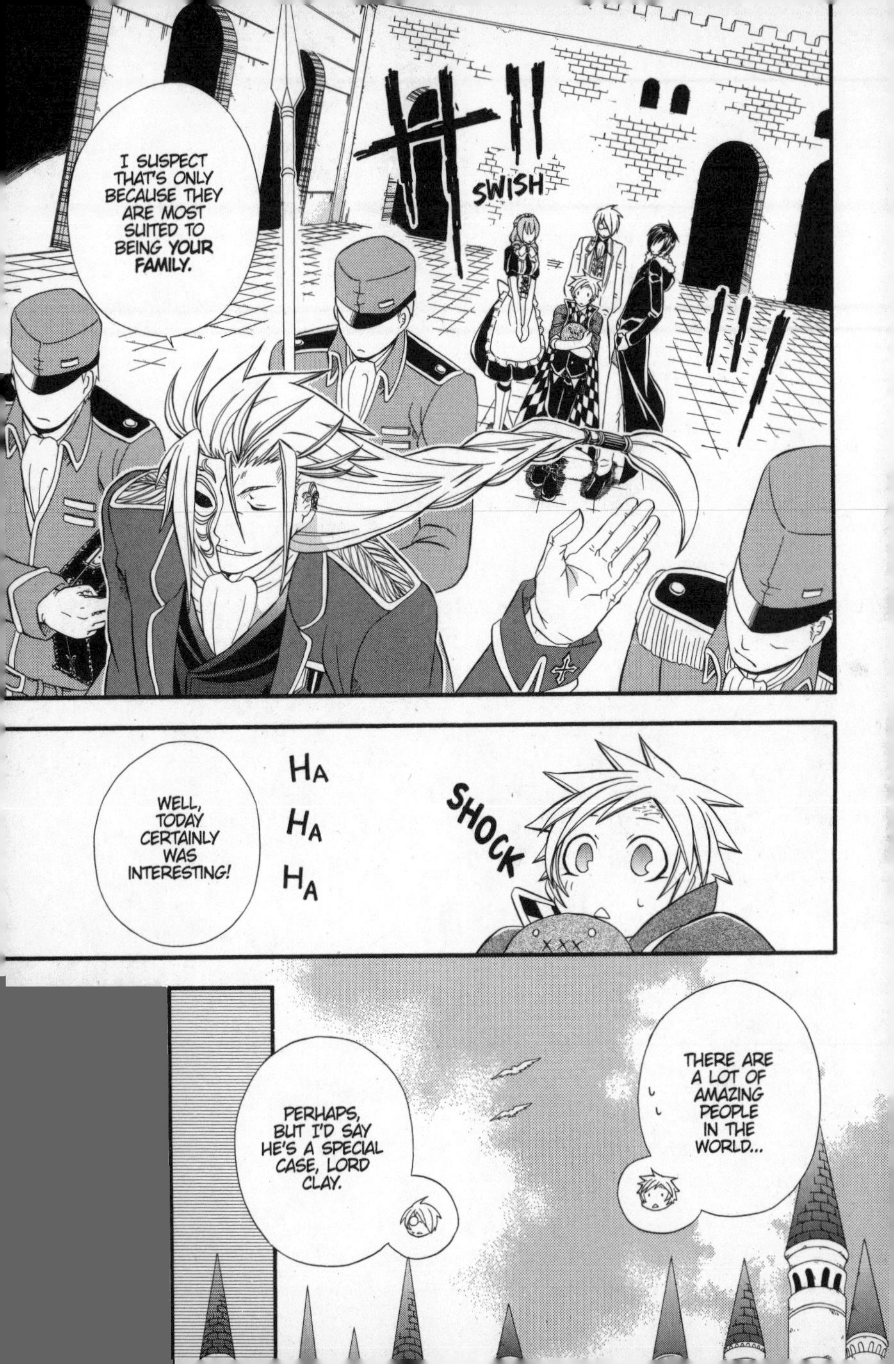
SWISH
I SUSPECT THAT'S ONLY BECAUSE THEY ARE MOST SUITED TO BEING YOUR FAMILY.
SHOCK
HA HA HA
WELL, TODAY CERTAINLY WAS INTERESTING!
THERE ARE A LOT OF AMAZING PEOPLE IN THE WORLD...
PERHAPS, BUT I'D SAY HE'S A SPECIAL CASE, LORD CLAY.

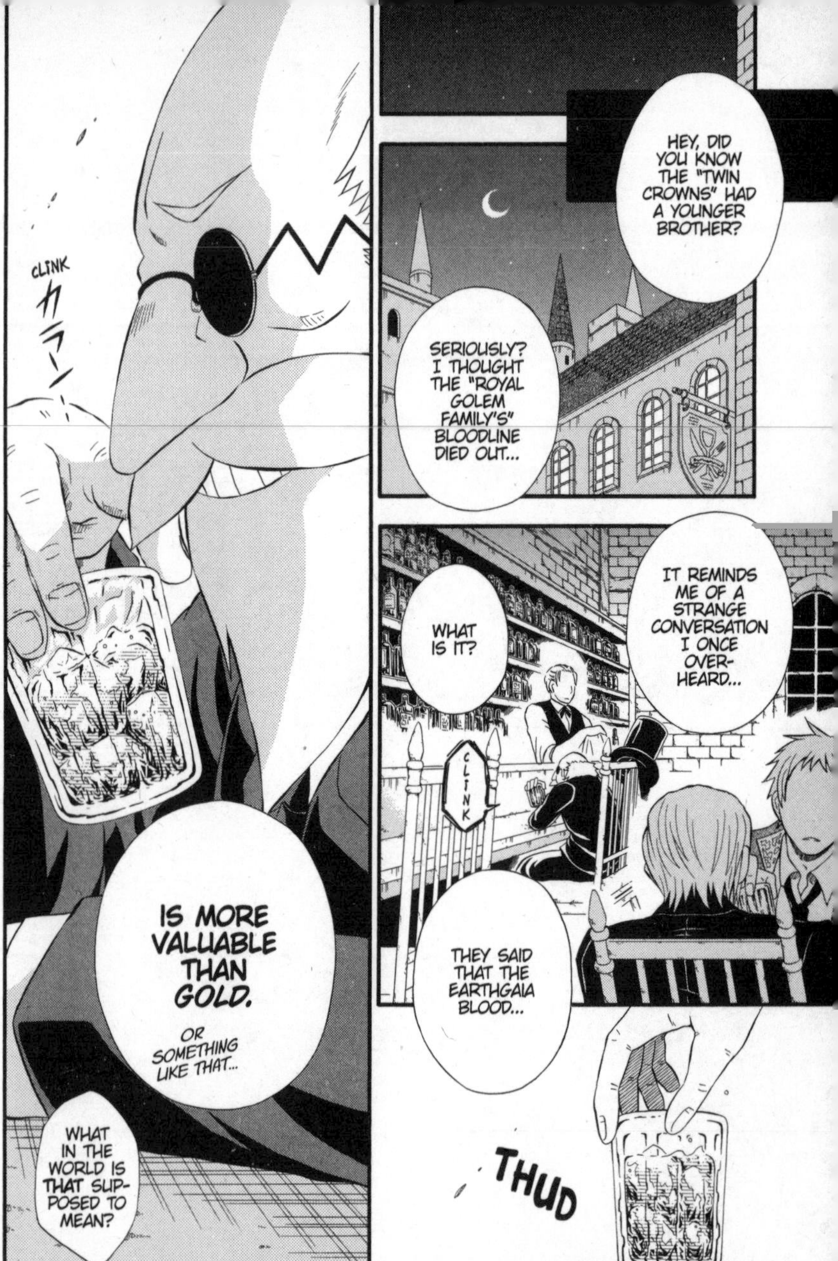
HEY, DID YOU KNOW THE "TWIN CROWNS" HAD A YOUNGER BROTHER?
SERIOUSLY? I THOUGHT THE "ROYAL GOLEM FAMILY'S" BLOODLINE DIED OUT...
IT REMINDS ME OF A STRANGE CONVERSATION I ONCE OVER-HEARD...
WHAT IS IT?
CLINK
THEY SAID THAT THE EARTHGAIA BLOOD...
THUD
CLINK
カラーン
IS MORE VALUABLE THAN GOLD.
OR SOMETHING LIKE THAT...
WHAT IN THE WORLD IS THAT SUP-POSED TO MEAN?

Chapter 3: The Blood of Earthgaia (Part 1)

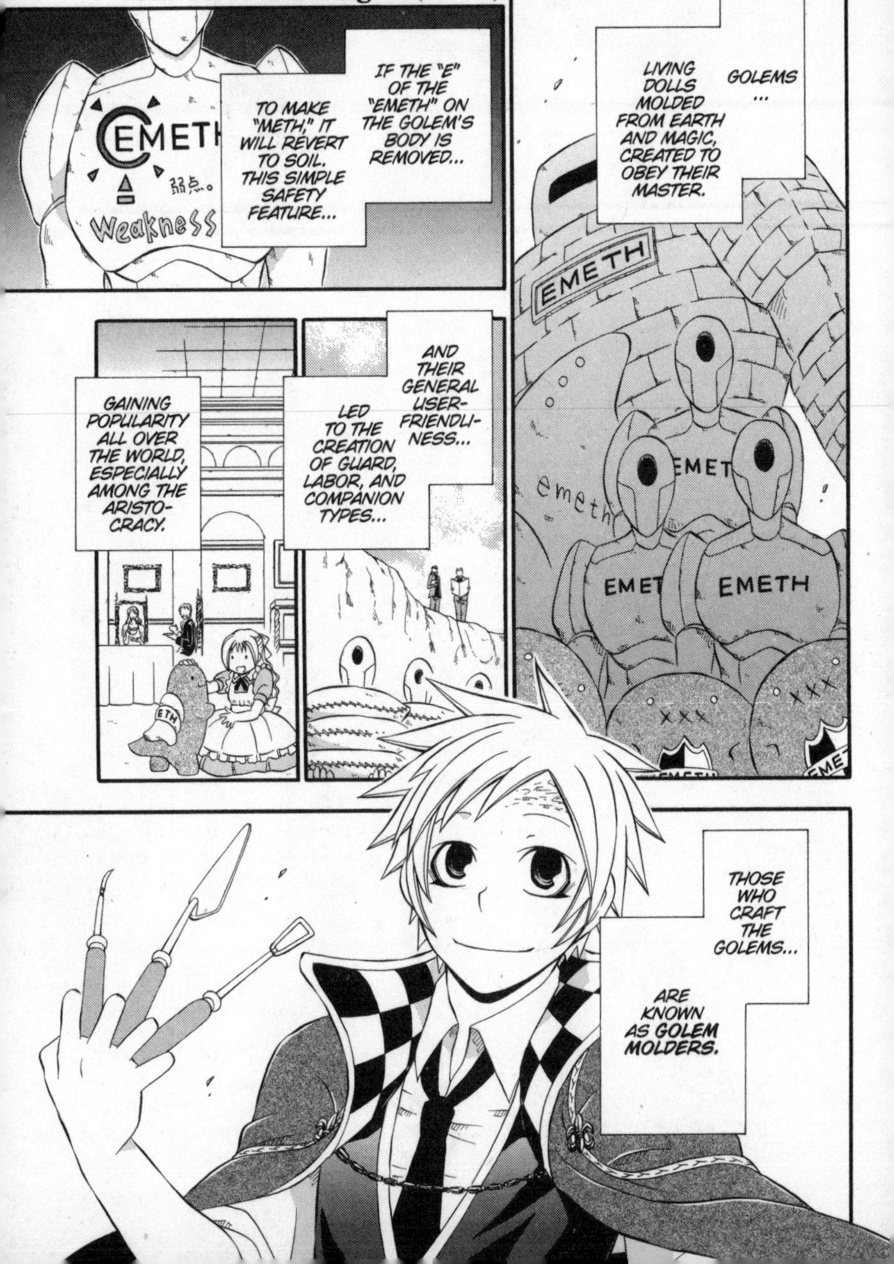
GOLEMS...
LIVING DOLLS MOLDED FROM EARTH AND MAGIC, CREATED TO OBEY THEIR MASTER.
EMETH
EMETH
emeth
IF THE "E" OF THE "EMETH" ON THE GOLEM'S BODY IS REMOVED...
TO MAKE "METH," IT WILL REVERT TO SOIL. THIS SIMPLE SAFETY FEATURE...
EMETH
弱点。
Weakness
AND THEIR GENERAL USER-FRIENDLI-NESS...
LED TO THE CREATION OF GUARD, LABOR, AND COMPANION TYPES...
GAINING POPULARITY ALL OVER THE WORLD, ESPECIALLY AMONG THE ARISTO-CRACY.
THOSE WHO CRAFT THE GOLEMS...
ARE KNOWN AS GOLEM MOLDERS.

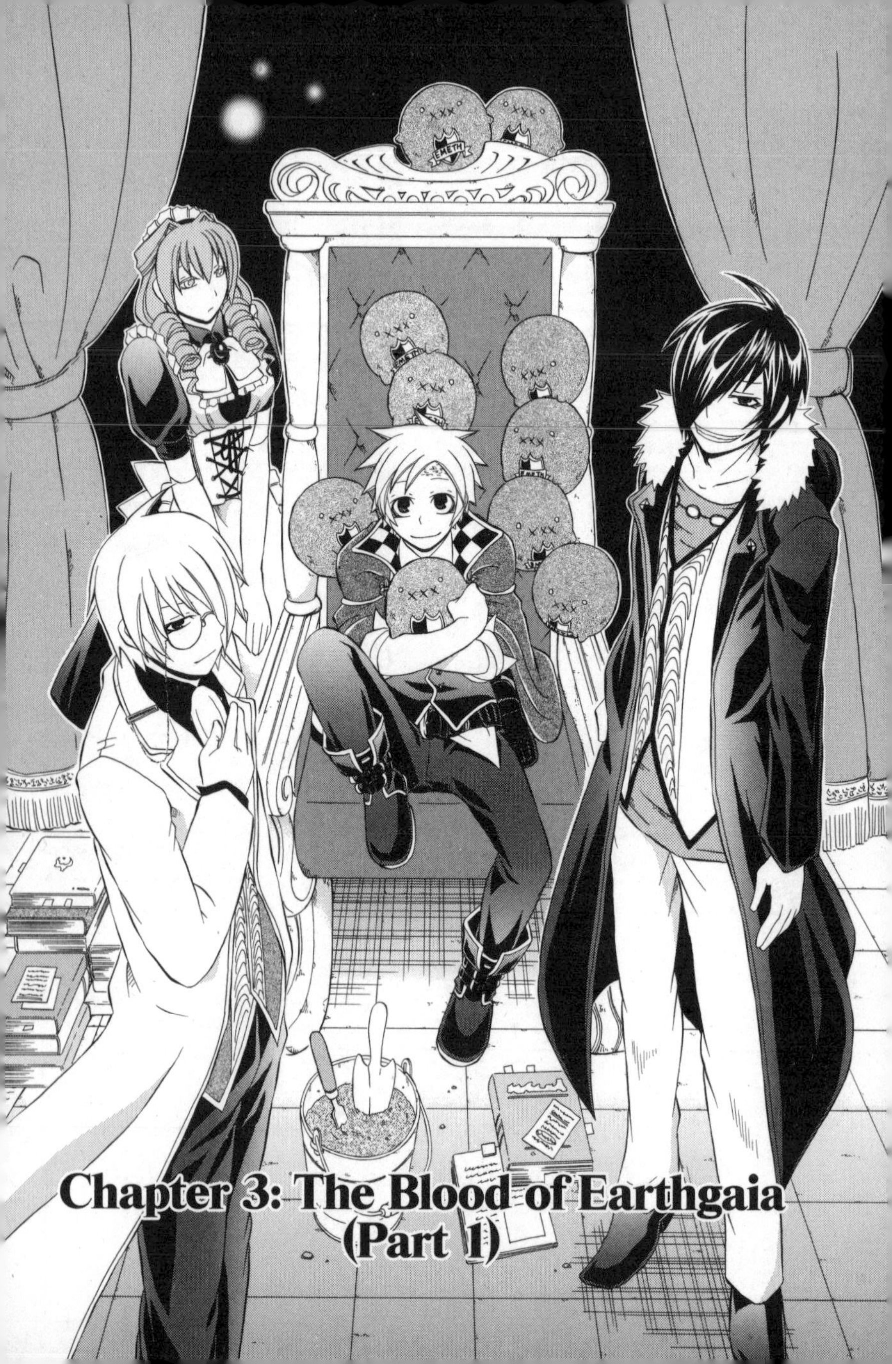

Chapter 3: The Blood of Earthgaia (Part 1)

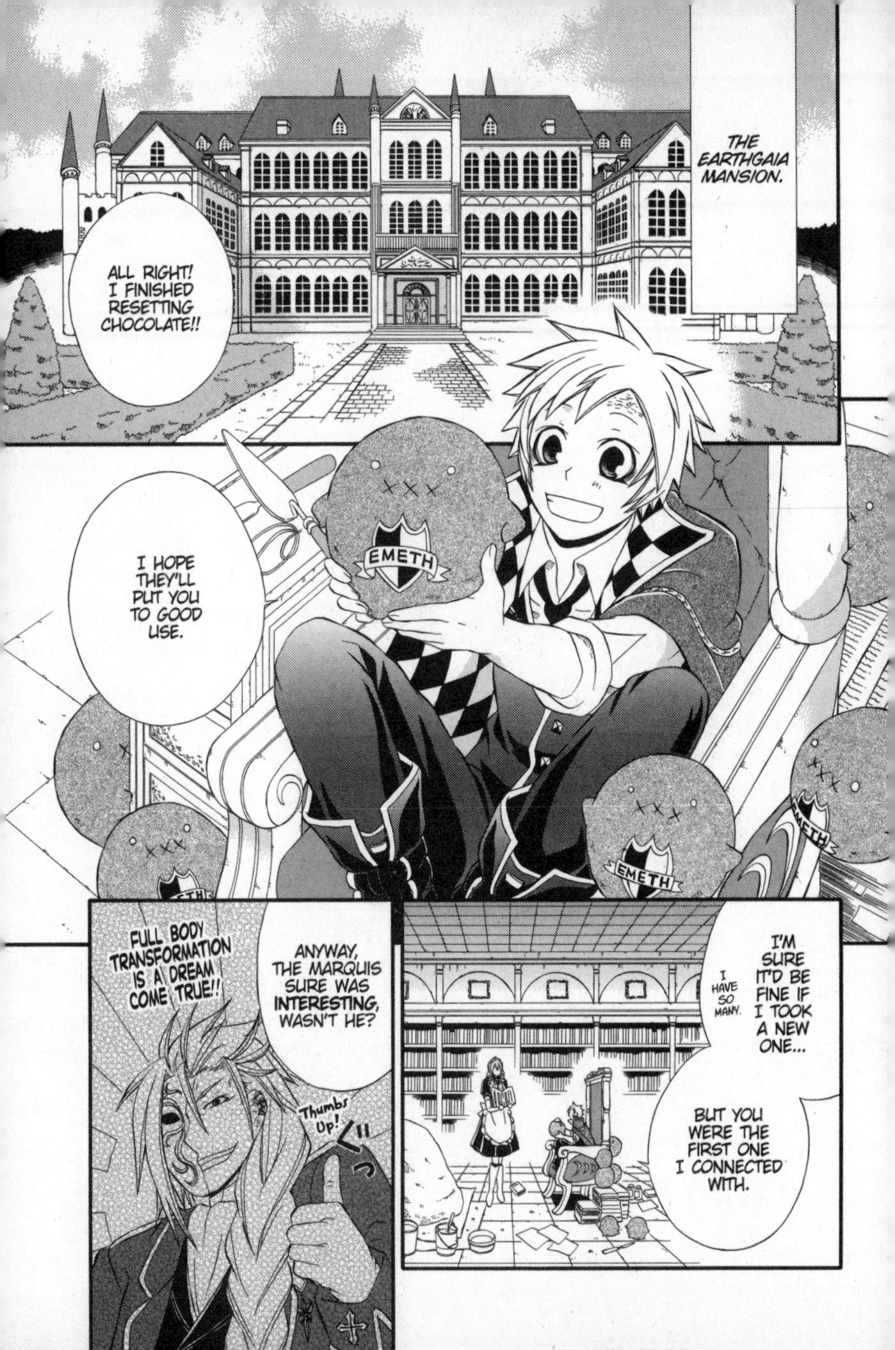
THE EARTHGAIA MANSION.
ALL RIGHT! I FINISHED RESETTING CHOCOLATE!!
I HOPE THEY'LL PUT YOU TO GOOD USE.
I'M SURE IT'D BE FINE IF I TOOK A NEW ONE...
I HAVE SO MANY.
BUT YOU WERE THE FIRST ONE I CONNECTED WITH.
ANYWAY, THE MARQUIS SURE WAS INTERESTING, WASN'T HE?
FULL BODY TRANSFORMATION IS A DREAM COME TRUE!!
Thumbs Up!

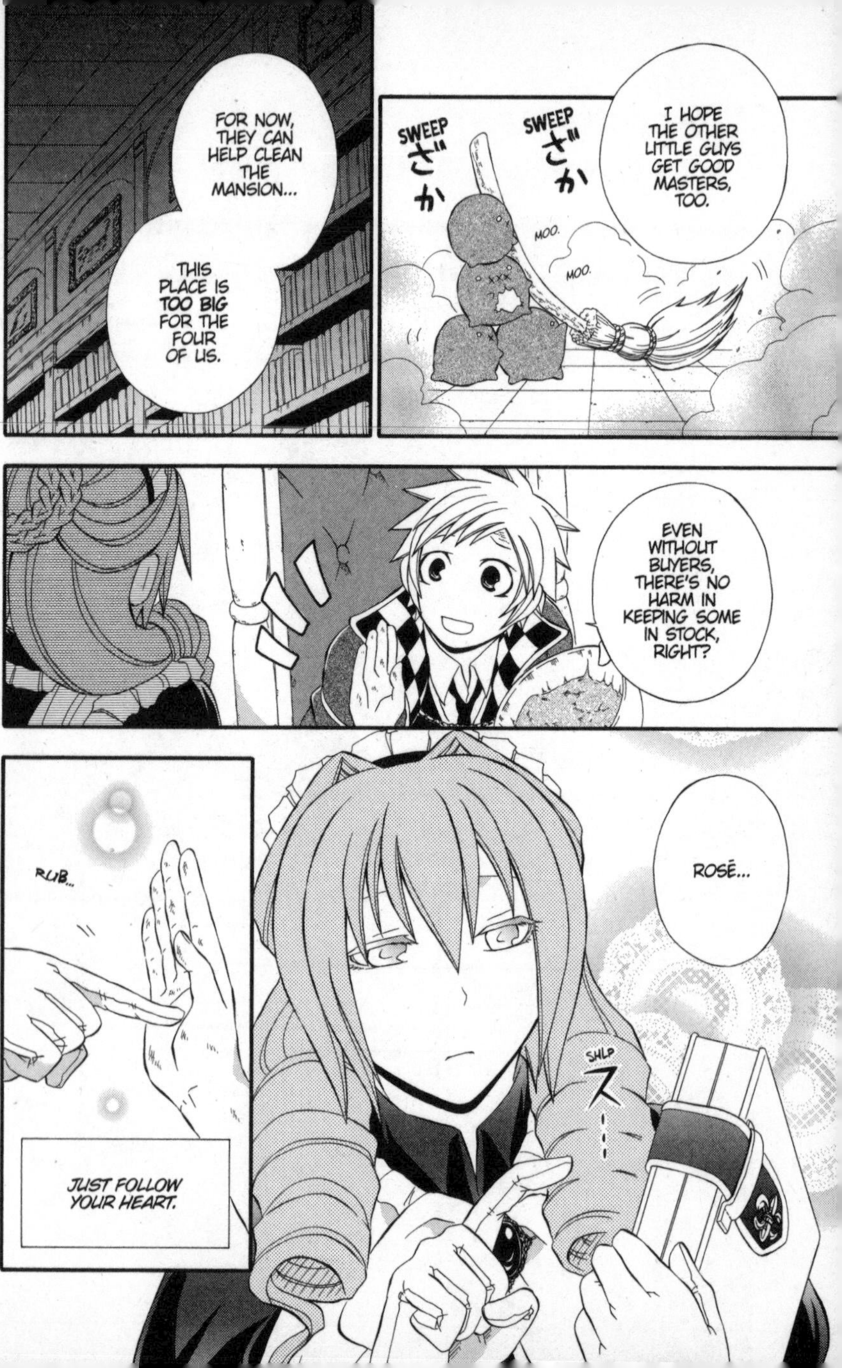
I HOPE THE OTHER LITTLE GUYS GET GOOD MASTERS, TOO.
SWEEP ざか
SWEEP ざか
MOO.
MOO.
FOR NOW, THEY CAN HELP CLEAN THE MANSION...
THIS PLACE IS TOO BIG FOR THE FOUR OF US.
EVEN WITHOUT BUYERS, THERE'S NO HARM IN KEEPING SOME IN STOCK, RIGHT?
ROSÉ...
SHLP ス...
RUB...
JUST FOLLOW YOUR HEART.

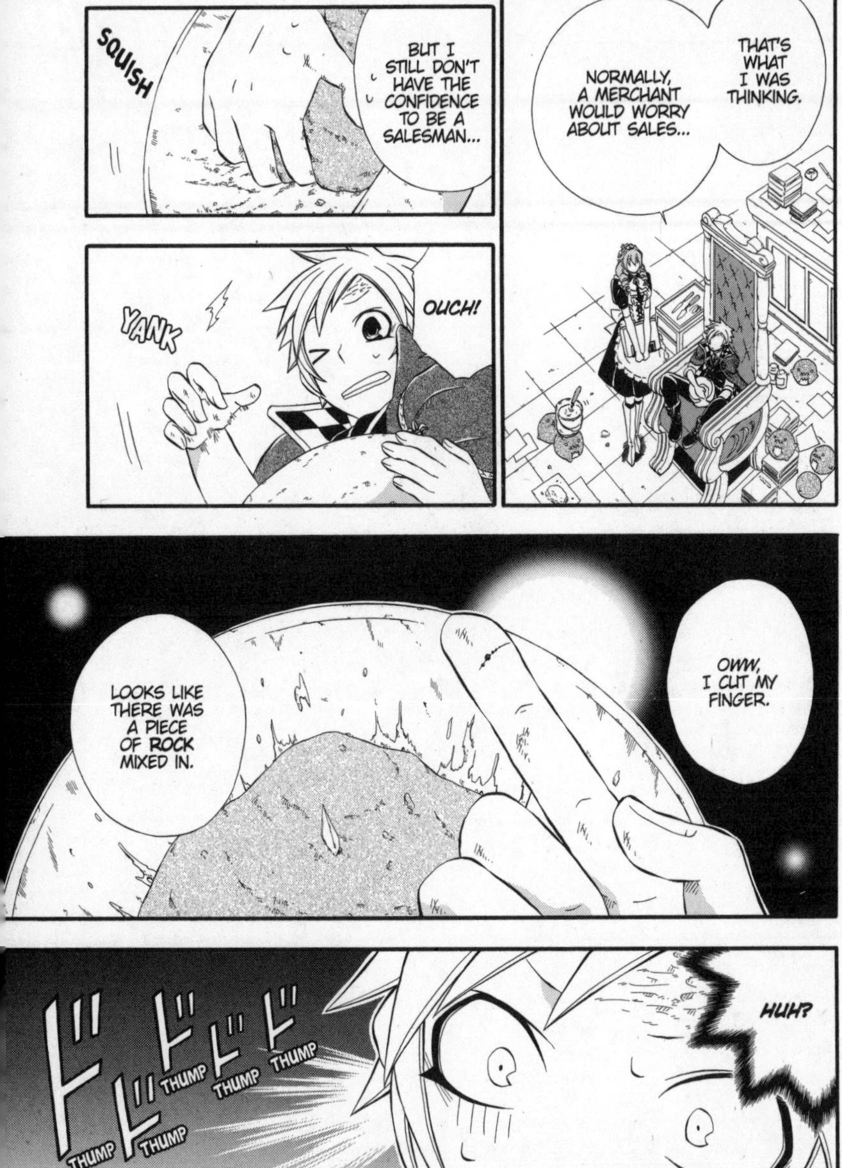
THAT'S WHAT I WAS THINKING.
NORMALLY, A MERCHANT WOULD WORRY ABOUT SALES...
BUT I STILL DON'T HAVE THE CONFIDENCE TO BE A SALESMAN...
SQUISH
OUCH!
YANK
OWW, I CUT MY FINGER.
LOOKS LIKE THERE WAS A PIECE OF ROCK MIXED IN.
HUH?
ドドドドド
THUMP THUMP THUMP THUMP THUMP

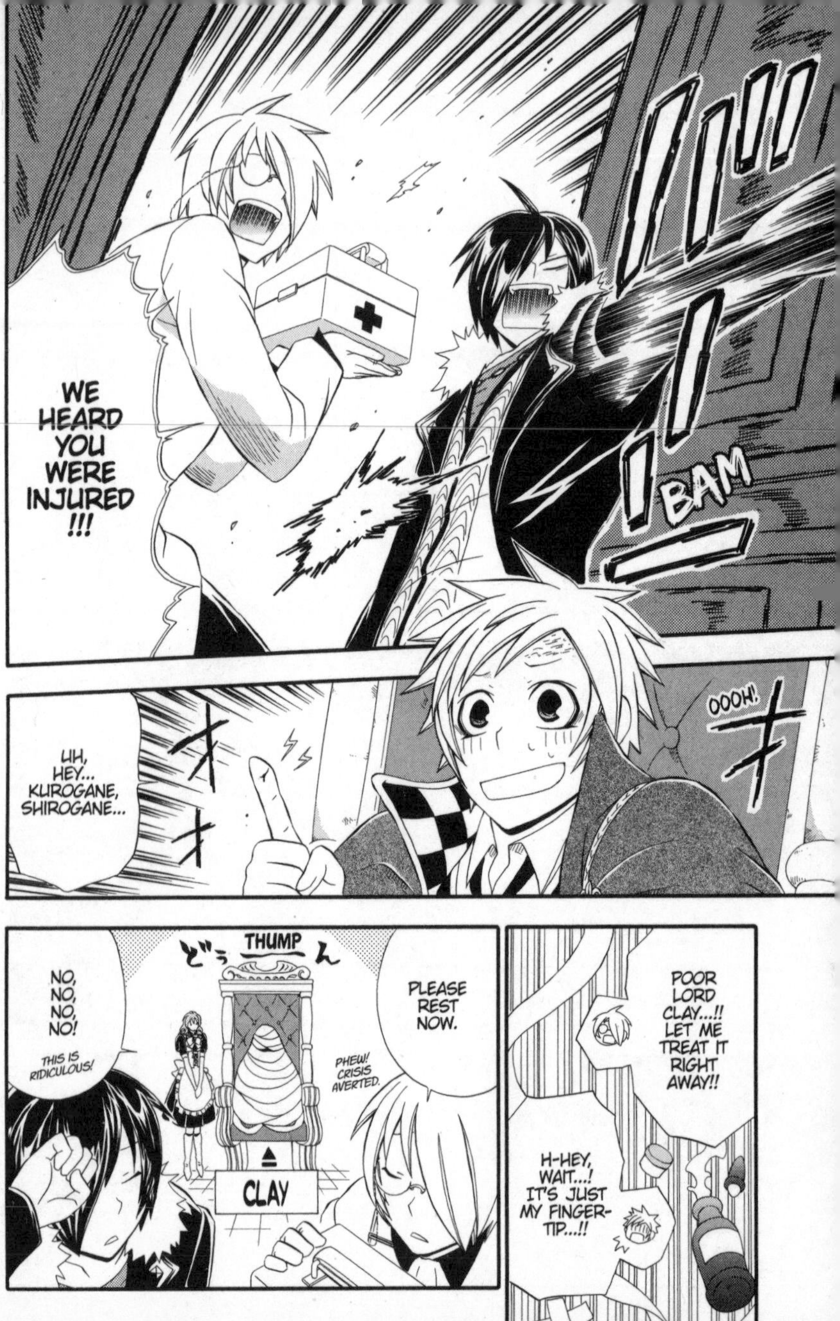
BAM
WE HEARD YOU WERE INJURED!!!
OOOH!
UH, HEY... KUROGANE, SHIROGANE...
POOR LORD CLAY...!! LET ME TREAT IT RIGHT AWAY!!
H-HEY, WAIT...! IT'S JUST MY FINGER-TIP...!!
PLEASE REST NOW.
どぅ THUMP ん
PHEW! CRISIS AVERTED.
NO, NO, NO, NO!
THIS IS RIDICULOUS!
CLAY

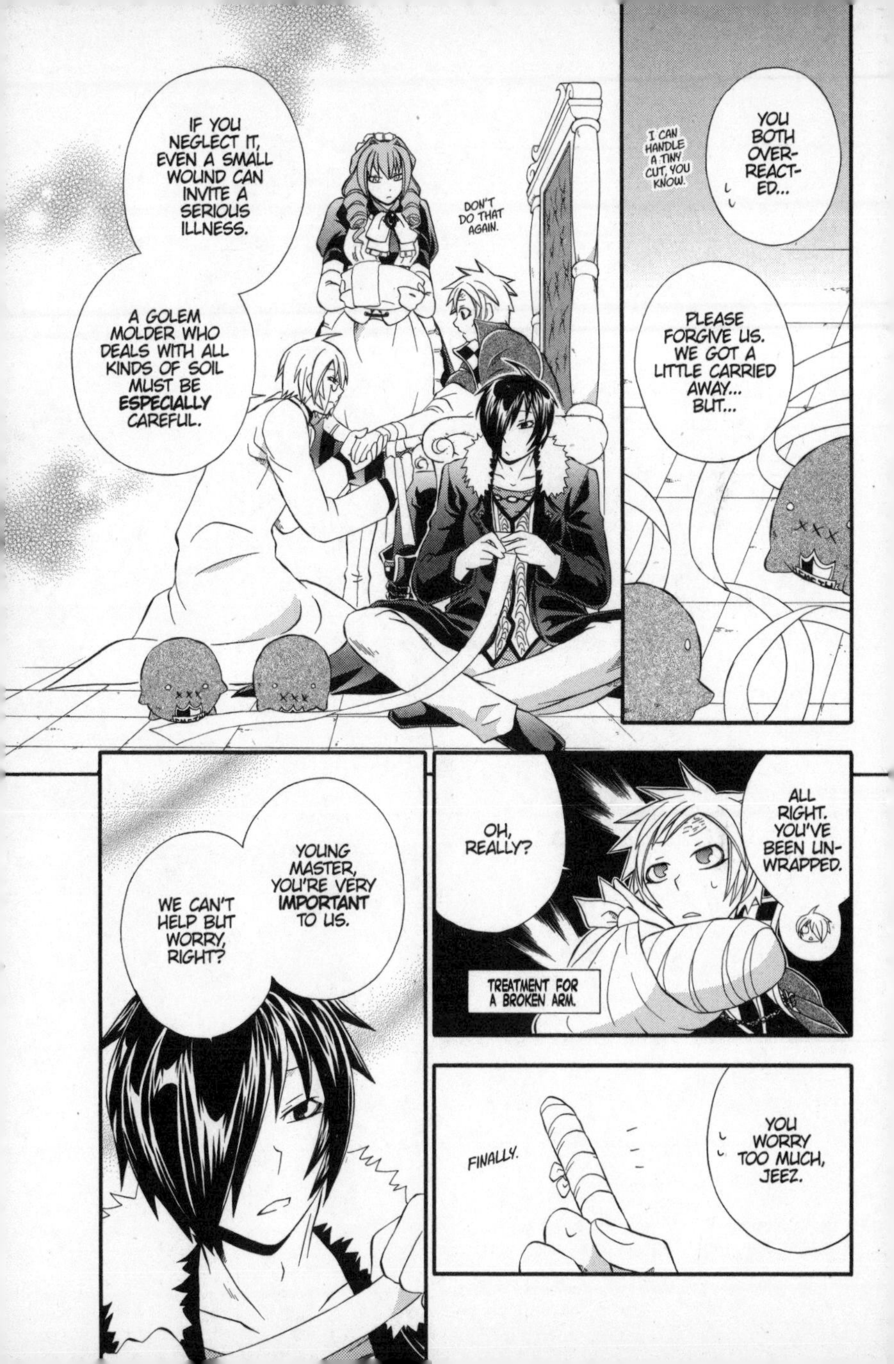
YOU BOTH OVER-REACTED...
I CAN HANDLE A TINY CUT, YOU KNOW.
PLEASE FORGIVE US. WE GOT A LITTLE CARRIED AWAY... BUT...
IF YOU NEGLECT IT, EVEN A SMALL WOUND CAN INVITE A SERIOUS ILLNESS.
A GOLEM MOLDER WHO DEALS WITH ALL KINDS OF SOIL MUST BE ESPECIALLY CAREFUL.
DON'T DO THAT AGAIN.
ALL RIGHT. YOU'VE BEEN UN-WRAPPED.
OH, REALLY?
TREATMENT FOR A BROKEN ARM.
YOU WORRY TOO MUCH, JEEZ.
FINALLY.
YOUNG MASTER, YOU'RE VERY IMPORTANT TO US.
WE CAN'T HELP BUT WORRY, RIGHT?

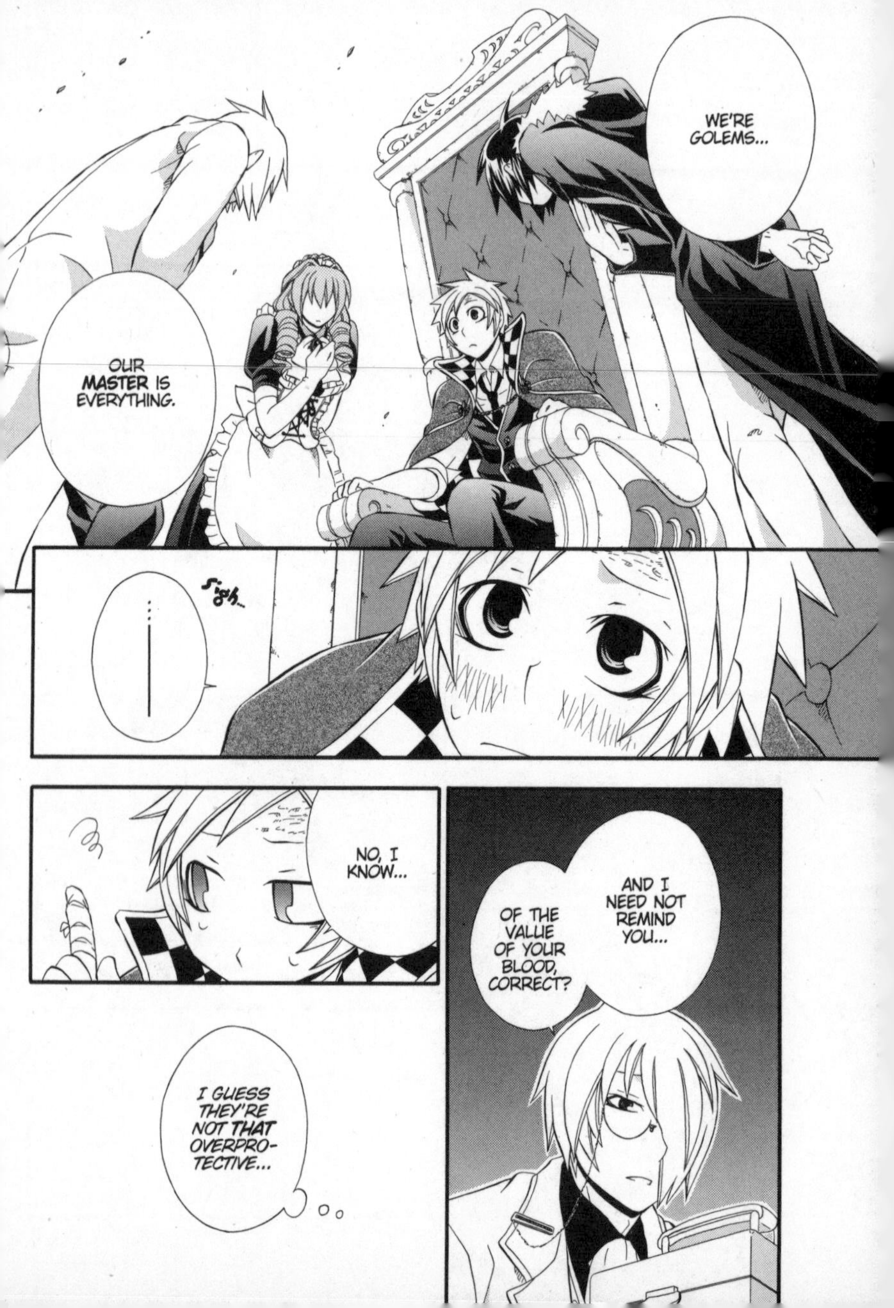
WE'RE GOLEMS...
OUR MASTER IS EVERYTHING.
Sigh..
...
AND I NEED NOT REMIND YOU...
OF THE VALUE OF YOUR BLOOD, CORRECT?
NO, I KNOW...
I GUESS THEY'RE NOT THAT OVERPROTECTIVE...

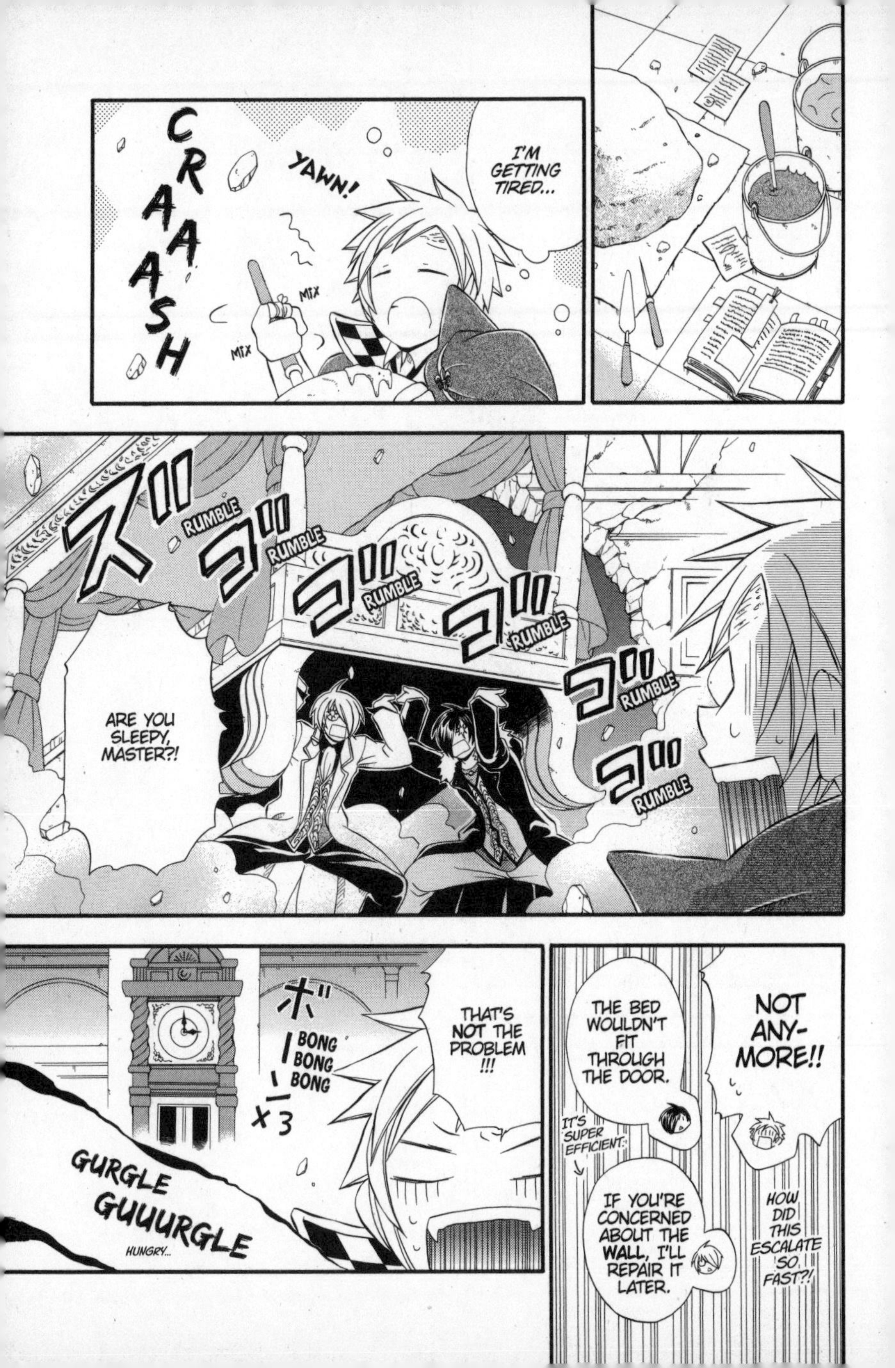
I'M GETTING TIRED...
YAWN!
CRAAASH
MIX
MIX
RUMBLE
RUMBLE
RUMBLE
RUMBLE
RUMBLE
RUMBLE
ARE YOU SLEEPY, MASTER?!
NOT ANYMORE!!
THE BED WOULDN'T FIT THROUGH THE DOOR.
IT'S SUPER EFFICIENT.
IF YOU'RE CONCERNED ABOUT THE WALL, I'LL REPAIR IT LATER.
HOW DID THIS ESCALATE SO FAST?!
THAT'S NOT THE PROBLEM!!!
BONG BONG BONG
x3
GURGLE GUUURGLE
HUNGRY...

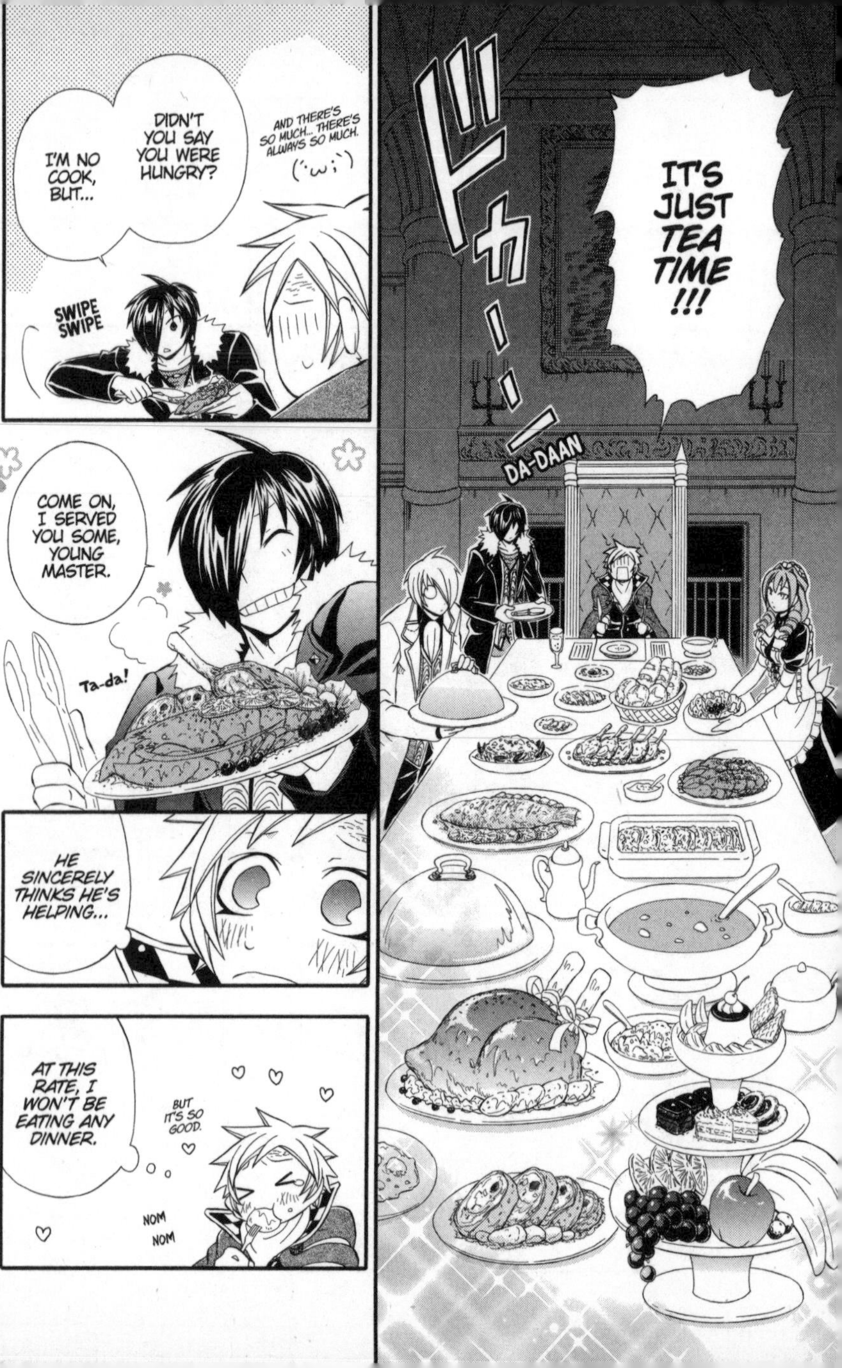
IT'S JUST TEA TIME!!!
DA-DAAN
AND THERE'S SO MUCH... THERE'S ALWAYS SO MUCH.
DIDN'T YOU SAY YOU WERE HUNGRY?
I'M NO COOK, BUT...
SWIPE SWIPE
COME ON, I SERVED YOU SOME, YOUNG MASTER.
Ta-da!
HE SINCERELY THINKS HE'S HELPING...
AT THIS RATE, I WON'T BE EATING ANY DINNER.
BUT IT'S SO GOOD.
NOM NOM

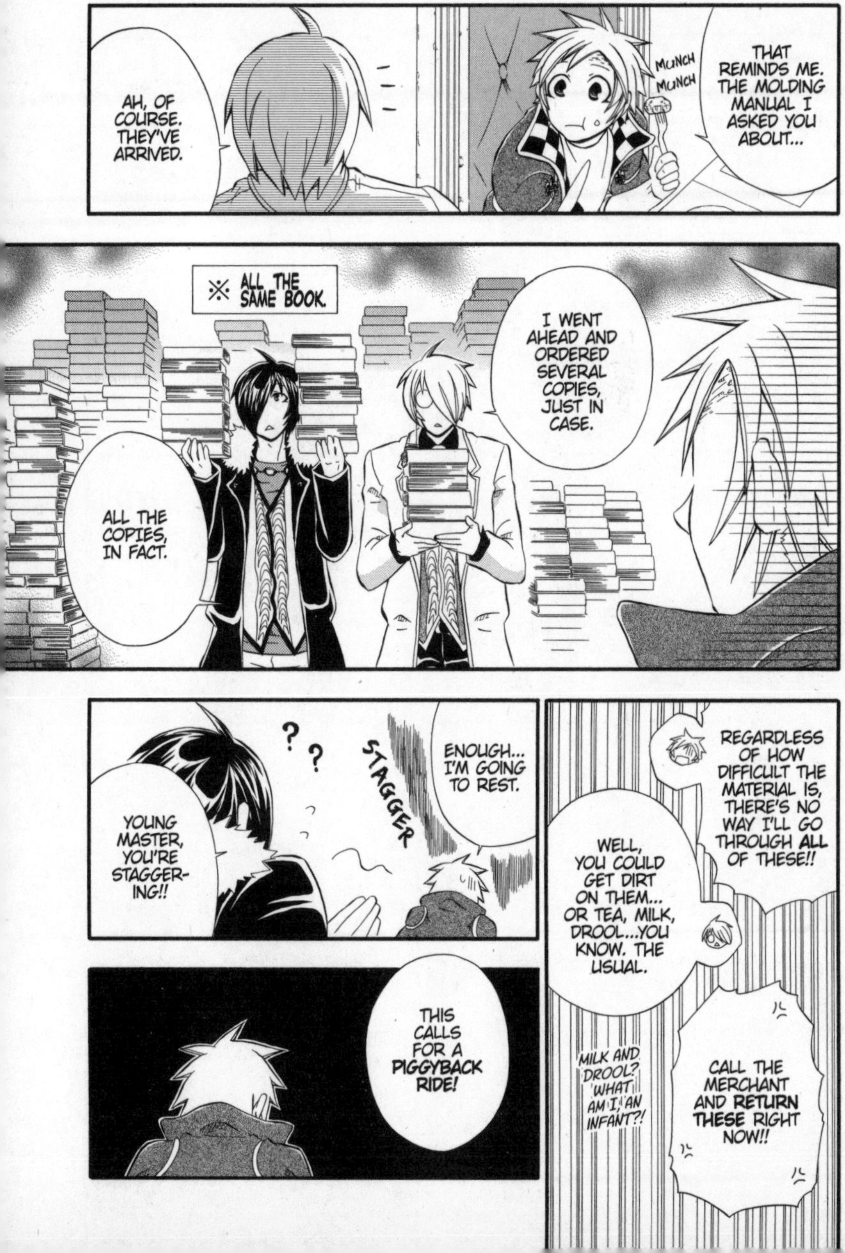
MUNCH MUNCH
THAT REMINDS ME. THE MOLDING MANUAL I ASKED YOU ABOUT...
AH, OF COURSE. THEY'VE ARRIVED.
I WENT AHEAD AND ORDERED SEVERAL COPIES, JUST IN CASE.
※ ALL THE SAME BOOK.
ALL THE COPIES, IN FACT.
REGARDLESS OF HOW DIFFICULT THE MATERIAL IS, THERE'S NO WAY I'LL GO THROUGH **ALL** OF THESE!!
WELL, YOU COULD GET DIRT ON THEM... OR TEA, MILK, DROOL...YOU KNOW. THE USUAL.
CALL THE MERCHANT AND **RETURN THESE** RIGHT NOW!!
MILK AND DROOL? WHAT AM I, AN INFANT?!
ENOUGH... I'M GOING TO REST.
STAGGER
? ?
YOUNG MASTER, YOU'RE STAGGER-ING!!
THIS CALLS FOR A **PIGGYBACK** RIDE!

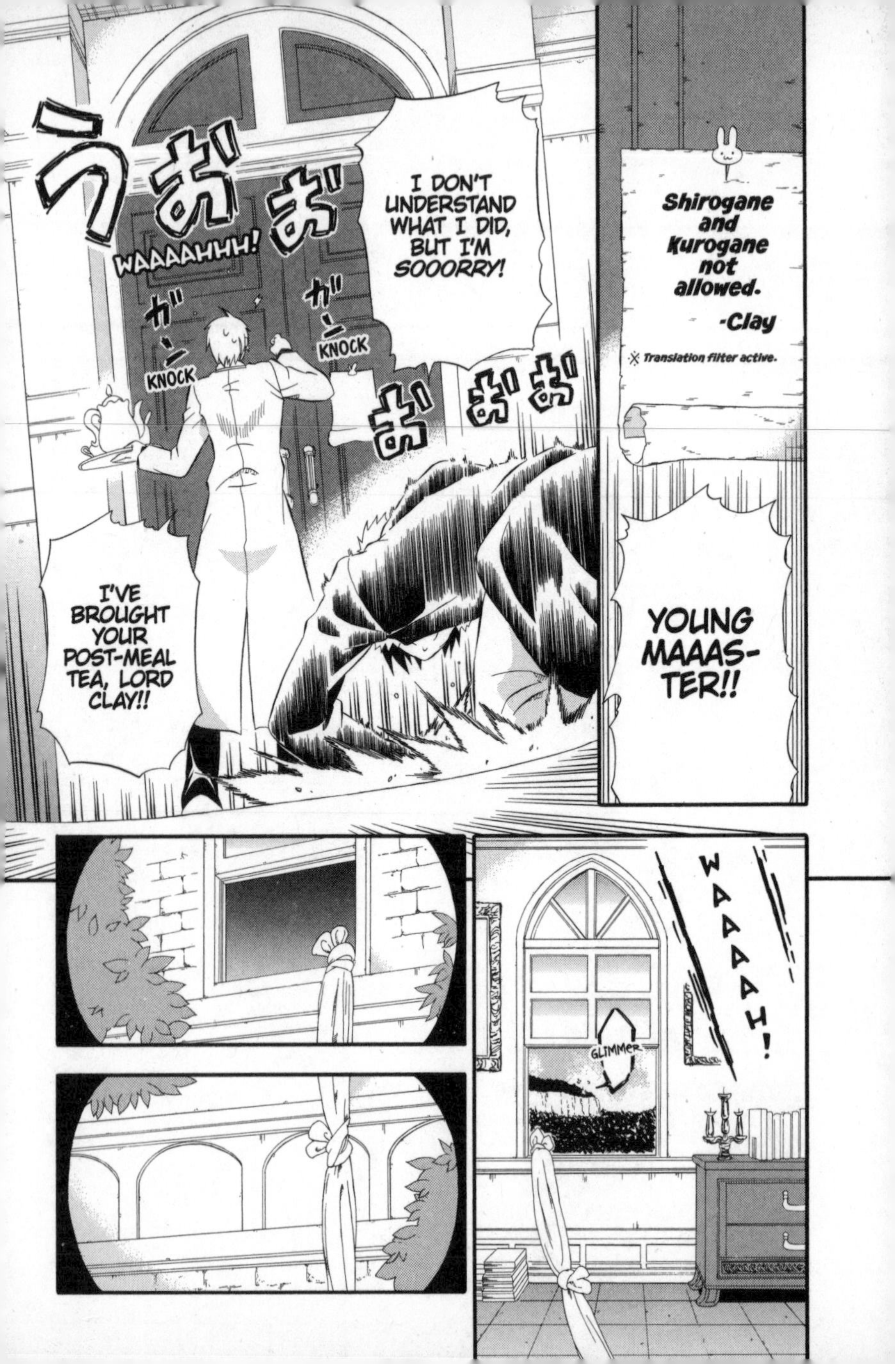
Shirogane and Kurogane not allowed.
-Clay
※ Translation filter active.
YOUNG MAAASTER!!
うおお
WAAAAHHH!
おおお
I DON'T UNDERSTAND WHAT I DID, BUT I'M SOOORRY!
ガン
KNOCK
ガン
KNOCK
I'VE BROUGHT YOUR POST-MEAL TEA, LORD CLAY!!
WAAAAAH!
GLIMMER

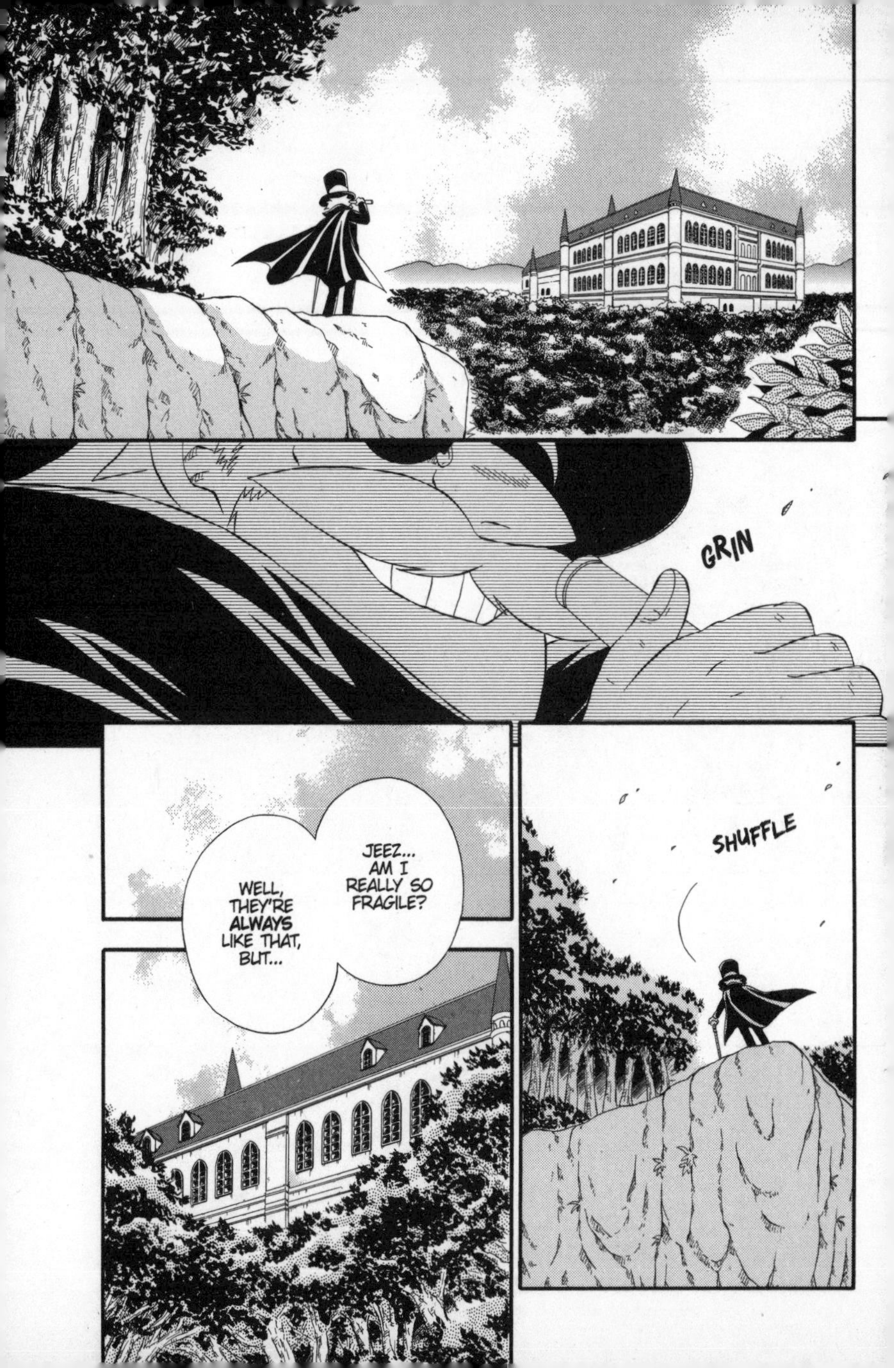
GRIN
SHUFFLE
JEEZ... AM I REALLY SO FRAGILE?
WELL, THEY'RE ALWAYS LIKE THAT, BUT...

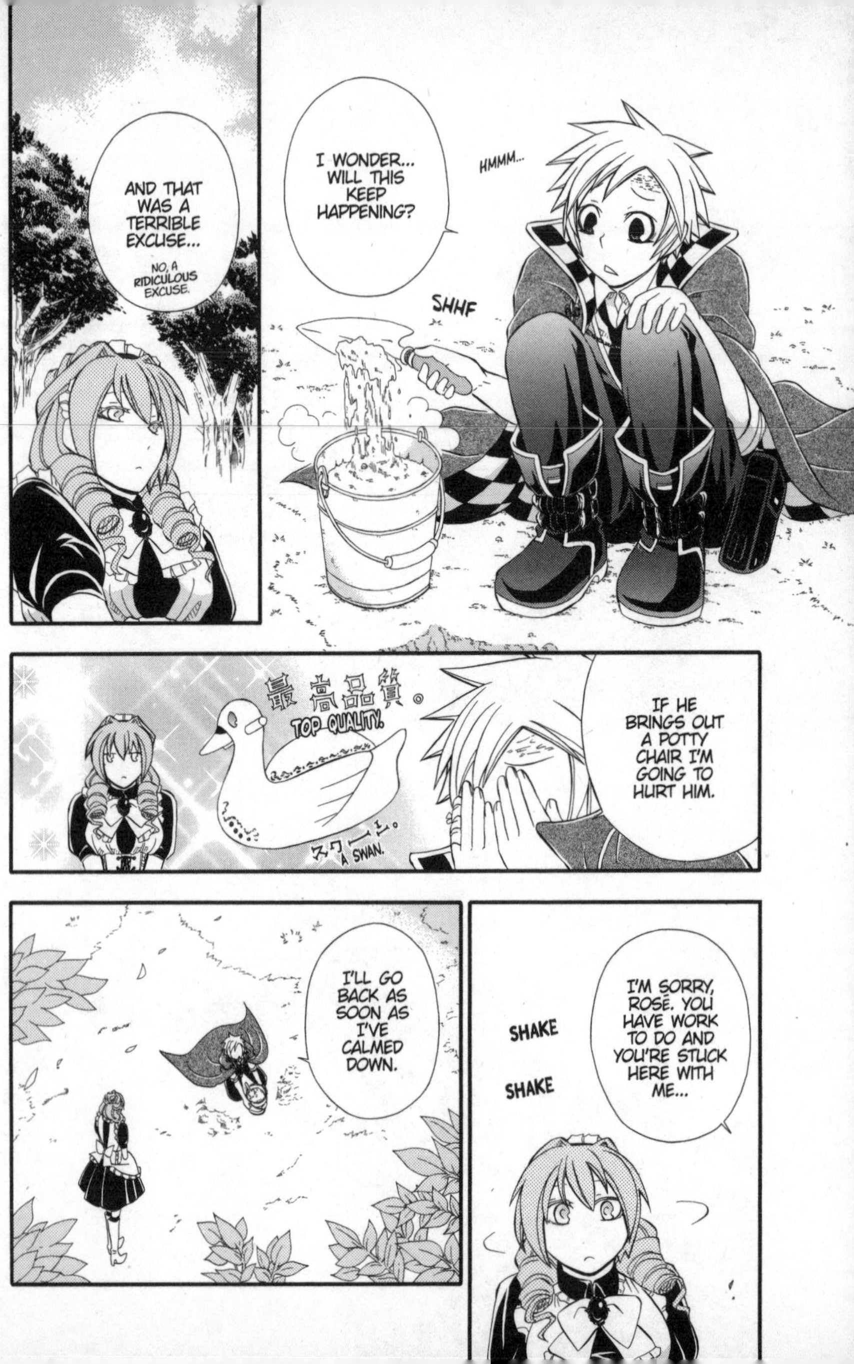
I WONDER... WILL THIS KEEP HAPPENING?
HMMM...
SHHF
AND THAT WAS A TERRIBLE EXCUSE...
NO, A RIDICULOUS EXCUSE.
IF HE BRINGS OUT A POTTY CHAIR I'M GOING TO HURT HIM.
最高品質。
TOP QUALITY.
スワ～ン。
A SWAN.
I'M SORRY, ROSÉ. YOU HAVE WORK TO DO AND YOU'RE STUCK HERE WITH ME...
SHAKE
SHAKE
I'LL GO BACK AS SOON AS I'VE CALMED DOWN.

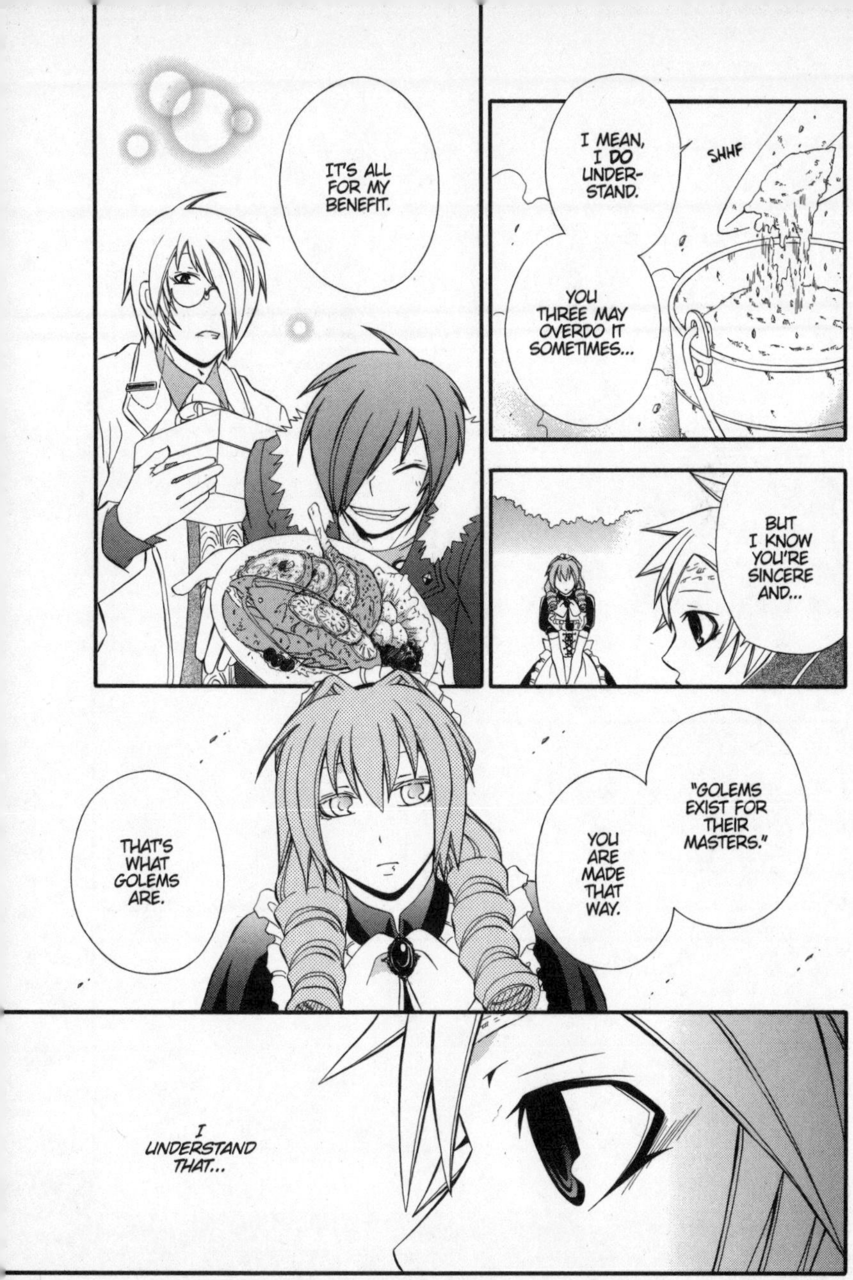
I MEAN, I DO UNDER-STAND.
SHHF
YOU THREE MAY OVERDO IT SOMETIMES...
BUT I KNOW YOU'RE SINCERE AND...
IT'S ALL FOR MY BENEFIT.
"GOLEMS EXIST FOR THEIR MASTERS."
YOU ARE MADE THAT WAY.
THAT'S WHAT GOLEMS ARE.
I UNDERSTAND THAT...

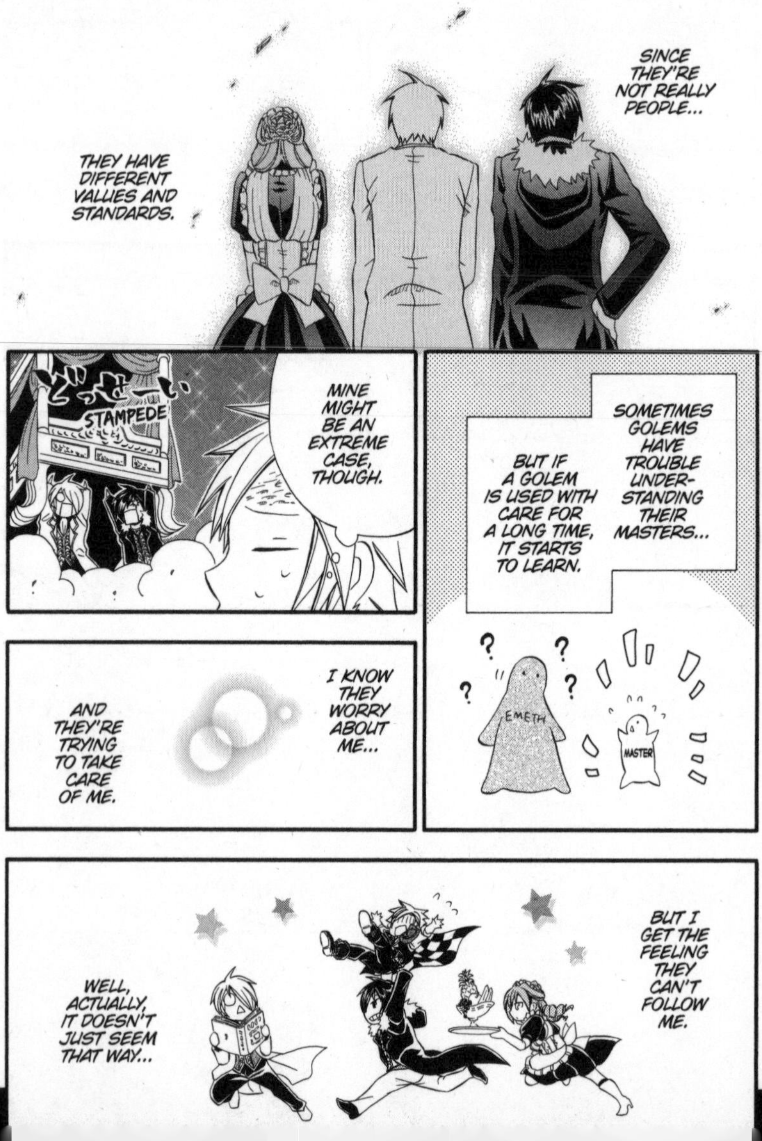

SINCE THEY'RE NOT REALLY PEOPLE...
THEY HAVE DIFFERENT VALUES AND STANDARDS.
SOMETIMES GOLEMS HAVE TROUBLE UNDER-STANDING THEIR MASTERS...
BUT IF A GOLEM IS USED WITH CARE FOR A LONG TIME, IT STARTS TO LEARN.
EMETH
MASTER
MINE MIGHT BE AN EXTREME CASE, THOUGH.
STAMPEDE
I KNOW THEY WORRY ABOUT ME...
AND THEY'RE TRYING TO TAKE CARE OF ME.
BUT I GET THE FEELING THEY CAN'T FOLLOW ME.
WELL, ACTUALLY, IT DOESN'T JUST SEEM THAT WAY...

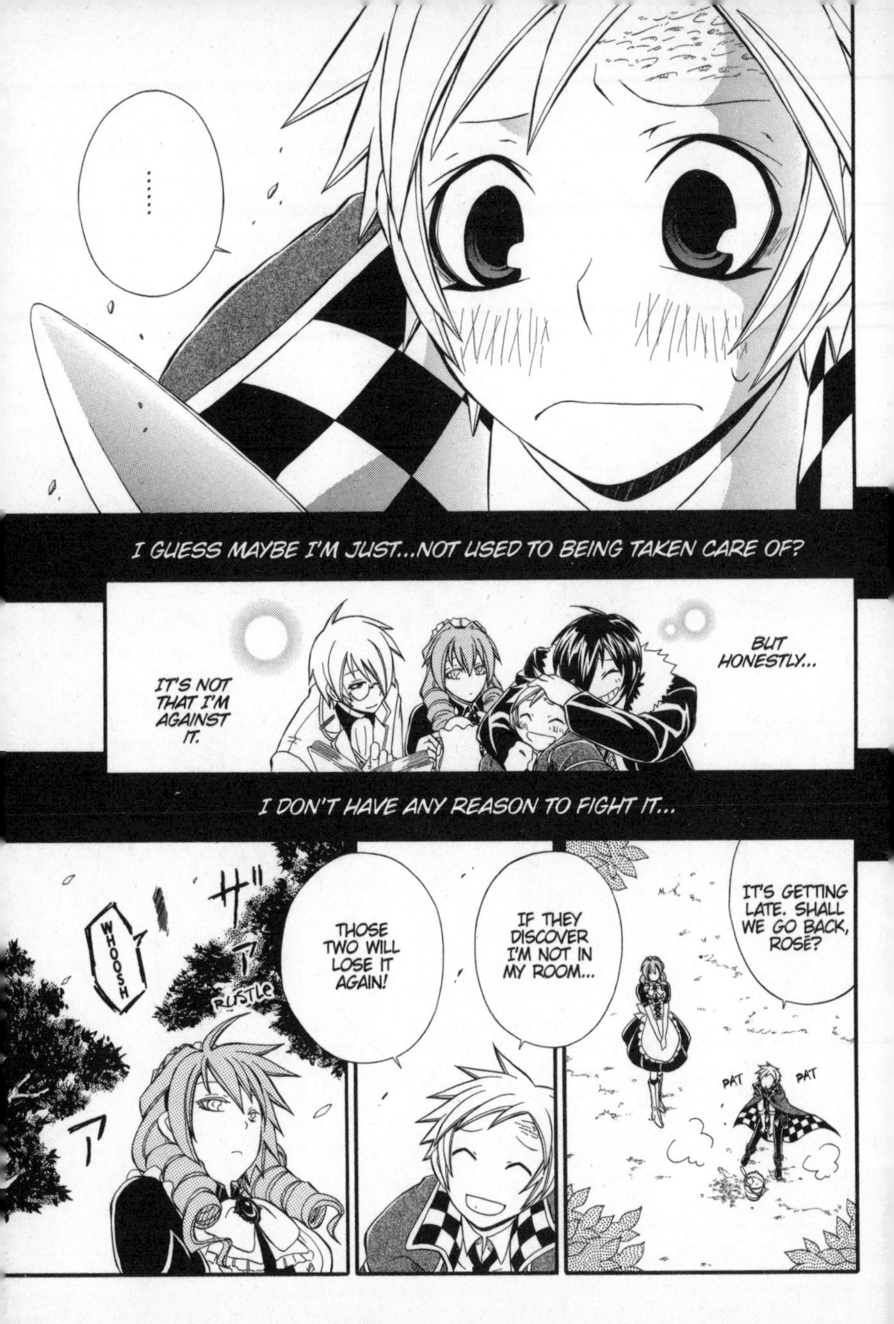
......
I GUESS MAYBE I'M JUST...NOT USED TO BEING TAKEN CARE OF?
BUT HONESTLY...
IT'S NOT THAT I'M AGAINST IT.
I DON'T HAVE ANY REASON TO FIGHT IT...
IT'S GETTING LATE. SHALL WE GO BACK, ROSÉ?
PAT
PAT
IF THEY DISCOVER I'M NOT IN MY ROOM...
THOSE TWO WILL LOSE IT AGAIN!
RUSTLE
WHOOSH

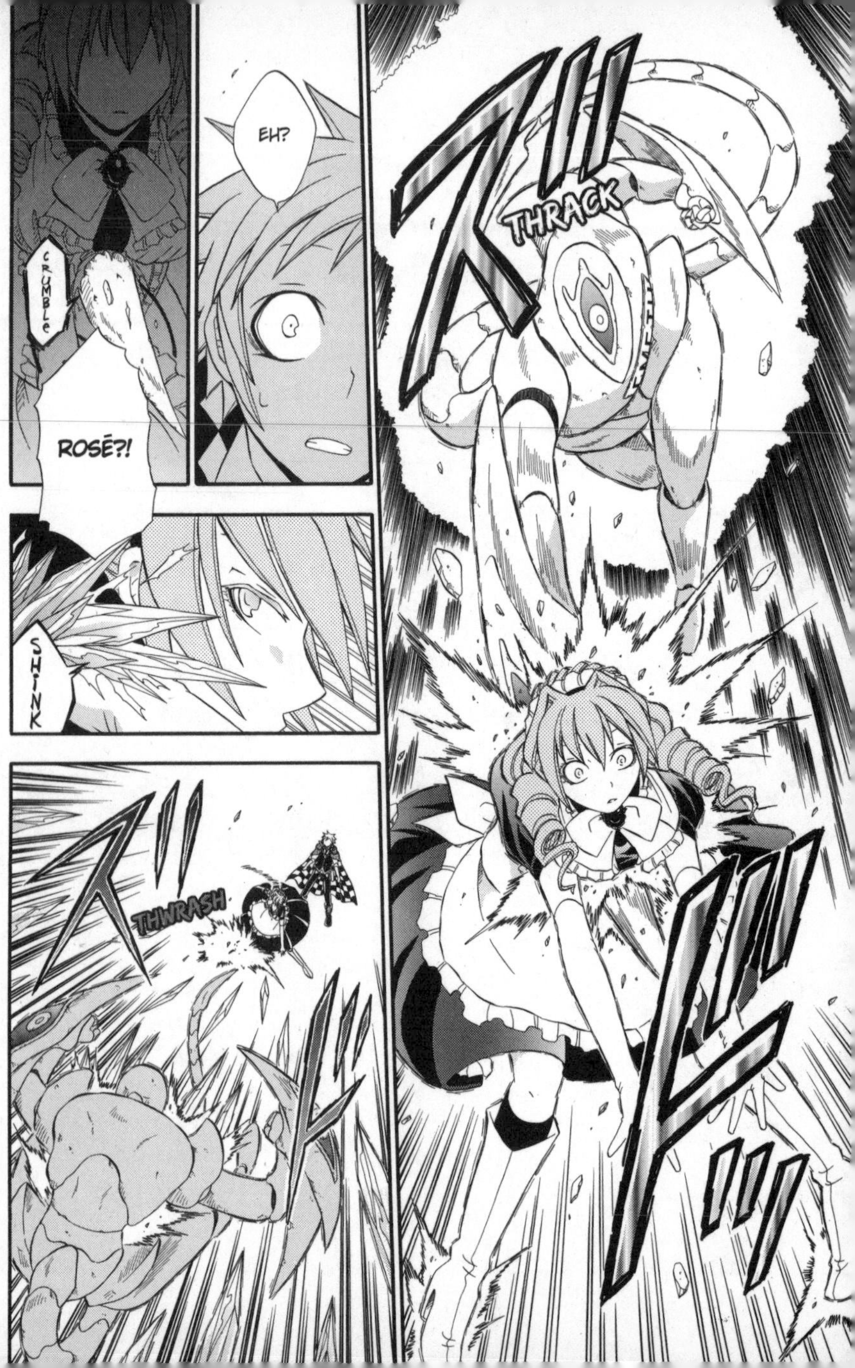
THRACK
EH?
CRUMBLE
ROSÉ?!
SHINK
THWRASH

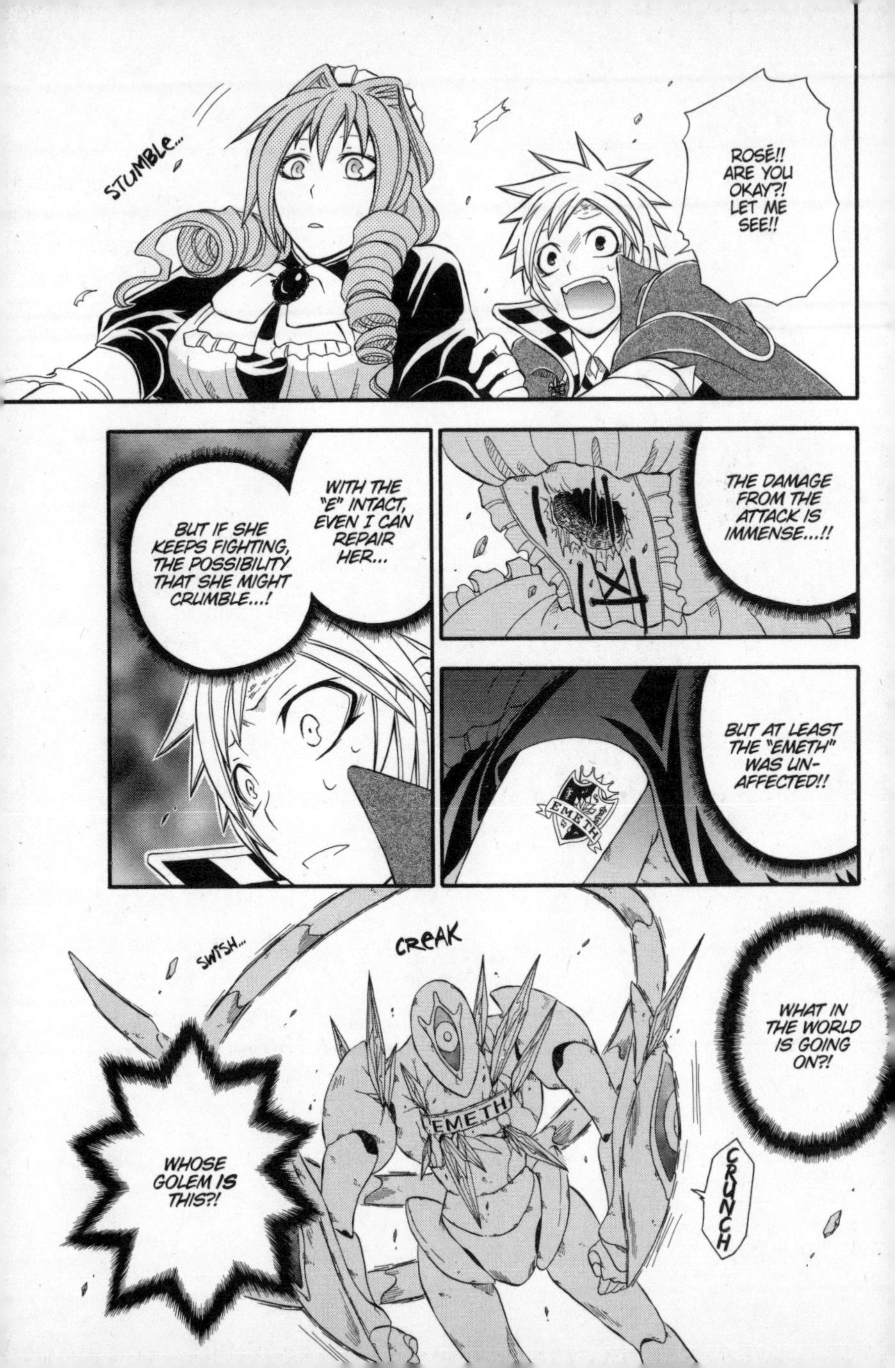
ROSÉ!! ARE YOU OKAY?! LET ME SEE!!
STUMBLE...
THE DAMAGE FROM THE ATTACK IS IMMENSE...!!
BUT AT LEAST THE "EMETH" WAS UN-AFFECTED!!
EMETH
WITH THE "E" INTACT, EVEN I CAN REPAIR HER...
BUT IF SHE KEEPS FIGHTING, THE POSSIBILITY THAT SHE MIGHT CRUMBLE...!
WHAT IN THE WORLD IS GOING ON?!
CRUNCH
CREAK
SWISH...
EMETH
WHOSE GOLEM IS THIS?!

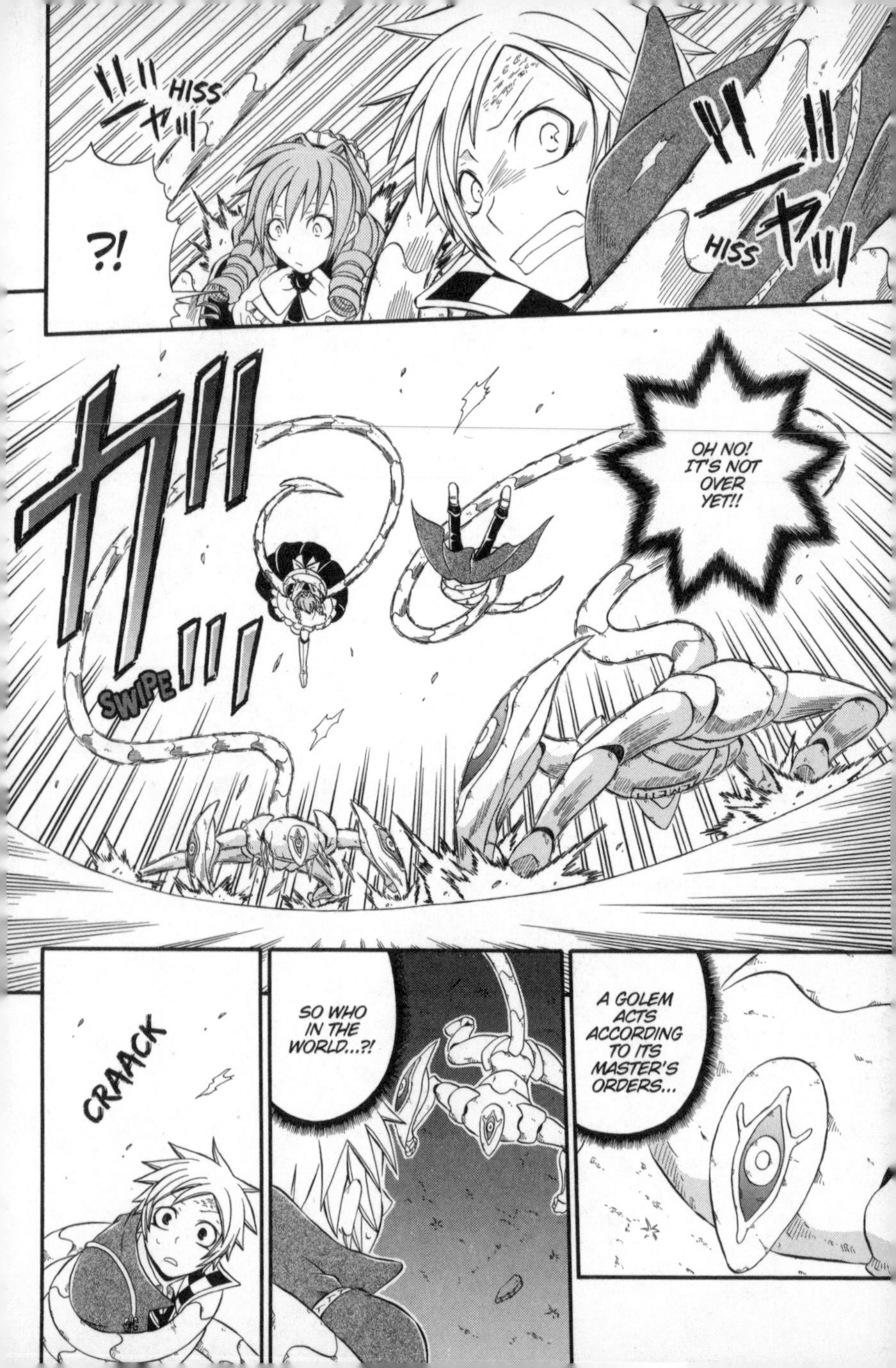
HISS
HISS
?!
OH NO! IT'S NOT OVER YET!!
SWIPE
A GOLEM ACTS ACCORDING TO ITS MASTER'S ORDERS...
SO WHO IN THE WORLD...?!
CRAACK

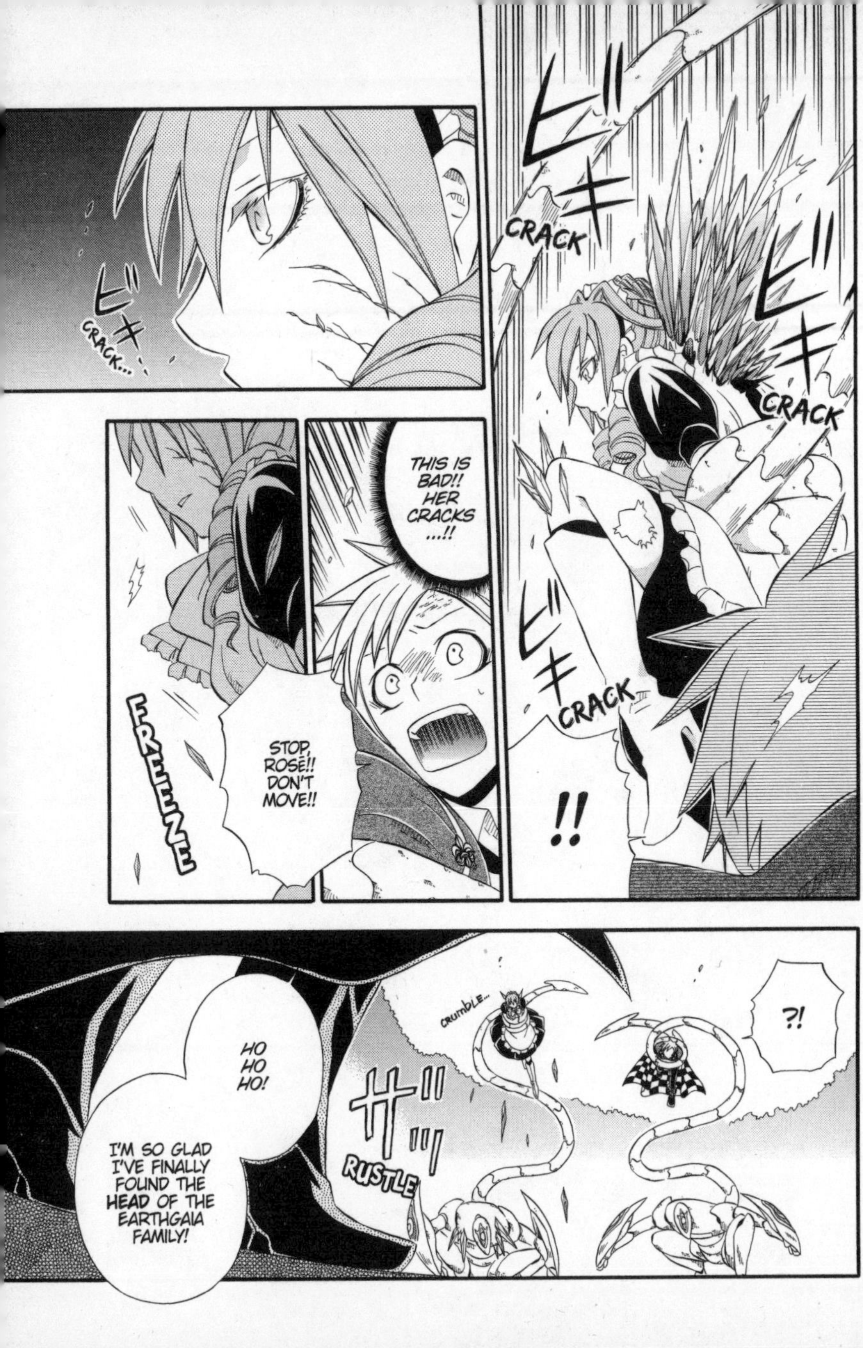
CRACK
CRACK
CRACK
!!
CRACK...
THIS IS BAD!! HER CRACKS ...!!
STOP, ROSÉ!! DON'T MOVE!!
FREEZE
?!
CRUMBLE...
RUSTLE
HO HO HO!
I'M SO GLAD I'VE FINALLY FOUND THE HEAD OF THE EARTHGAIA FAMILY!

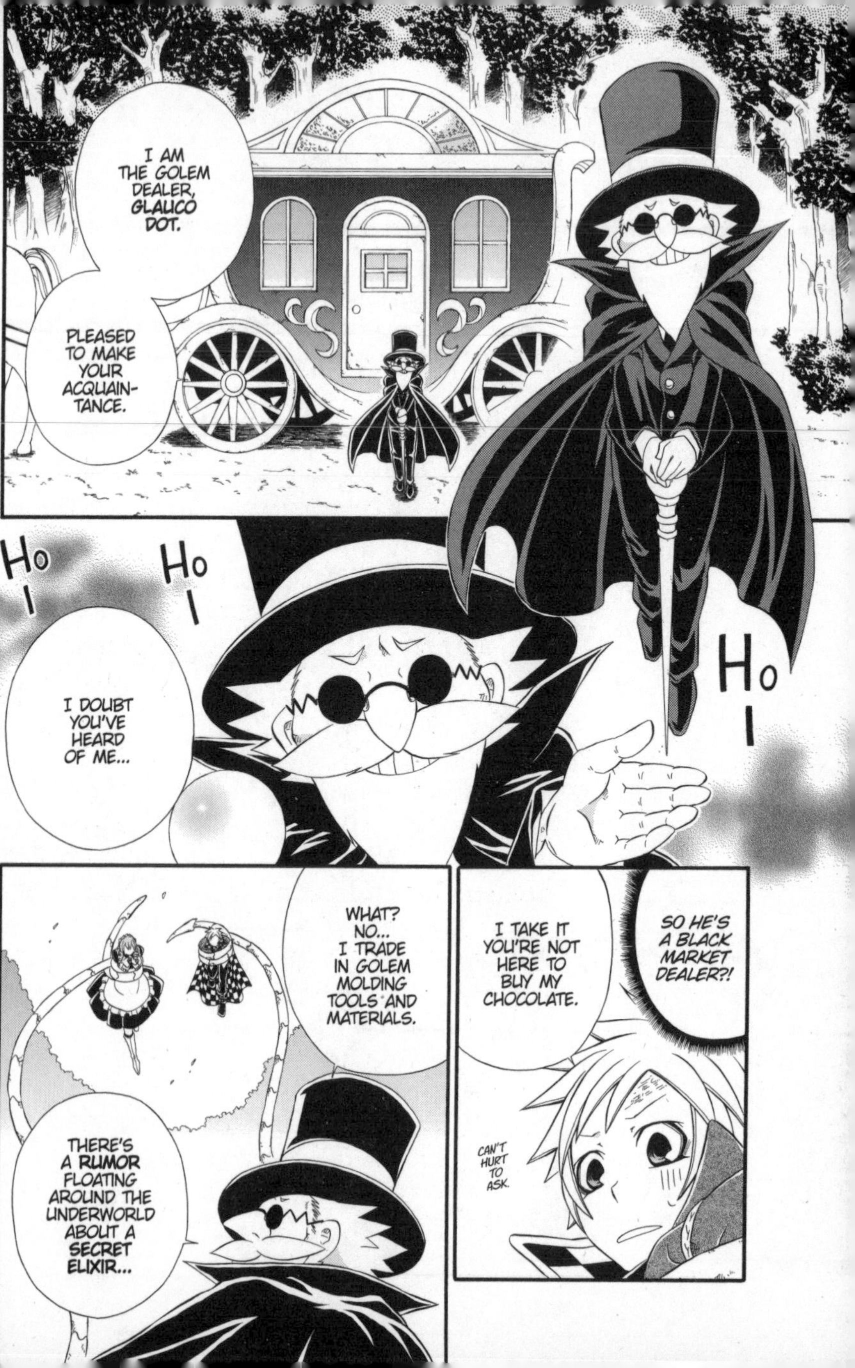
I AM THE GOLEM DEALER, GLAUCO DOT.
PLEASED TO MAKE YOUR ACQUAINTANCE.
HO
HO
HO
I DOUBT YOU'VE HEARD OF ME...
SO HE'S A BLACK MARKET DEALER?!
I TAKE IT YOU'RE NOT HERE TO BUY MY CHOCOLATE.
CAN'T HURT TO ASK.
WHAT? NO... I TRADE IN GOLEM MOLDING TOOLS AND MATERIALS.
THERE'S A RUMOR FLOATING AROUND THE UNDERWORLD ABOUT A SECRET ELIXIR...

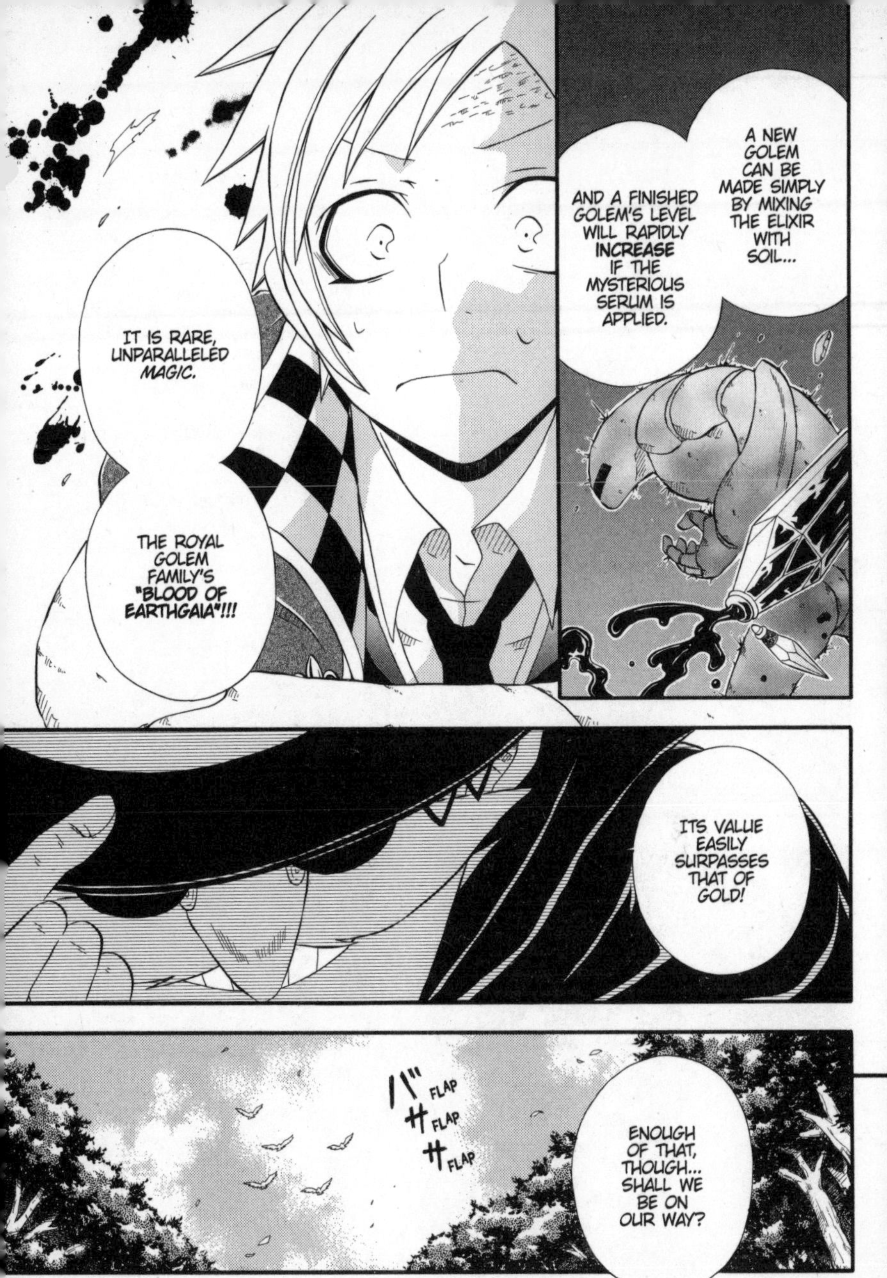
A NEW GOLEM CAN BE MADE SIMPLY BY MIXING THE ELIXIR WITH SOIL...
AND A FINISHED GOLEM'S LEVEL WILL RAPIDLY INCREASE IF THE MYSTERIOUS SERUM IS APPLIED.
IT IS RARE, UNPARALLELED MAGIC.
THE ROYAL GOLEM FAMILY'S "BLOOD OF EARTHGAIA"!!!
ITS VALUE EASILY SURPASSES THAT OF GOLD!
バ FLAP
サ FLAP
サ FLAP
ENOUGH OF THAT, THOUGH... SHALL WE BE ON OUR WAY?

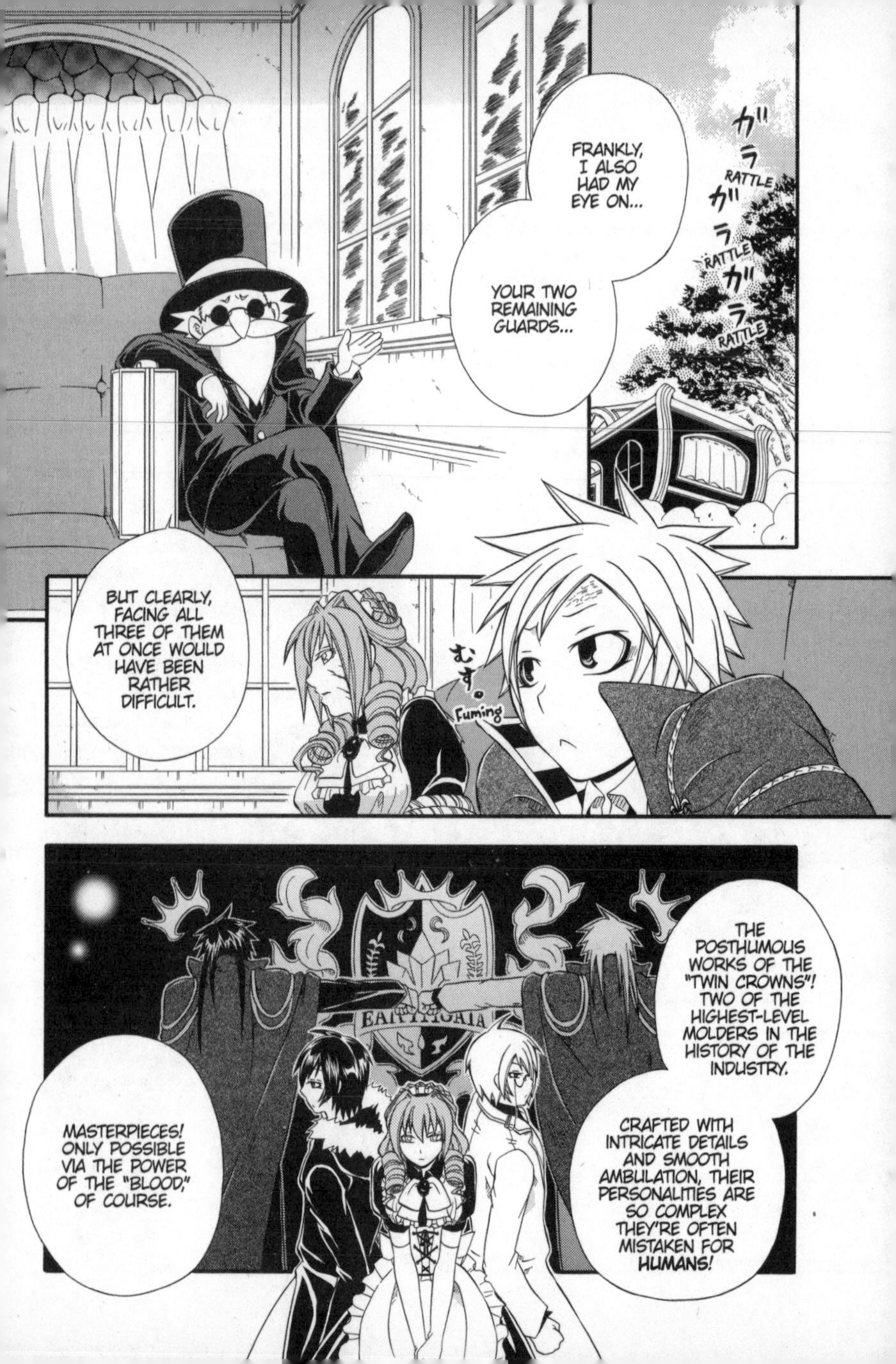
ガラ
RATTLE
ガラ
RATTLE
ガラ
RATTLE
FRANKLY, I ALSO HAD MY EYE ON...
YOUR TWO REMAINING GUARDS...
BUT CLEARLY, FACING ALL THREE OF THEM AT ONCE WOULD HAVE BEEN RATHER DIFFICULT.
むす。
Fuming
THE POSTHUMOUS WORKS OF THE "TWIN CROWNS"! TWO OF THE HIGHEST-LEVEL MOLDERS IN THE HISTORY OF THE INDUSTRY.
CRAFTED WITH INTRICATE DETAILS AND SMOOTH AMBULATION, THEIR PERSONALITIES ARE SO COMPLEX THEY'RE OFTEN MISTAKEN FOR HUMANS!
MASTERPIECES! ONLY POSSIBLE VIA THE POWER OF THE "BLOOD," OF COURSE.

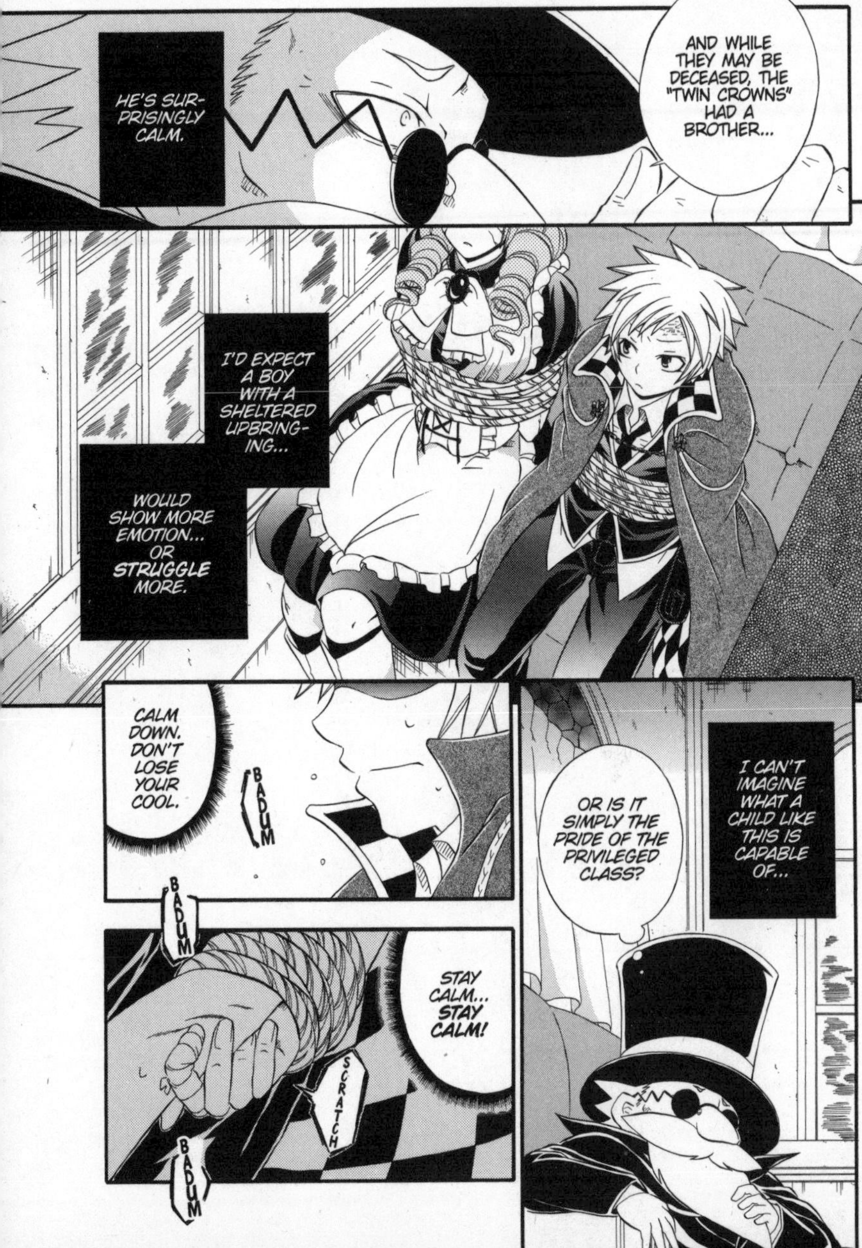
AND WHILE THEY MAY BE DECEASED, THE "TWIN CROWNS" HAD A BROTHER...
HE'S SUR-PRISINGLY CALM.
I'D EXPECT A BOY WITH A SHELTERED UPBRING-ING...
WOULD SHOW MORE EMOTION... OR STRUGGLE MORE.
I CAN'T IMAGINE WHAT A CHILD LIKE THIS IS CAPABLE OF...
OR IS IT SIMPLY THE PRIDE OF THE PRIVILEGED CLASS?
CALM DOWN. DON'T LOSE YOUR COOL.
BADUM
BADUM
STAY CALM... STAY CALM!
SCRATCH
BADUM

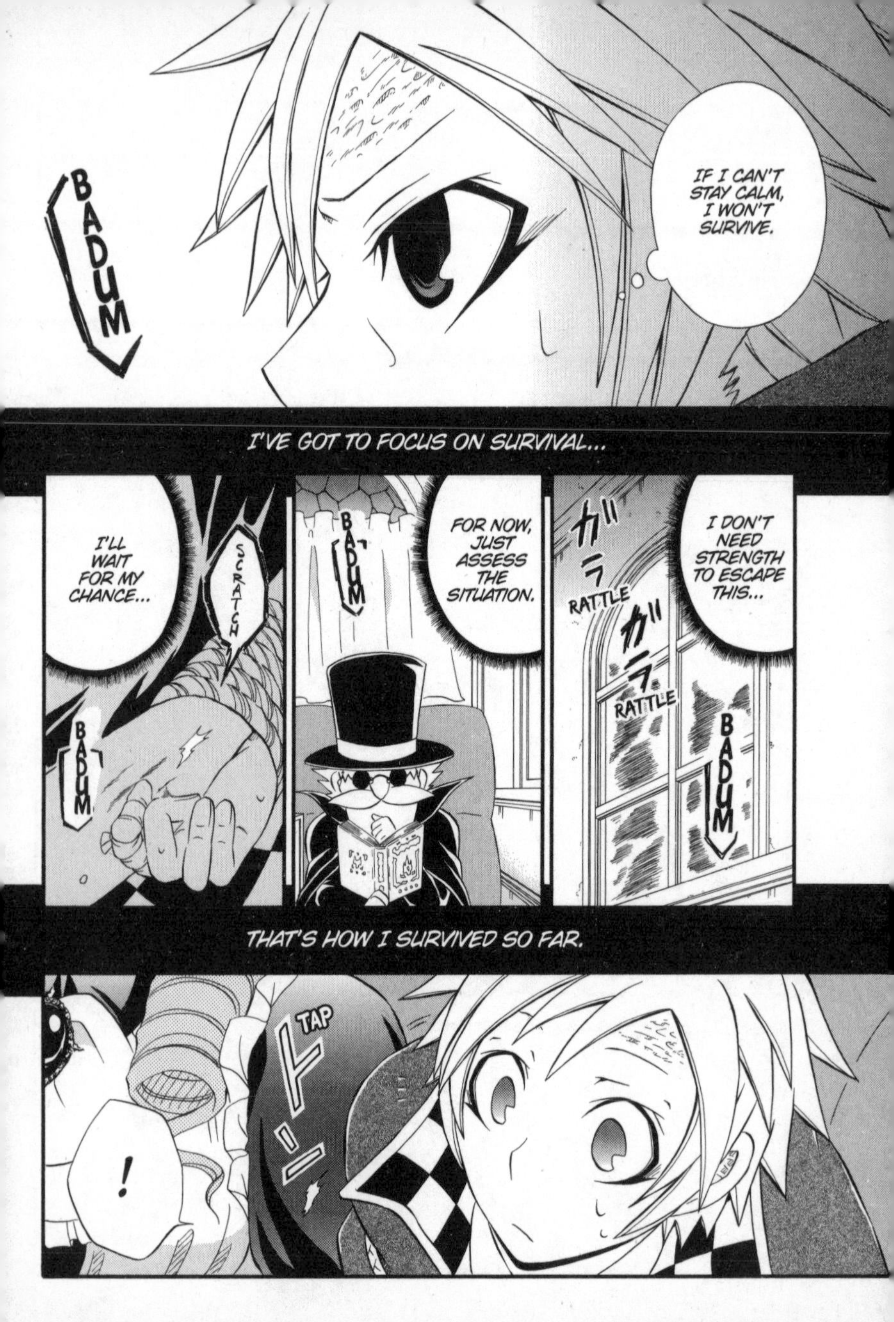
IF I CAN'T STAY CALM, I WON'T SURVIVE.
BADUM
I'VE GOT TO FOCUS ON SURVIVAL...
I DON'T NEED STRENGTH TO ESCAPE THIS...
ガラ
RATTLE
ガラ
RATTLE
BADUM
FOR NOW, JUST ASSESS THE SITUATION.
BADUM
I'LL WAIT FOR MY CHANCE...
SCRATCH
BADUM
THAT'S HOW I SURVIVED SO FAR.
TAP
!

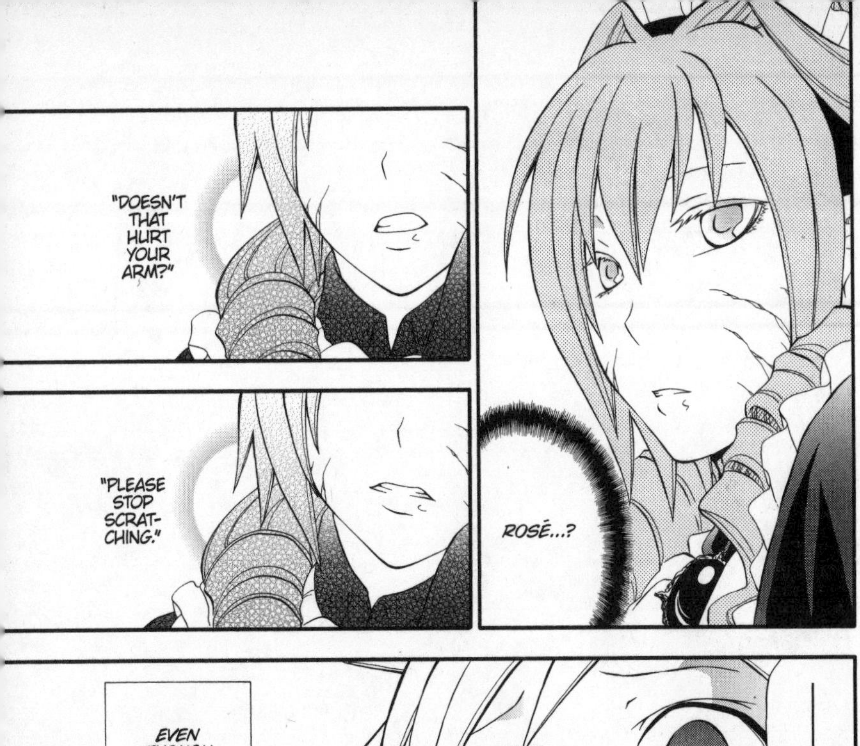
ROSÉ...?
"DOESN'T THAT HURT YOUR ARM?"
"PLEASE STOP SCRATCHING."
!...
EVEN THOUGH YOU'RE THE ONE COVERED IN CRACKS...
YOU'RE STILL JUST WORRIED ABOUT ME.
RUB...
THESE GOLEMS LOVE ME...

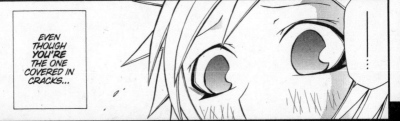

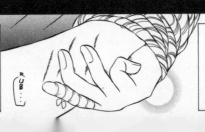

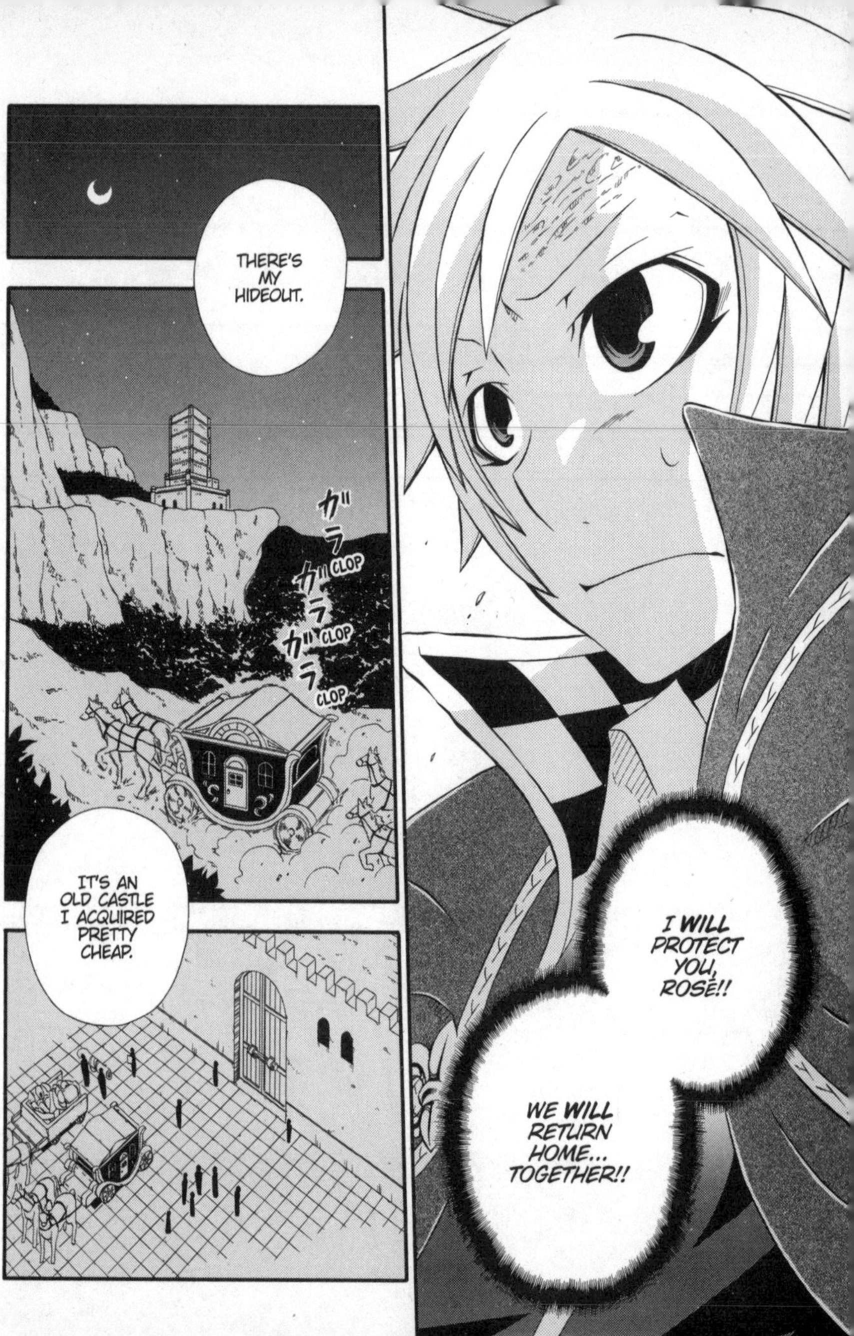
I WILL PROTECT YOU, ROSE!!
WE WILL RETURN HOME... TOGETHER!!
THERE'S MY HIDEOUT.
ガラ CLOP
ガラ CLOP
ガラ CLOP
IT'S AN OLD CASTLE I ACQUIRED PRETTY CHEAP.

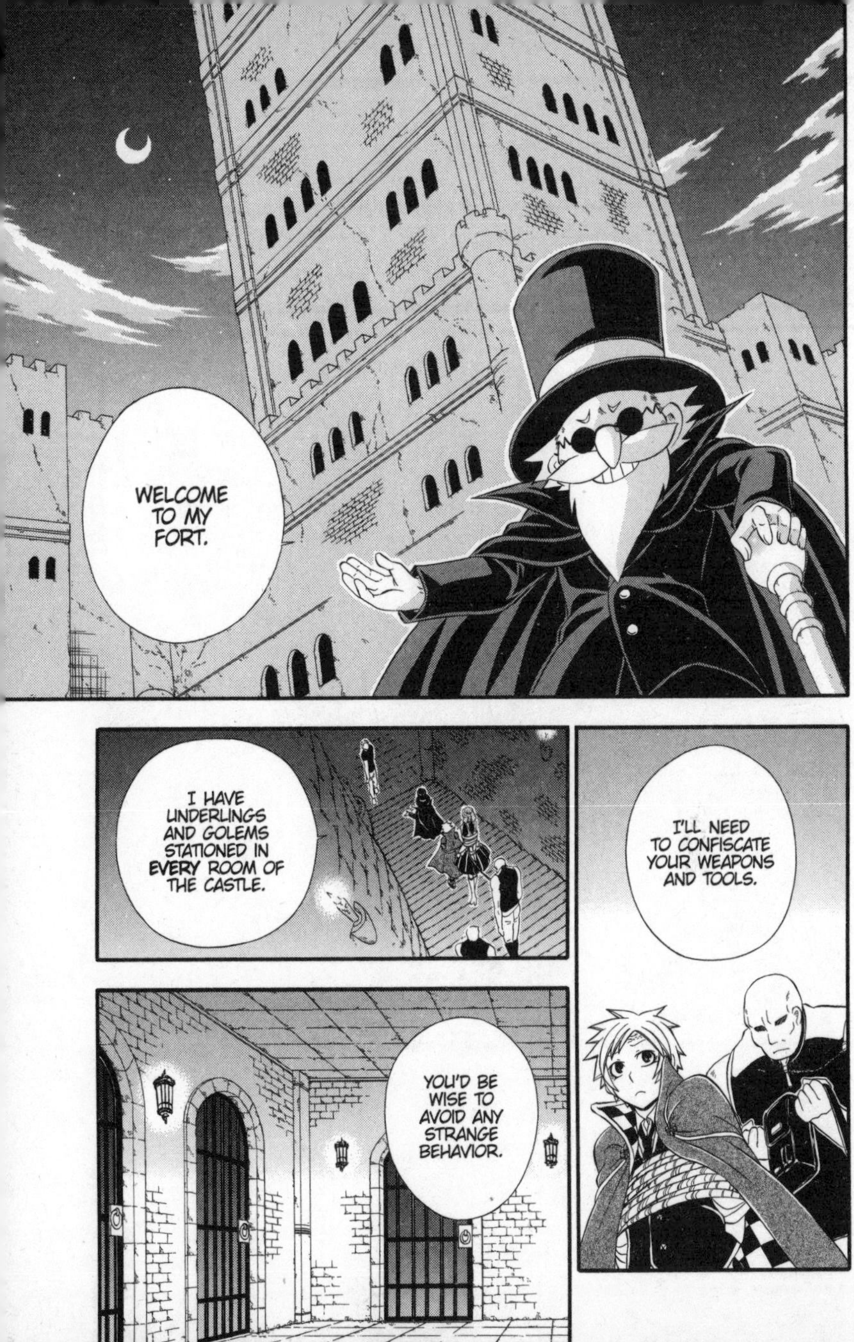
WELCOME TO MY FORT.
I'LL NEED TO CONFISCATE YOUR WEAPONS AND TOOLS.
I HAVE UNDERLINGS AND GOLEMS STATIONED IN EVERY ROOM OF THE CASTLE.
YOU'D BE WISE TO AVOID ANY STRANGE BEHAVIOR.

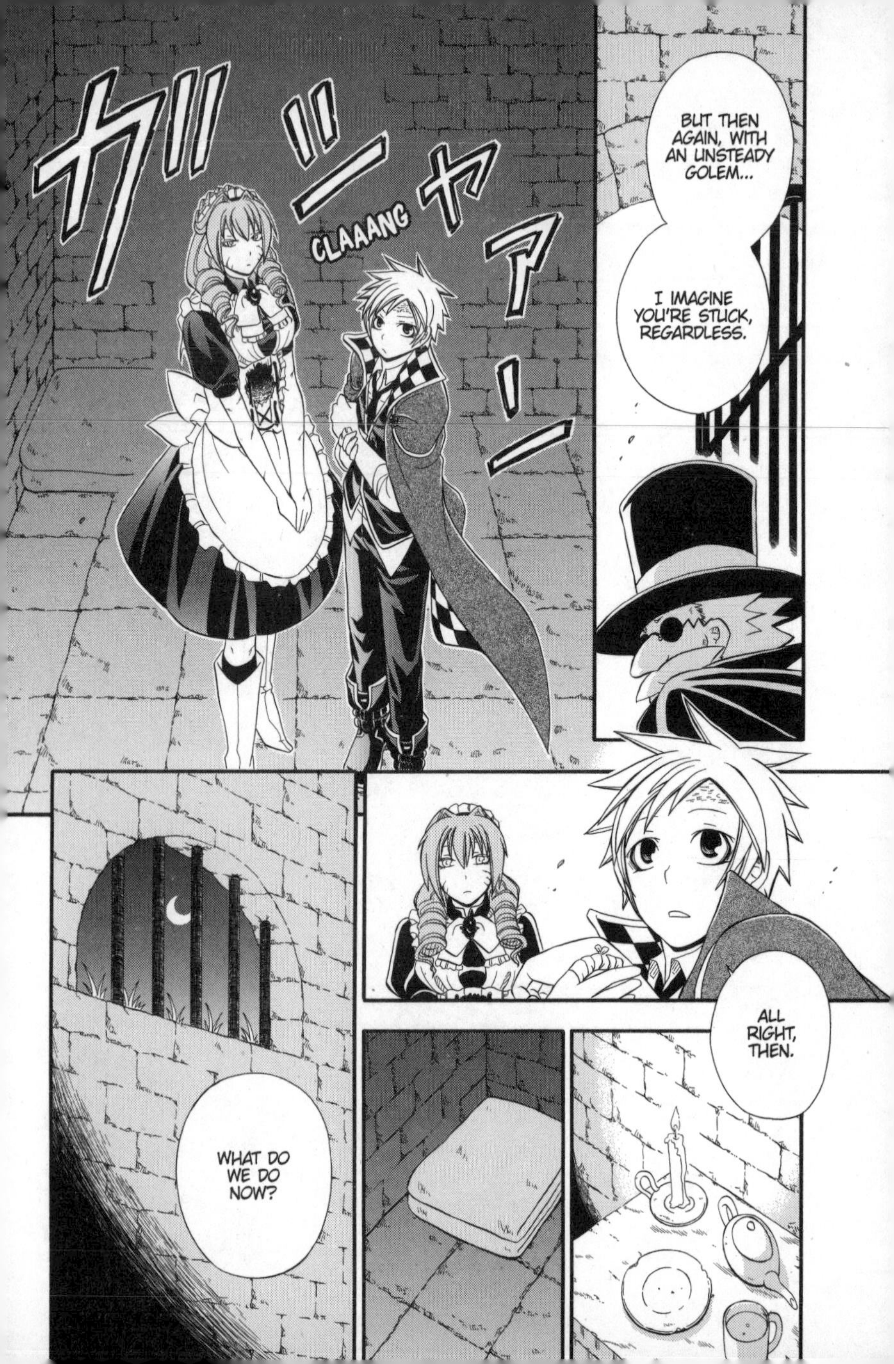
BUT THEN AGAIN, WITH AN UNSTEADY GOLEM...
I IMAGINE YOU'RE STUCK, REGARDLESS.
CLAAANG
ALL RIGHT, THEN.
WHAT DO WE DO NOW?

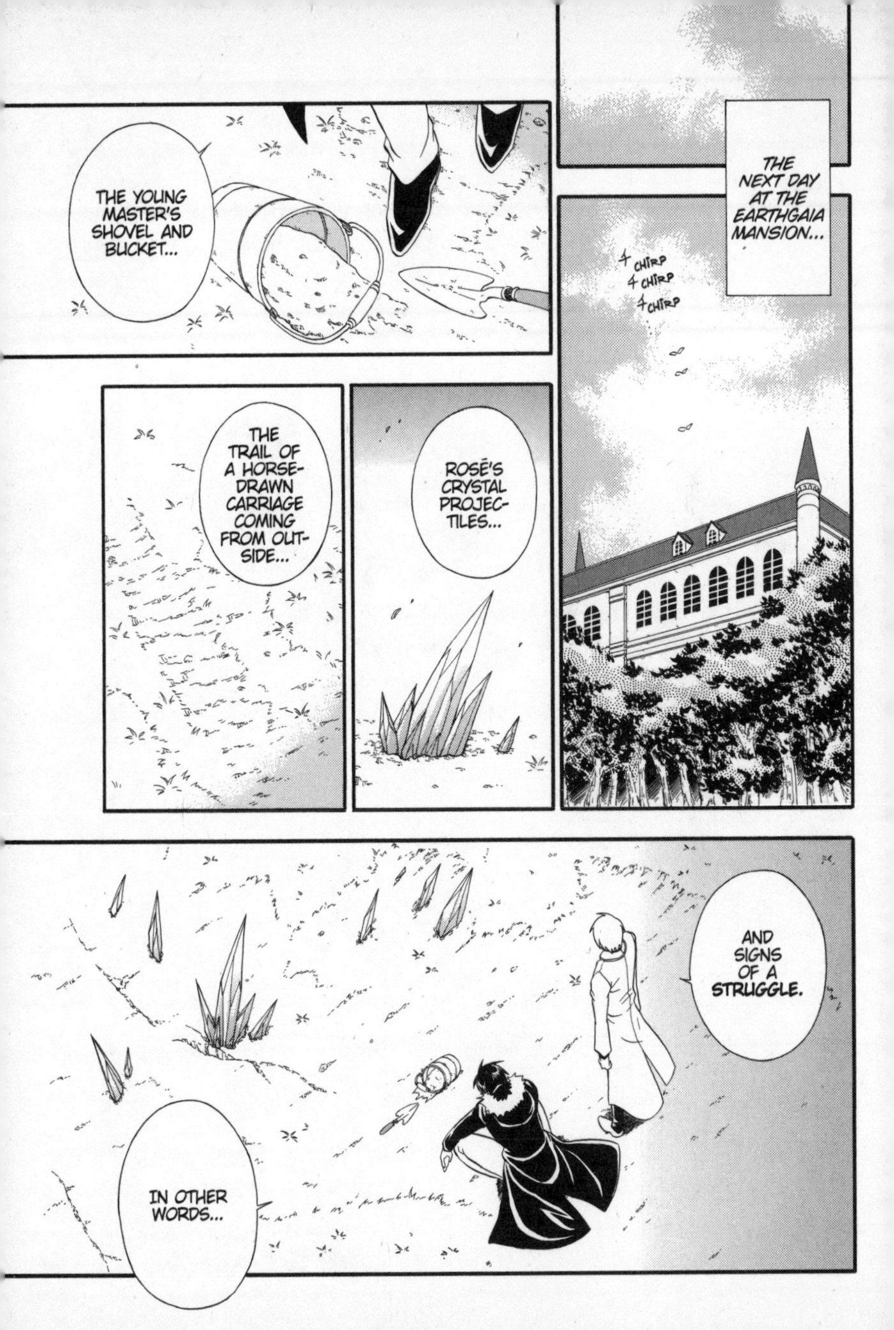
THE NEXT DAY AT THE EARTHGAIA MANSION...
CHIRP
CHIRP
CHIRP
THE YOUNG MASTER'S SHOVEL AND BUCKET...
ROSÉ'S CRYSTAL PROJEC-TILES...
THE TRAIL OF A HORSE-DRAWN CARRIAGE COMING FROM OUT-SIDE...
AND SIGNS OF A STRUGGLE.
IN OTHER WORDS...

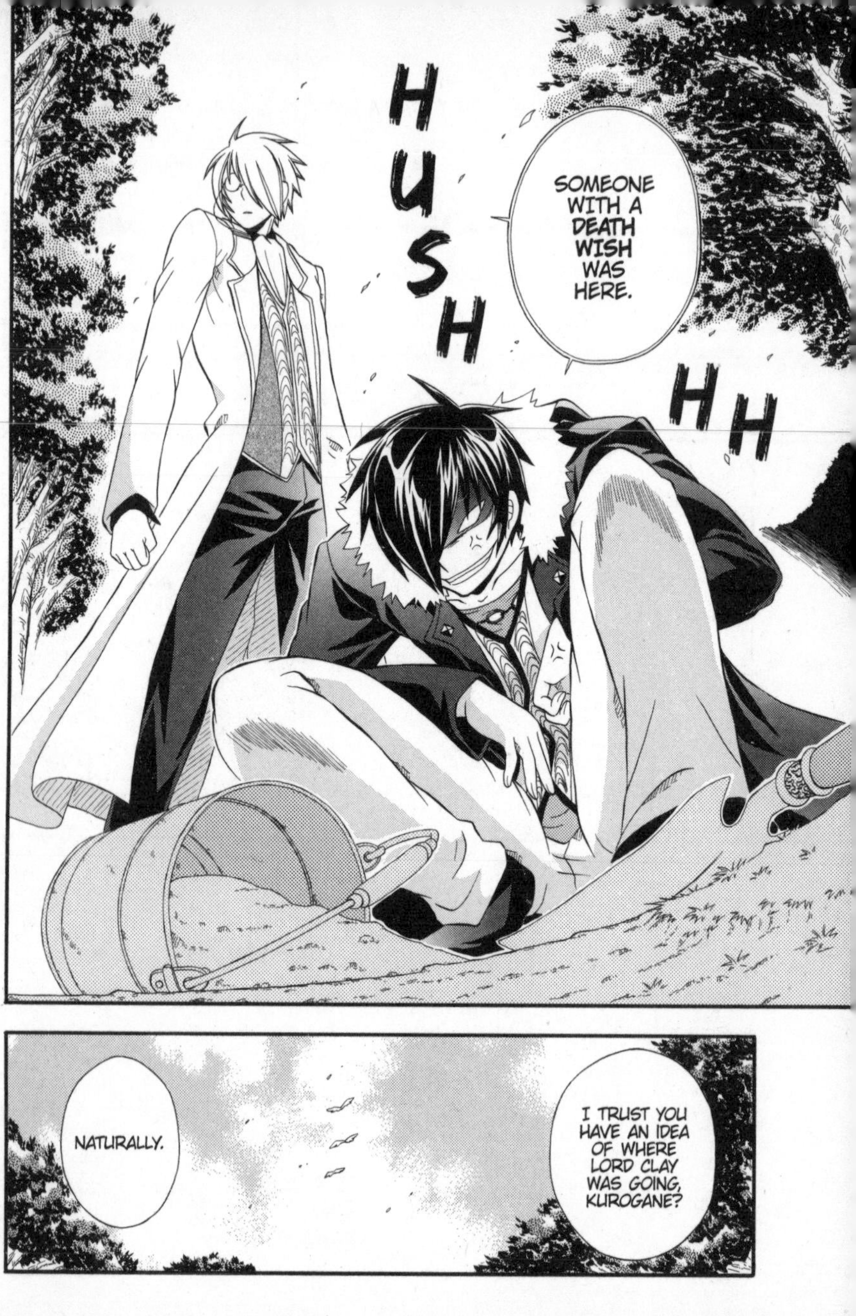
HUSHHH
SOMEONE WITH A DEATH WISH WAS HERE.
I TRUST YOU HAVE AN IDEA OF WHERE LORD CLAY WAS GOING, KUROGANE?
NATURALLY.

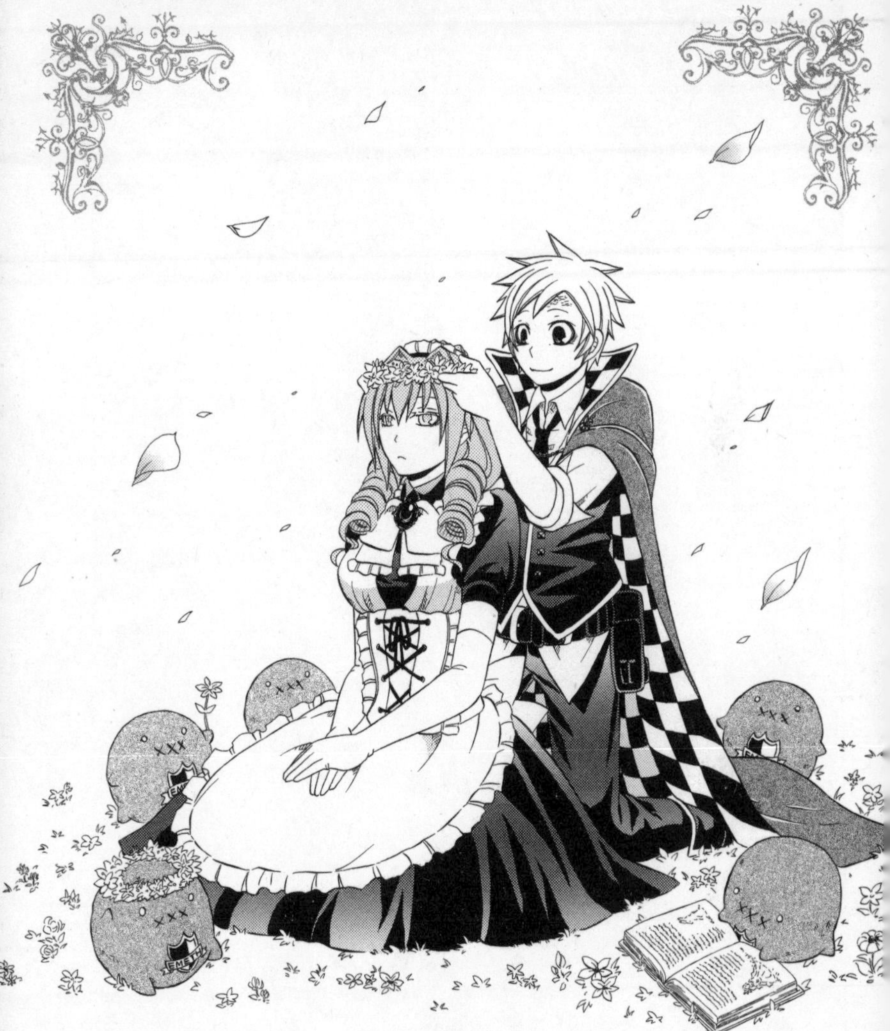
EMETH

Chapter 4: The Blood of Earthgaia (Part 2)

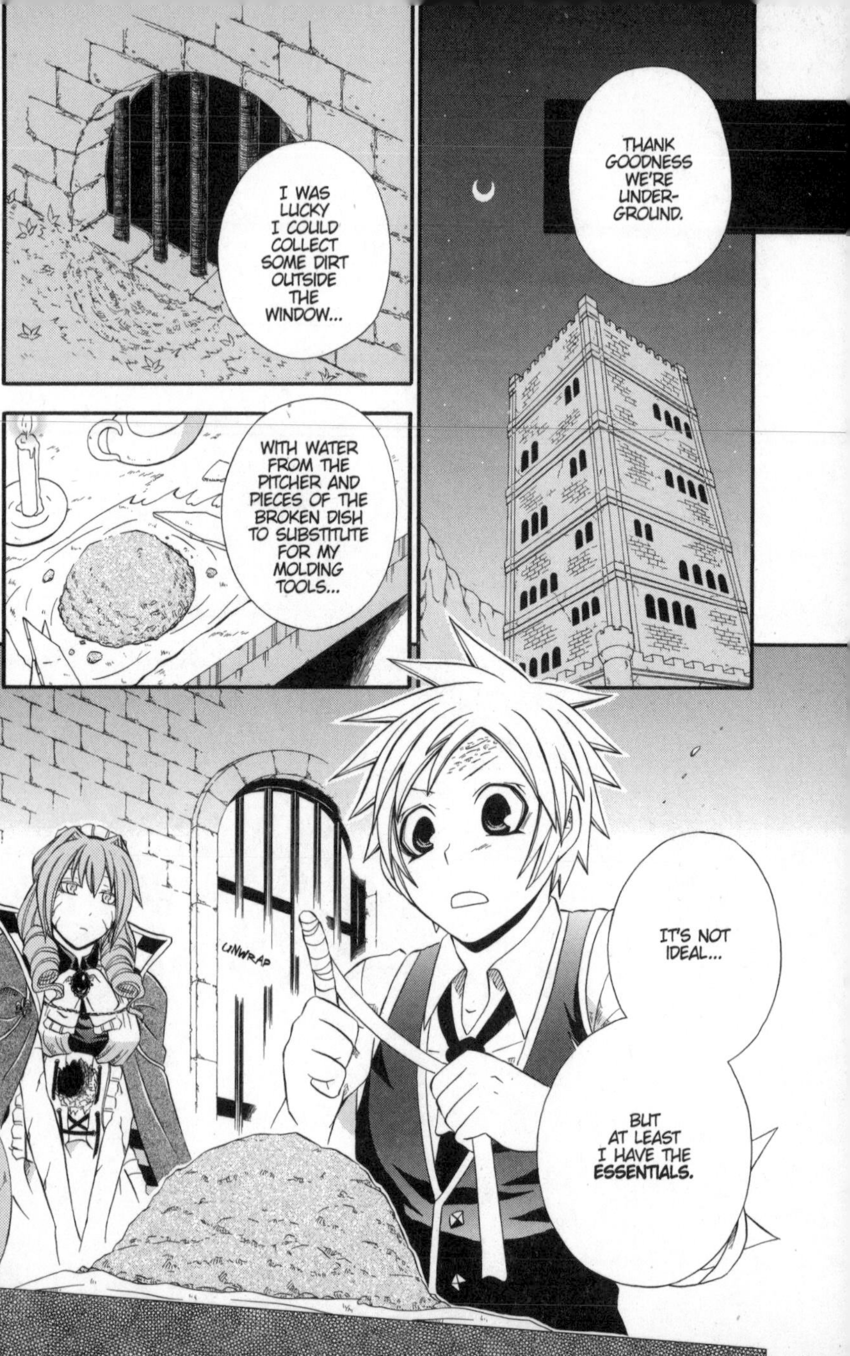
THANK GOODNESS WE'RE UNDER-GROUND.
I WAS LUCKY I COULD COLLECT SOME DIRT OUTSIDE THE WINDOW...
WITH WATER FROM THE PITCHER AND PIECES OF THE BROKEN DISH TO SUBSTITUTE FOR MY MOLDING TOOLS...
IT'S NOT IDEAL...
BUT AT LEAST I HAVE THE ESSENTIALS.
UNWRAP

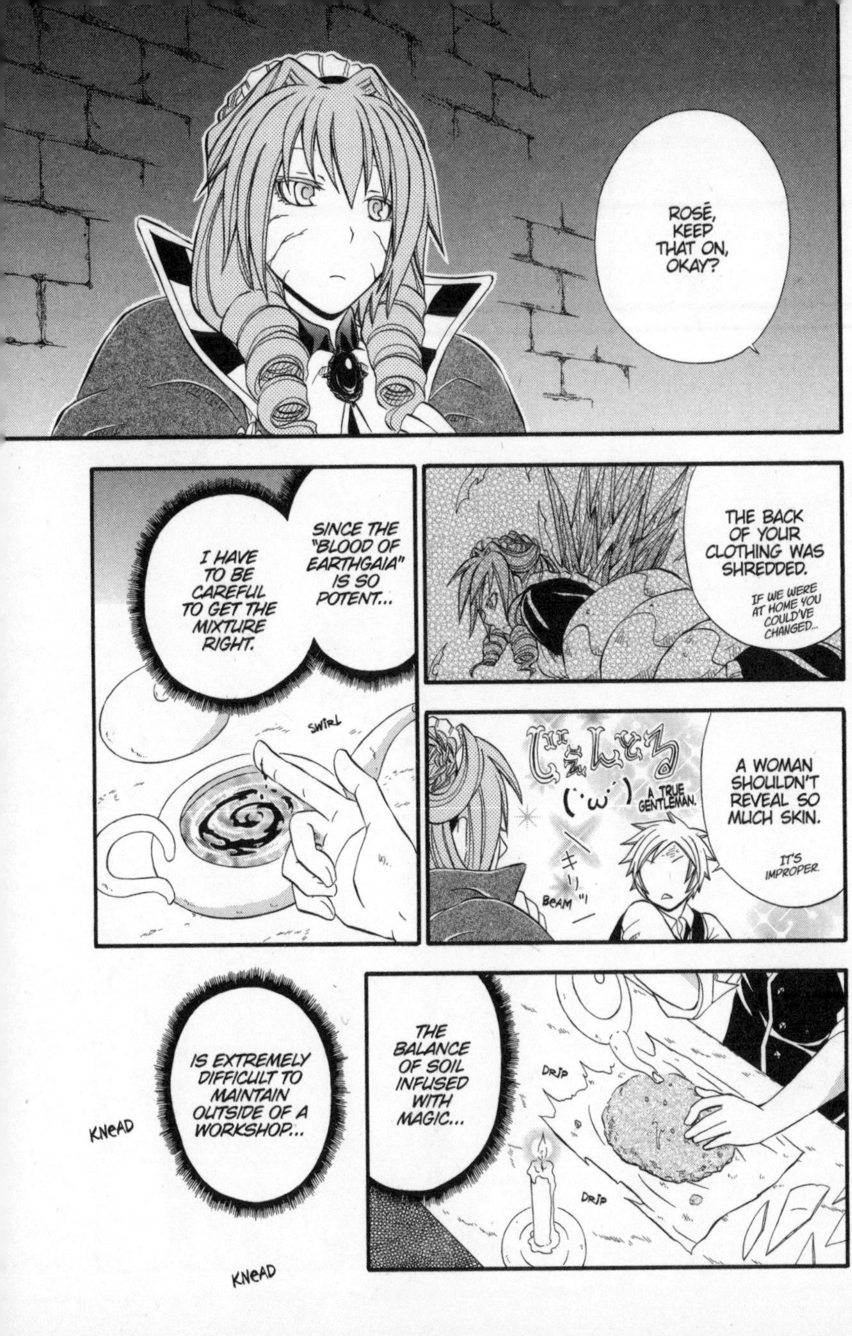
ROSÉ, KEEP THAT ON, OKAY?
THE BACK OF YOUR CLOTHING WAS SHREDDED.
IF WE WERE AT HOME YOU COULD'VE CHANGED...
A WOMAN SHOULDN'T REVEAL SO MUCH SKIN.
A TRUE GENTLEMAN.
IT'S IMPROPER.
BEAM
SINCE THE "BLOOD OF EARTHGAIA" IS SO POTENT...
I HAVE TO BE CAREFUL TO GET THE MIXTURE RIGHT.
SWIRL
THE BALANCE OF SOIL INFUSED WITH MAGIC...
DRIP
DRIP
IS EXTREMELY DIFFICULT TO MAINTAIN OUTSIDE OF A WORKSHOP...
KNEAD
KNEAD

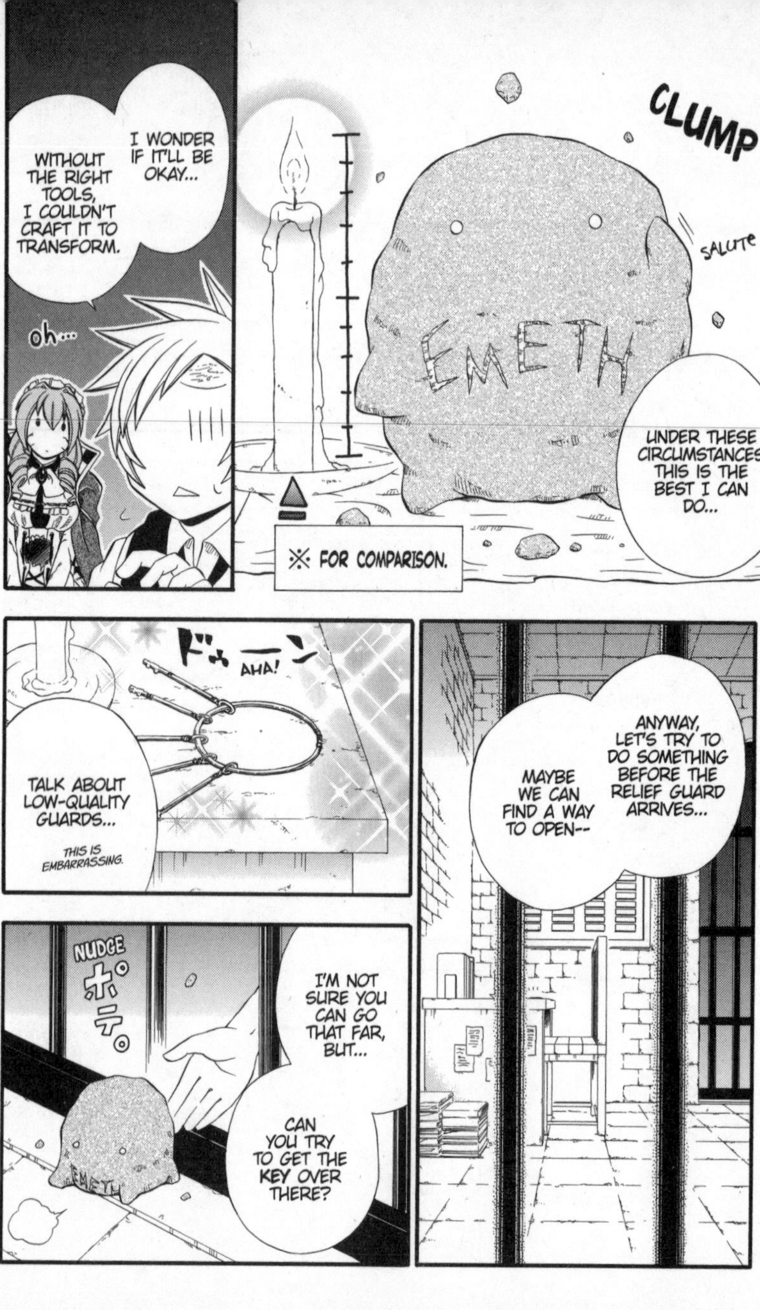
CLUMP
SALUTE
EMETH
UNDER THESE CIRCUMSTANCES THIS IS THE BEST I CAN DO...
※ FOR COMPARISON.
I WONDER IF IT'LL BE OKAY...
WITHOUT THE RIGHT TOOLS, I COULDN'T CRAFT IT TO TRANSFORM.
oh...
ANYWAY, LET'S TRY TO DO SOMETHING BEFORE THE RELIEF GUARD ARRIVES...
MAYBE WE CAN FIND A WAY TO OPEN--
ドゥーン
AHA!
TALK ABOUT LOW-QUALITY GUARDS...
THIS IS EMBARRASSING.
I'M NOT SURE YOU CAN GO THAT FAR, BUT...
CAN YOU TRY TO GET THE KEY OVER THERE?
NUDGE
ポテ。
EMETH

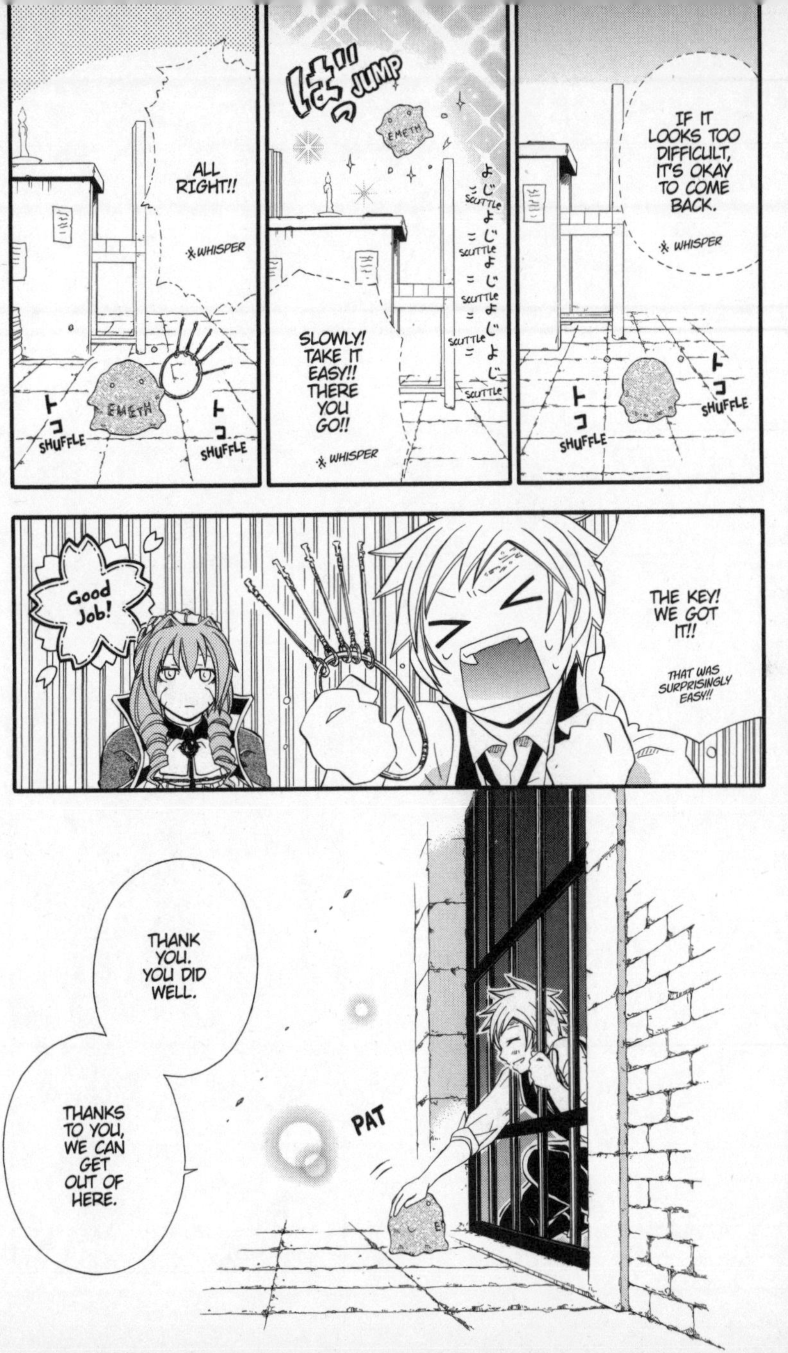

IF IT LOOKS TOO DIFFICULT, IT'S OKAY TO COME BACK.
※ WHISPER
トコ SHUFFLE
トコ SHUFFLE
はっ JUMP
よじ SCUTTLE
よじ SCUTTLE
よじ SCUTTLE
よじ SCUTTLE
よじ SCUTTLE
SLOWLY! TAKE IT EASY!! THERE YOU GO!!
※ WHISPER
EMETH
ALL RIGHT!!
※ WHISPER
トコ SHUFFLE
トコ SHUFFLE
EMETH
THE KEY! WE GOT IT!!
THAT WAS SURPRISINGLY EASY!!
Good Job!
THANK YOU. YOU DID WELL.
THANKS TO YOU, WE CAN GET OUT OF HERE.
PAT

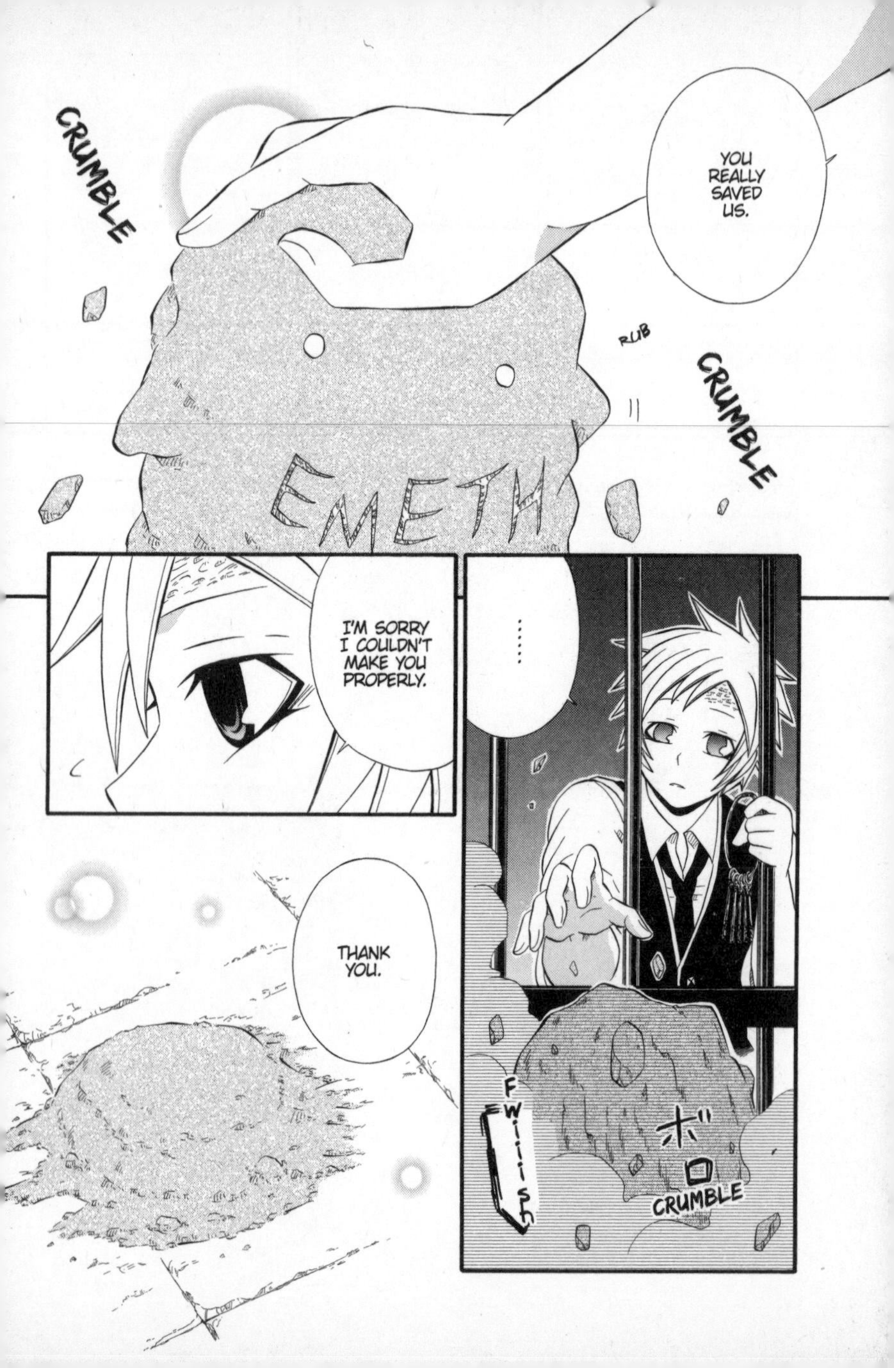
YOU REALLY SAVED US.
CRUMBLE
RUB
CRUMBLE
EMETH
......
ボロ
CRUMBLE
FWiiish
I'M SORRY I COULDN'T MAKE YOU PROPERLY.
THANK YOU.

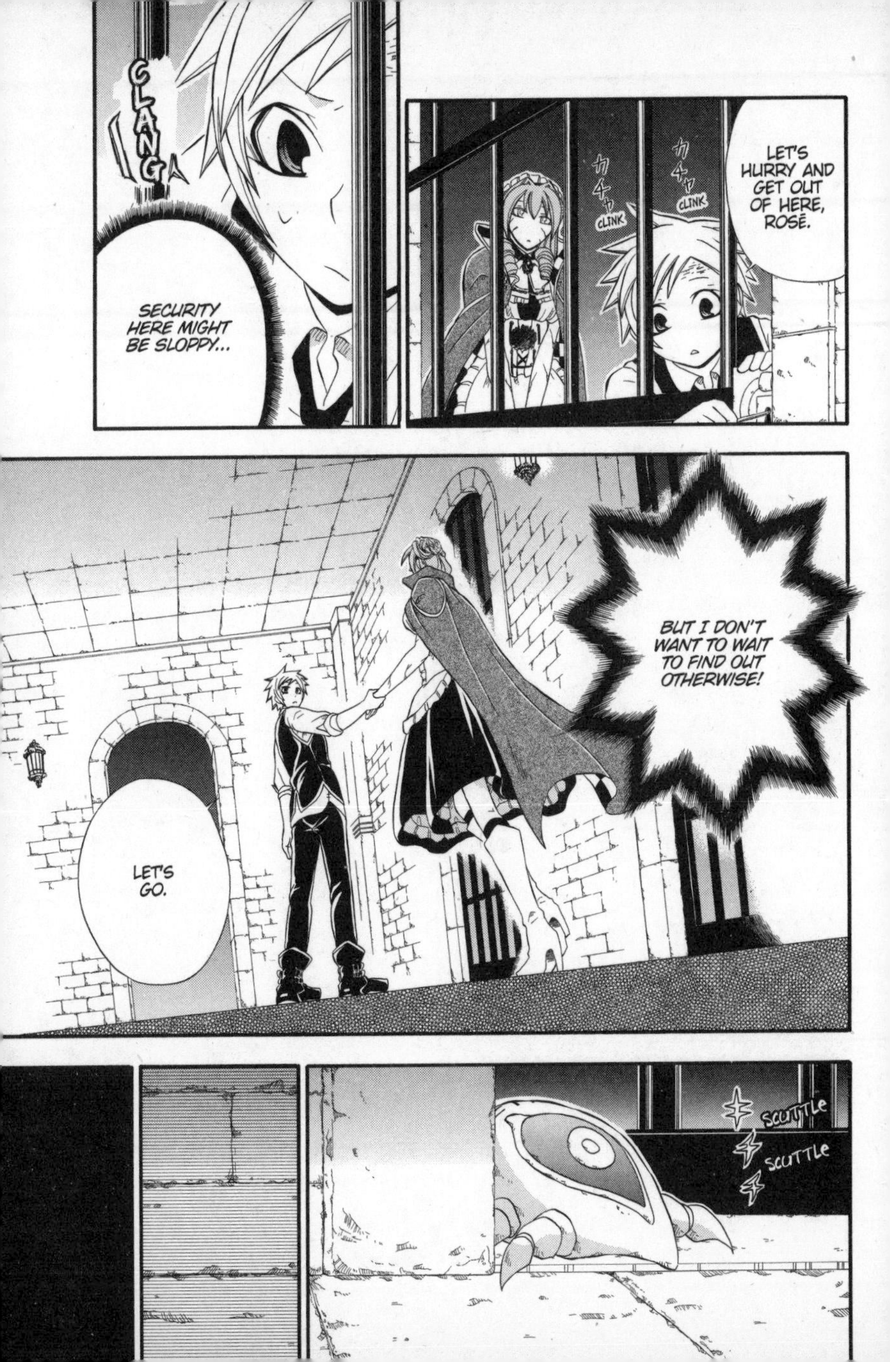
LET'S HURRY AND GET OUT OF HERE, ROSÉ.
カチャ CLINK
カチャ CLINK
CLANG
SECURITY HERE MIGHT BE SLOPPY...
BUT I DON'T WANT TO WAIT TO FIND OUT OTHERWISE!
LET'S GO.
SCUTTLE
SCUTTLE

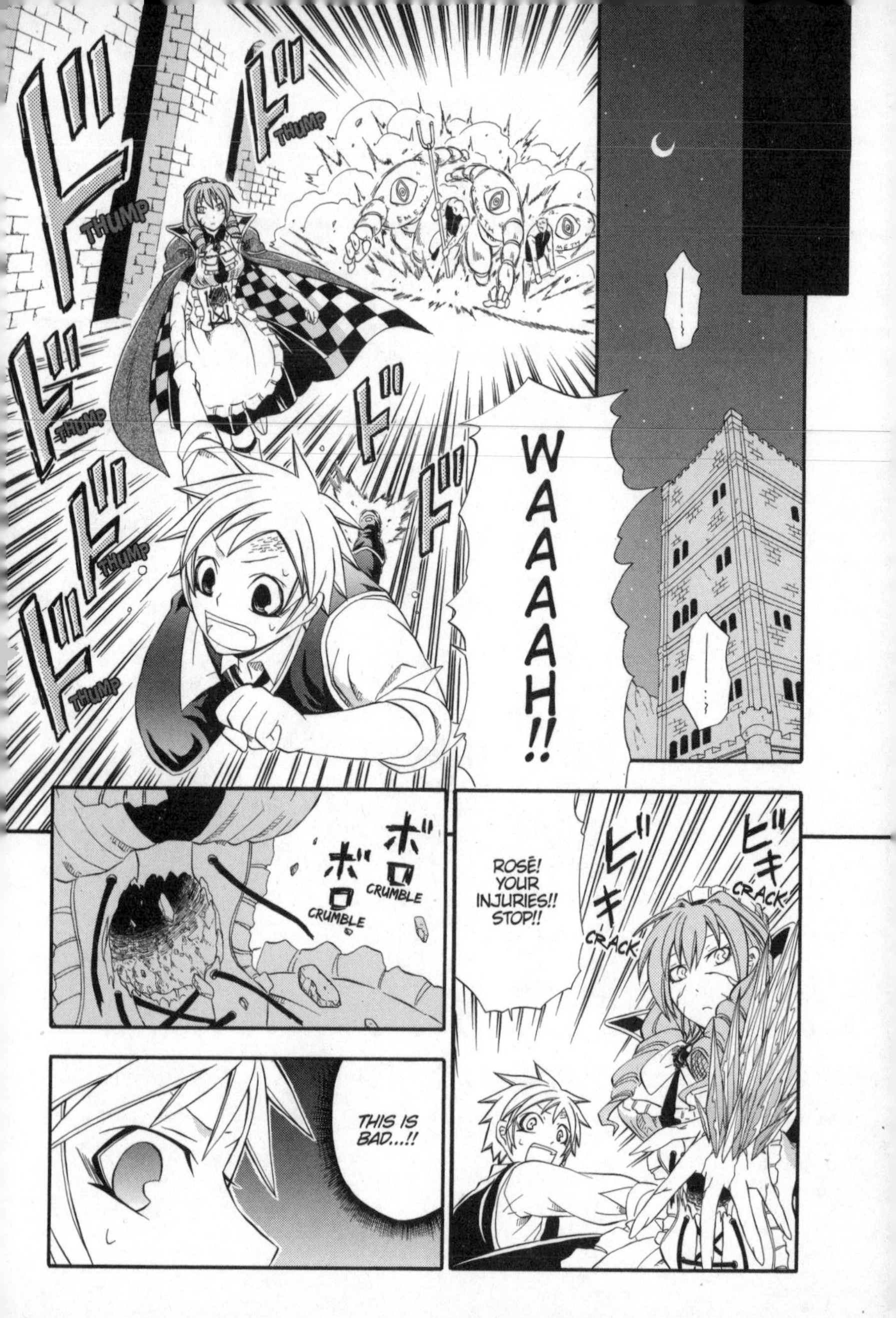

!
...?
WAAAAAH!!
THUMP
THUMP
THUMP
THUMP
THUMP
ビキ
CRACK
ビキ
CRACK
ROSÉ! YOUR INJURIES!! STOP!!
ボロ
CRUMBLE
ボロ
CRUMBLE
THIS IS BAD...!!

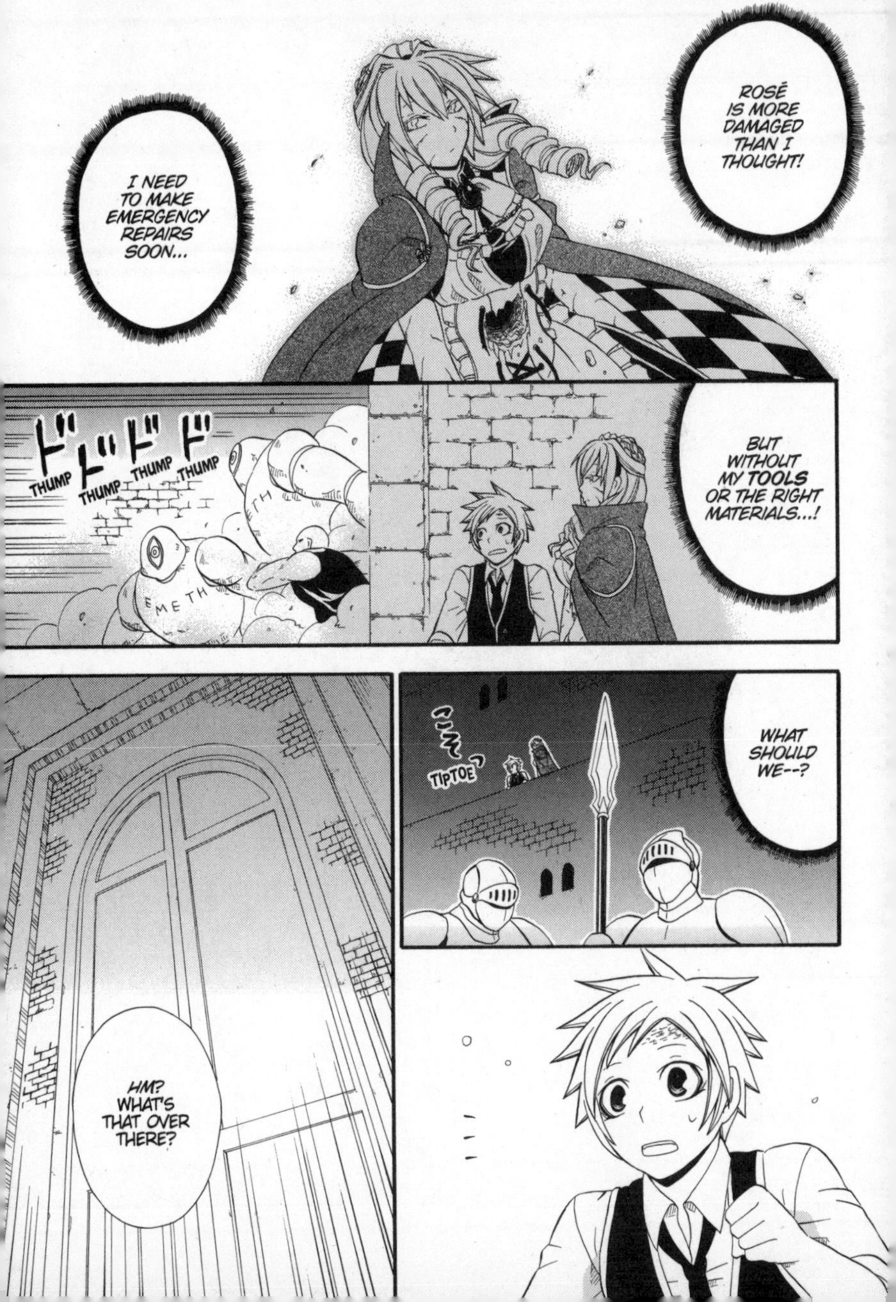
ROSÉ IS MORE DAMAGED THAN I THOUGHT!
I NEED TO MAKE EMERGENCY REPAIRS SOON...
BUT WITHOUT MY TOOLS OR THE RIGHT MATERIALS...!
ドドドド
THUMP THUMP THUMP THUMP
WHAT SHOULD WE--?
TIPTOE
HM? WHAT'S THAT OVER THERE?

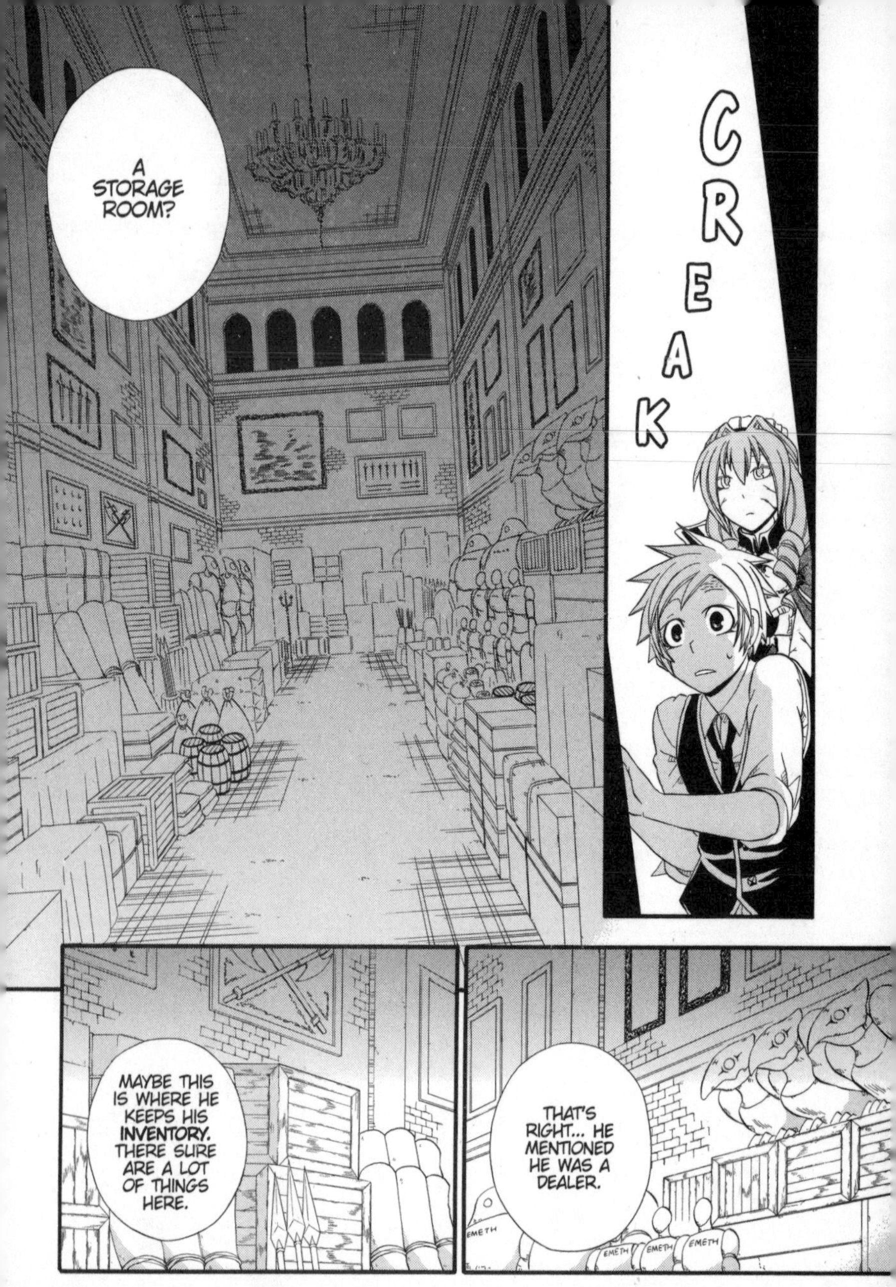
A STORAGE ROOM?
CREAK
MAYBE THIS IS WHERE HE KEEPS HIS **INVENTORY.** THERE SURE ARE A LOT OF THINGS HERE.
THAT'S RIGHT... HE MENTIONED HE WAS A DEALER.
EMETH
EMETH
EMETH
EMETH

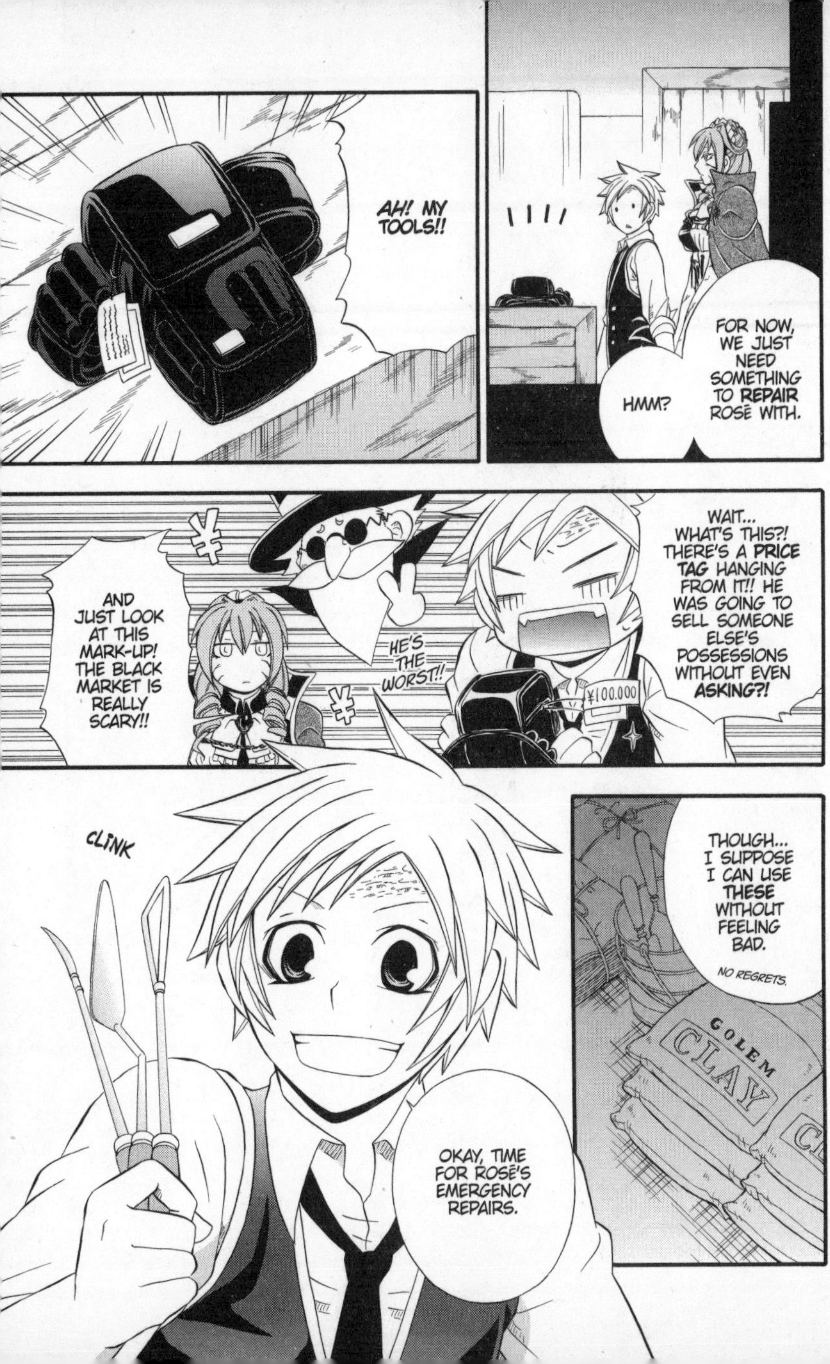
FOR NOW, WE JUST NEED SOMETHING TO **REPAIR** ROSÉ WITH.
HMM?
AH! MY TOOLS!!
WAIT... WHAT'S THIS?! THERE'S A **PRICE TAG** HANGING FROM IT!! HE WAS GOING TO SELL SOMEONE ELSE'S POSSESSIONS WITHOUT EVEN **ASKING?!**
¥100.000
HE'S THE WORST!!
AND JUST LOOK AT THIS MARK-UP! THE BLACK MARKET IS REALLY SCARY!!
THOUGH... I SUPPOSE I CAN USE **THESE** WITHOUT FEELING BAD.
NO REGRETS.
GOLEM CLAY
CLINK
OKAY, TIME FOR ROSÉ'S EMERGENCY REPAIRS.

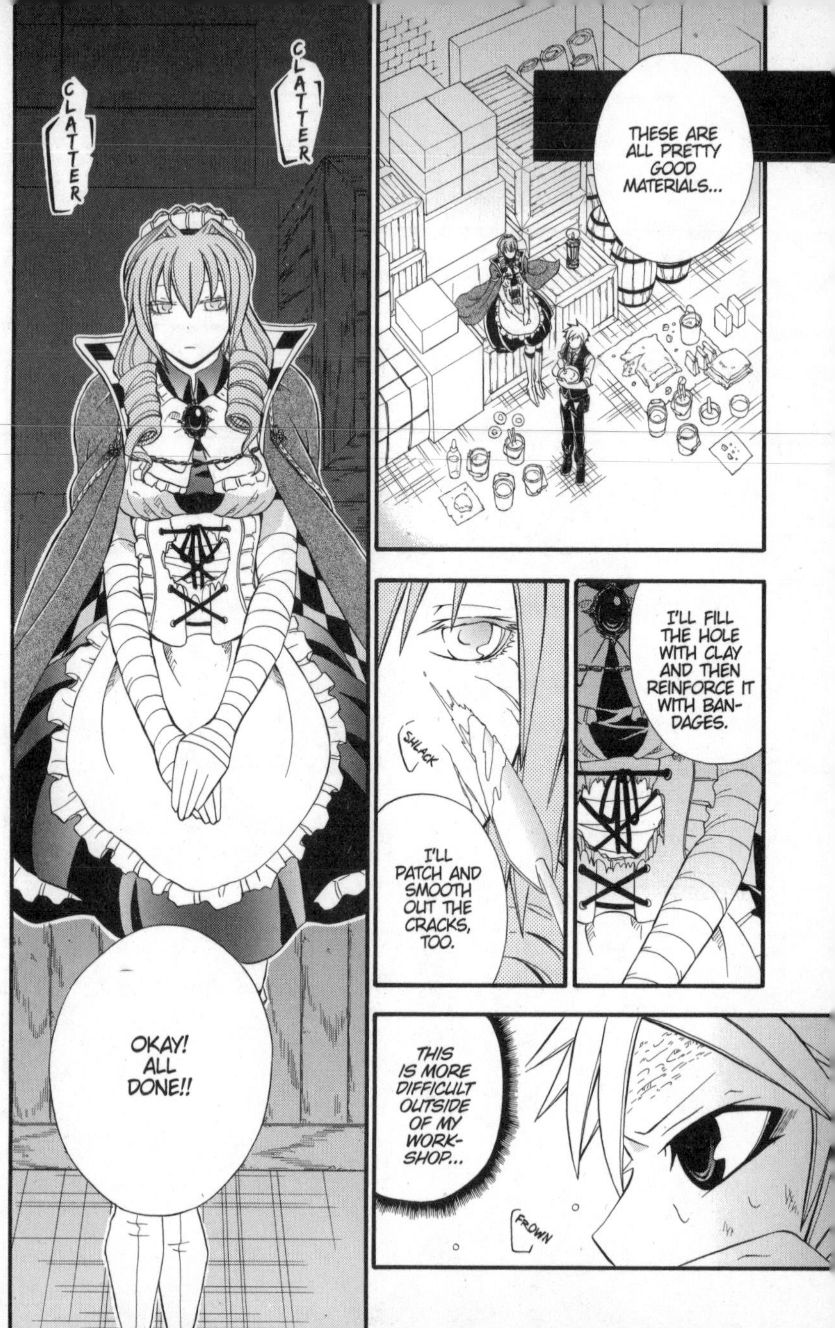
THESE ARE ALL PRETTY GOOD MATERIALS...
I'LL FILL THE HOLE WITH CLAY AND THEN REINFORCE IT WITH BAN-DAGES.
SHLACK
I'LL PATCH AND SMOOTH OUT THE CRACKS, TOO.
THIS IS MORE DIFFICULT OUTSIDE OF MY WORK-SHOP...
FROWN
CLATTER
CLATTER
OKAY! ALL DONE!!

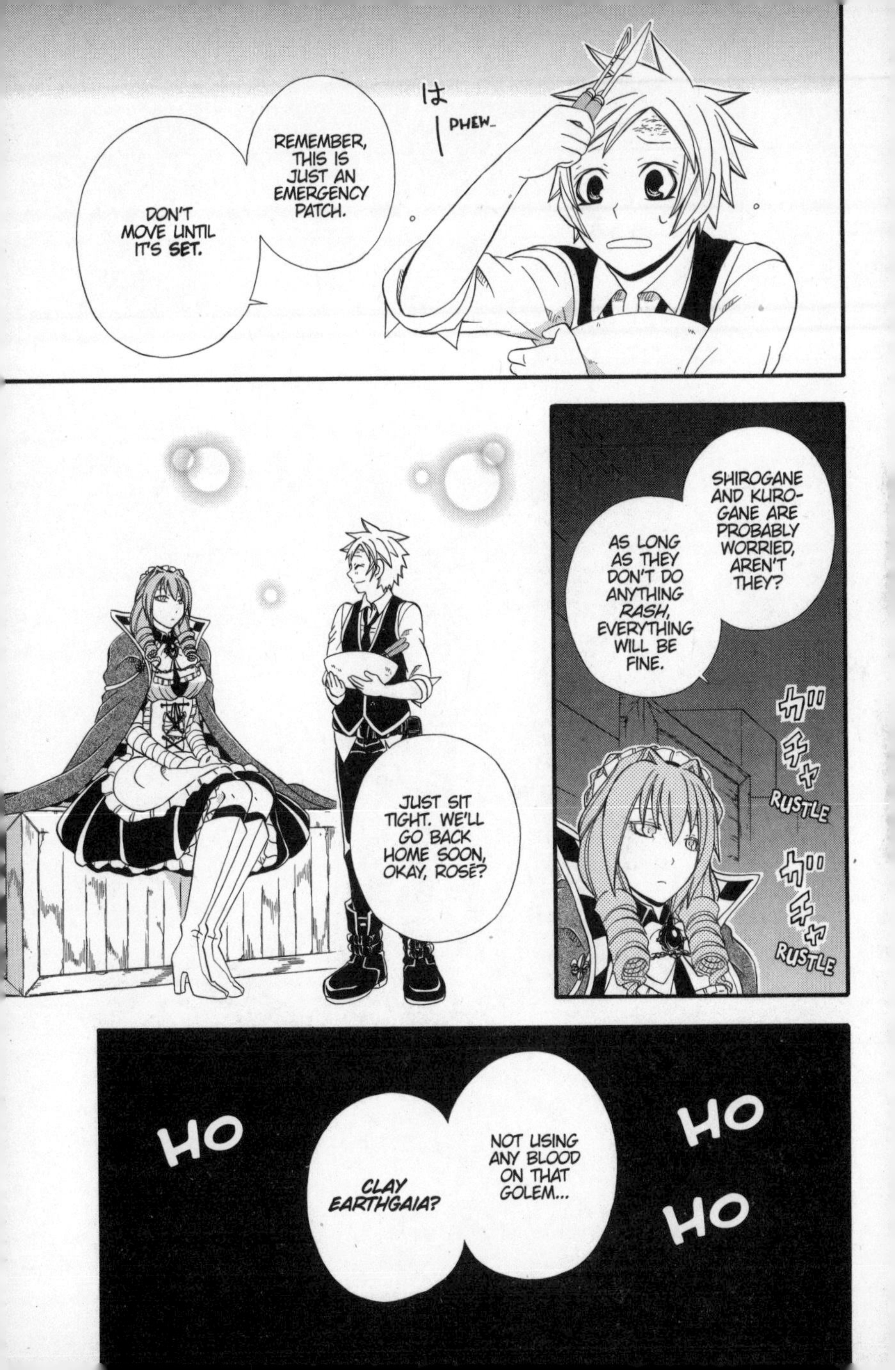
は
PHEW...
REMEMBER, THIS IS JUST AN EMERGENCY PATCH.
DON'T MOVE UNTIL IT'S SET.
SHIROGANE AND KUROGANE ARE PROBABLY WORRIED, AREN'T THEY?
AS LONG AS THEY DON'T DO ANYTHING *RASH*, EVERYTHING WILL BE FINE.
ガチャ
RUSTLE
ガチャ
RUSTLE
JUST SIT TIGHT. WE'LL GO BACK HOME SOON, OKAY, ROSÉ?
HO
HO
HO
NOT USING ANY BLOOD ON THAT GOLEM...
CLAY EARTHGAIA?

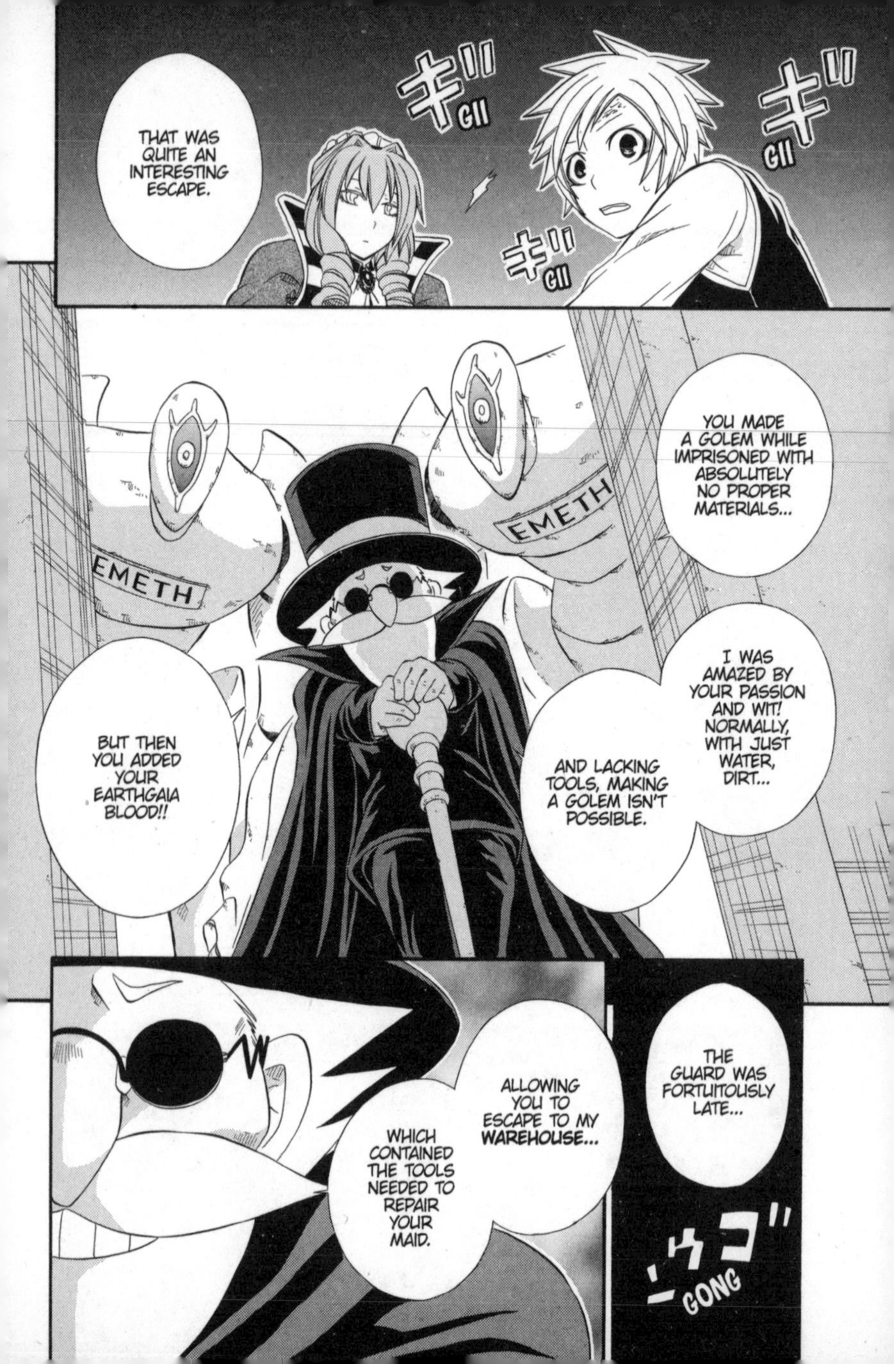
GII
GII
GII
THAT WAS QUITE AN INTERESTING ESCAPE.
YOU MADE A GOLEM WHILE IMPRISONED WITH ABSOLUTLEY NO PROPER MATERIALS...
EMETH
EMETH
I WAS AMAZED BY YOUR PASSION AND WIT! NORMALLY, WITH JUST WATER, DIRT...
AND LACKING TOOLS, MAKING A GOLEM ISN'T POSSIBLE.
BUT THEN YOU ADDED YOUR EARTHGAIA BLOOD!!
THE GUARD WAS FORTUITOUSLY LATE...
GONG
ALLOWING YOU TO ESCAPE TO MY WAREHOUSE...
WHICH CONTAINED THE TOOLS NEEDED TO REPAIR YOUR MAID.

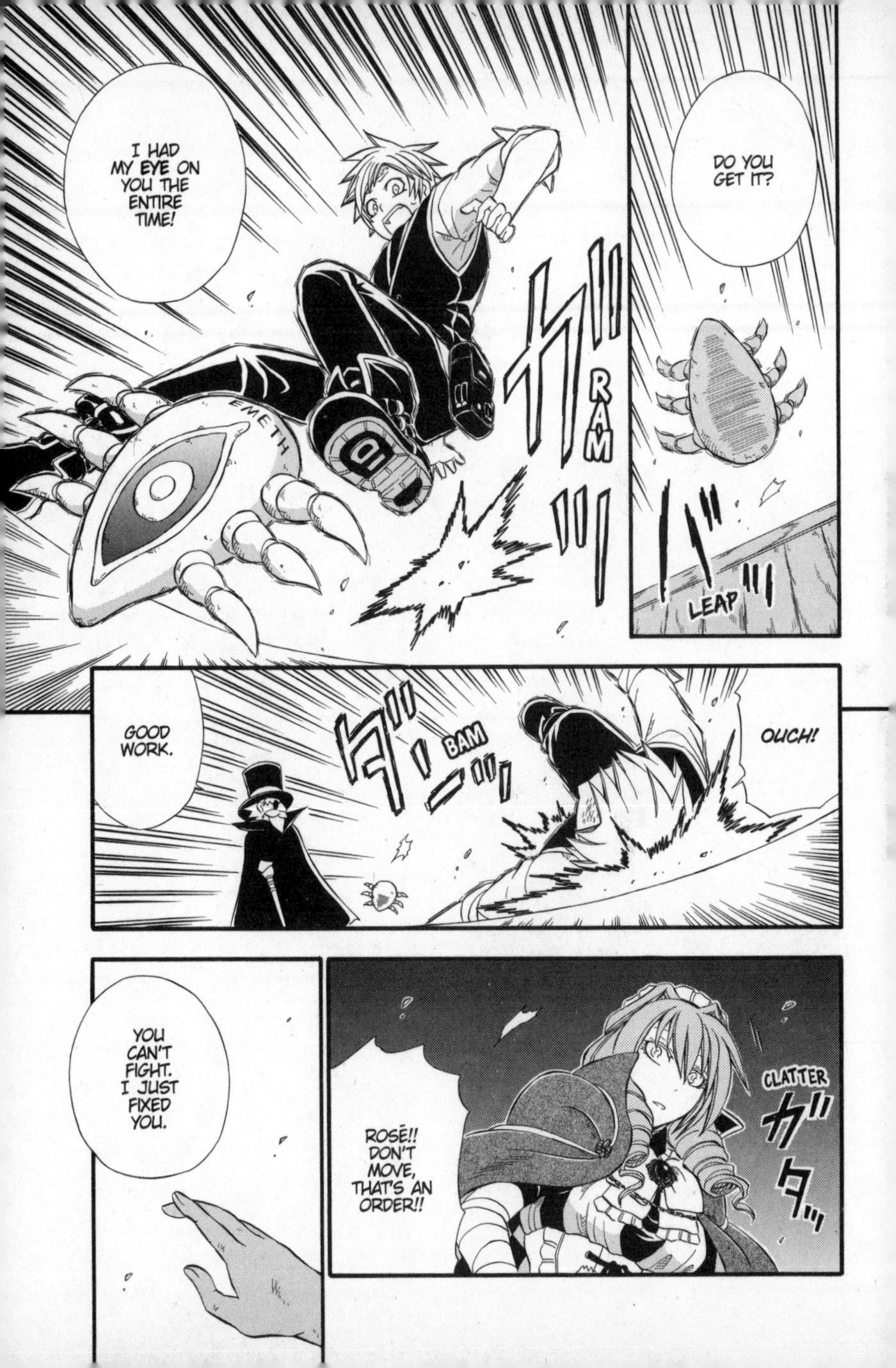
DO YOU GET IT?
LEAP
I HAD MY EYE ON YOU THE ENTIRE TIME!
RAM
EMETH
OUCH!
BAM
GOOD WORK.
CLATTER
ROSĒ!! DON'T MOVE, THAT'S AN ORDER!!
YOU CAN'T FIGHT. I JUST FIXED YOU.

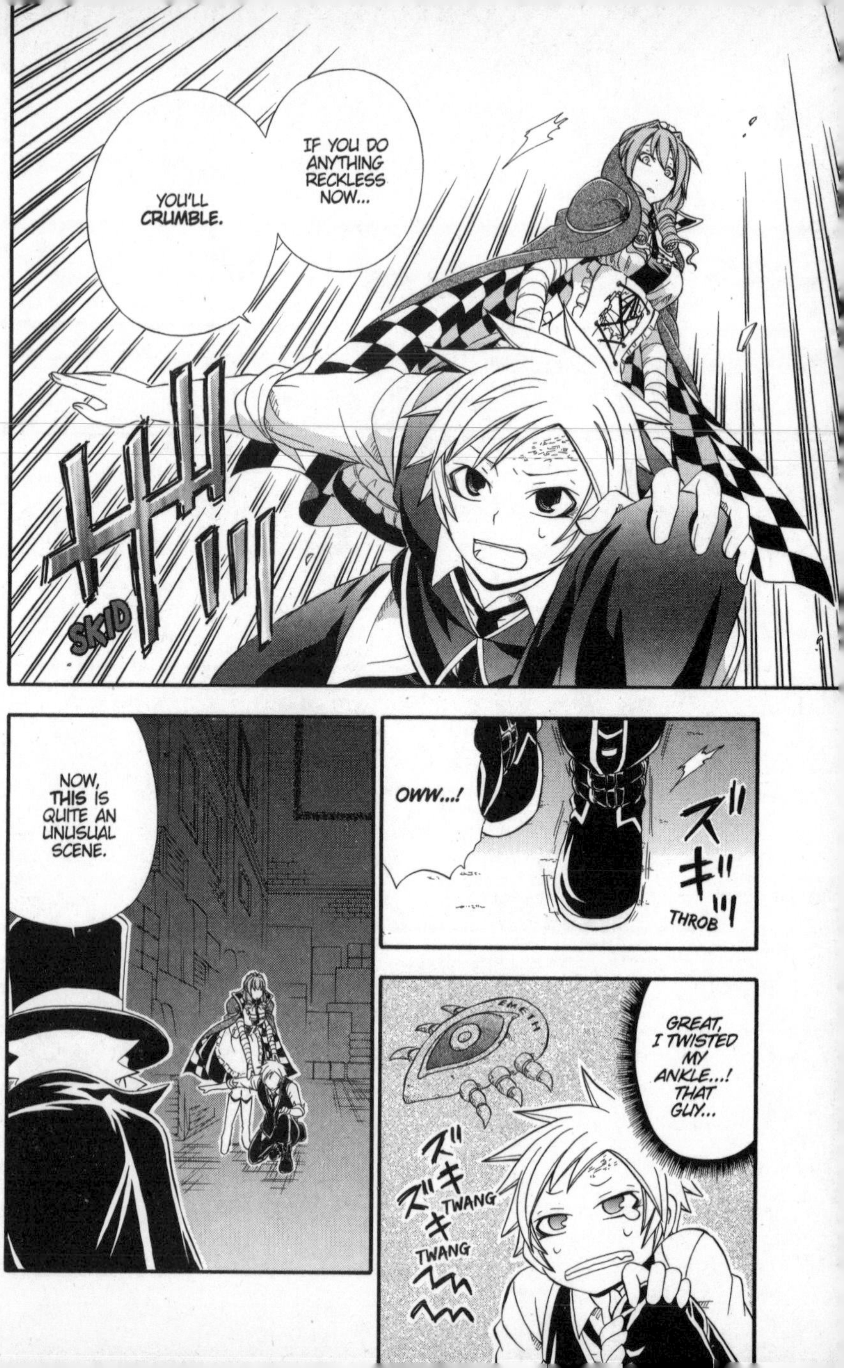
IF YOU DO ANYTHING RECKLESS NOW...
YOU'LL CRUMBLE.
SKID
OWW...!
THROB
GREAT, I TWISTED MY ANKLE...! THAT GUY...
EMETH
TWANG
TWANG
NOW, THIS IS QUITE AN UNUSUAL SCENE.

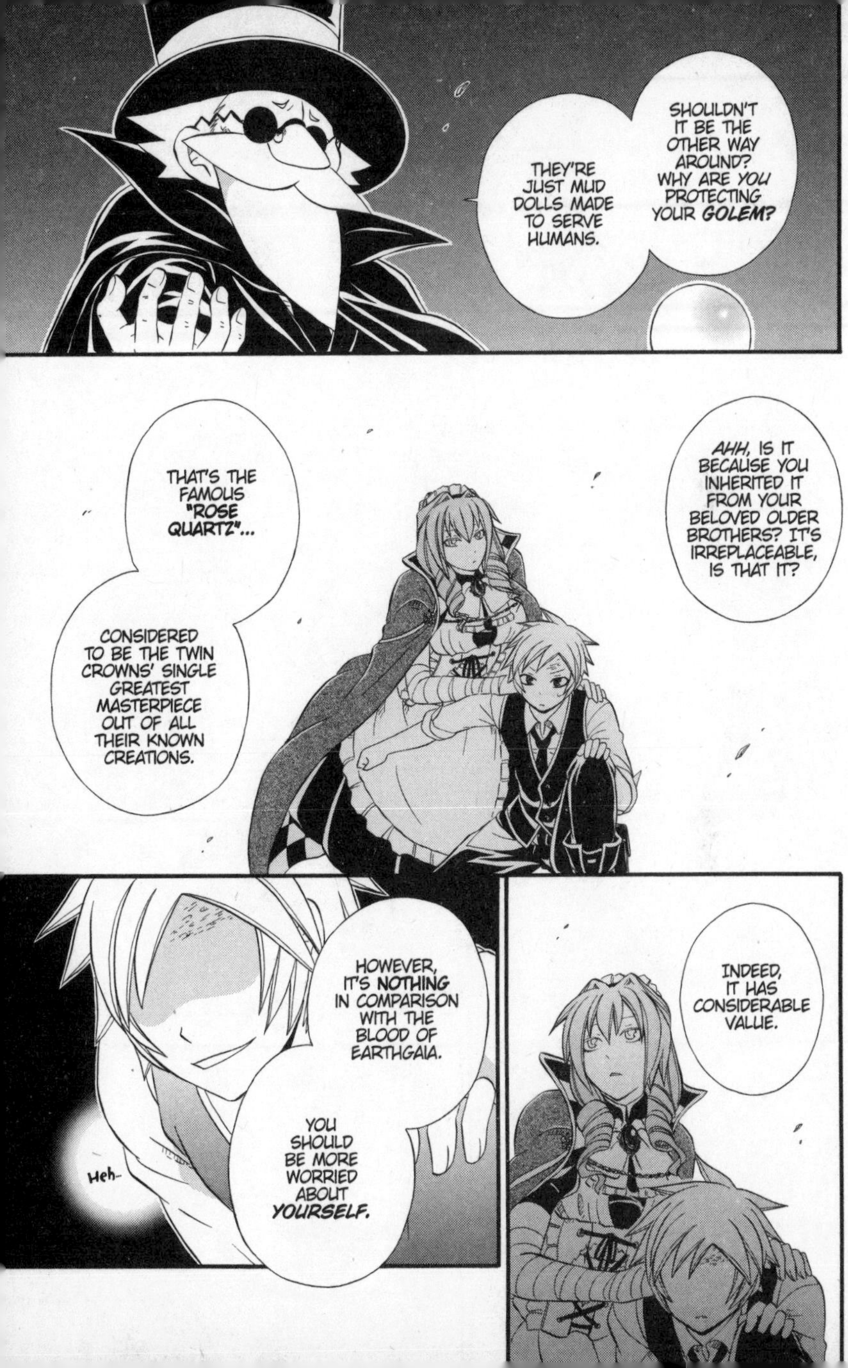
SHOULDN'T IT BE THE OTHER WAY AROUND? WHY ARE *YOU* PROTECTING YOUR **GOLEM?**
THEY'RE JUST MUD DOLLS MADE TO SERVE HUMANS.
AHH, IS IT BECAUSE YOU INHERITED IT FROM YOUR BELOVED OLDER BROTHERS? IT'S IRREPLACEABLE, IS THAT IT?
THAT'S THE FAMOUS **"ROSE QUARTZ"...**
CONSIDERED TO BE THE TWIN CROWNS' SINGLE GREATEST MASTERPIECE OUT OF ALL THEIR KNOWN CREATIONS.
INDEED, IT HAS CONSIDERABLE VALUE.
HOWEVER, IT'S **NOTHING** IN COMPARISON WITH THE BLOOD OF EARTHGAIA.
YOU SHOULD BE MORE WORRIED ABOUT ***YOURSELF.***
Heh..

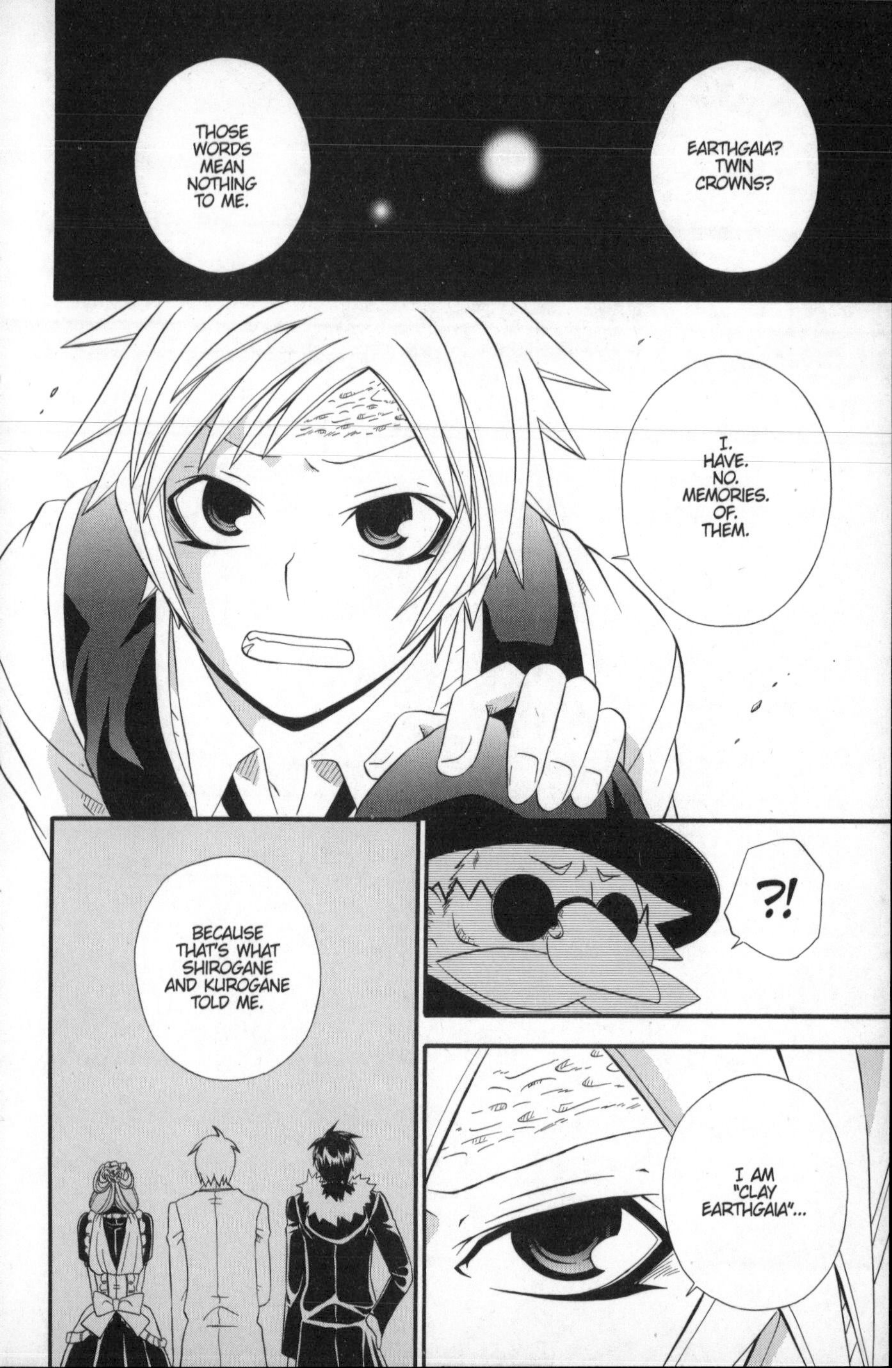
EARTHGAIA? TWIN CROWNS?
THOSE WORDS MEAN NOTHING TO ME.
I. HAVE. NO. MEMORIES. OF. THEM.
?!
I AM "CLAY EARTHGAIA"...
BECAUSE THAT'S WHAT SHIROGANE AND KUROGANE TOLD ME.

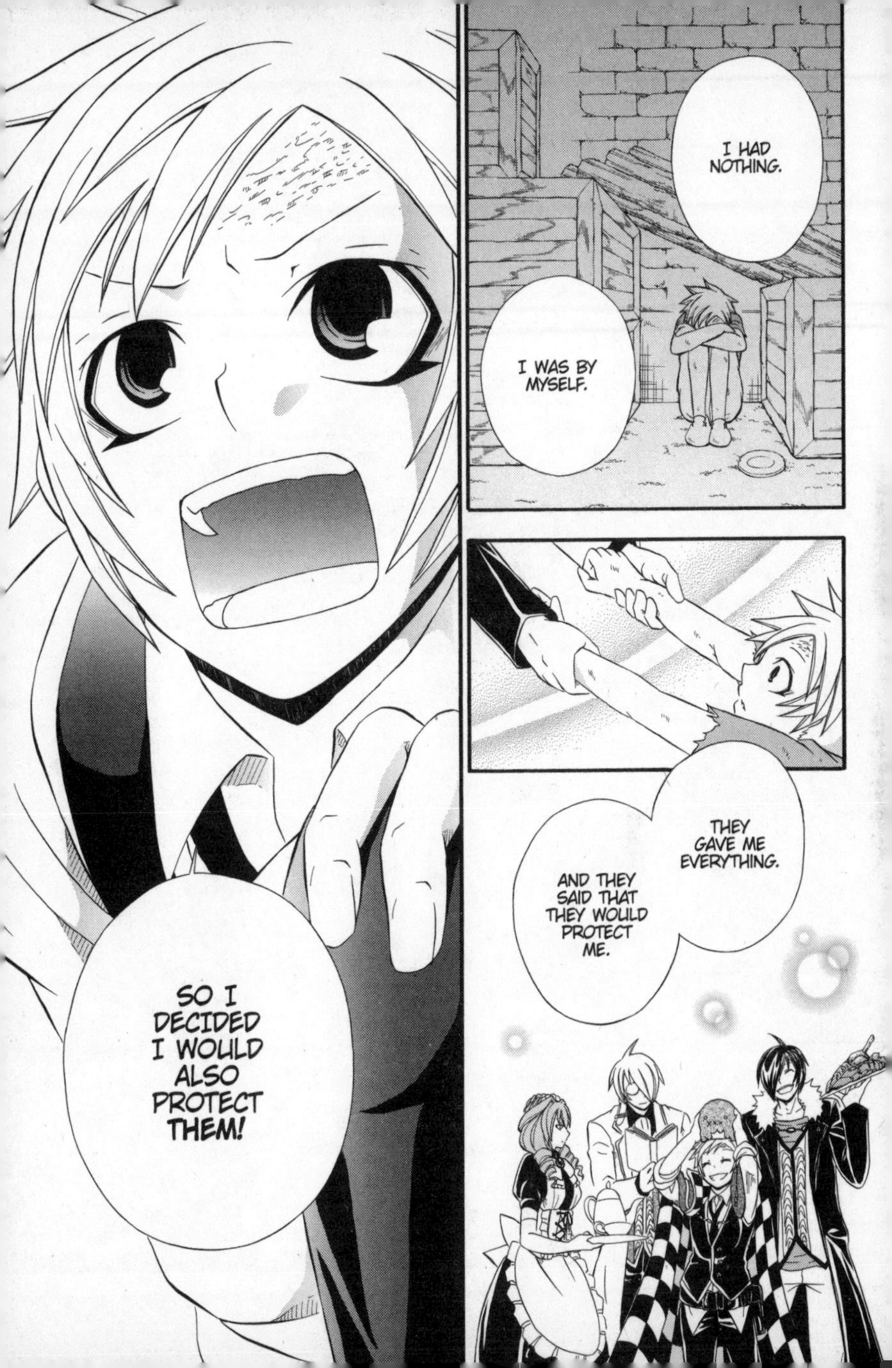
I HAD NOTHING.
I WAS BY MYSELF.
THEY GAVE ME EVERYTHING.
AND THEY SAID THAT THEY WOULD PROTECT ME.
SO I DECIDED I WOULD ALSO PROTECT THEM!

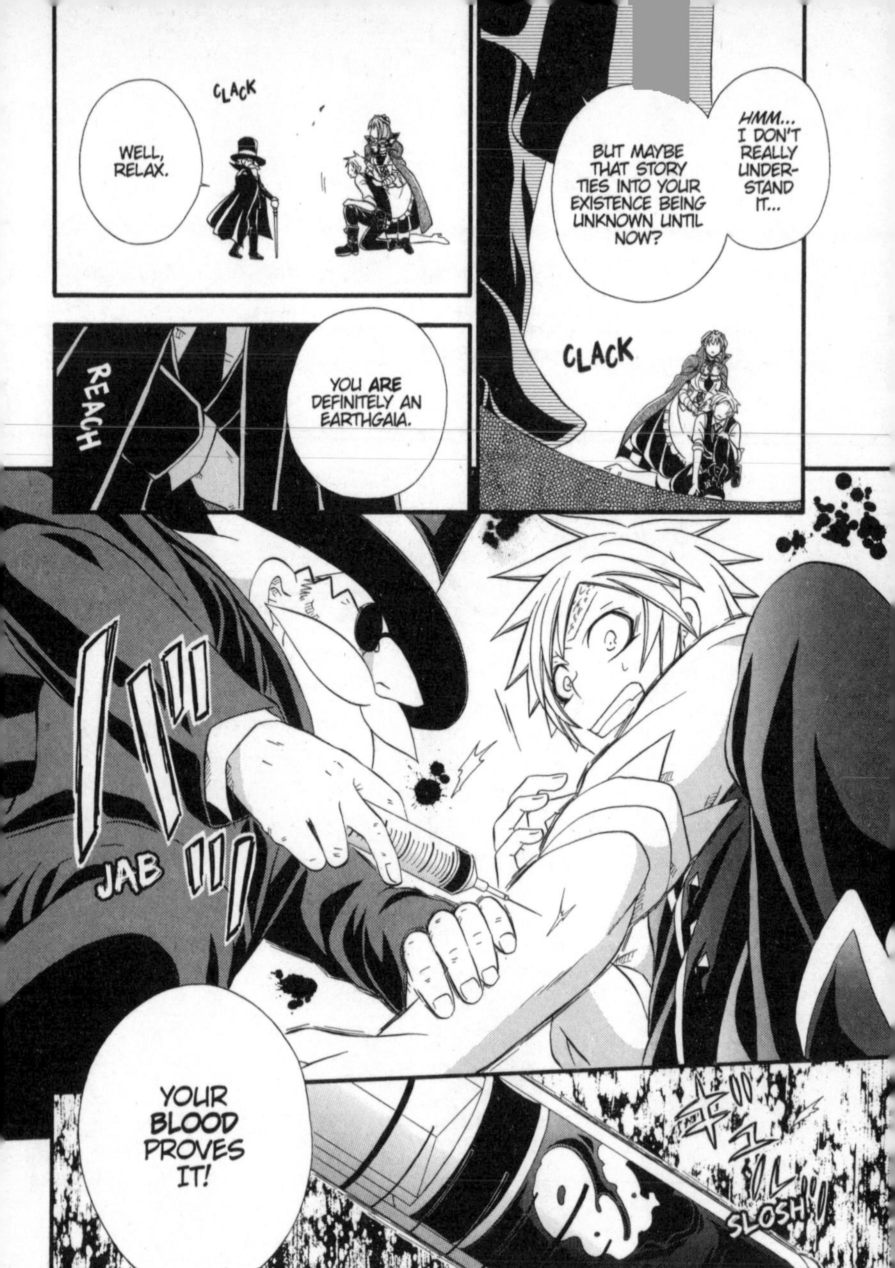
HMM... I DON'T REALLY UNDER-STAND IT...
BUT MAYBE THAT STORY TIES INTO YOUR EXISTENCE BEING UNKNOWN UNTIL NOW?
CLACK
CLACK
WELL, RELAX.
REACH
YOU ARE DEFINITELY AN EARTHGAIA.
JAB
YOUR BLOOD PROVES IT!
SLOSH

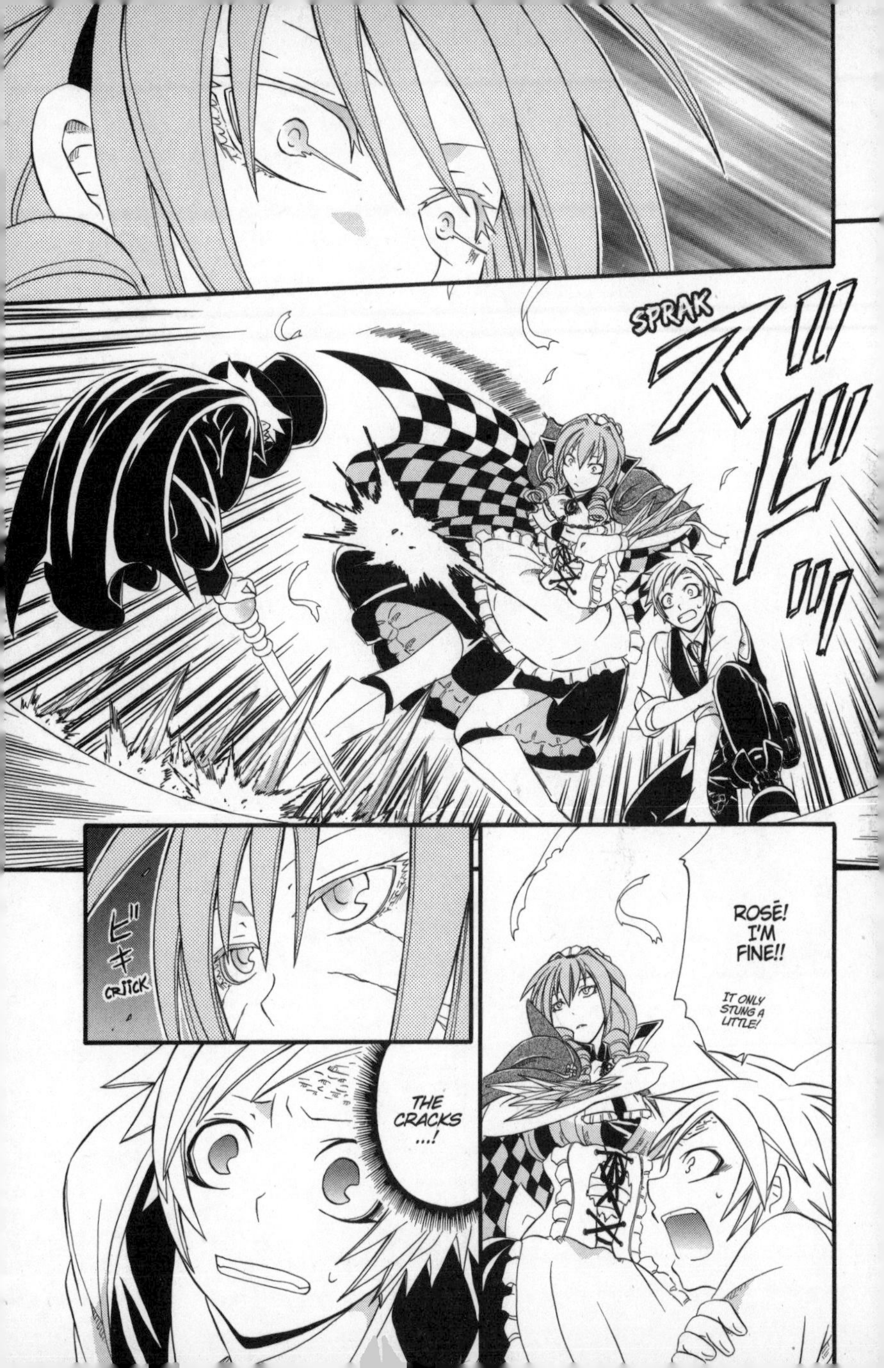
SPRAK
ROSÉ! I'M FINE!!
IT ONLY STUNG A LITTLE!
ビキ
CRiCK
THE CRACKS ...!

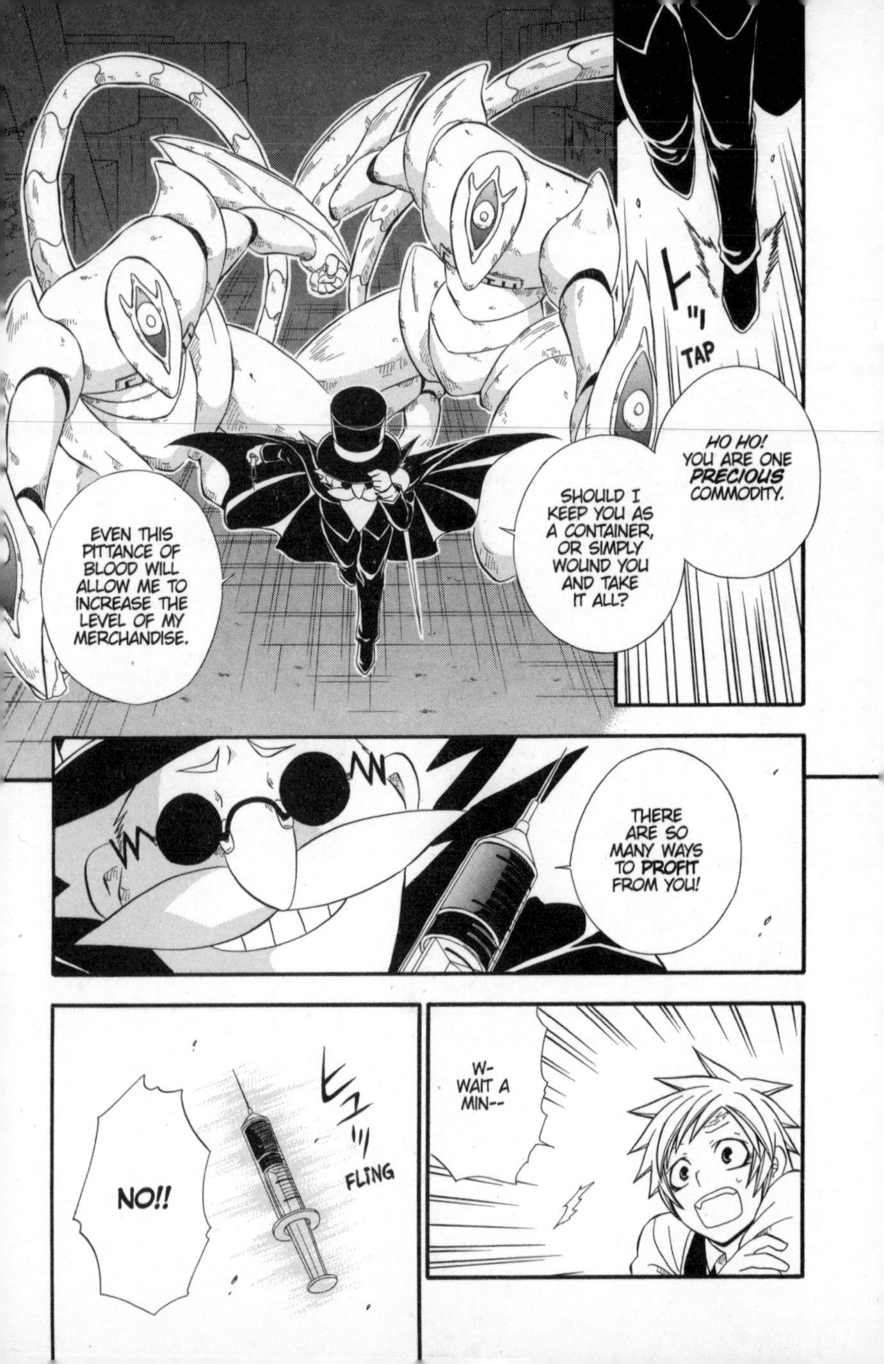

TAP
HO HO! YOU ARE ONE ***PRECIOUS*** COMMODITY.
SHOULD I KEEP YOU AS A CONTAINER, OR SIMPLY WOUND YOU AND TAKE IT ALL?
EVEN THIS PITTANCE OF BLOOD WILL ALLOW ME TO INCREASE THE LEVEL OF MY MERCHANDISE.
THERE ARE SO MANY WAYS TO **PROFIT** FROM YOU!
W-WAIT A MIN--
NO!!
FLING

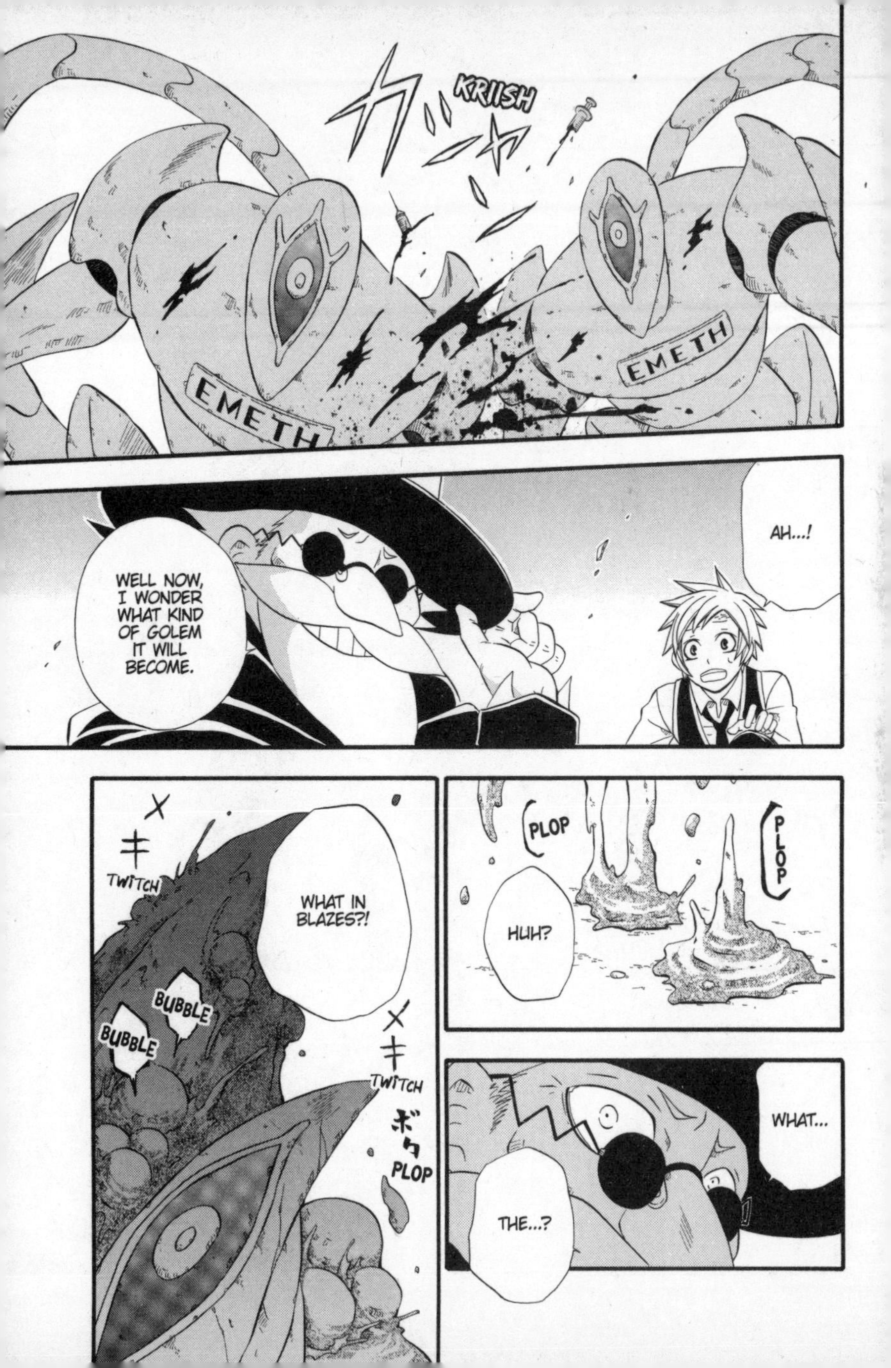
KRIISH
AH...!
WELL NOW, I WONDER WHAT KIND OF GOLEM IT WILL BECOME.
PLOP
PLOP
HUH?
WHAT...
THE...?
WHAT IN BLAZES?!
TWITCH
BUBBLE
BUBBLE
TWITCH
PLOP

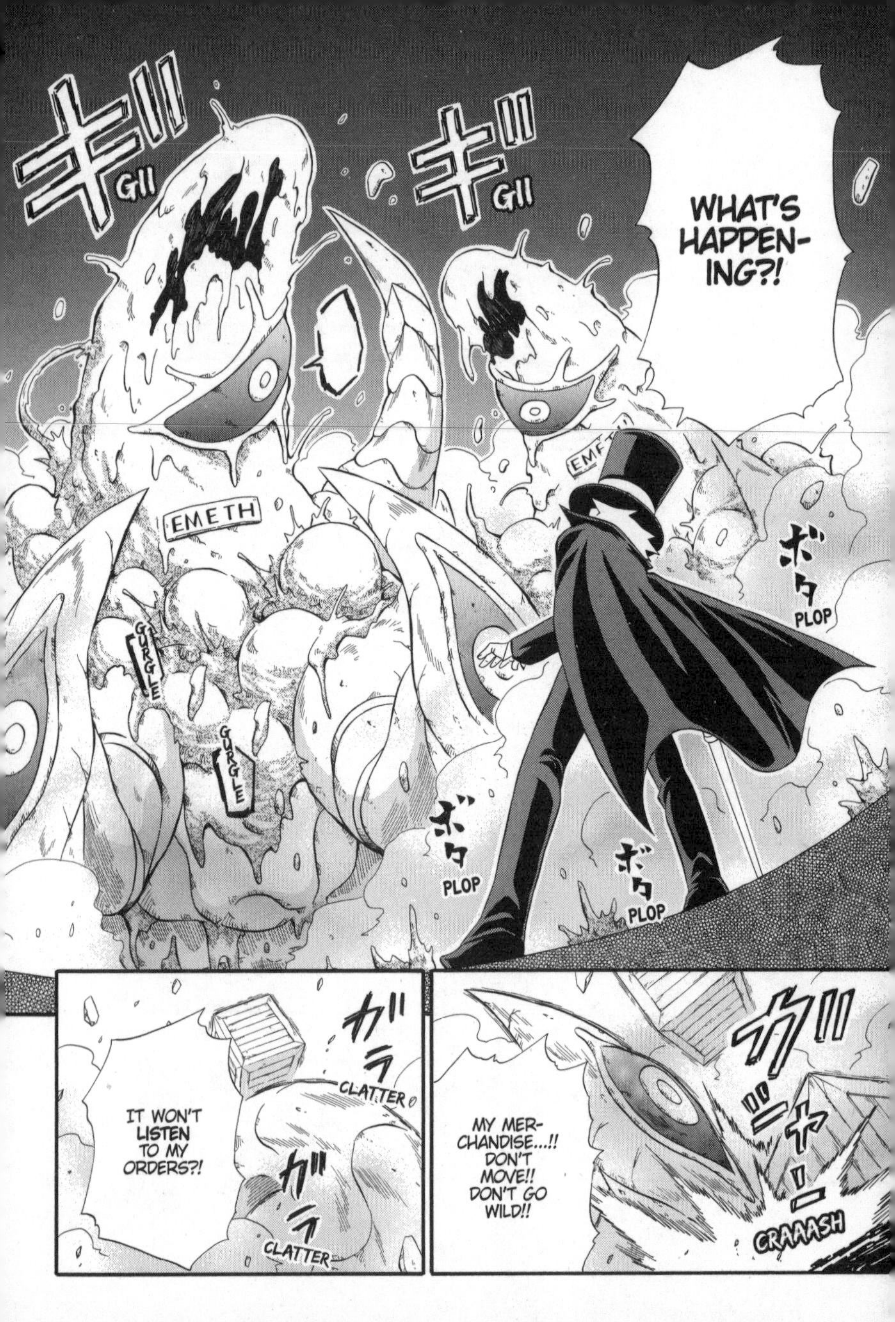
WHAT'S HAPPEN-ING?!
ギ GII
ギ GII
EMETH
ボタ PLOP
EMETH
GURGLE
GURGLE
ボタ PLOP
ボタ PLOP
ガシャーン CRAAASH
MY MER-CHANDISE...!! DON'T MOVE!! DON'T GO WILD!!
ガラ CLATTER
IT WON'T LISTEN TO MY ORDERS?!
ガラ CLATTER

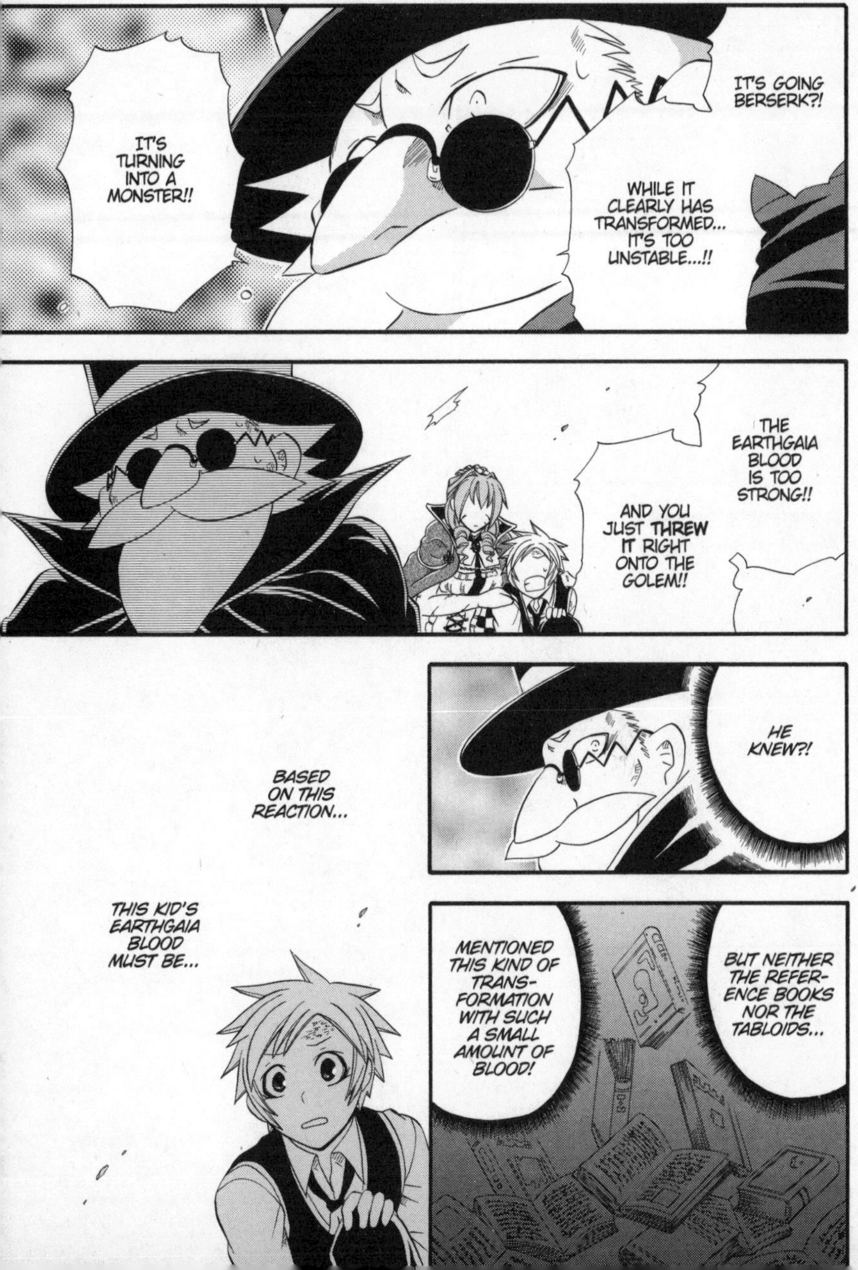
IT'S GOING BERSERK?!
WHILE IT CLEARLY HAS TRANSFORMED... IT'S TOO UNSTABLE...!!
IT'S TURNING INTO A MONSTER!!
THE EARTHGAIA BLOOD IS TOO STRONG!!
AND YOU JUST THREW IT RIGHT ONTO THE GOLEM!!
HE KNEW?!
BASED ON THIS REACTION...
BUT NEITHER THE REFERENCE BOOKS NOR THE TABLOIDS...
MENTIONED THIS KIND OF TRANSFORMATION WITH SUCH A SMALL AMOUNT OF BLOOD!
THIS KID'S EARTHGAIA BLOOD MUST BE...

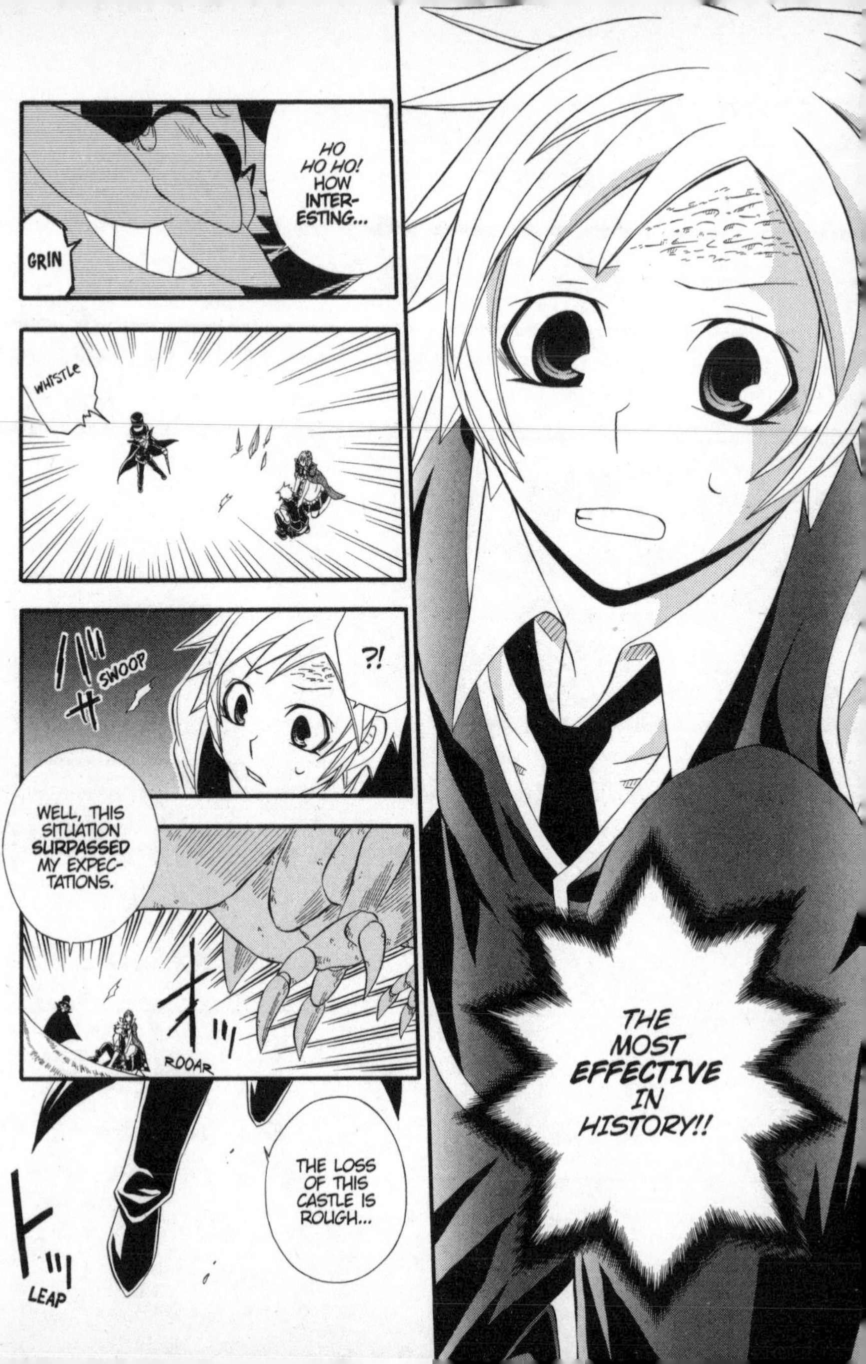
THE MOST EFFECTIVE IN HISTORY!!
HO HO HO! HOW INTER-ESTING...
GRIN
WHISTLE
?!
SWOOP
WELL, THIS SITUATION SURPASSED MY EXPECTATIONS.
ROOAR
THE LOSS OF THIS CASTLE IS ROUGH...
LEAP

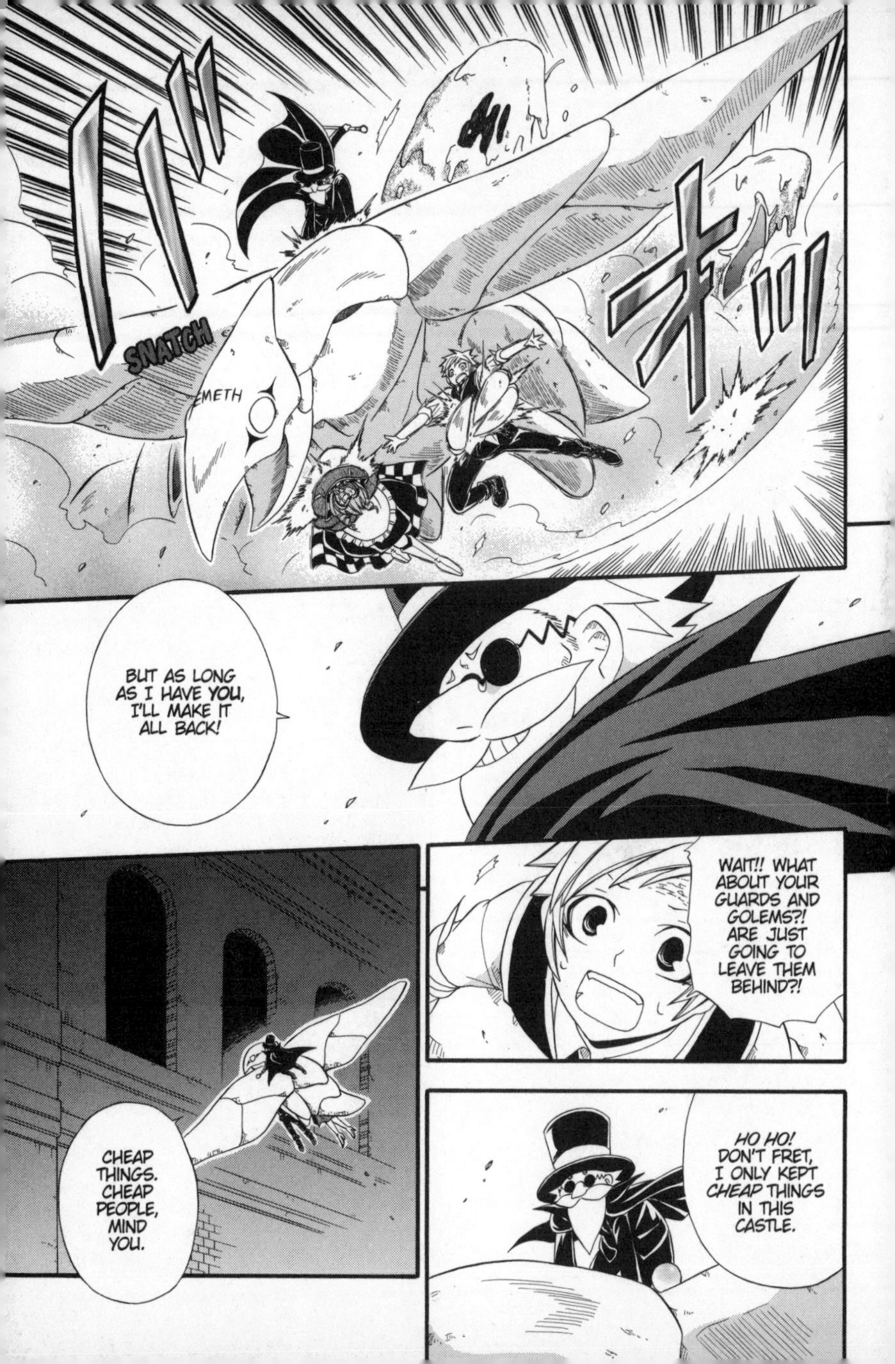
SNATCH
EMETH
BUT AS LONG AS I HAVE YOU, I'LL MAKE IT ALL BACK!
WAIT!! WHAT ABOUT YOUR GUARDS AND GOLEMS?! ARE JUST GOING TO LEAVE THEM BEHIND?!
HO HO! DON'T FRET, I ONLY KEPT *CHEAP* THINGS IN THIS CASTLE.
CHEAP THINGS. CHEAP PEOPLE, MIND YOU.

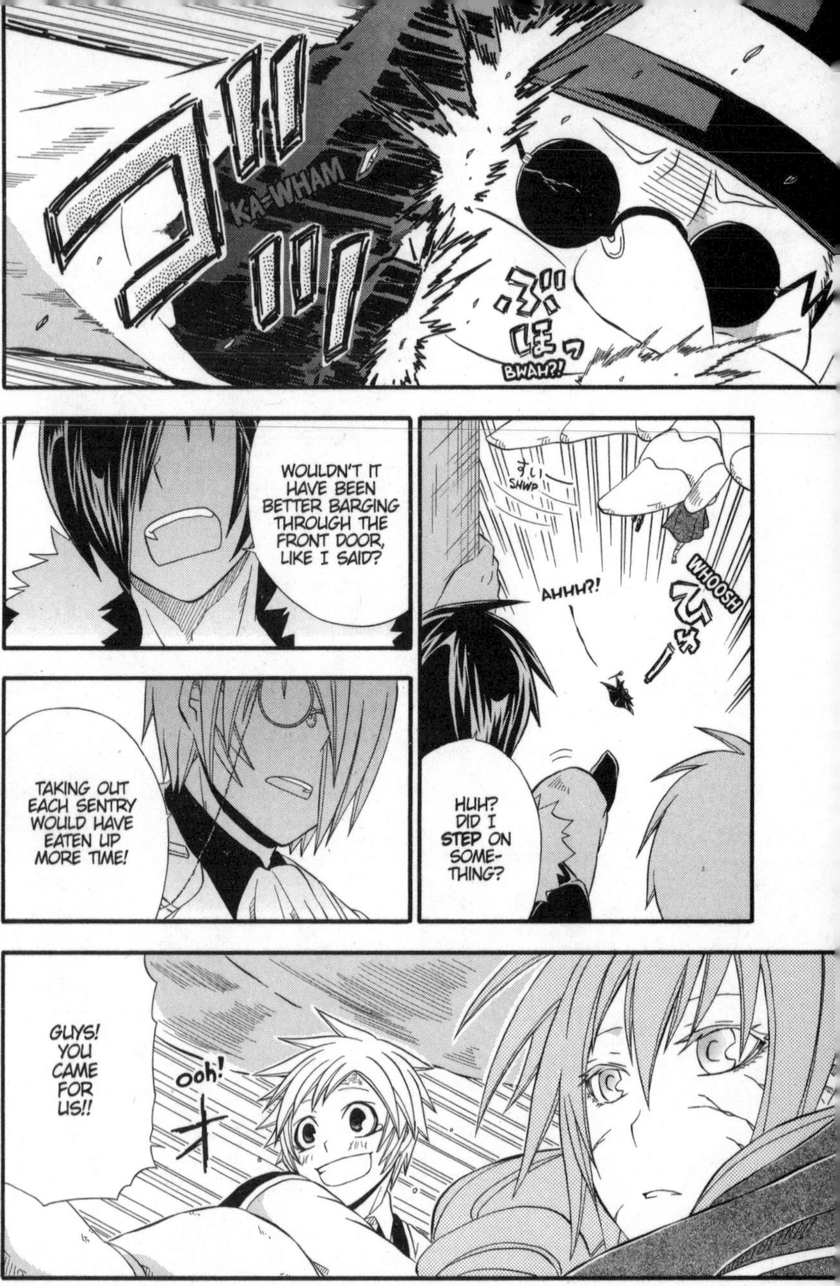
KA=WHAM
BWAH?!
すい SHWP
WHOOSH
AHHH?!
HUH? DID I STEP ON SOME-THING?
WOULDN'T IT HAVE BEEN BETTER BARGING THROUGH THE FRONT DOOR, LIKE I SAID?
TAKING OUT EACH SENTRY WOULD HAVE EATEN UP MORE TIME!
GUYS! YOU CAME FOR US!!
ooh!

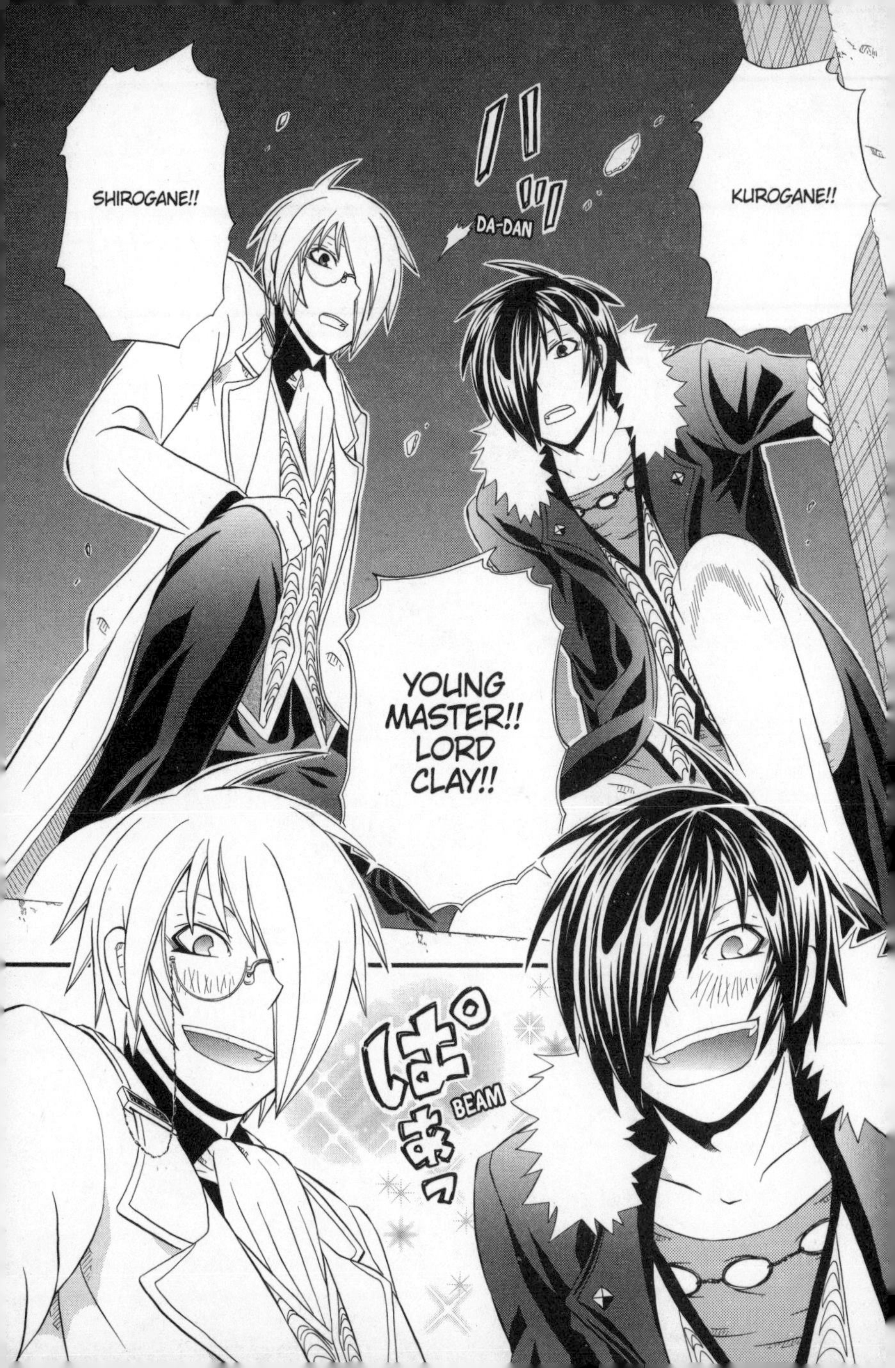
KUROGANE!!
DA-DAN
SHIROGANE!!
YOUNG MASTER!! LORD CLAY!!
ぱぁっ
BEAM

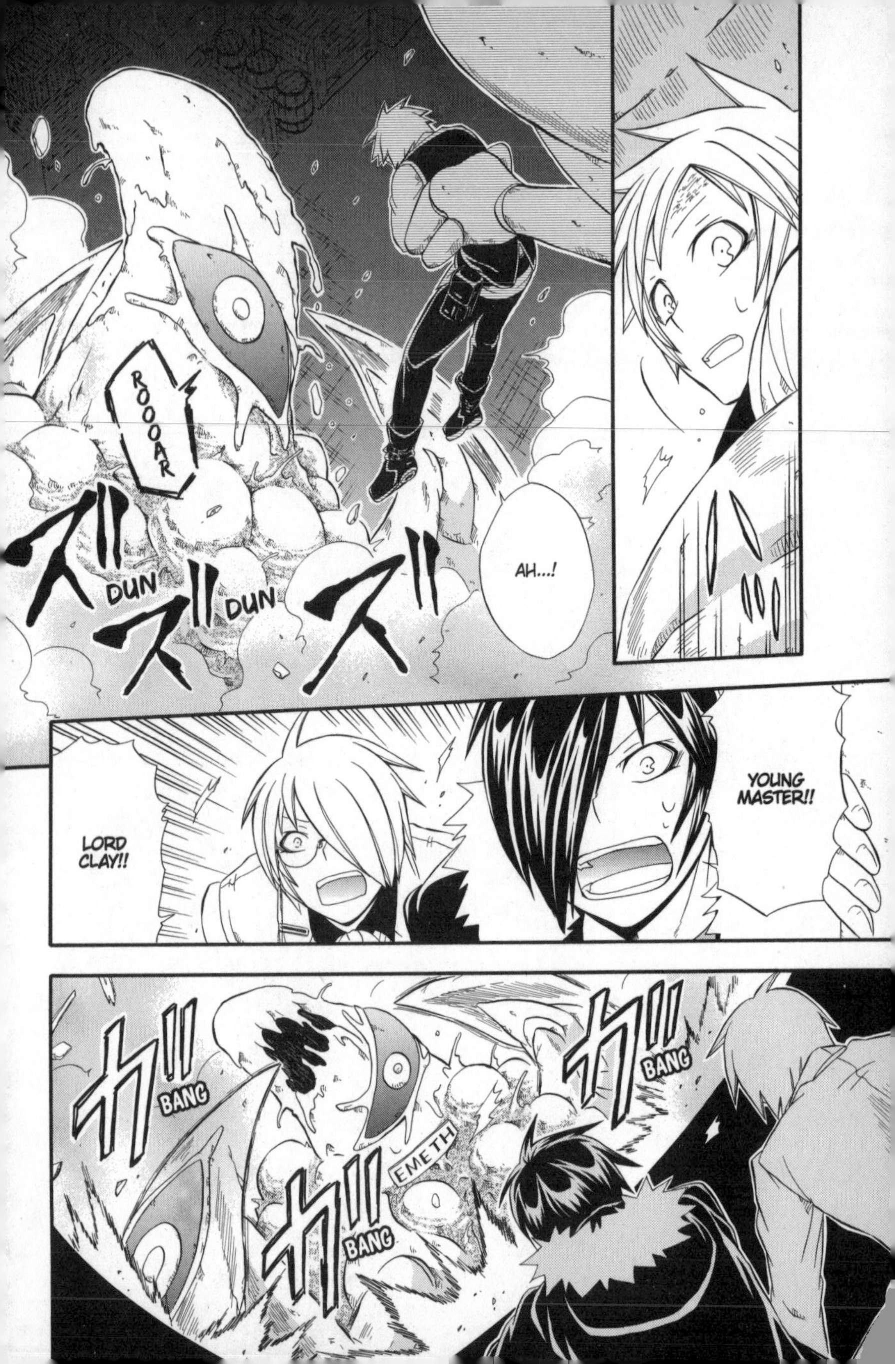
ROOOAR
ズ!!
DUN
ズ!!
DUN
ズ!!
AH...!
YOUNG MASTER!!
LORD CLAY!!
ガ!!
BANG
EMETH
ガ!!
BANG
ガ!!
BANG

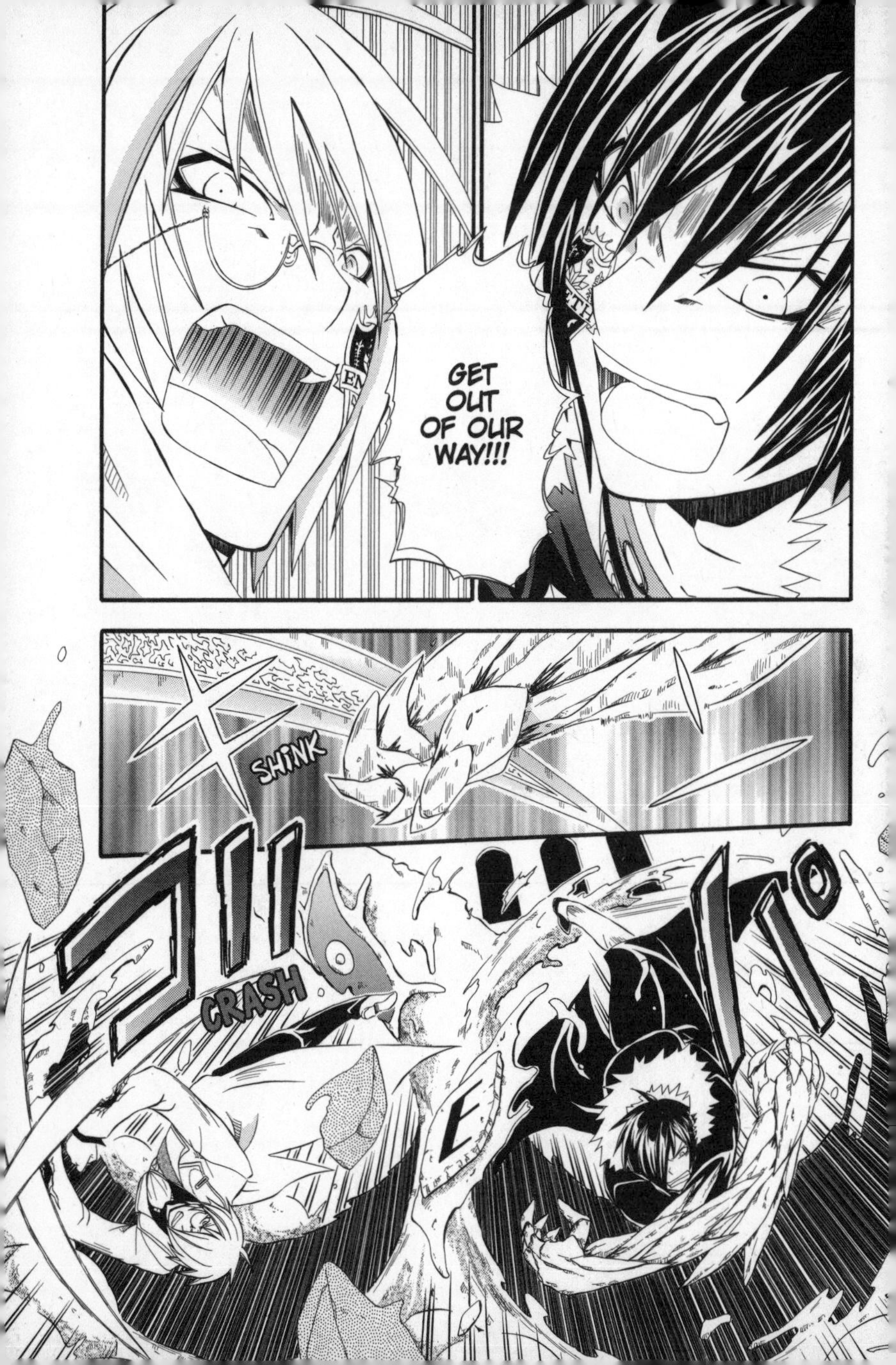
GET OUT OF OUR WAY!!!
SHINK
CRASH

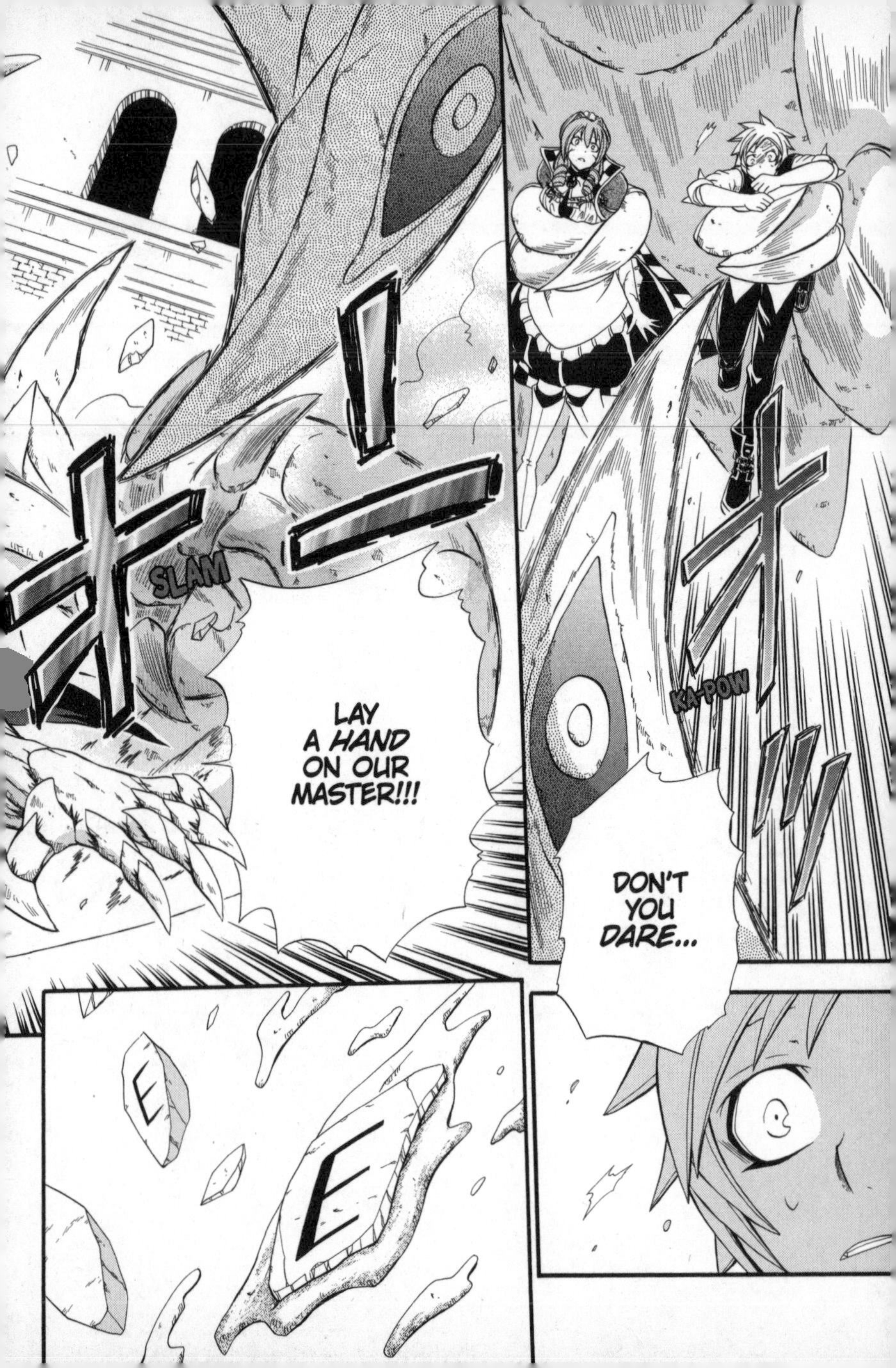
KA-POW
DON'T YOU DARE...
SLAM
LAY A *HAND* ON OUR MASTER!!!

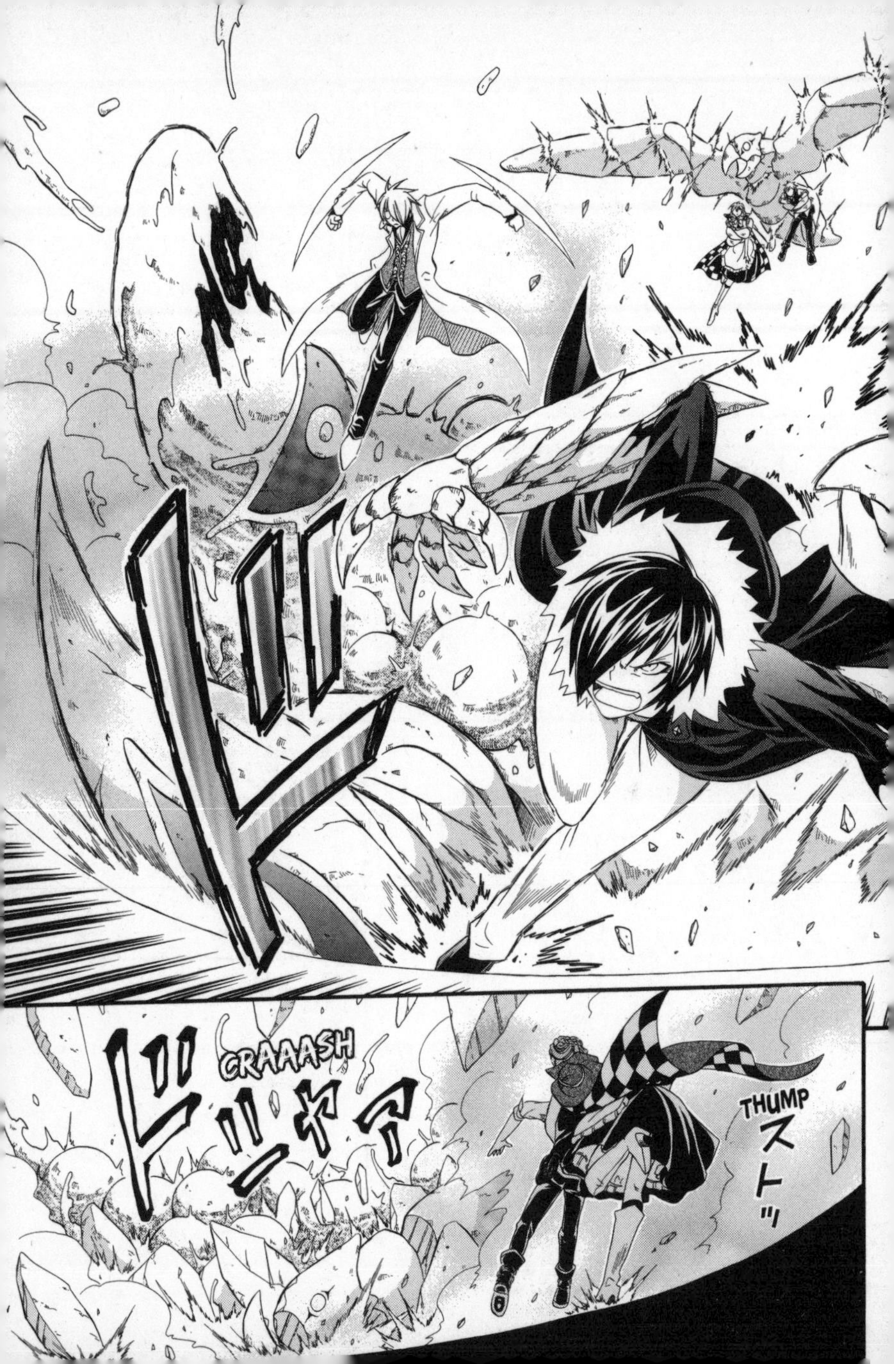
THUMP
ストッ
CRAAASH

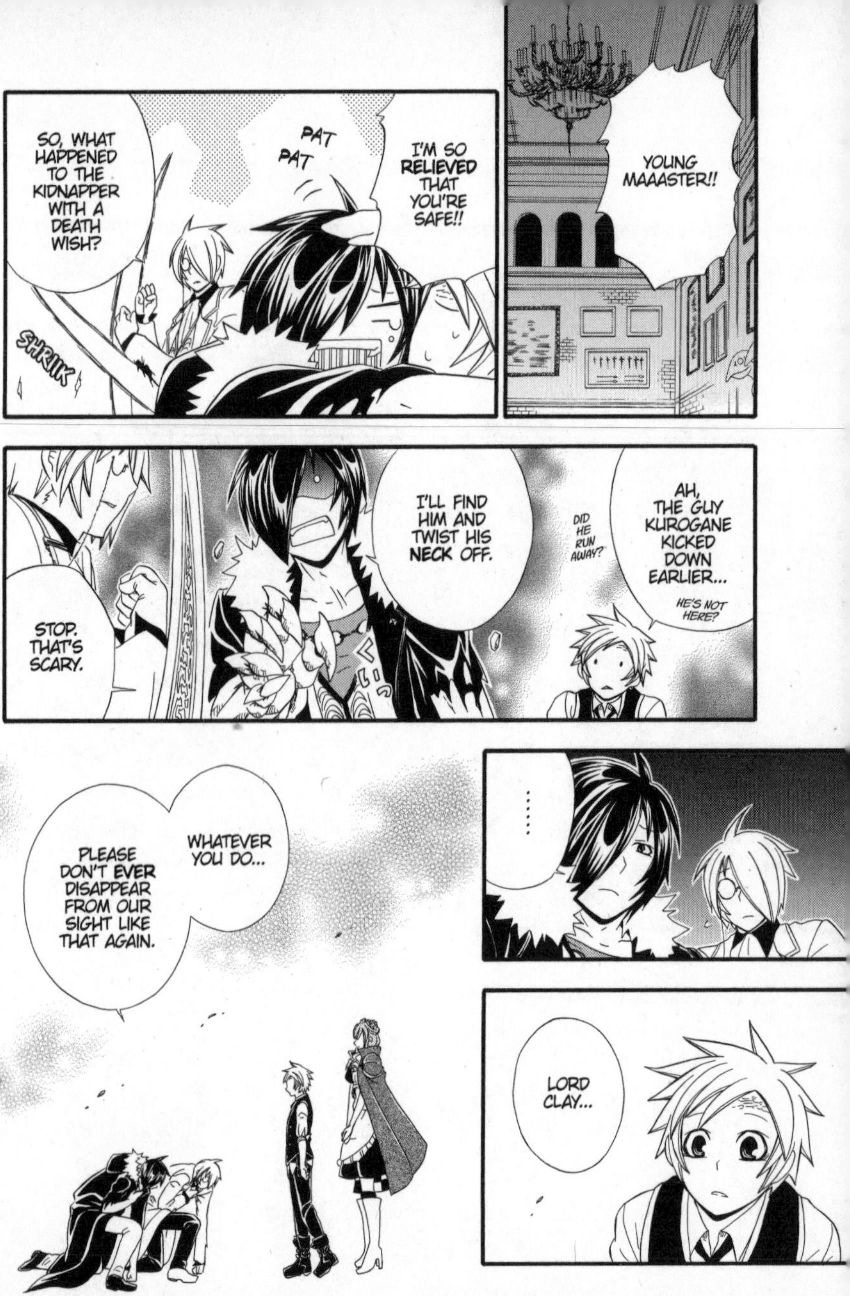
YOUNG MAAASTER!!
I'M SO RELIEVED THAT YOU'RE SAFE!!
PAT PAT
SO, WHAT HAPPENED TO THE KIDNAPPER WITH A DEATH WISH?
SHRIIK
AH, THE GUY KUROGANE KICKED DOWN EARLIER...
DID HE RUN AWAY?
HE'S NOT HERE?
I'LL FIND HIM AND TWIST HIS NECK OFF.
STOP. THAT'S SCARY.
......
LORD CLAY...
WHATEVER YOU DO...
PLEASE DON'T EVER DISAPPEAR FROM OUR SIGHT LIKE THAT AGAIN.

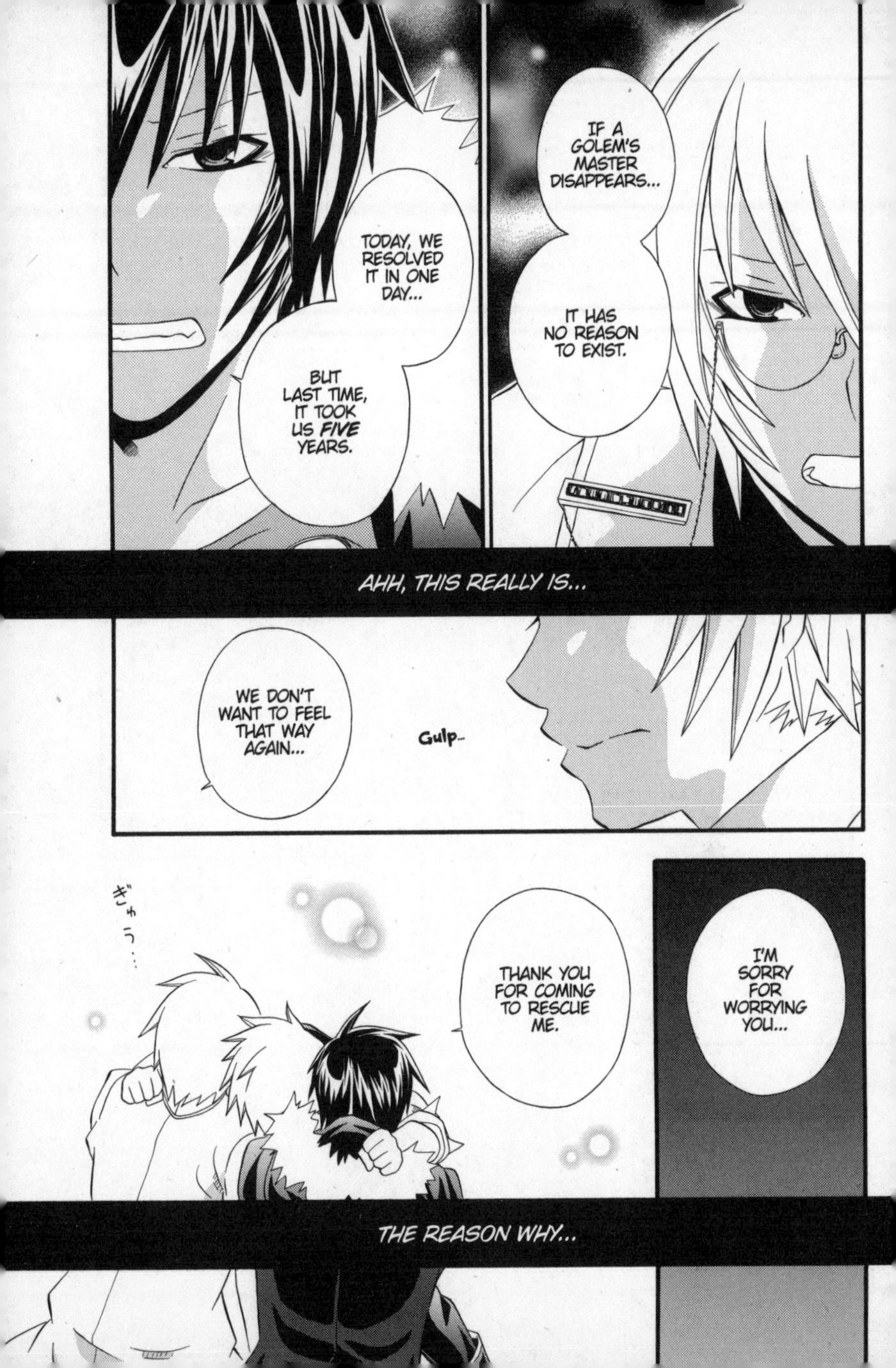
IF A GOLEM'S MASTER DISAPPEARS...
IT HAS NO REASON TO EXIST.
TODAY, WE RESOLVED IT IN ONE DAY...
BUT LAST TIME, IT TOOK US *FIVE* YEARS.
AHH, THIS REALLY IS...
Gulp...
WE DON'T WANT TO FEEL THAT WAY AGAIN...
I'M SORRY FOR WORRYING YOU...
THANK YOU FOR COMING TO RESCUE ME.
ぎゅう…
THE REASON WHY...

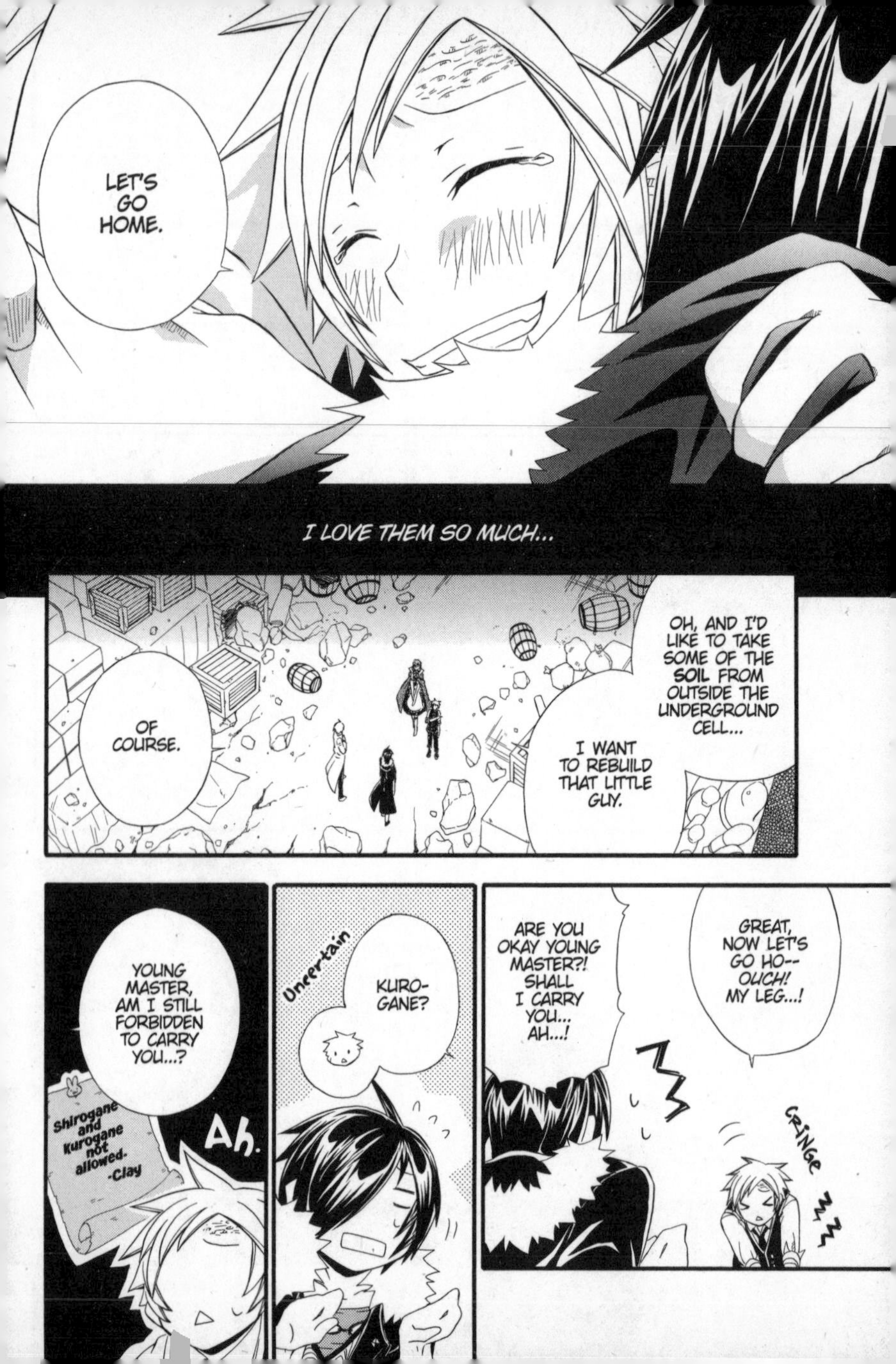
LET'S GO HOME.
I LOVE THEM SO MUCH...
OH, AND I'D LIKE TO TAKE SOME OF THE SOIL FROM OUTSIDE THE UNDERGROUND CELL...
I WANT TO REBUILD THAT LITTLE GUY.
OF COURSE.
GREAT, NOW LET'S GO HO-- OUCH! MY LEG...!
ARE YOU OKAY YOUNG MASTER?! SHALL I CARRY YOU... AH...!
CRINGE
Uncertain
KURO-GANE?
YOUNG MASTER, AM I STILL FORBIDDEN TO CARRY YOU...?
Shirogane and Kurogane not allowed. -Clay
Ah.

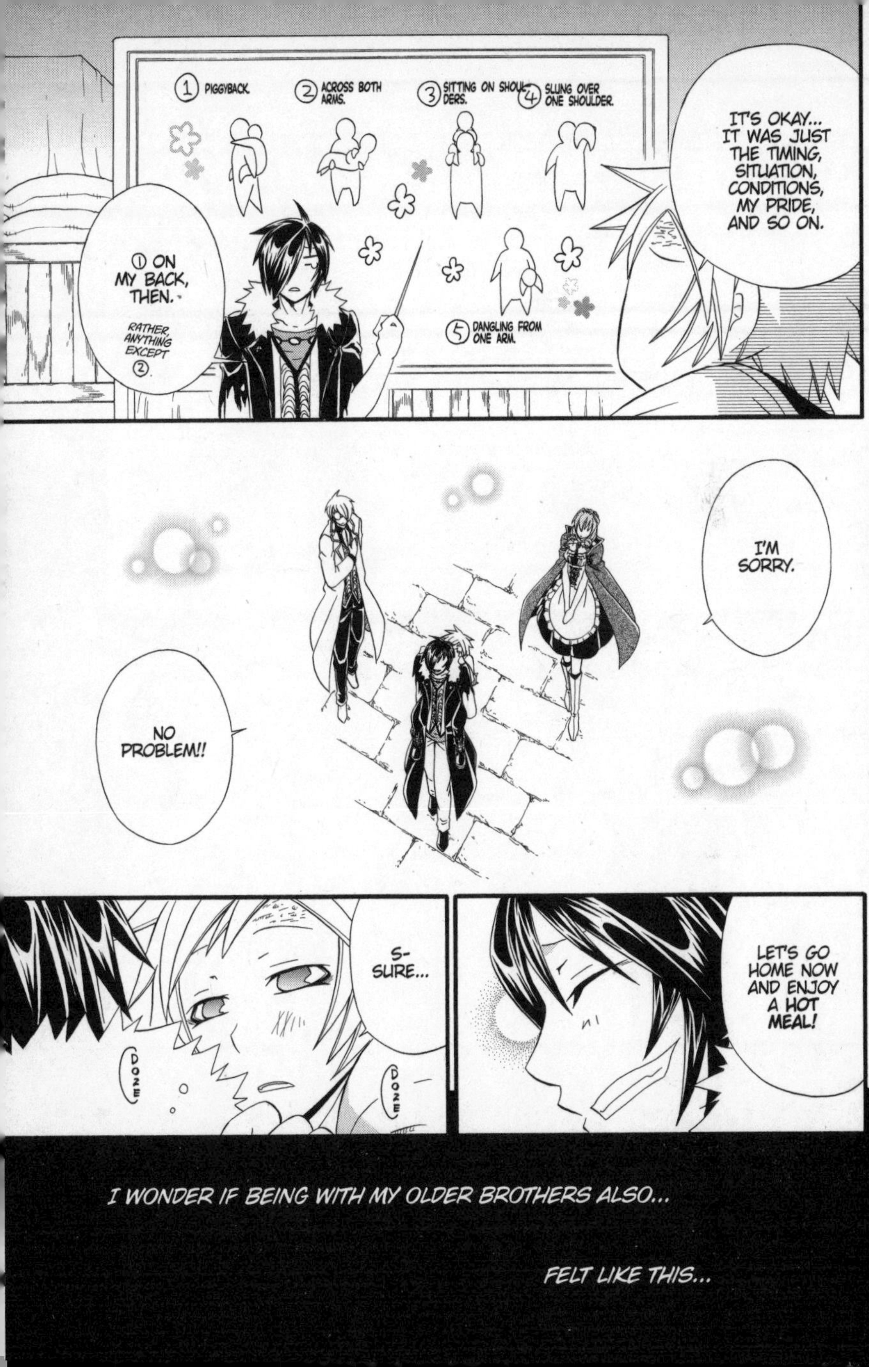
IT'S OKAY... IT WAS JUST THE TIMING, SITUATION, CONDITIONS, MY PRIDE, AND SO ON.
1 PIGGYBACK.
2 ACROSS BOTH ARMS.
3 SITTING ON SHOULDERS.
4 SLUNG OVER ONE SHOULDER.
5 DANGLING FROM ONE ARM.
① ON MY BACK, THEN.
RATHER, ANYTHING EXCEPT ②.
I'M SORRY.
NO PROBLEM!!
LET'S GO HOME NOW AND ENJOY A HOT MEAL!
S-SURE...
DOZE
DOZE
I WONDER IF BEING WITH MY OLDER BROTHERS ALSO...
FELT LIKE THIS...

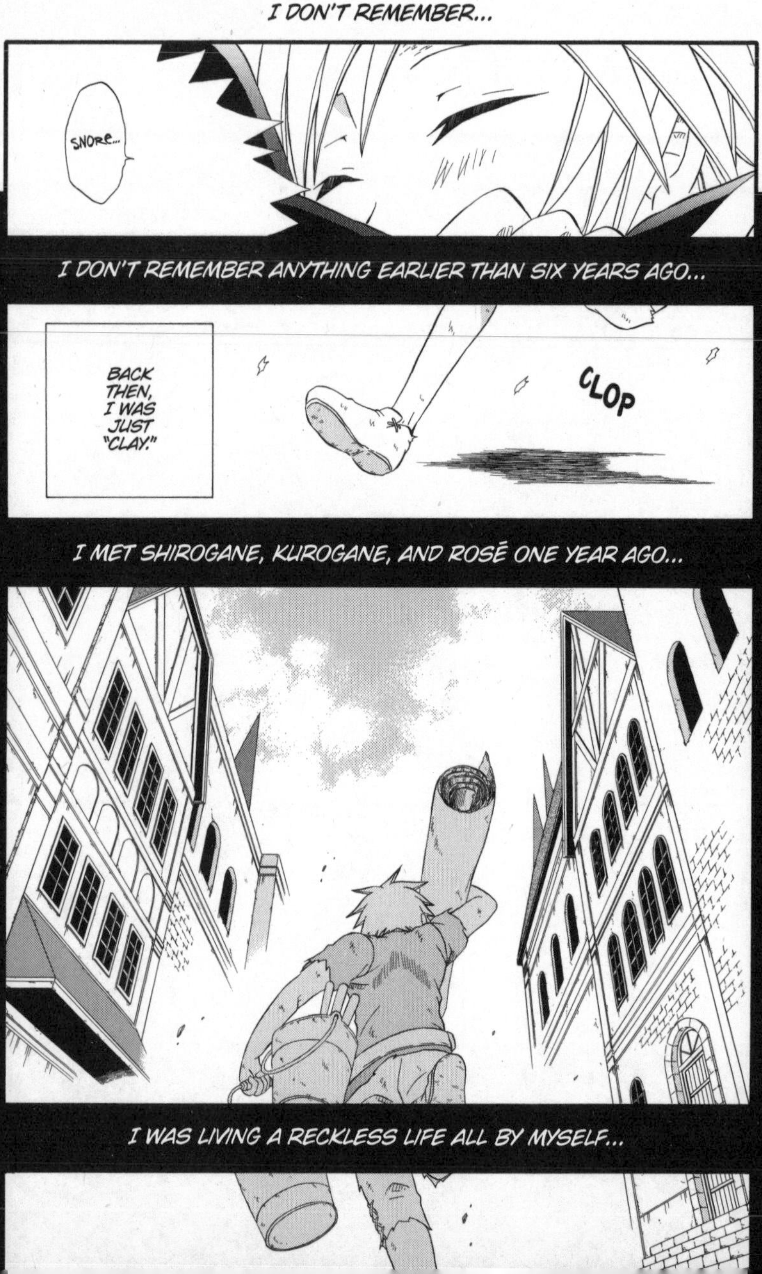
I DON'T REMEMBER...
SNORE...
I DON'T REMEMBER ANYTHING EARLIER THAN SIX YEARS AGO...
CLOP
BACK THEN, I WAS JUST "CLAY."
I MET SHIROGANE, KUROGANE, AND ROSÉ ONE YEAR AGO...
I WAS LIVING A RECKLESS LIFE ALL BY MYSELF...

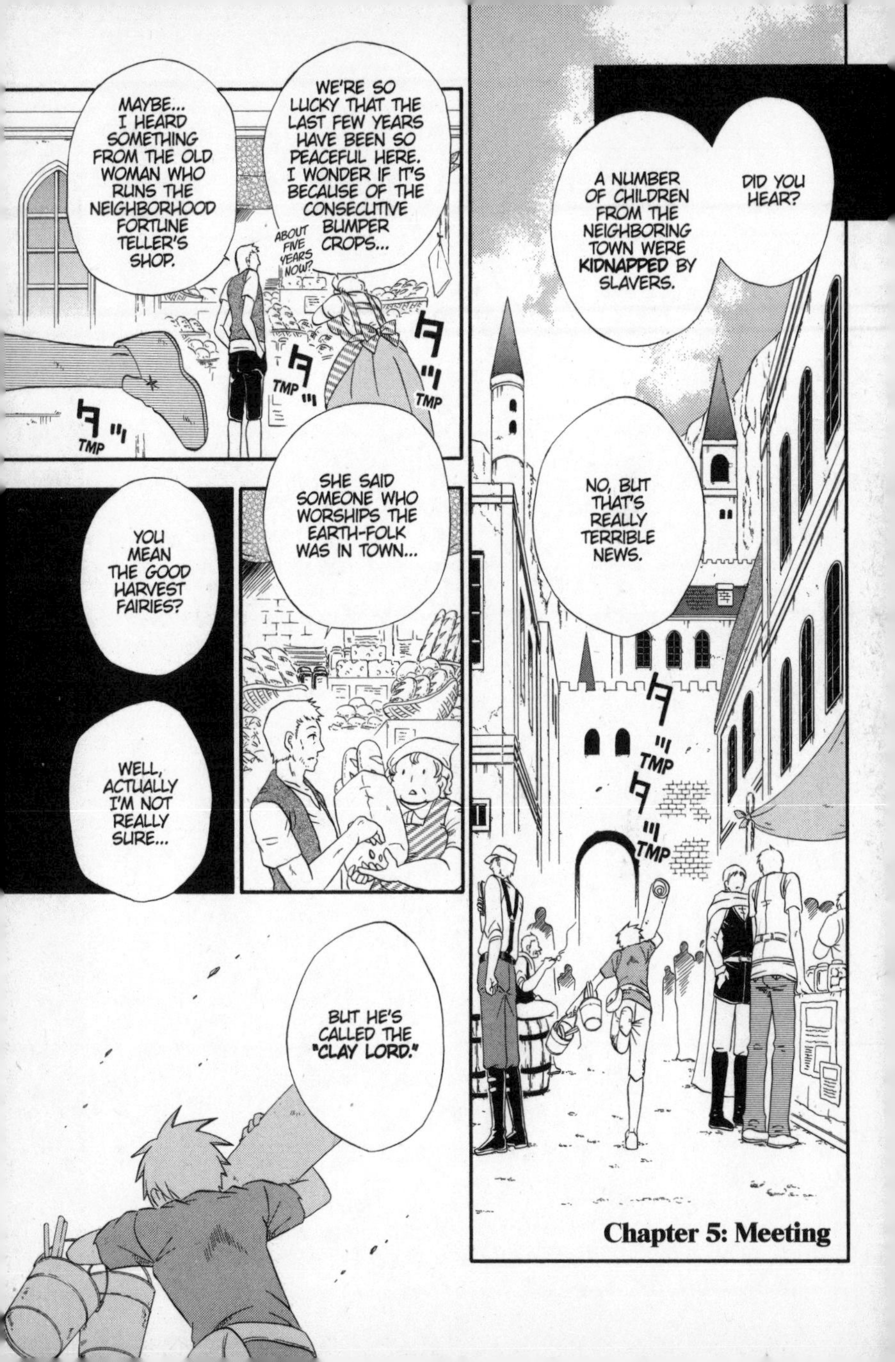
DID YOU HEAR?
A NUMBER OF CHILDREN FROM THE NEIGHBORING TOWN WERE KIDNAPPED BY SLAVERS.
NO, BUT THAT'S REALLY TERRIBLE NEWS.
TMP
TMP
Chapter 5: Meeting
WE'RE SO LUCKY THAT THE LAST FEW YEARS HAVE BEEN SO PEACEFUL HERE. I WONDER IF IT'S BECAUSE OF THE CONSECUTIVE BUMPER CROPS...
ABOUT FIVE YEARS NOW?
MAYBE... I HEARD SOMETHING FROM THE OLD WOMAN WHO RUNS THE NEIGHBORHOOD FORTUNE TELLER'S SHOP.
TMP
TMP
TMP
SHE SAID SOMEONE WHO WORSHIPS THE EARTH-FOLK WAS IN TOWN...
YOU MEAN THE GOOD HARVEST FAIRIES?
WELL, ACTUALLY I'M NOT REALLY SURE...
BUT HE'S CALLED THE "CLAY LORD."

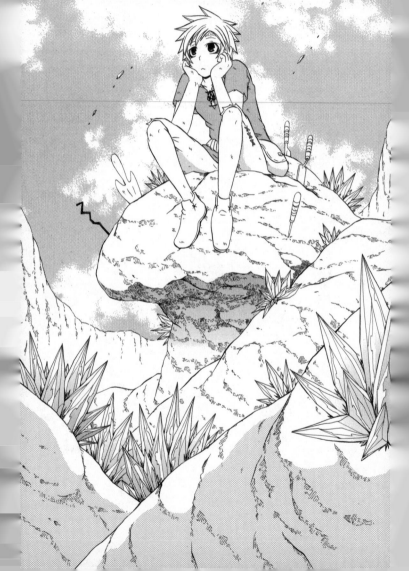

Chapter 5: Meeting

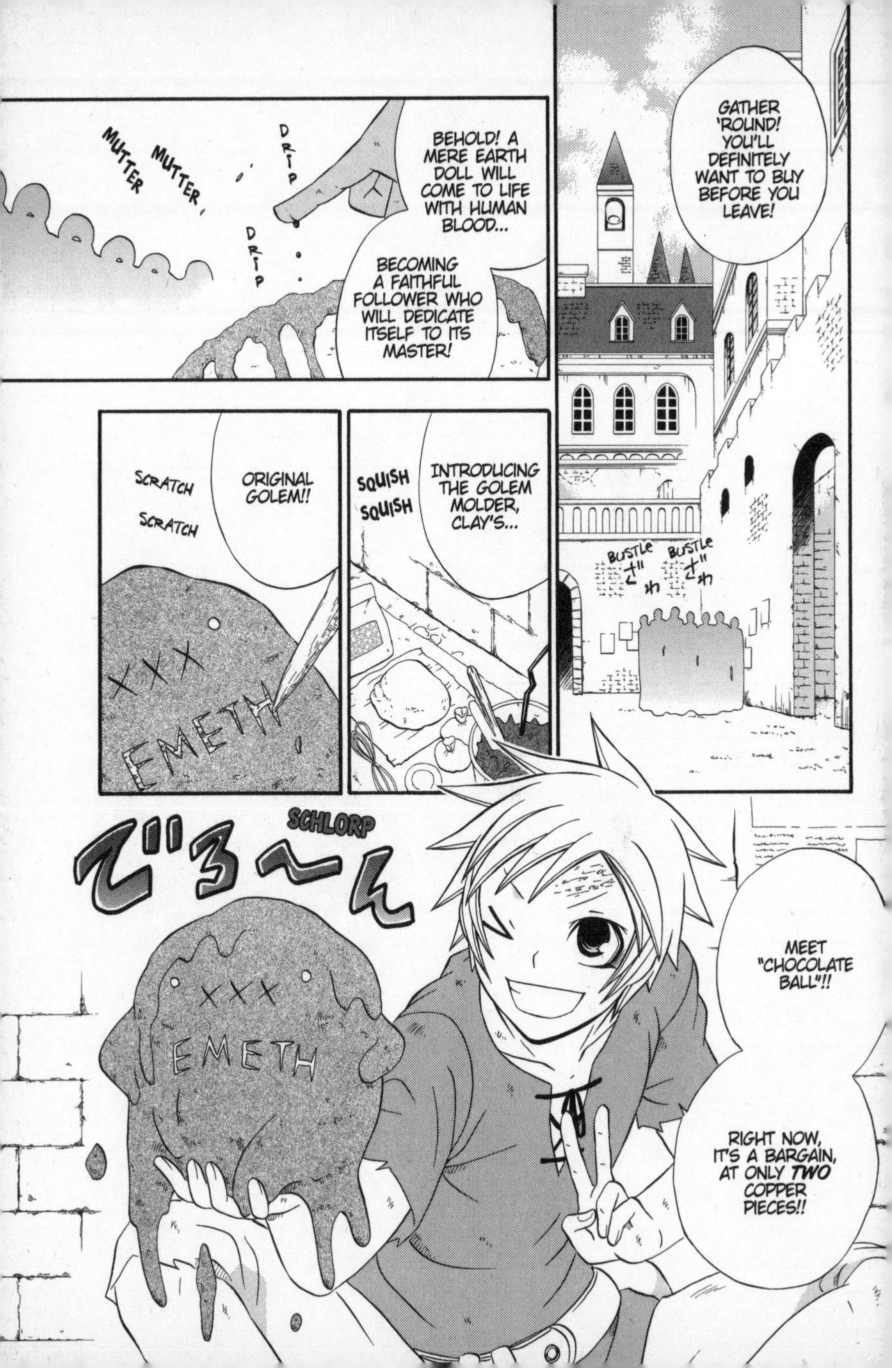
GATHER 'ROUND! YOU'LL DEFINITELY WANT TO BUY BEFORE YOU LEAVE!
BUSTLE ざわ
BUSTLE ざわ
BEHOLD! A MERE EARTH DOLL WILL COME TO LIFE WITH HUMAN BLOOD...
BECOMING A FAITHFUL FOLLOWER WHO WILL DEDICATE ITSELF TO ITS MASTER!
DRIP
DRIP
MUTTER,
MUTTER
INTRODUCING THE GOLEM MOLDER, CLAY'S...
SQUISH
SQUISH
ORIGINAL GOLEM!!
SCRATCH
SCRATCH
EMETH
MEET "CHOCOLATE BALL"!!
RIGHT NOW, IT'S A BARGAIN, AT ONLY TWO COPPER PIECES!!
SCHLORP
でろ〜ん
EMETH

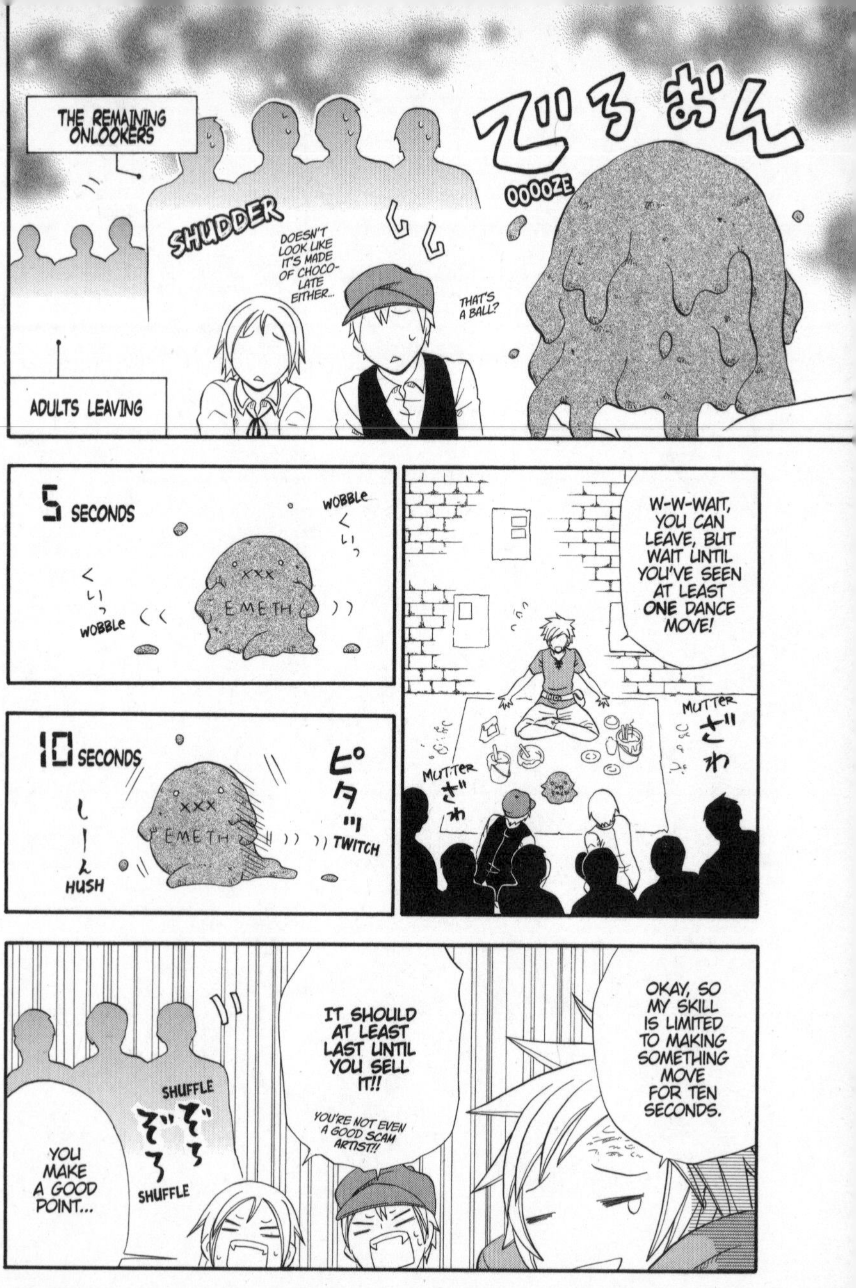
でろおん
OOOOZE
THAT'S A BALL?
SHUDDER
しし
DOESN'T LOOK LIKE IT'S MADE OF CHOCO-LATE EITHER...
THE REMAINING ONLOOKERS
ADULTS LEAVING
W-W-WAIT, YOU CAN LEAVE, BUT WAIT UNTIL YOU'VE SEEN AT LEAST ONE DANCE MOVE!
MUTTER ざわ
MUTTER ざわ
5 SECONDS
WOBBLE くいっ
くいっ WOBBLE
EMETH
10 SECONDS
ピタッ TWITCH
しーん HUSH
EMETH
OKAY, SO MY SKILL IS LIMITED TO MAKING SOMETHING MOVE FOR TEN SECONDS.
IT SHOULD AT LEAST LAST UNTIL YOU SELL IT!!
YOU'RE NOT EVEN A GOOD SCAM ARTIST!!
SHUFFLE ぞろぞろ SHUFFLE
YOU MAKE A GOOD POINT...

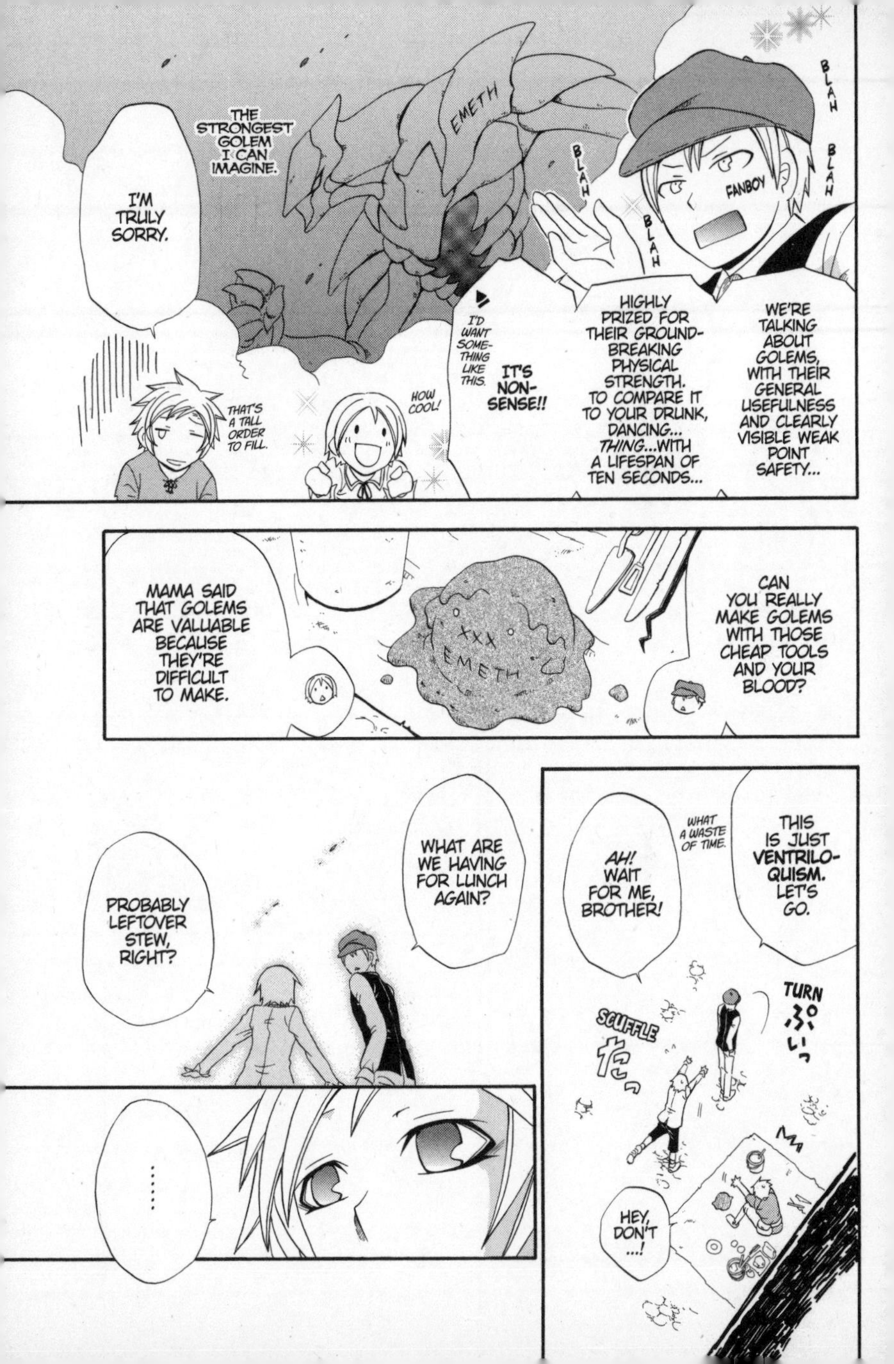
BLAH BLAH
FANBOY
BLAH BLAH
WE'RE TALKING ABOUT GOLEMS, WITH THEIR GENERAL USEFULNESS AND CLEARLY VISIBLE WEAK POINT SAFETY...
HIGHLY PRIZED FOR THEIR GROUND-BREAKING PHYSICAL STRENGTH. TO COMPARE IT TO YOUR DRUNK, DANCING... THING...WITH A LIFESPAN OF TEN SECONDS...
IT'S NON-SENSE!!
EMETH
I'D WANT SOME-THING LIKE THIS.
HOW COOL!
THAT'S A TALL ORDER TO FILL.
THE STRONGEST GOLEM I CAN IMAGINE.
I'M TRULY SORRY.
CAN YOU REALLY MAKE GOLEMS WITH THOSE CHEAP TOOLS AND YOUR BLOOD?
XXX EMETH
MAMA SAID THAT GOLEMS ARE VALUABLE BECAUSE THEY'RE DIFFICULT TO MAKE.
THIS IS JUST VENTRILO-QUISM. LET'S GO.
WHAT A WASTE OF TIME.
AH! WAIT FOR ME, BROTHER!
TURN
ぷいっ
SCUFFLE
たっ
HEY, DON'T ...!
WHAT ARE WE HAVING FOR LUNCH AGAIN?
PROBABLY LEFTOVER STEW, RIGHT?
......

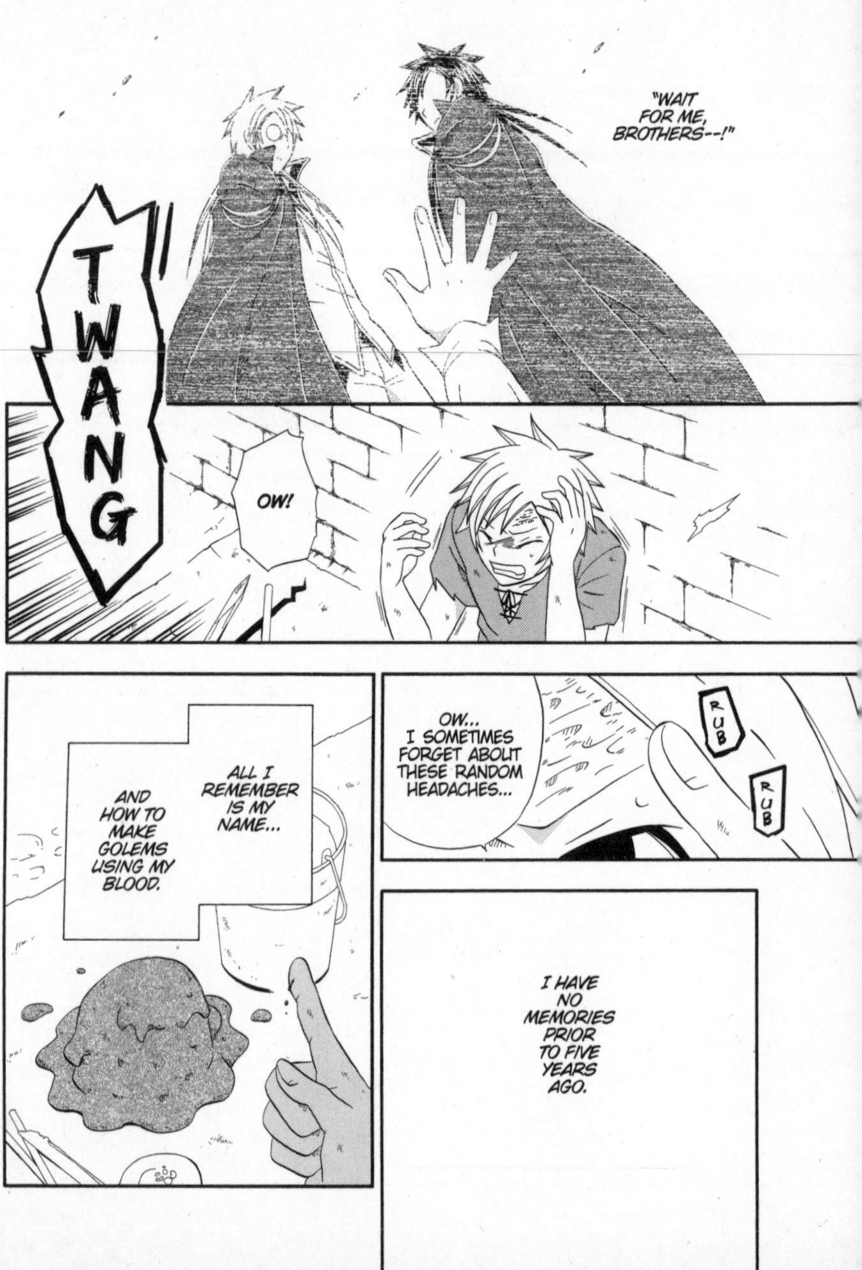
"WAIT FOR ME, BROTHERS--!"
TWANG
OW!
OW... I SOMETIMES FORGET ABOUT THESE RANDOM HEADACHES...
RUB
RUB
I HAVE NO MEMORIES PRIOR TO FIVE YEARS AGO.
ALL I REMEMBER IS MY NAME...
AND HOW TO MAKE GOLEMS USING MY BLOOD.

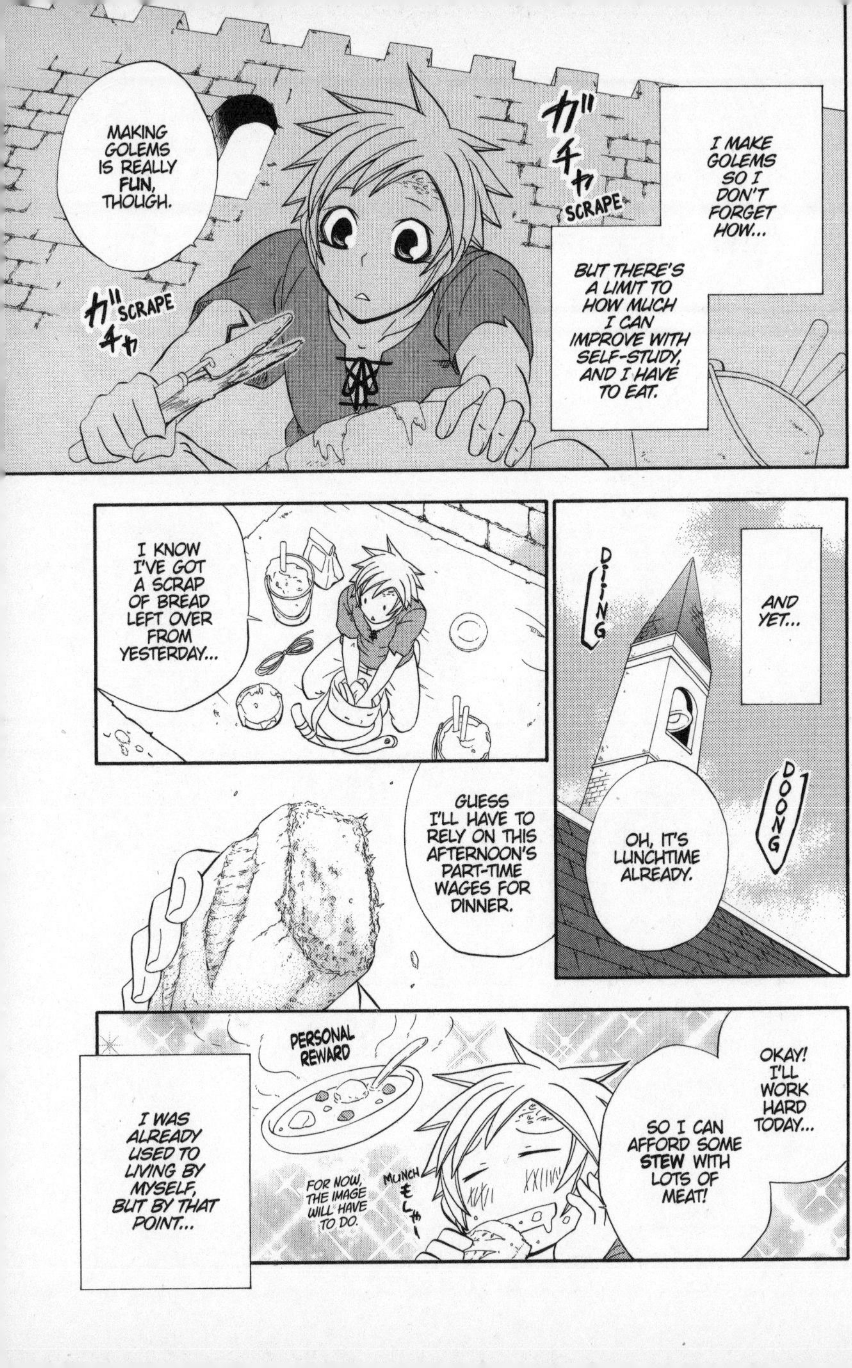
I MAKE GOLEMS SO I DON'T FORGET HOW...
BUT THERE'S A LIMIT TO HOW MUCH I CAN IMPROVE WITH SELF-STUDY, AND I HAVE TO EAT.
ガチャ SCRAPE
MAKING GOLEMS IS REALLY FUN, THOUGH.
ガチャ SCRAPE
AND YET...
DIIING
DOOONG
OH, IT'S LUNCHTIME ALREADY.
I KNOW I'VE GOT A SCRAP OF BREAD LEFT OVER FROM YESTERDAY...
GUESS I'LL HAVE TO RELY ON THIS AFTERNOON'S PART-TIME WAGES FOR DINNER.
OKAY! I'LL WORK HARD TODAY...
SO I CAN AFFORD SOME STEW WITH LOTS OF MEAT!
PERSONAL REWARD
MUNCH もしゃ
FOR NOW, THE IMAGE WILL HAVE TO DO.
I WAS ALREADY USED TO LIVING BY MYSELF, BUT BY THAT POINT...

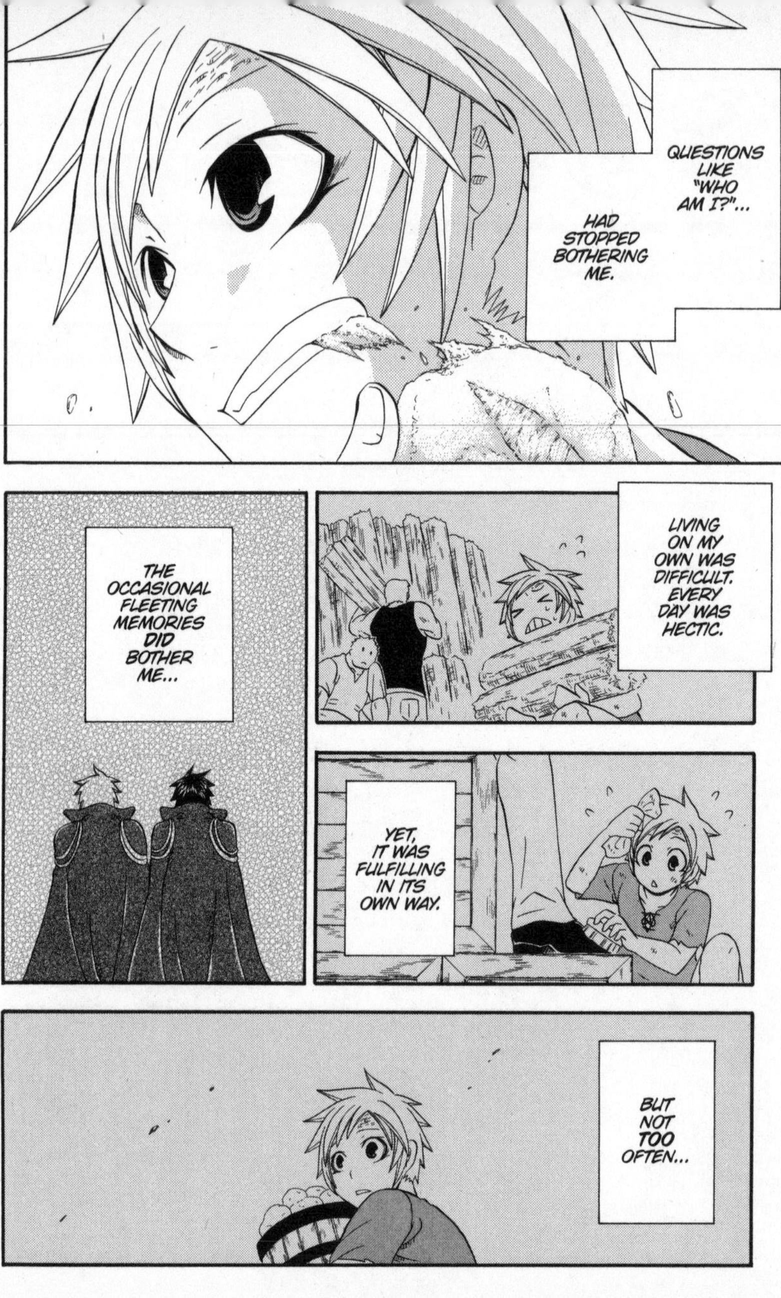
QUESTIONS LIKE "WHO AM I?"...
HAD STOPPED BOTHERING ME.
LIVING ON MY OWN WAS DIFFICULT. EVERY DAY WAS HECTIC.
YET, IT WAS FULFILLING IN ITS OWN WAY.
THE OCCASIONAL FLEETING MEMORIES DID BOTHER ME...
BUT NOT TOO OFTEN...

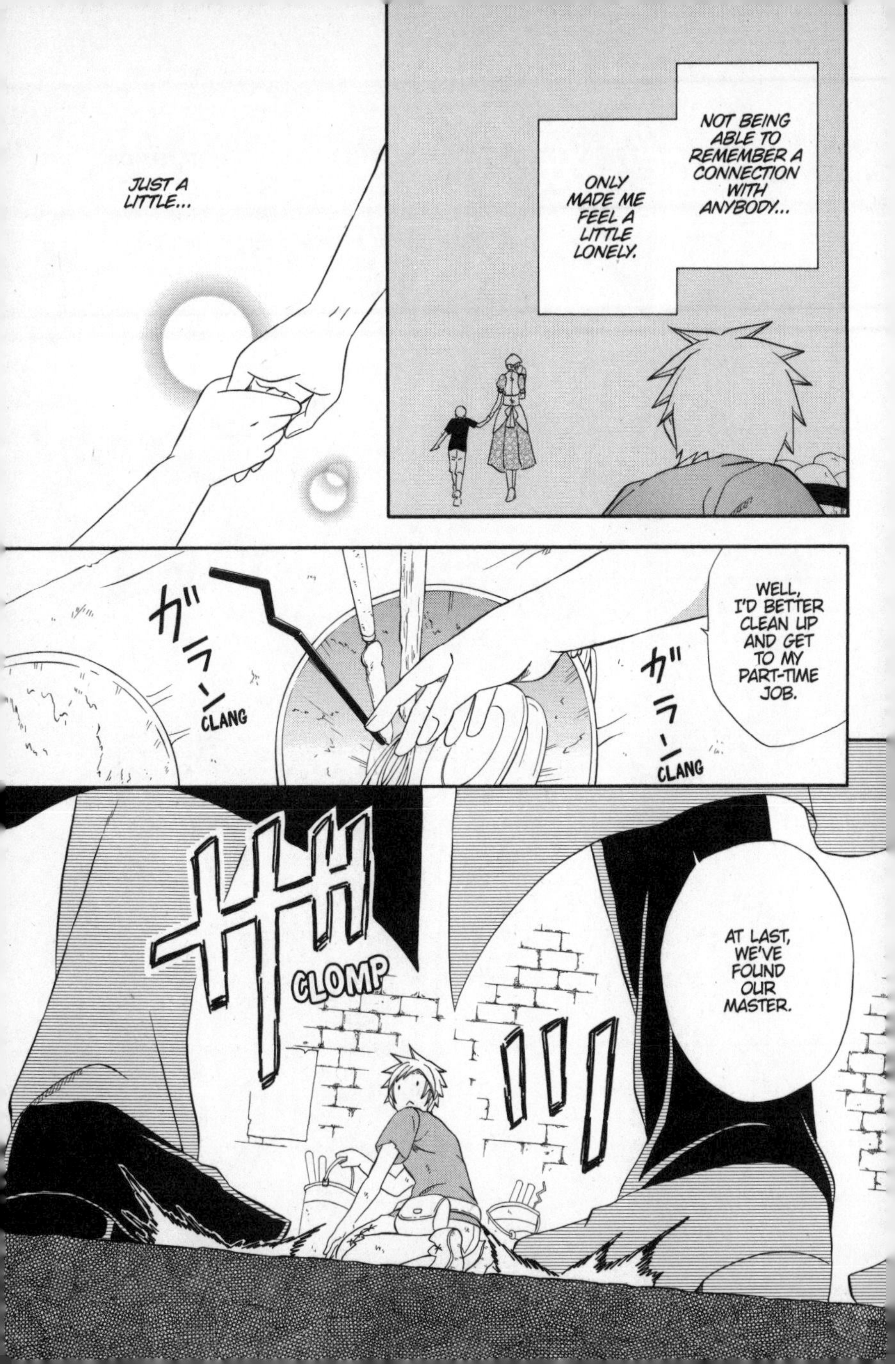
NOT BEING ABLE TO REMEMBER A CONNECTION WITH ANYBODY...
ONLY MADE ME FEEL A LITTLE LONELY.
JUST A LITTLE...
WELL, I'D BETTER CLEAN UP AND GET TO MY PART-TIME JOB.
ガラーン
CLANG
ガラーン
CLANG
AT LAST, WE'VE FOUND OUR MASTER.
CLOMP

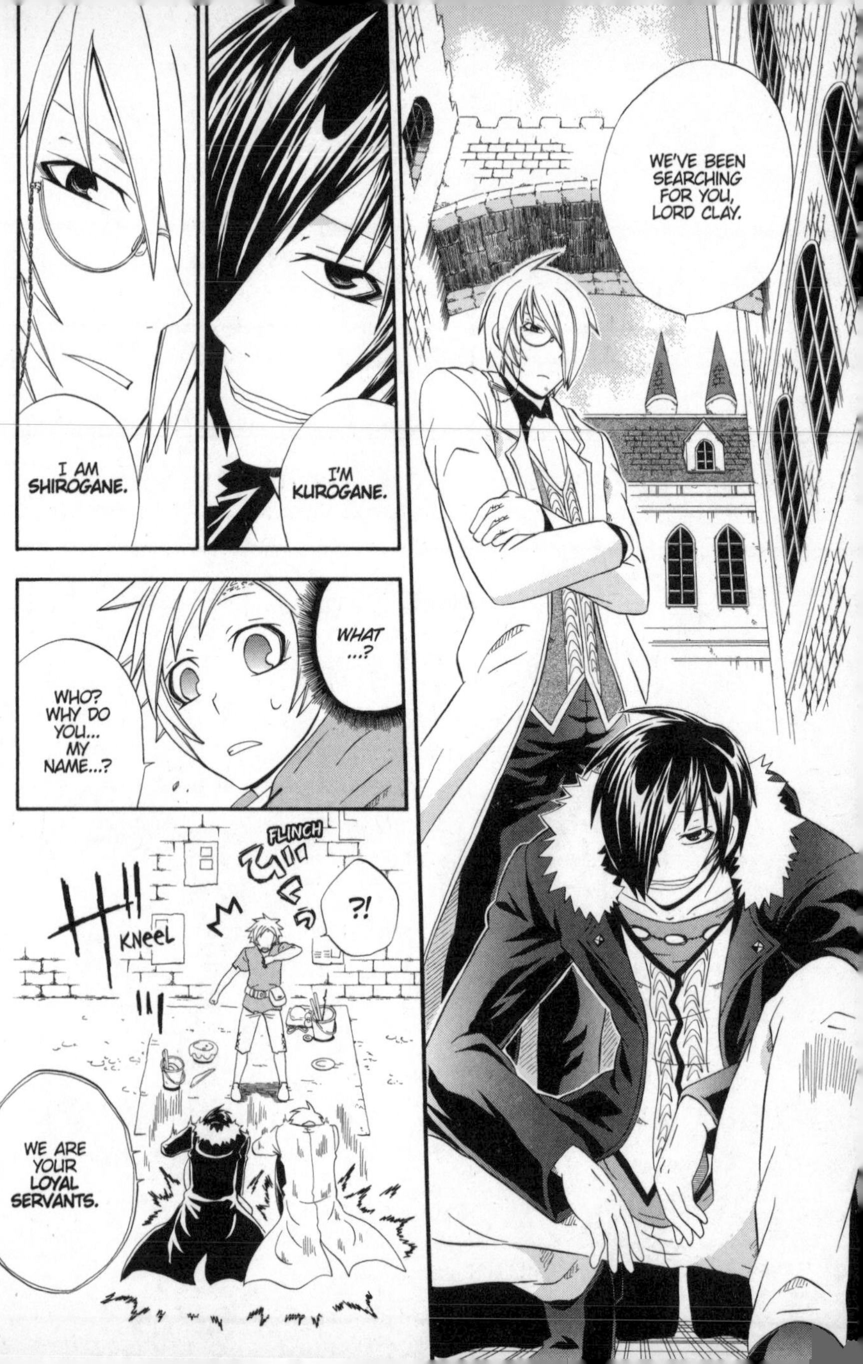
WE'VE BEEN SEARCHING FOR YOU, LORD CLAY.
I'M KUROGANE.
I AM SHIROGANE.
WHAT ...?
WHO? WHY DO YOU... MY NAME...?
FLINCH
?!
Kneel
WE ARE YOUR LOYAL SERVANTS.

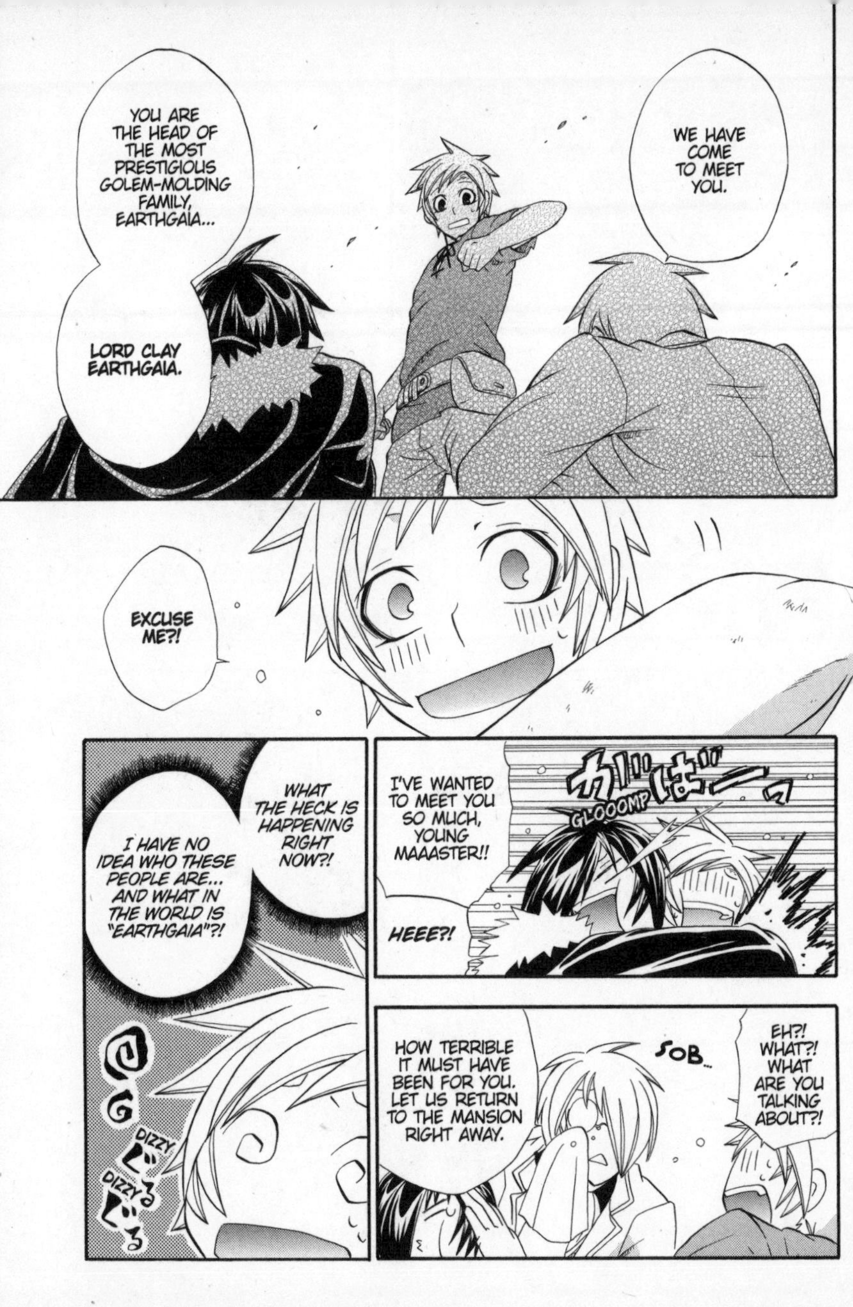
WE HAVE COME TO MEET YOU.
YOU ARE THE HEAD OF THE MOST PRESTIGIOUS GOLEM-MOLDING FAMILY, EARTHGAIA...
LORD CLAY EARTHGAIA.
EXCUSE ME?!
I'VE WANTED TO MEET YOU SO MUCH, YOUNG MAAASTER!!
GLOOOMP
HEEE?!
EH?! WHAT?! WHAT ARE YOU TALKING ABOUT?!
SOB...
HOW TERRIBLE IT MUST HAVE BEEN FOR YOU. LET US RETURN TO THE MANSION RIGHT AWAY.
WHAT THE HECK IS HAPPENING RIGHT NOW?!
I HAVE NO IDEA WHO THESE PEOPLE ARE... AND WHAT IN THE WORLD IS "EARTHGAIA"?!
DIZZY
DIZZY

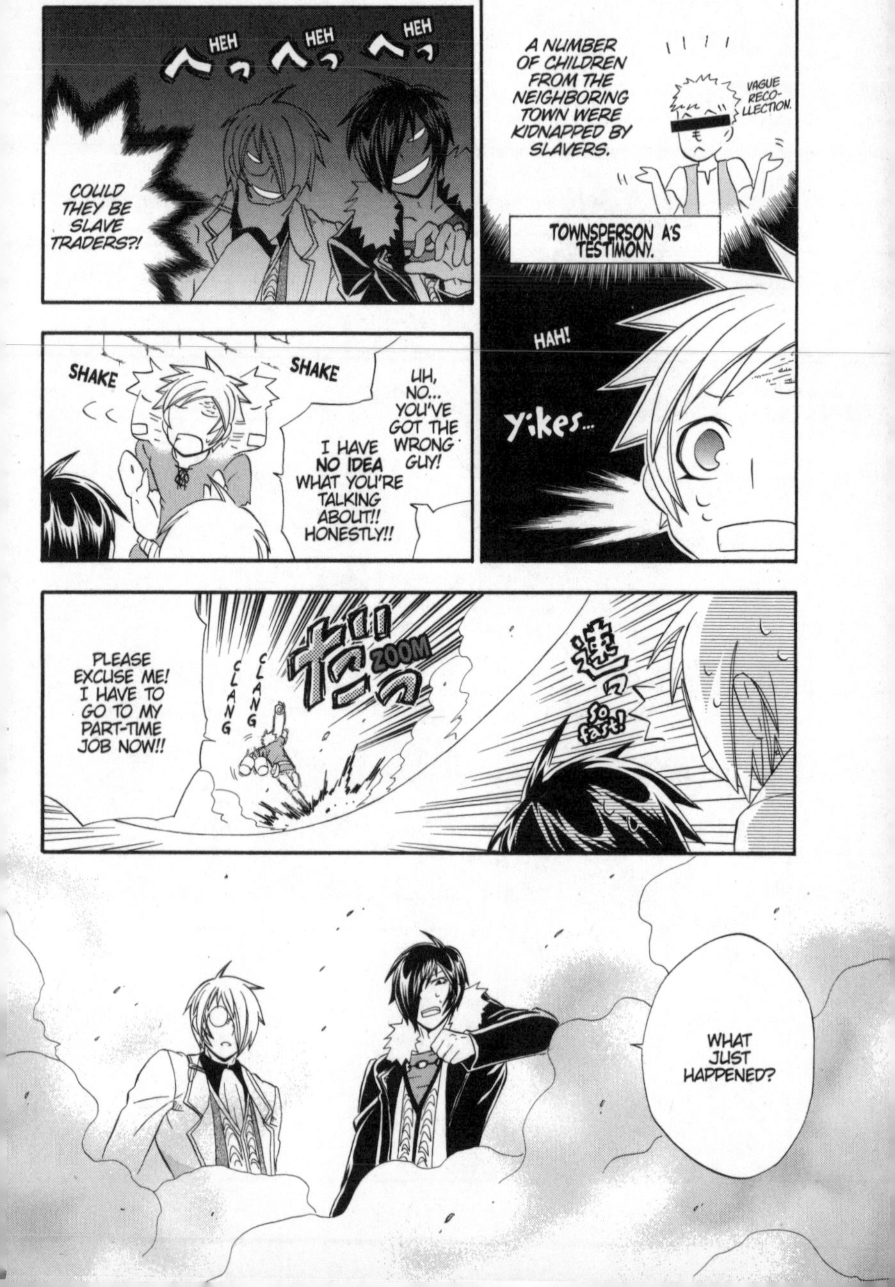
A NUMBER OF CHILDREN FROM THE NEIGHBORING TOWN WERE KIDNAPPED BY SLAVERS.
VAGUE RECOLLECTION.
TOWNSPERSON A'S TESTIMONY.
HAH!
yikes...
HEH HEH HEH
COULD THEY BE SLAVE TRADERS?!
SHAKE SHAKE
UH, NO... YOU'VE GOT THE WRONG GUY!
I HAVE NO IDEA WHAT YOU'RE TALKING ABOUT!! HONESTLY!!
SO FAST!
ZOOM
CLANG CLANG
PLEASE EXCUSE ME! I HAVE TO GO TO MY PART-TIME JOB NOW!!
WHAT JUST HAPPENED?

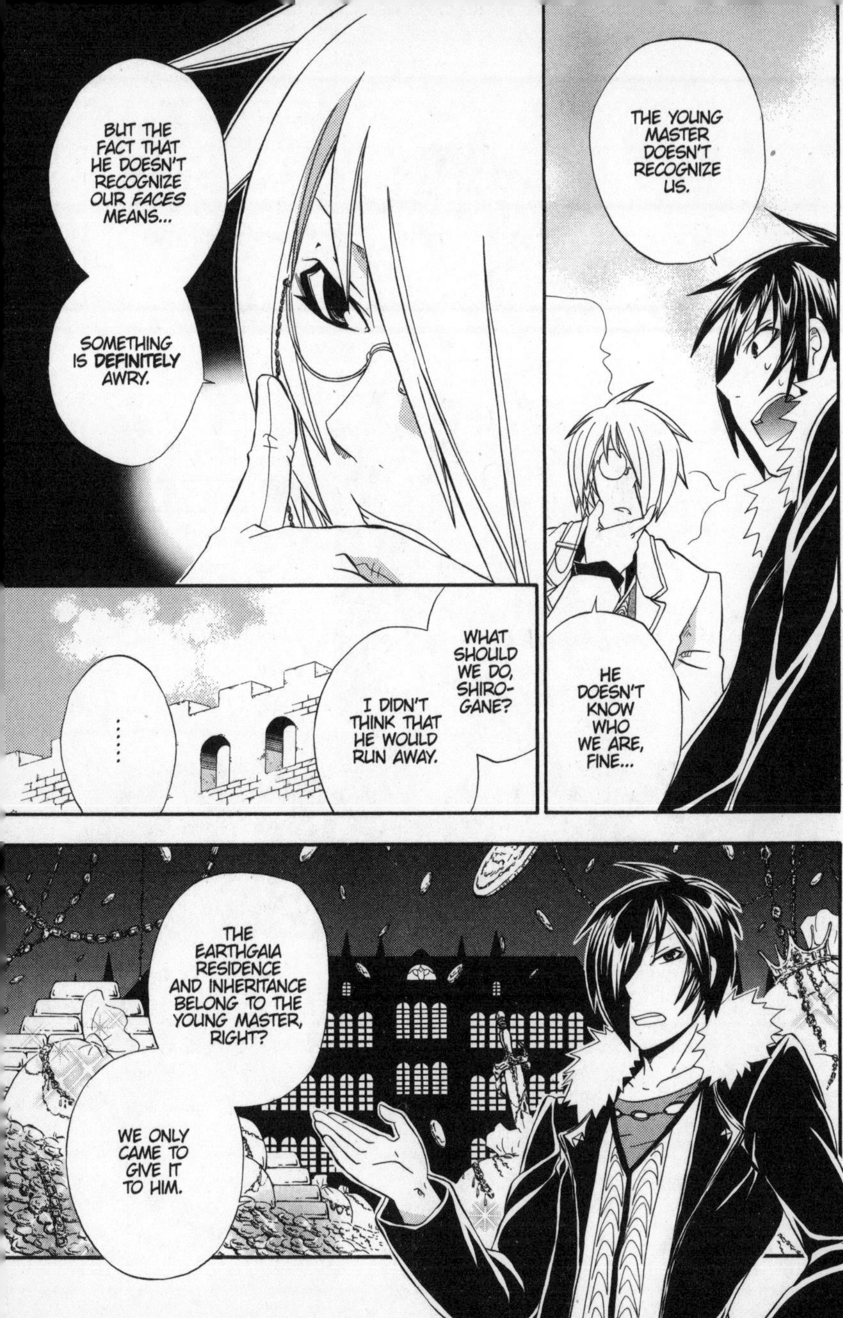
THE YOUNG MASTER DOESN'T RECOGNIZE US.
HE DOESN'T KNOW WHO WE ARE, FINE...
BUT THE FACT THAT HE DOESN'T RECOGNIZE OUR *FACES* MEANS...
SOMETHING IS **DEFINITELY** AWRY.
WHAT SHOULD WE DO, SHIRO-GANE?
I DIDN'T THINK THAT HE WOULD RUN AWAY.
......
THE EARTHGAIA RESIDENCE AND INHERITANCE BELONG TO THE YOUNG MASTER, RIGHT?
WE ONLY CAME TO GIVE IT TO HIM.

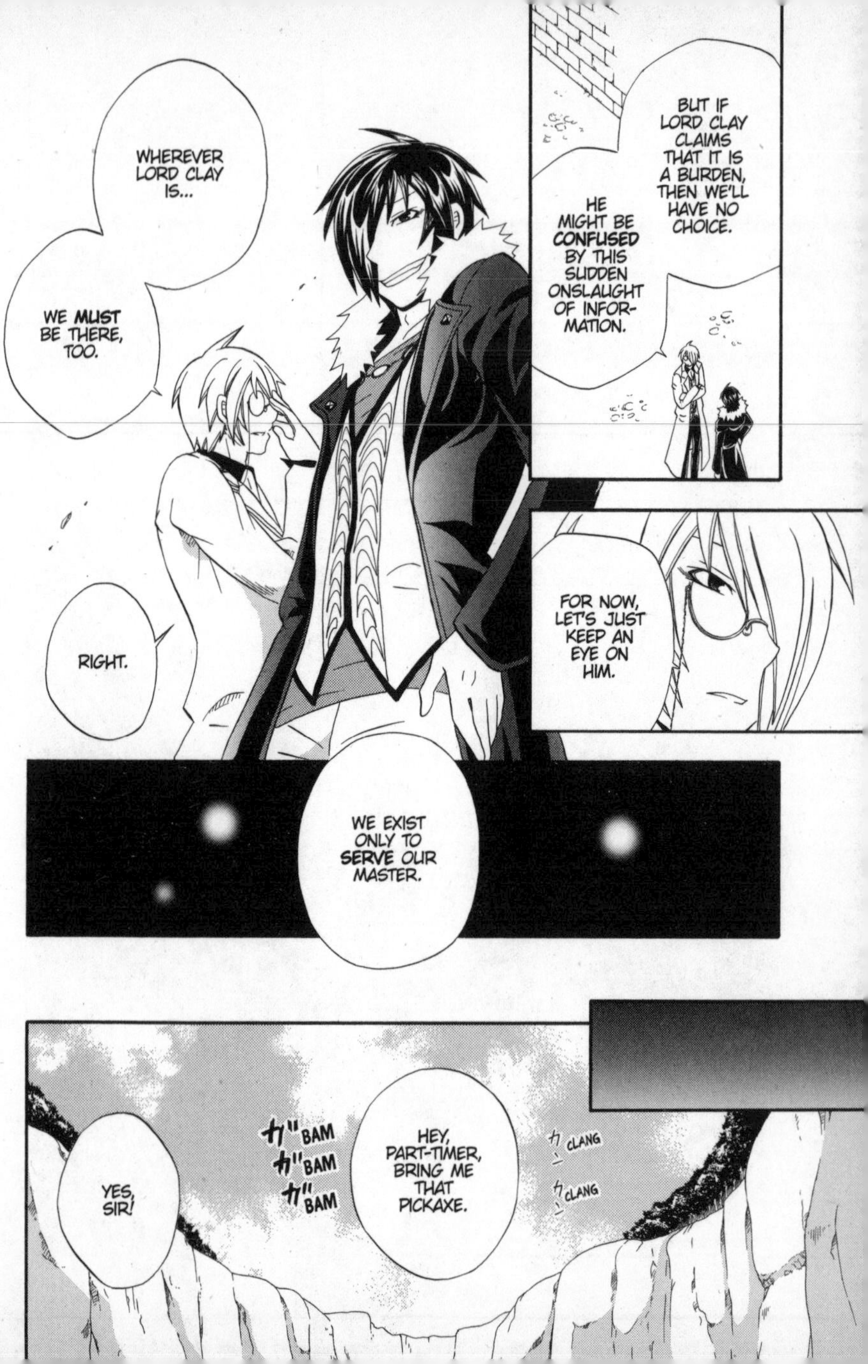
BUT IF LORD CLAY CLAIMS THAT IT IS A BURDEN, THEN WE'LL HAVE NO CHOICE.
HE MIGHT BE CONFUSED BY THIS SUDDEN ONSLAUGHT OF INFORMATION.
FOR NOW, LET'S JUST KEEP AN EYE ON HIM.
WHEREVER LORD CLAY IS...
WE MUST BE THERE, TOO.
RIGHT.
WE EXIST ONLY TO SERVE OUR MASTER.
CLANG
CLANG
HEY, PART-TIMER, BRING ME THAT PICKAXE.
BAM
BAM
BAM
YES, SIR!

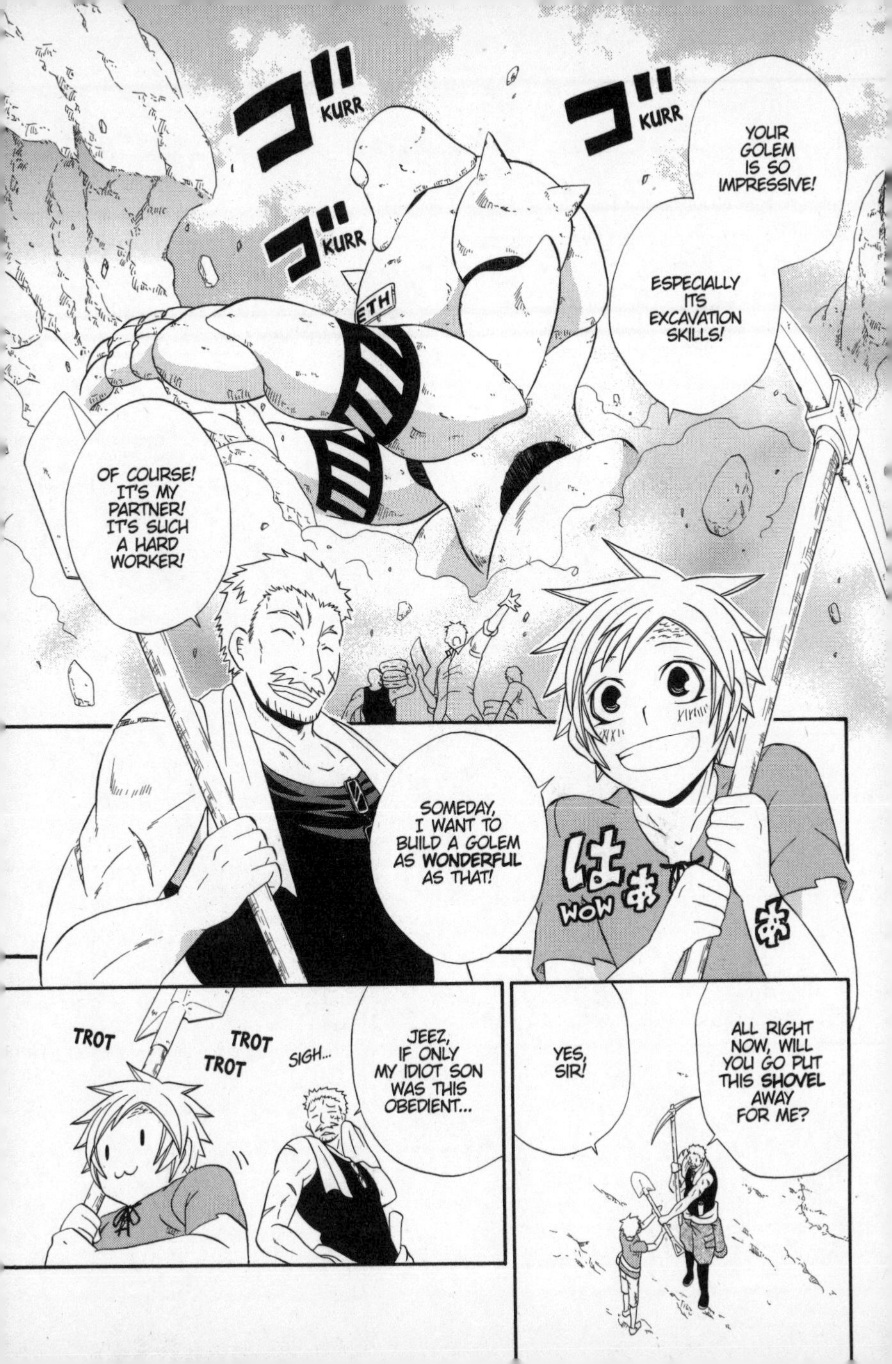
ゴ KURR
ゴ KURR
ゴ KURR
ETH
YOUR GOLEM IS SO IMPRESSIVE!
ESPECIALLY ITS EXCAVATION SKILLS!
OF COURSE! IT'S MY PARTNER! IT'S SUCH A HARD WORKER!
はああ WOW
SOMEDAY, I WANT TO BUILD A GOLEM AS WONDERFUL AS THAT!
ALL RIGHT NOW, WILL YOU GO PUT THIS SHOVEL AWAY FOR ME?
YES, SIR!
JEEZ, IF ONLY MY IDIOT SON WAS THIS OBEDIENT...
SIGH...
TROT
TROT
TROT

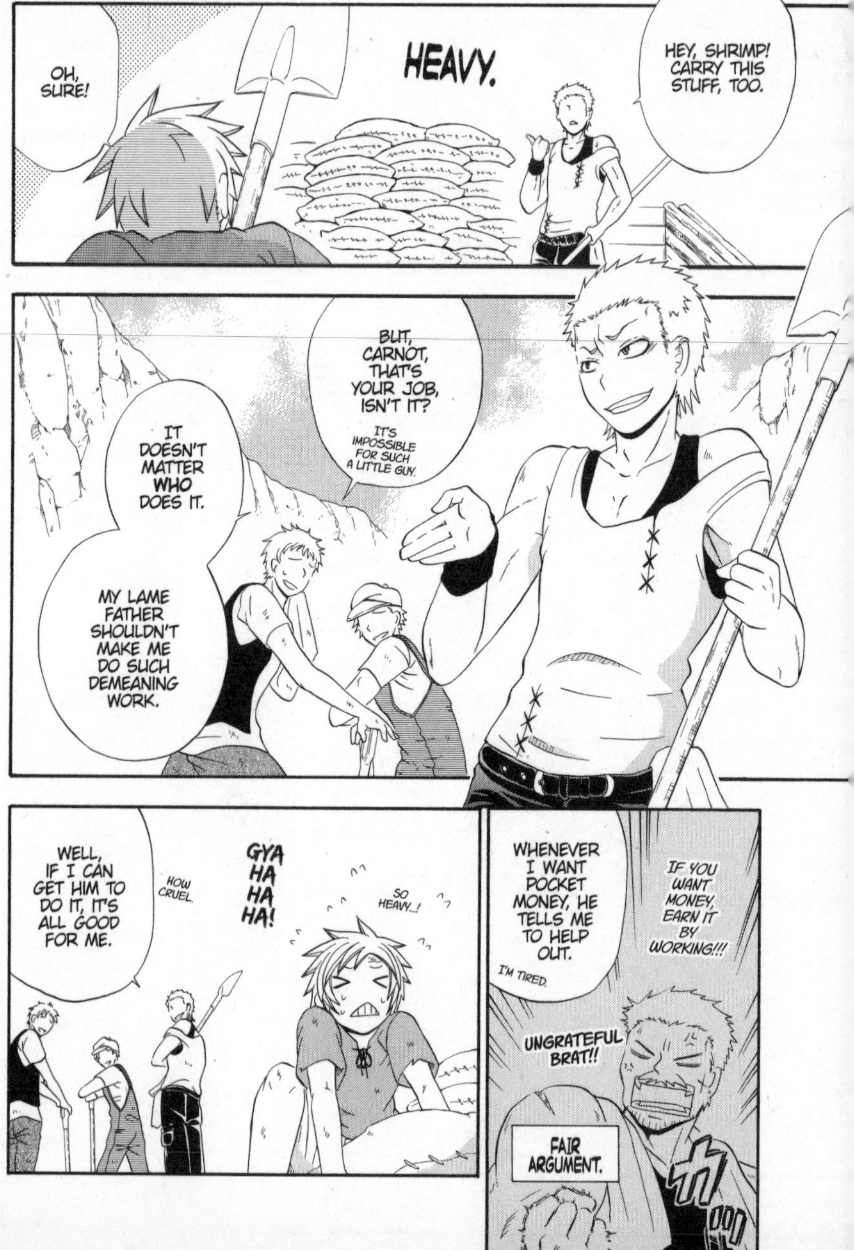
HEY, SHRIMP! CARRY THIS STUFF, TOO.
HEAVY.
OH, SURE!
BUT, CARNOT, THAT'S YOUR JOB, ISN'T IT?
IT'S IMPOSSIBLE FOR SUCH A LITTLE GUY.
IT DOESN'T MATTER WHO DOES IT.
MY LAME FATHER SHOULDN'T MAKE ME DO SUCH DEMEANING WORK.
WHENEVER I WANT POCKET MONEY, HE TELLS ME TO HELP OUT.
IF YOU WANT MONEY, EARN IT BY WORKING!!!
I'M TIRED.
UNGRATEFUL BRAT!!
FAIR ARGUMENT.
SO HEAVY...!
GYA HA HA HA!
HOW CRUEL.
WELL, IF I CAN GET HIM TO DO IT, IT'S ALL GOOD FOR ME.

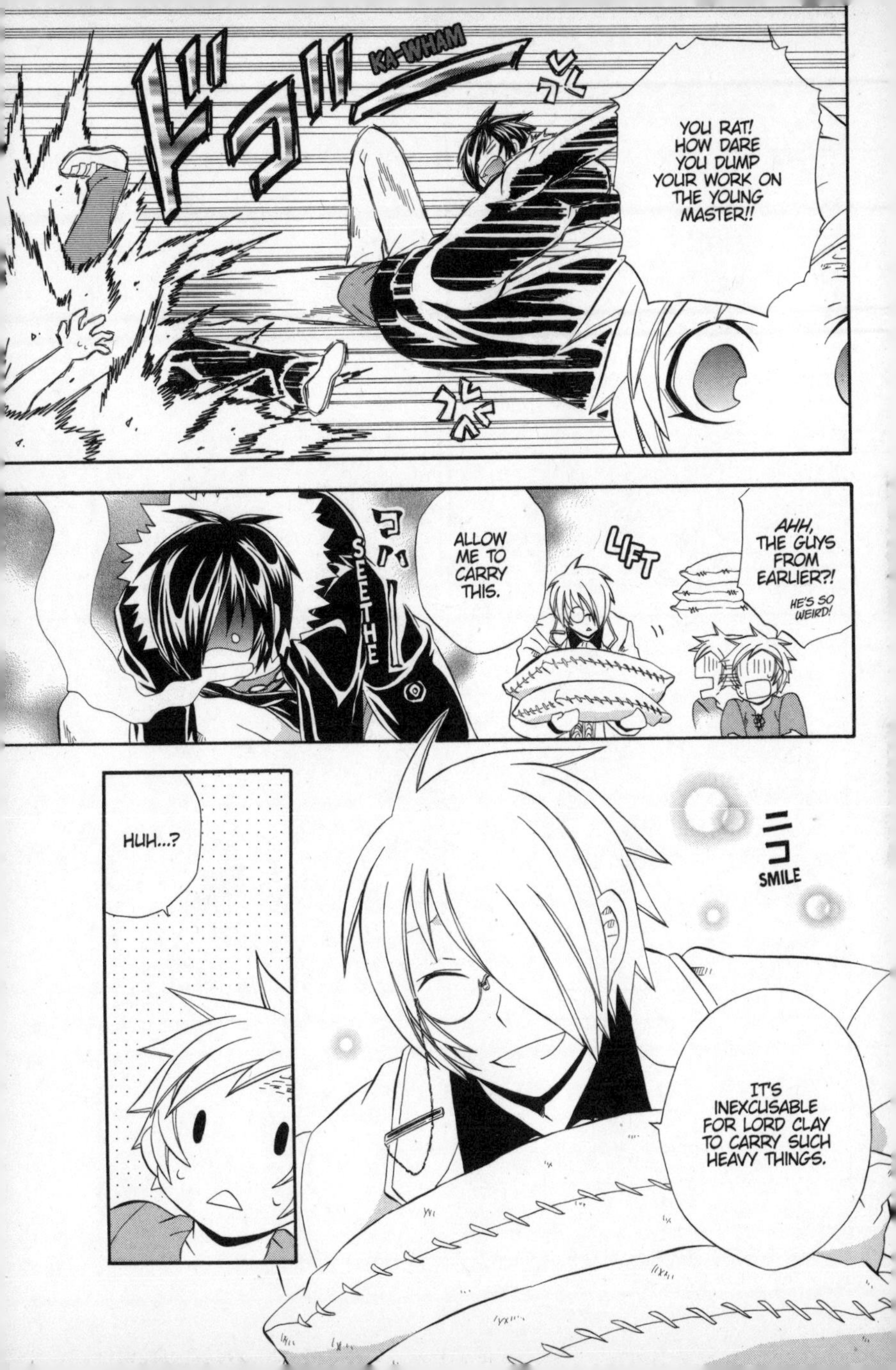
YOU RAT! HOW DARE YOU DUMP YOUR WORK ON THE YOUNG MASTER!!
KA-WHAM
AHH, THE GUYS FROM EARLIER?!
HE'S SO WEIRD!
LIFT
ALLOW ME TO CARRY THIS.
SEETHE
SMILE
IT'S INEXCUSABLE FOR LORD CLAY TO CARRY SUCH HEAVY THINGS.
HUH...?

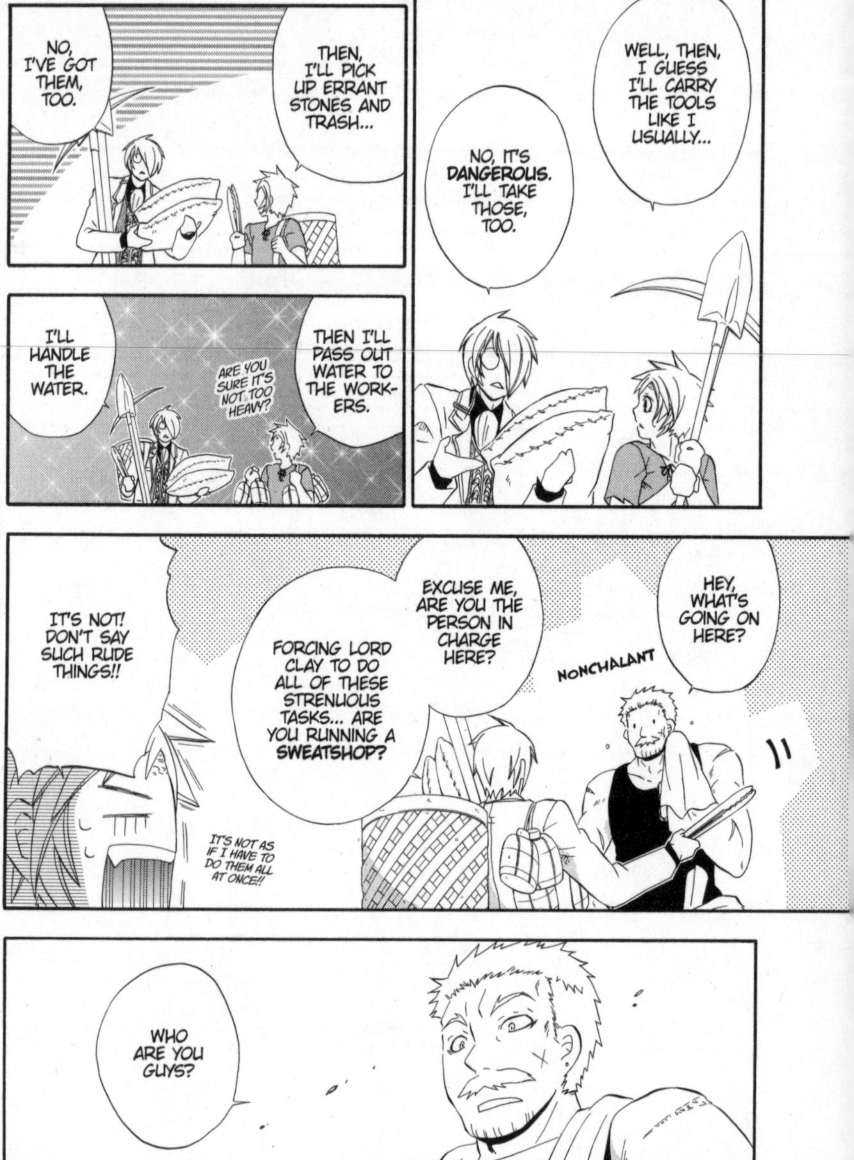
WELL, THEN, I GUESS I'LL CARRY THE TOOLS LIKE I USUALLY...
NO, IT'S DANGEROUS. I'LL TAKE THOSE, TOO.
THEN, I'LL PICK UP ERRANT STONES AND TRASH...
NO, I'VE GOT THEM, TOO.
THEN I'LL PASS OUT WATER TO THE WORK-ERS.
ARE YOU SURE IT'S NOT TOO HEAVY?
I'LL HANDLE THE WATER.
HEY, WHAT'S GOING ON HERE?
NONCHALANT
EXCUSE ME, ARE YOU THE PERSON IN CHARGE HERE?
FORCING LORD CLAY TO DO ALL OF THESE STRENUOUS TASKS... ARE YOU RUNNING A SWEATSHOP?
IT'S NOT! DON'T SAY SUCH RUDE THINGS!!
IT'S NOT AS IF I HAVE TO DO THEM ALL AT ONCE!!
WHO ARE YOU GUYS?

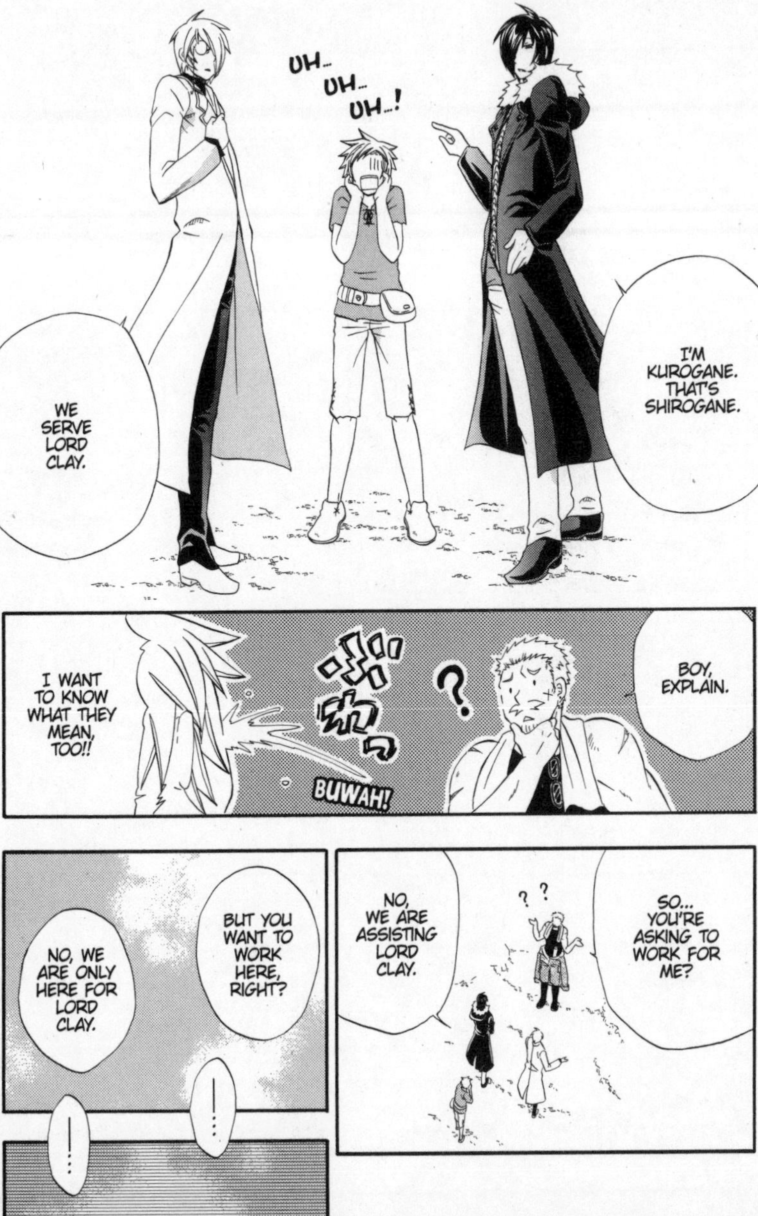
UH...
UH...
UH...!
I'M KUROGANE. THAT'S SHIROGANE.
WE SERVE LORD CLAY.
BOY, EXPLAIN.
?
I WANT TO KNOW WHAT THEY MEAN, TOO!!
BUWAH!
SO... YOU'RE ASKING TO WORK FOR ME?
? ?
NO, WE ARE ASSISTING LORD CLAY.
BUT YOU WANT TO WORK HERE, RIGHT?
NO, WE ARE ONLY HERE FOR LORD CLAY.
......!
......!

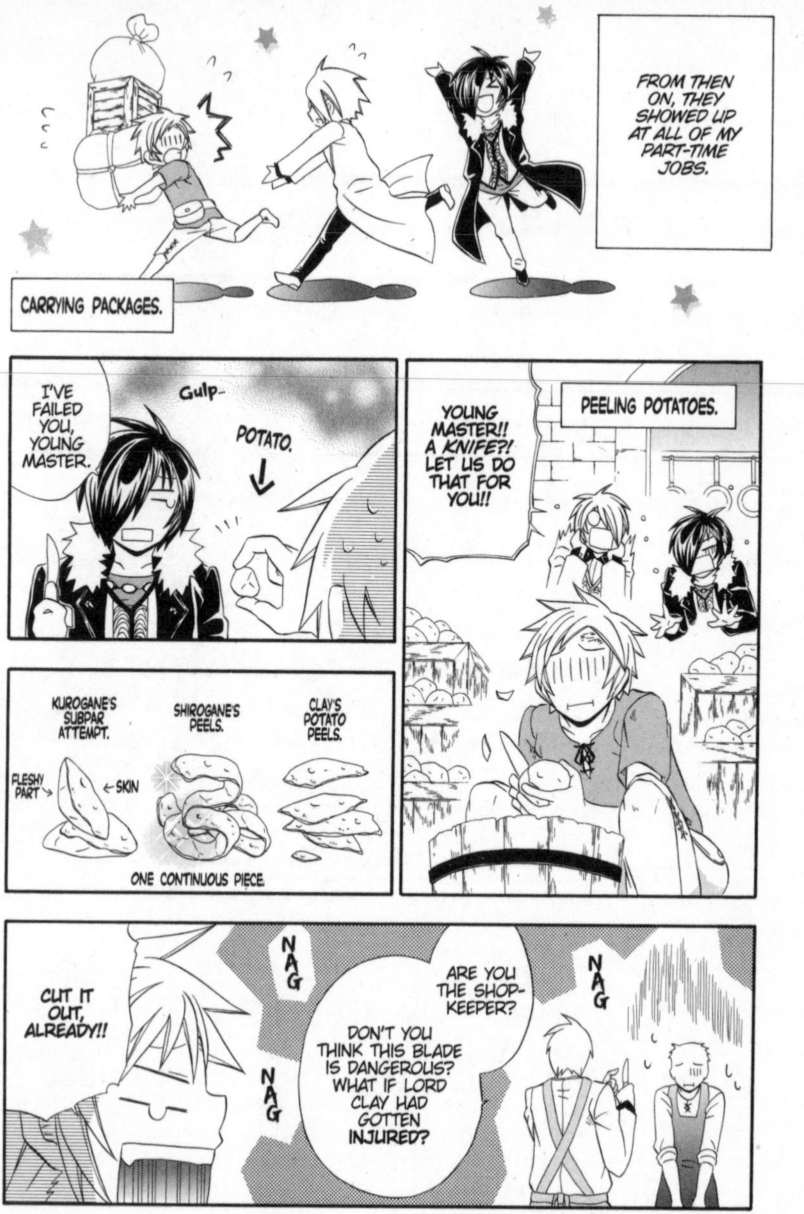
FROM THEN ON, THEY SHOWED UP AT ALL OF MY PART-TIME JOBS.
CARRYING PACKAGES.
PEELING POTATOES.
YOUNG MASTER!! A KNIFE?! LET US DO THAT FOR YOU!!
I'VE FAILED YOU, YOUNG MASTER.
Gulp-
POTATO.
KUROGANE'S SUBPAR ATTEMPT.
FLESHY PART
SKIN
SHIROGANE'S PEELS.
CLAY'S POTATO PEELS.
ONE CONTINUOUS PIECE.
NAG
ARE YOU THE SHOP-KEEPER?
DON'T YOU THINK THIS BLADE IS DANGEROUS? WHAT IF LORD CLAY HAD GOTTEN INJURED?
NAG
NAG
CUT IT OUT, ALREADY!!

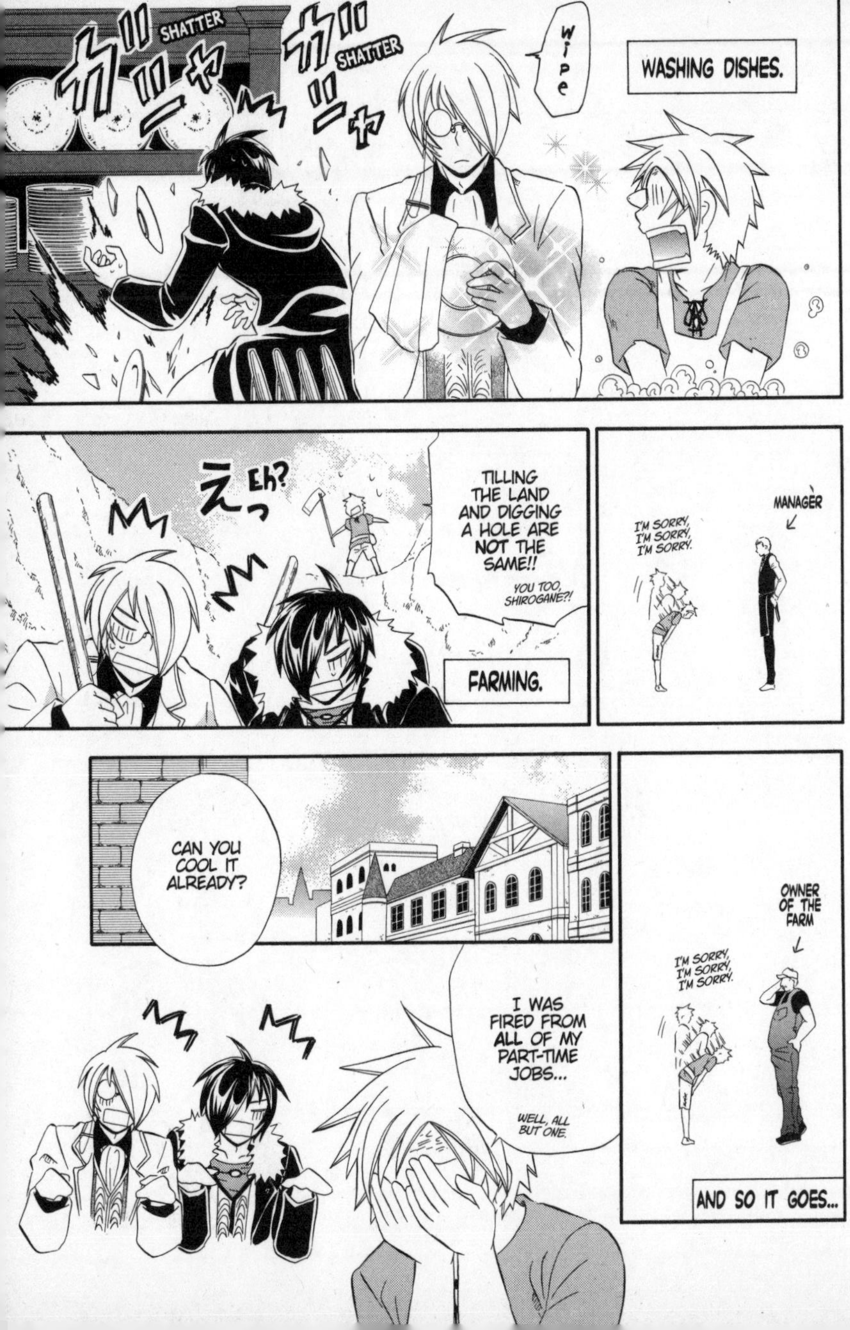
WASHING DISHES.
wipe
SHATTER
SHATTER
MANAGER
I'M SORRY, I'M SORRY, I'M SORRY.
TILLING THE LAND AND DIGGING A HOLE ARE NOT THE SAME!!
YOU TOO, SHIROGANE?!
Eh?
FARMING.
OWNER OF THE FARM
I'M SORRY, I'M SORRY, I'M SORRY.
AND SO IT GOES...
CAN YOU COOL IT ALREADY?
I WAS FIRED FROM ALL OF MY PART-TIME JOBS...
WELL, ALL BUT ONE.

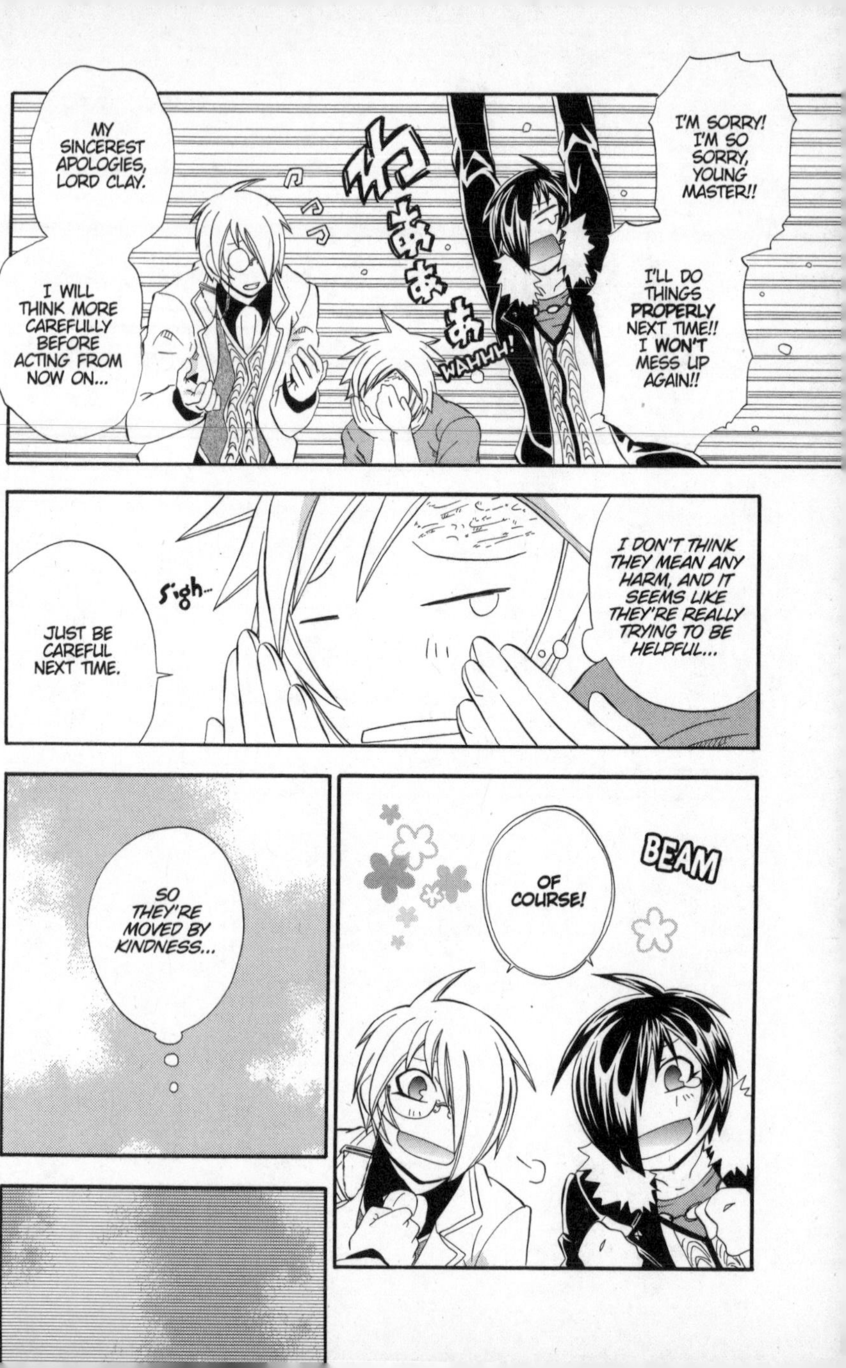
I'M SORRY! I'M SO SORRY, YOUNG MASTER!!
I'LL DO THINGS PROPERLY NEXT TIME!! I WON'T MESS UP AGAIN!!
わあああ
WAHHH!
MY SINCEREST APOLOGIES, LORD CLAY.
I WILL THINK MORE CAREFULLY BEFORE ACTING FROM NOW ON...
I DON'T THINK THEY MEAN ANY HARM, AND IT SEEMS LIKE THEY'RE REALLY TRYING TO BE HELPFUL...
Sigh...
JUST BE CAREFUL NEXT TIME.
BEAM
OF COURSE!
SO THEY'RE MOVED BY KINDNESS...

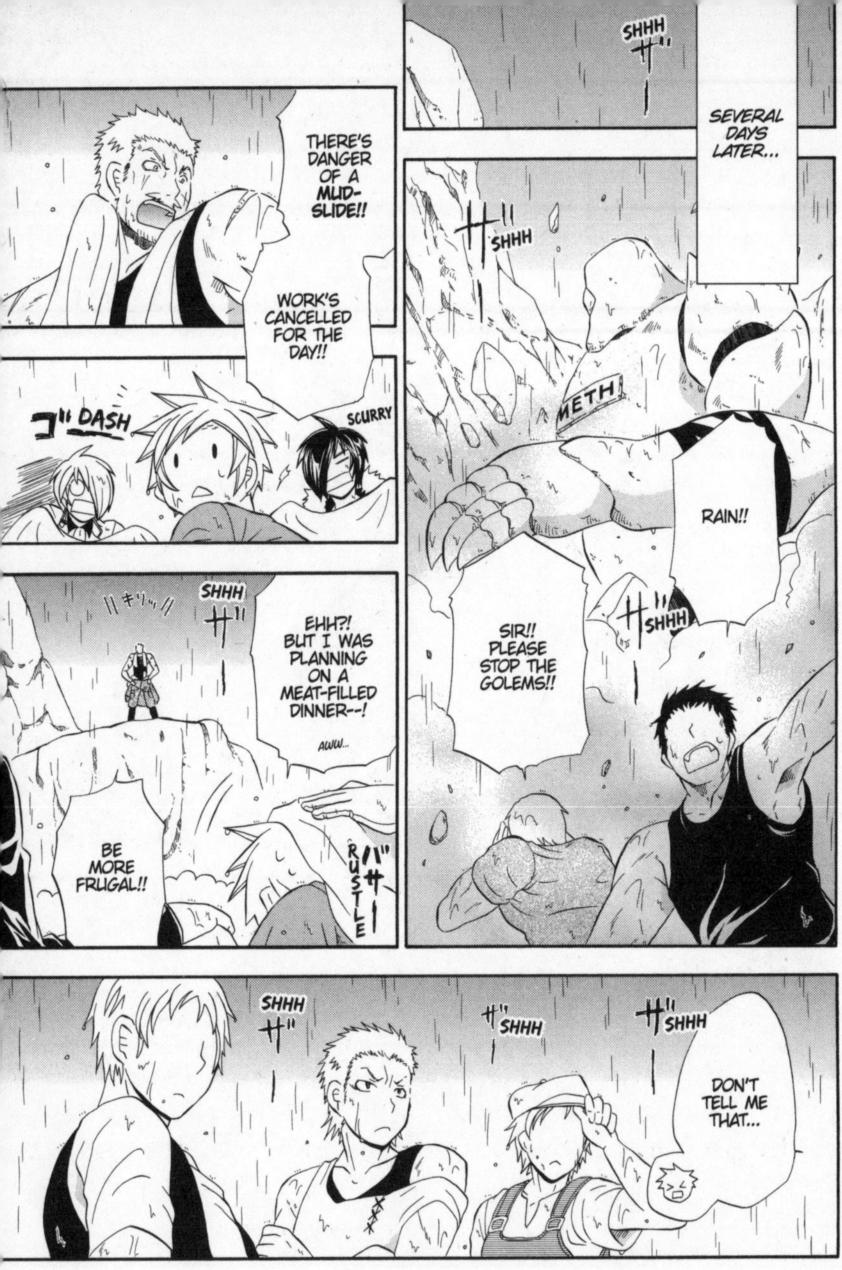
SHHH
ザ
SEVERAL DAYS LATER...
ザ SHHH
METH
RAIN!!
SIR!! PLEASE STOP THE GOLEMS!!
ザ SHHH
THERE'S DANGER OF A MUD-SLIDE!!
WORK'S CANCELLED FOR THE DAY!!
SCURRY
ゴ DASH
SHHH
ザ
キリッ
EHH?! BUT I WAS PLANNING ON A MEAT-FILLED DINNER--!
AWW...
RUSTLE
バサ
BE MORE FRUGAL!!
ザ SHHH
DON'T TELL ME THAT...
ザ SHHH
SHHH
ザ

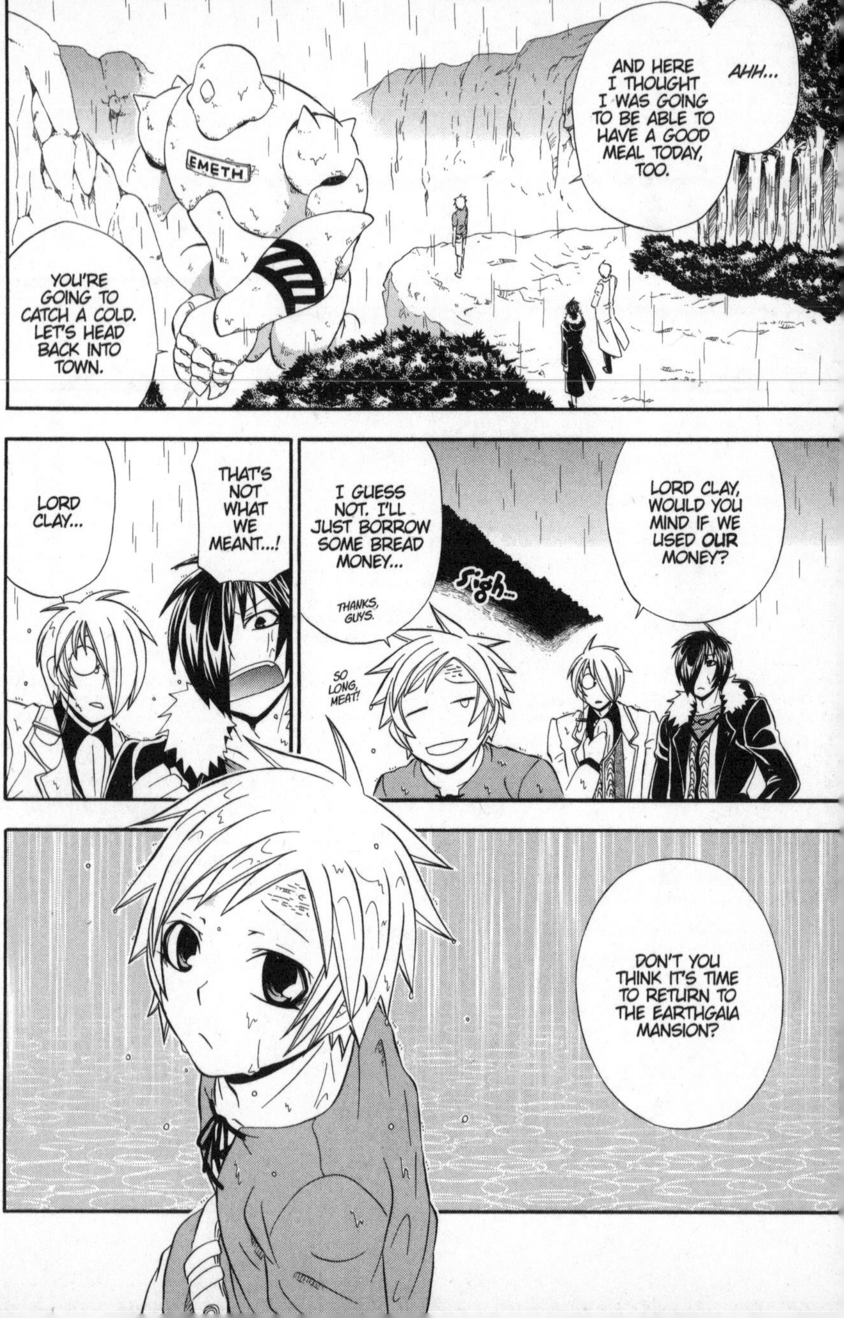
AHH...
AND HERE I THOUGHT I WAS GOING TO BE ABLE TO HAVE A GOOD MEAL TODAY, TOO.
EMETH
YOU'RE GOING TO CATCH A COLD. LET'S HEAD BACK INTO TOWN.
LORD CLAY, WOULD YOU MIND IF WE USED OUR MONEY?
Sigh...
I GUESS NOT. I'LL JUST BORROW SOME BREAD MONEY...
THANKS, GUYS.
SO LONG, MEAT!
THAT'S NOT WHAT WE MEANT...!
LORD CLAY...
DON'T YOU THINK IT'S TIME TO RETURN TO THE EARTHGAIA MANSION?

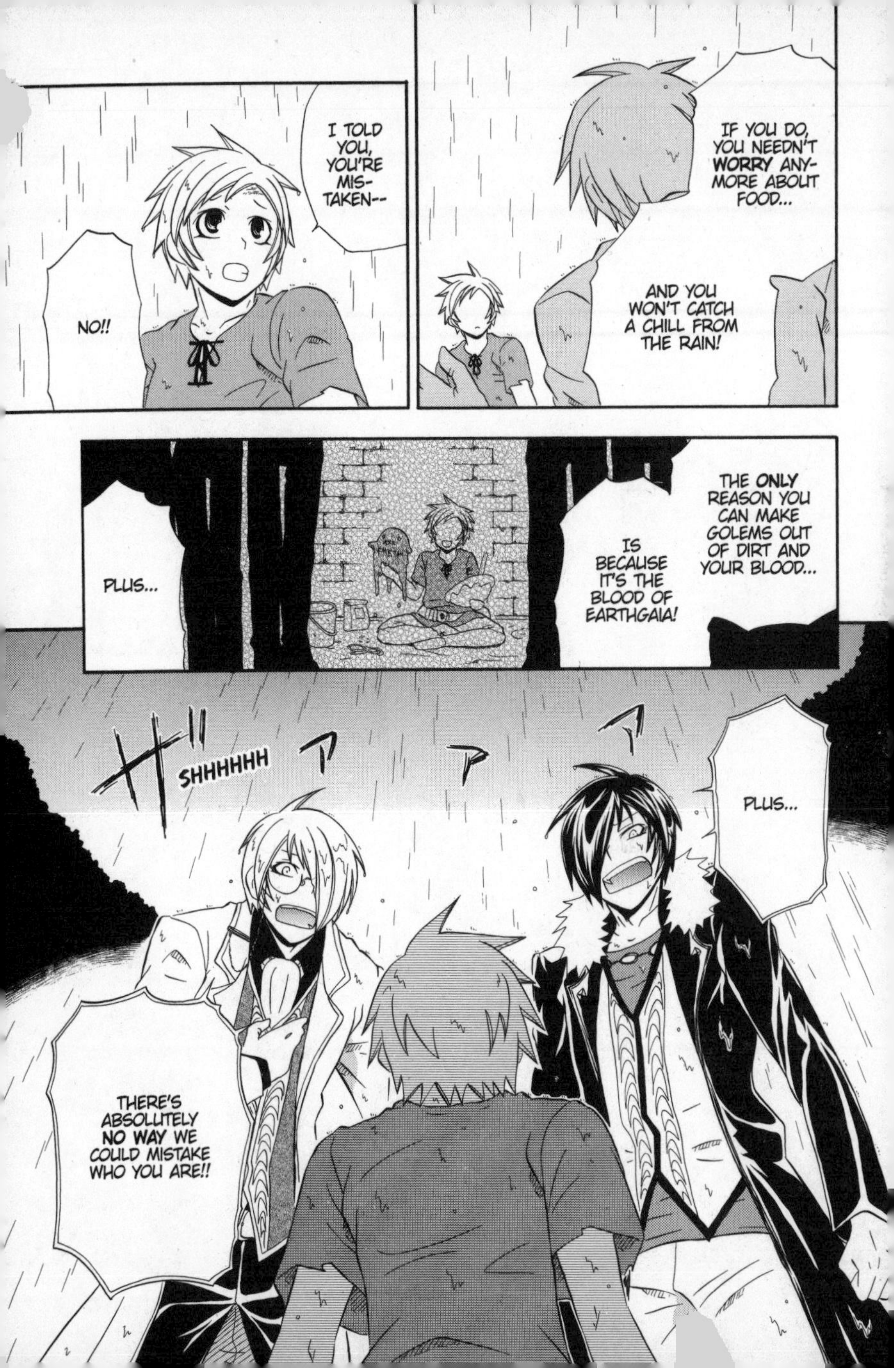
IF YOU DO, YOU NEEDN'T WORRY ANY-MORE ABOUT FOOD...
AND YOU WON'T CATCH A CHILL FROM THE RAIN!
I TOLD YOU, YOU'RE MIS-TAKEN--
NO!!
THE ONLY REASON YOU CAN MAKE GOLEMS OUT OF DIRT AND YOUR BLOOD...
IS BECAUSE IT'S THE BLOOD OF EARTHGAIA!
PLUS...
PLUS...
SHHHHHH
THERE'S ABSOLUTELY NO WAY WE COULD MISTAKE WHO YOU ARE!!

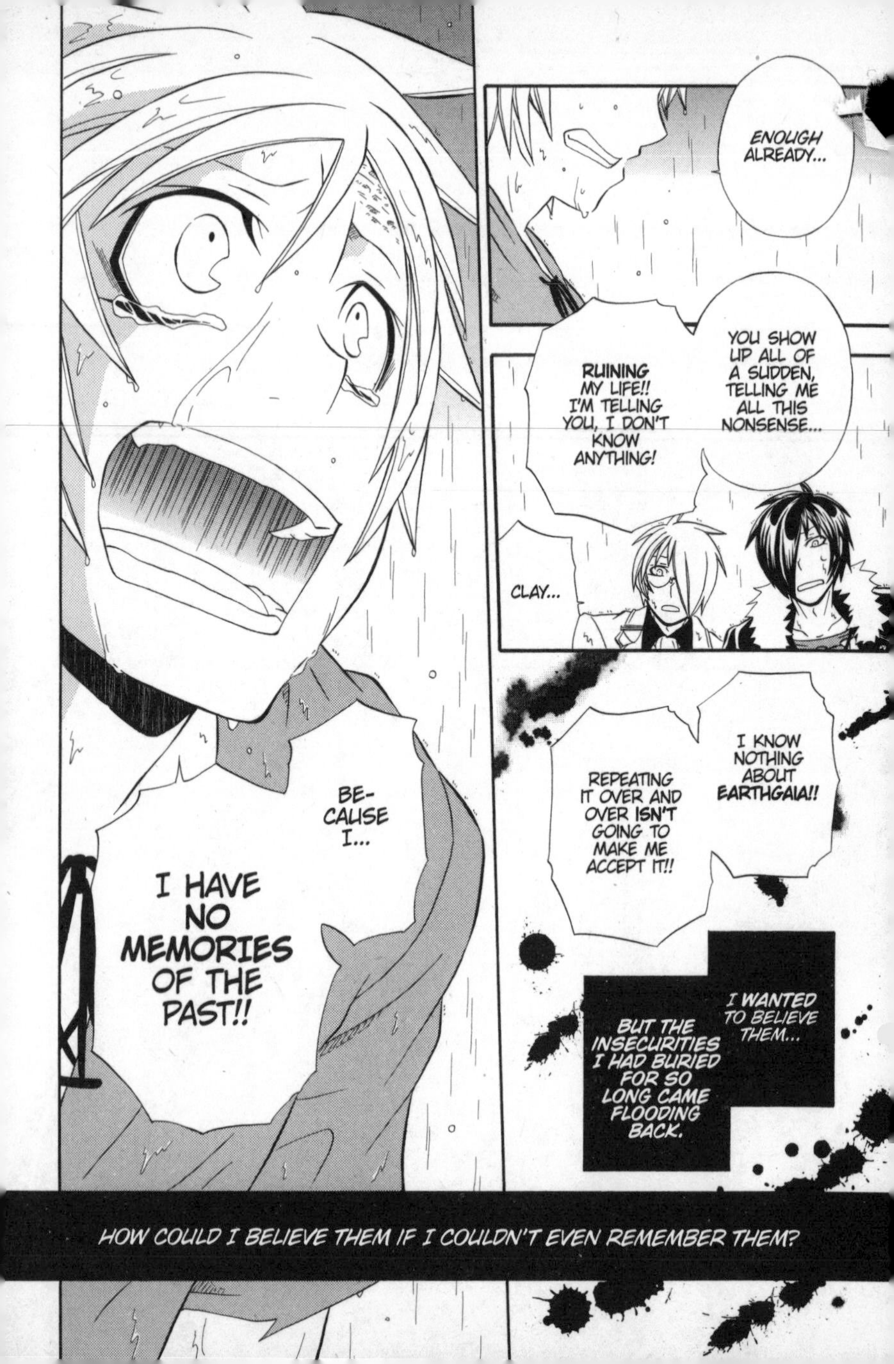
ENOUGH ALREADY...
YOU SHOW UP ALL OF A SUDDEN, TELLING ME ALL THIS NONSENSE...
RUINING MY LIFE!! I'M TELLING YOU, I DON'T KNOW ANYTHING!
CLAY...
I KNOW NOTHING ABOUT EARTHGAIA!!
REPEATING IT OVER AND OVER ISN'T GOING TO MAKE ME ACCEPT IT!!
I WANTED TO BELIEVE THEM...
BUT THE INSECURITIES I HAD BURIED FOR SO LONG CAME FLOODING BACK.
BE-CAUSE I...
I HAVE NO MEMORIES OF THE PAST!!
HOW COULD I BELIEVE THEM IF I COULDN'T EVEN REMEMBER THEM?

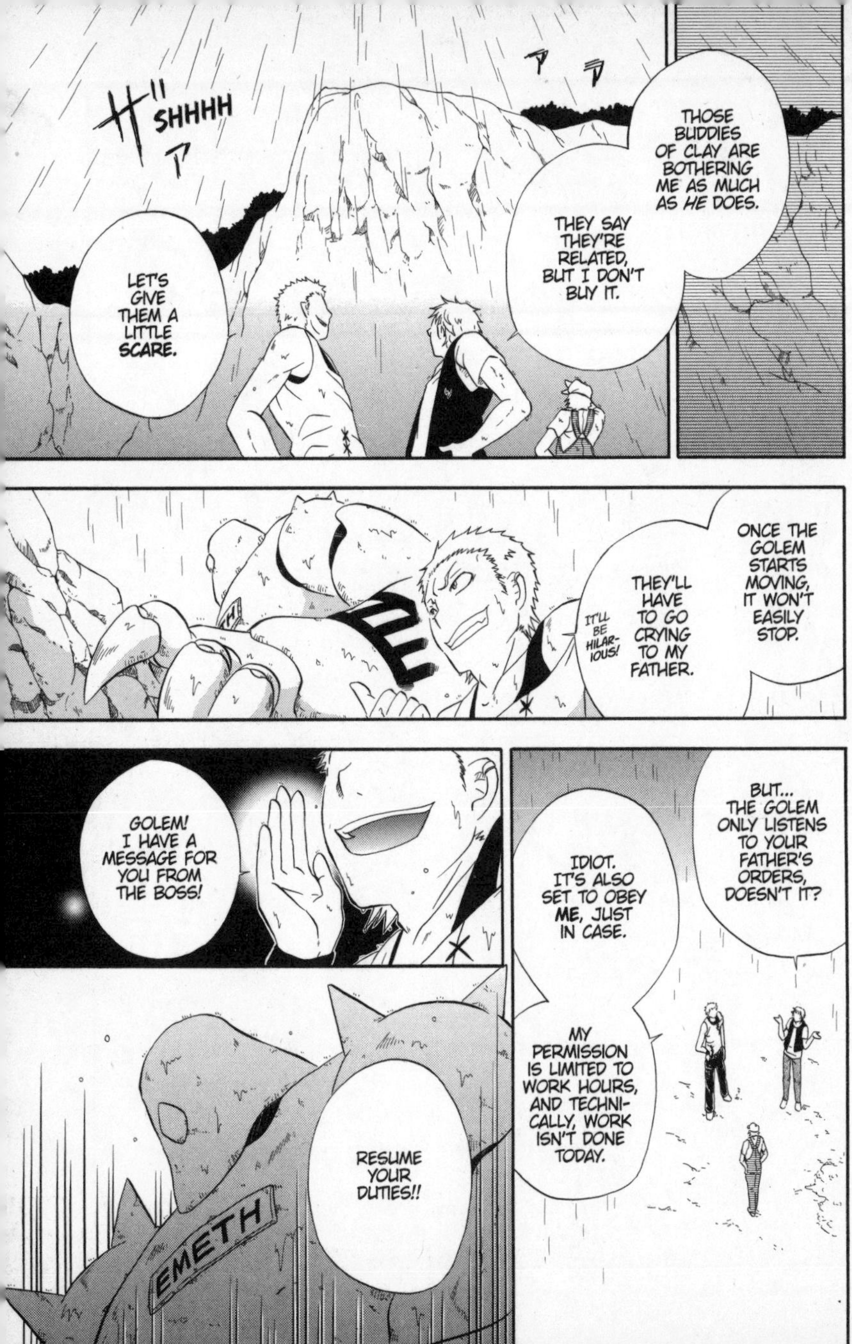
SHHHH
THOSE BUDDIES OF CLAY ARE BOTHERING ME AS MUCH AS *HE* DOES.
THEY SAY THEY'RE RELATED, BUT I DON'T BUY IT.
LET'S GIVE THEM A LITTLE SCARE.
ONCE THE GOLEM STARTS MOVING, IT WON'T EASILY STOP.
THEY'LL HAVE TO GO CRYING TO MY FATHER.
IT'LL BE HILAR-IOUS!
BUT... THE GOLEM ONLY LISTENS TO YOUR FATHER'S ORDERS, DOESN'T IT?
IDIOT. IT'S ALSO SET TO OBEY ME, JUST IN CASE.
MY PERMISSION IS LIMITED TO WORK HOURS, AND TECHNI-CALLY, WORK ISN'T DONE TODAY.
GOLEM! I HAVE A MESSAGE FOR YOU FROM THE BOSS!
RESUME YOUR DUTIES!!
EMETH

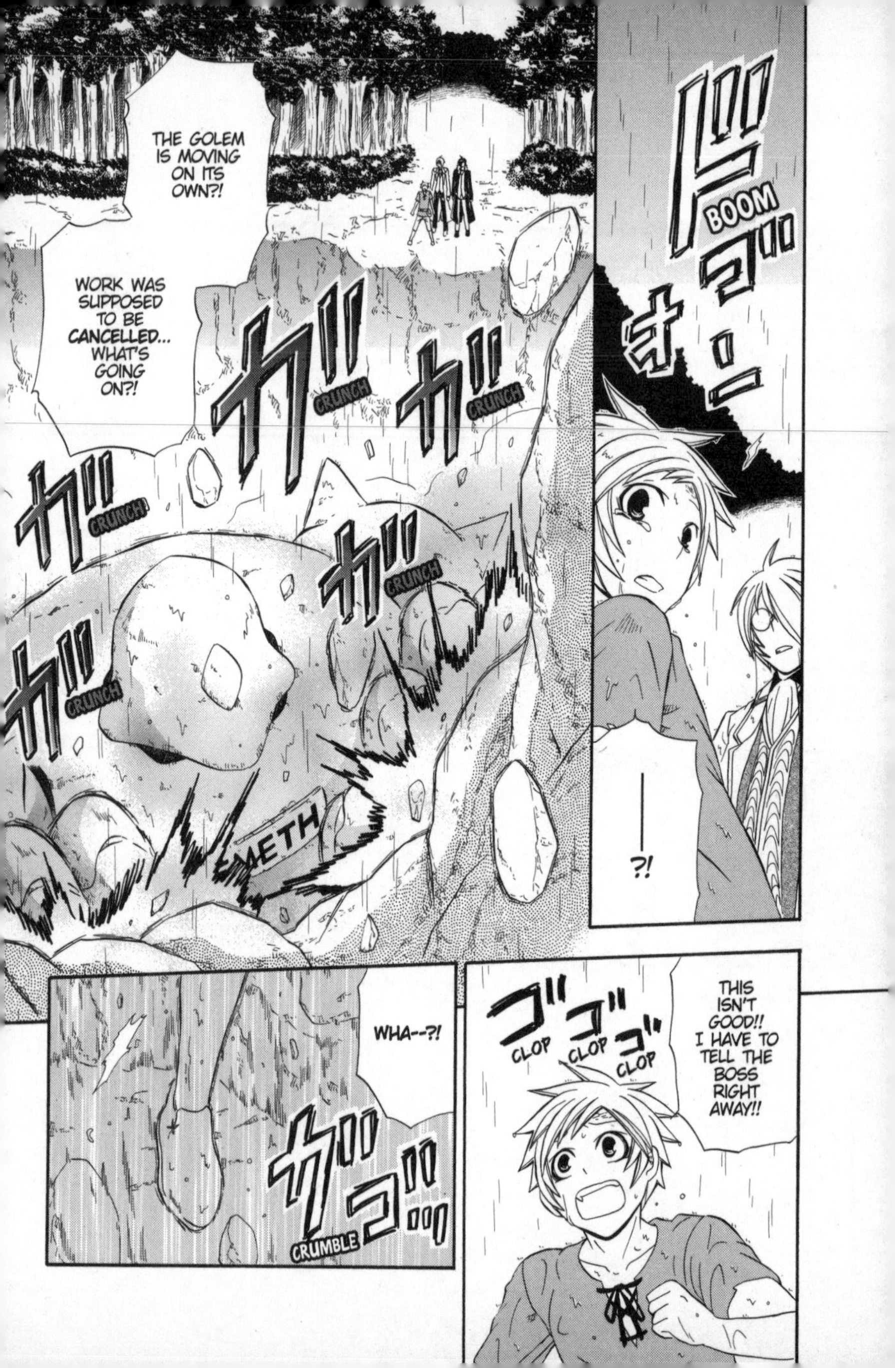
BOOM
?!
THE GOLEM IS MOVING ON ITS OWN?!
WORK WAS SUPPOSED TO BE CANCELLED... WHAT'S GOING ON?!
CRUNCH
CRUNCH
CRUNCH
CRUNCH
CRUNCH
METH
CLOP CLOP CLOP
THIS ISN'T GOOD!! I HAVE TO TELL THE BOSS RIGHT AWAY!!
WHA--?!
CRUMBLE

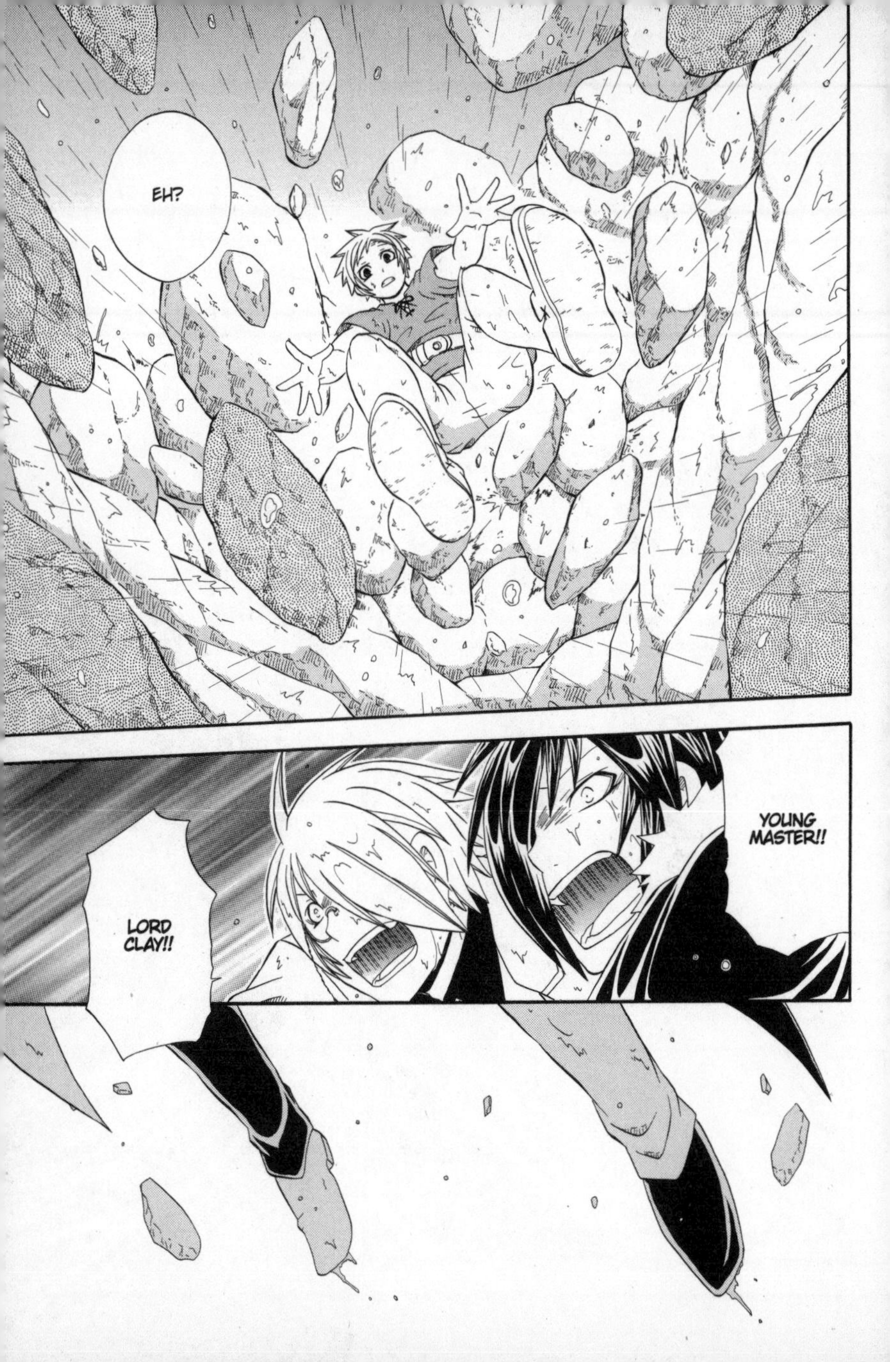
EH?
YOUNG MASTER!!
LORD CLAY!!

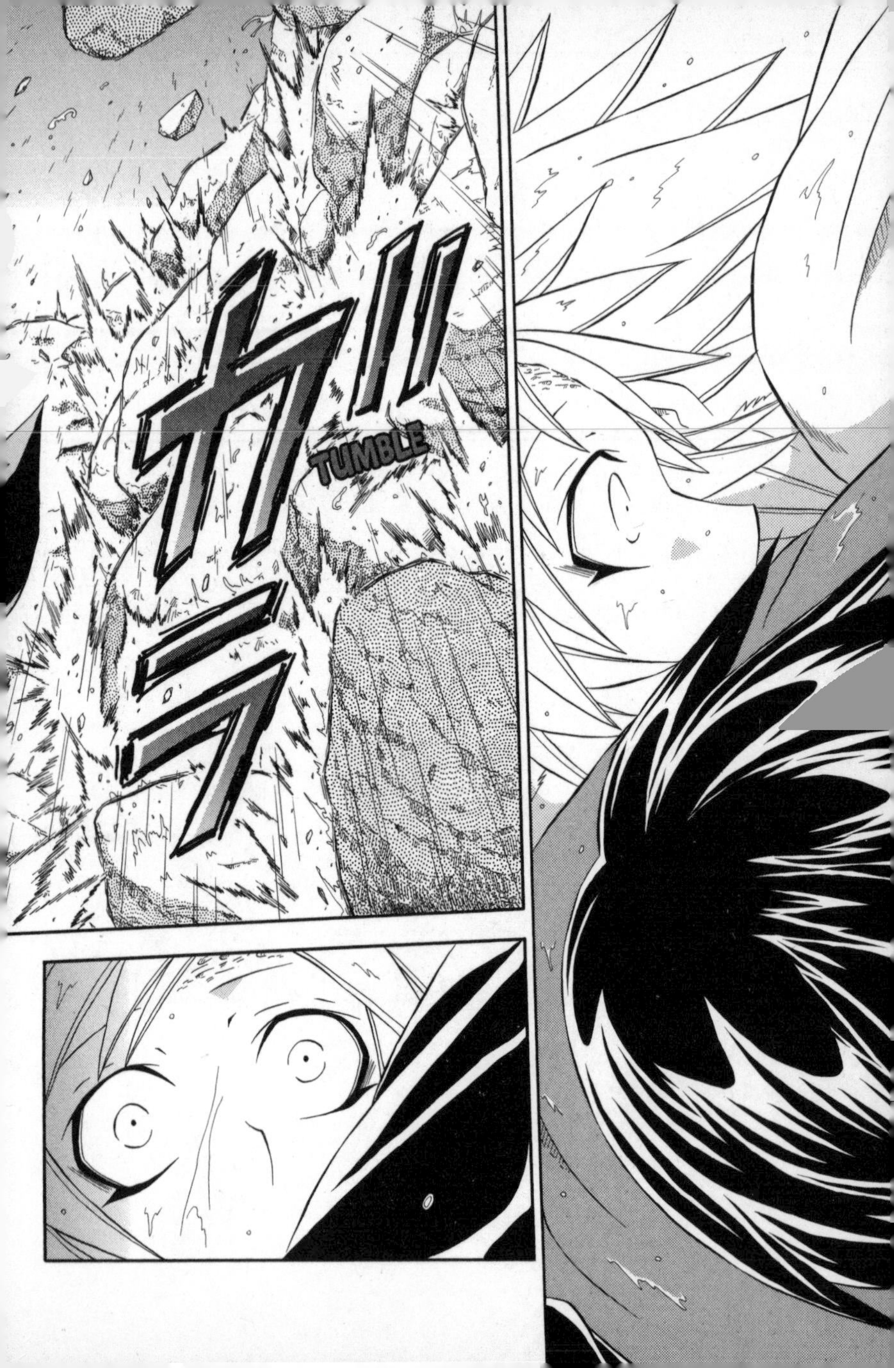
ガラ
TUMBLE

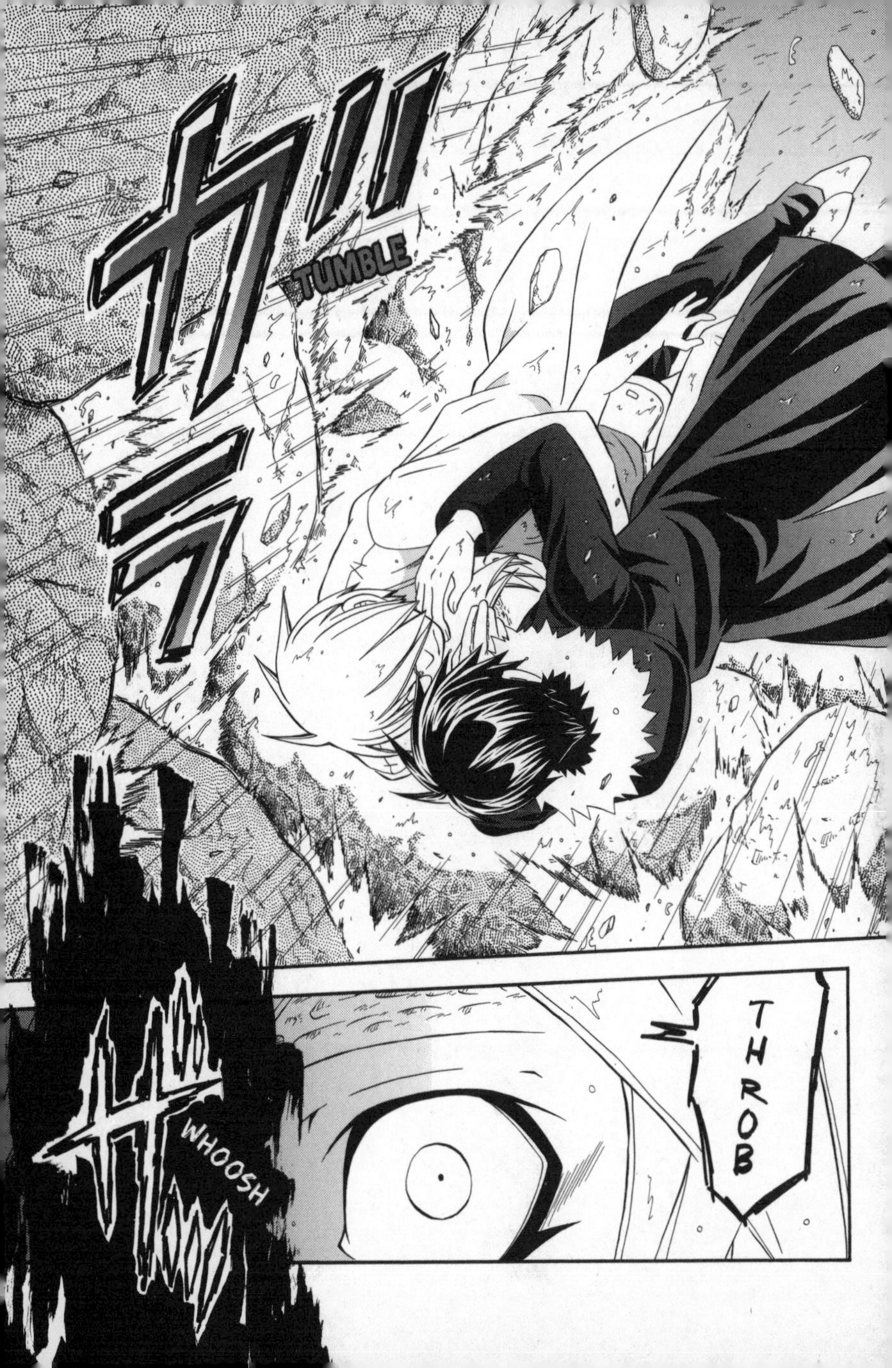
TUMBLE
THROB
WHOOSH

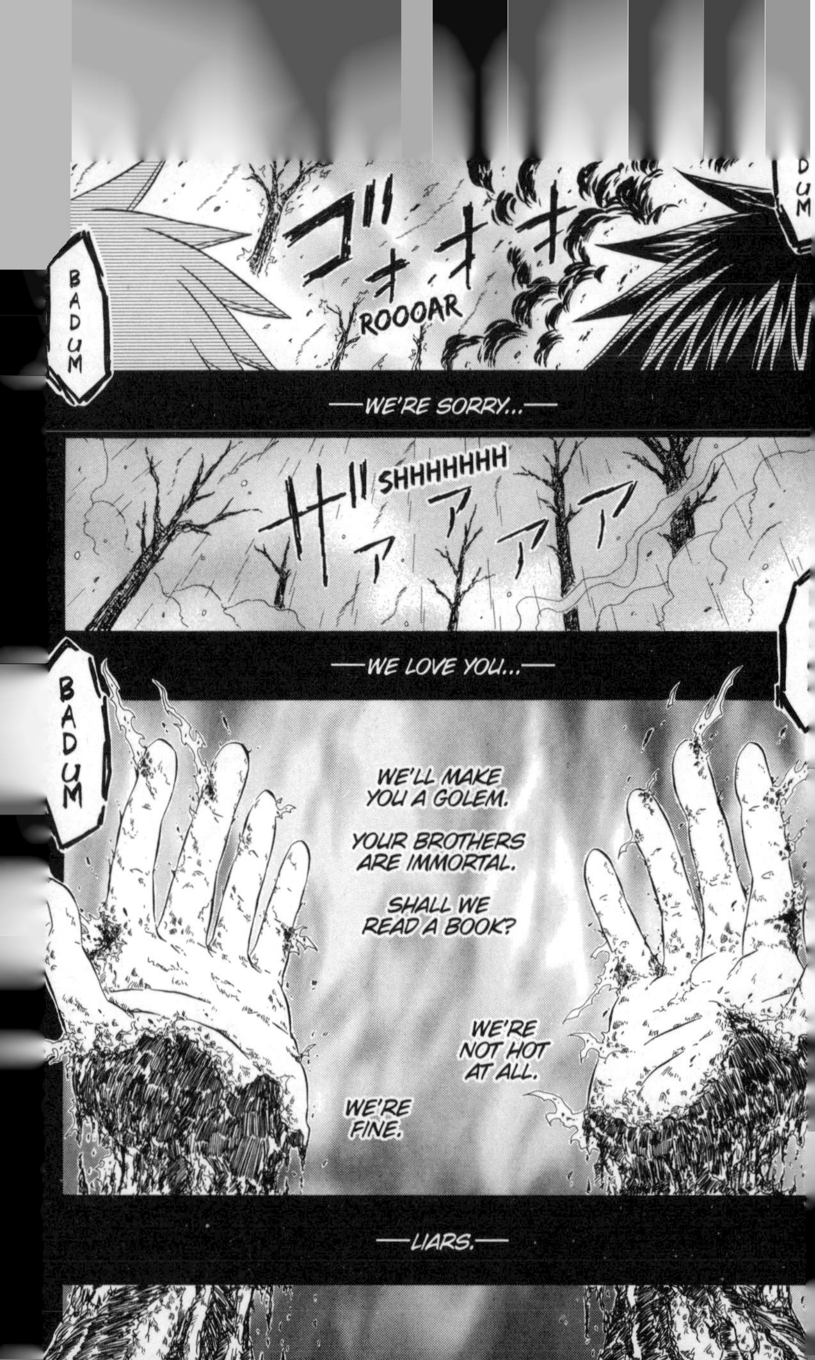
DUM
ゴォオオ
ROOOAR
BADUM
—WE'RE SORRY...—
ザァアアア
SHHHHHHH
—WE LOVE YOU...—
BADUM
WE'LL MAKE YOU A GOLEM.
YOUR BROTHERS ARE IMMORTAL.
SHALL WE READ A BOOK?
WE'RE NOT HOT AT ALL.
WE'RE FINE.
—LIARS.—

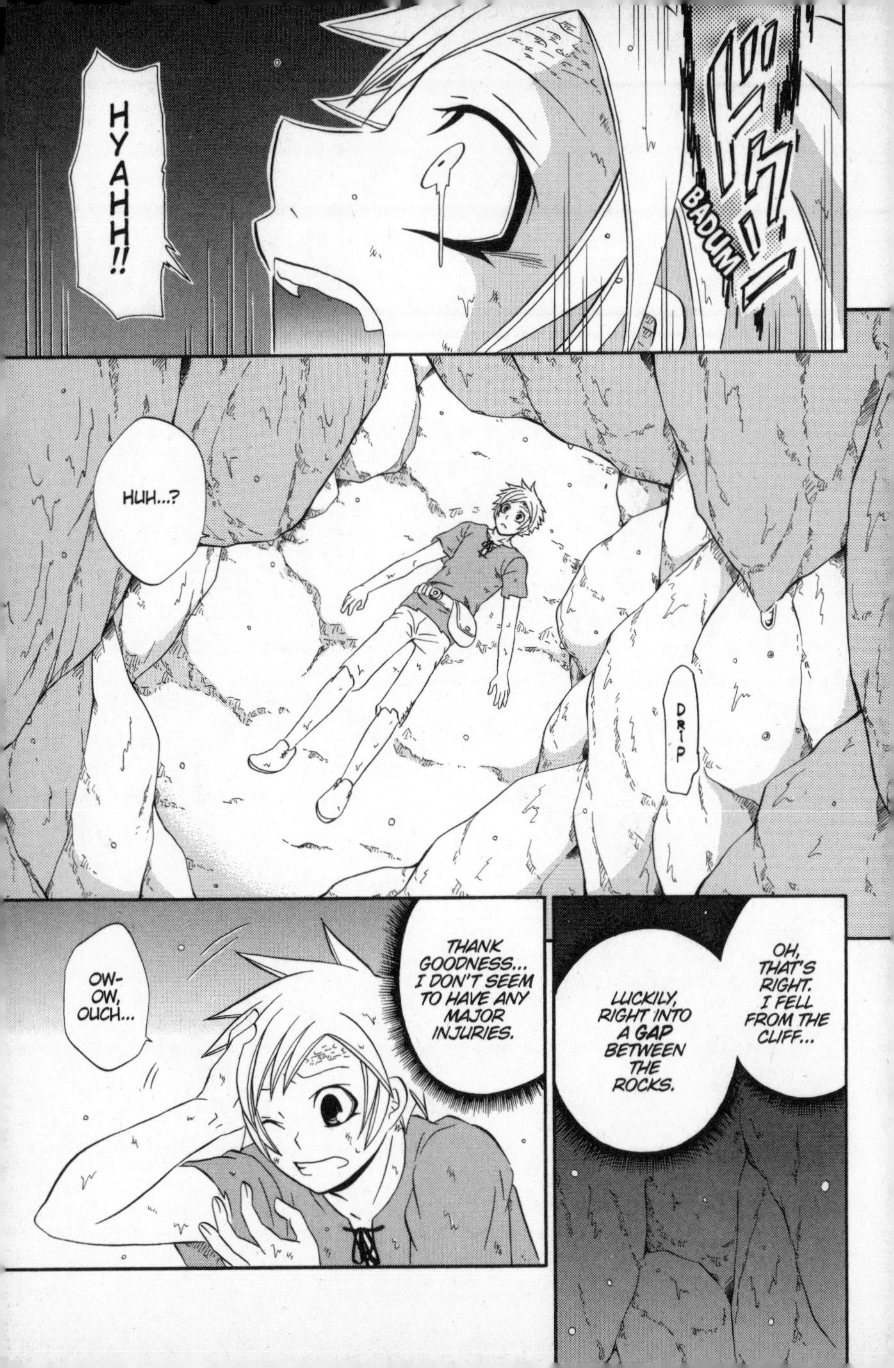
BADUM
HYAHH!!
HUH...?
DRIP
OH, THAT'S RIGHT. I FELL FROM THE CLIFF...
LUCKILY, RIGHT INTO A GAP BETWEEN THE ROCKS.
THANK GOODNESS... I DON'T SEEM TO HAVE ANY MAJOR INJURIES.
OW-OW, OUCH...

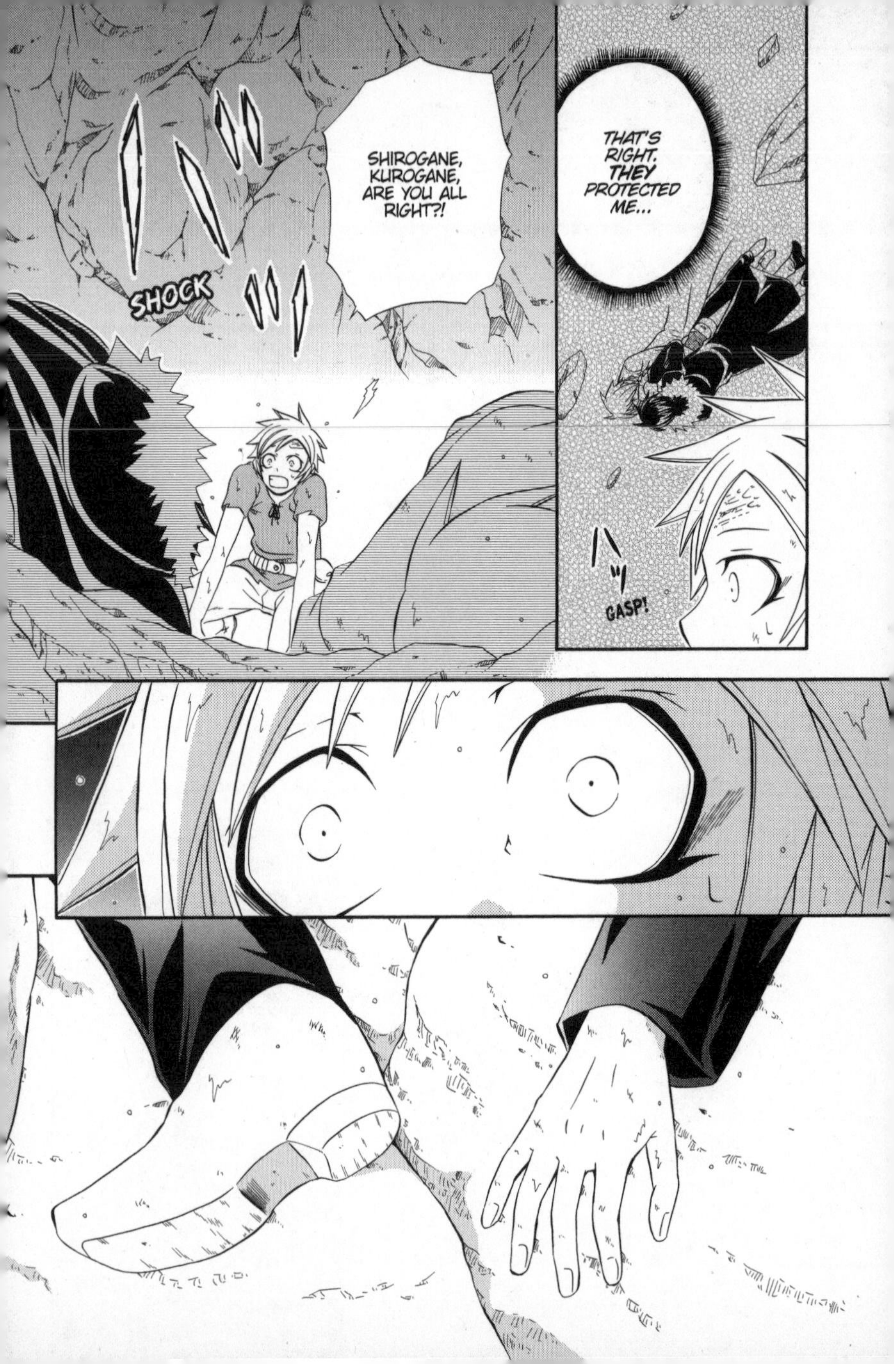
THAT'S RIGHT. THEY PROTECTED ME...
GASP!
SHIROGANE, KUROGANE, ARE YOU ALL RIGHT?!
SHOCK

KUROGANE... HIS ARM...

THAT LEG... SHIROGANE...!

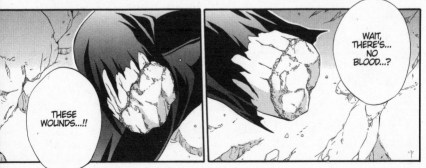

THESE WOUNDS...!!

WAIT, THERE'S... NO BLOOD...?

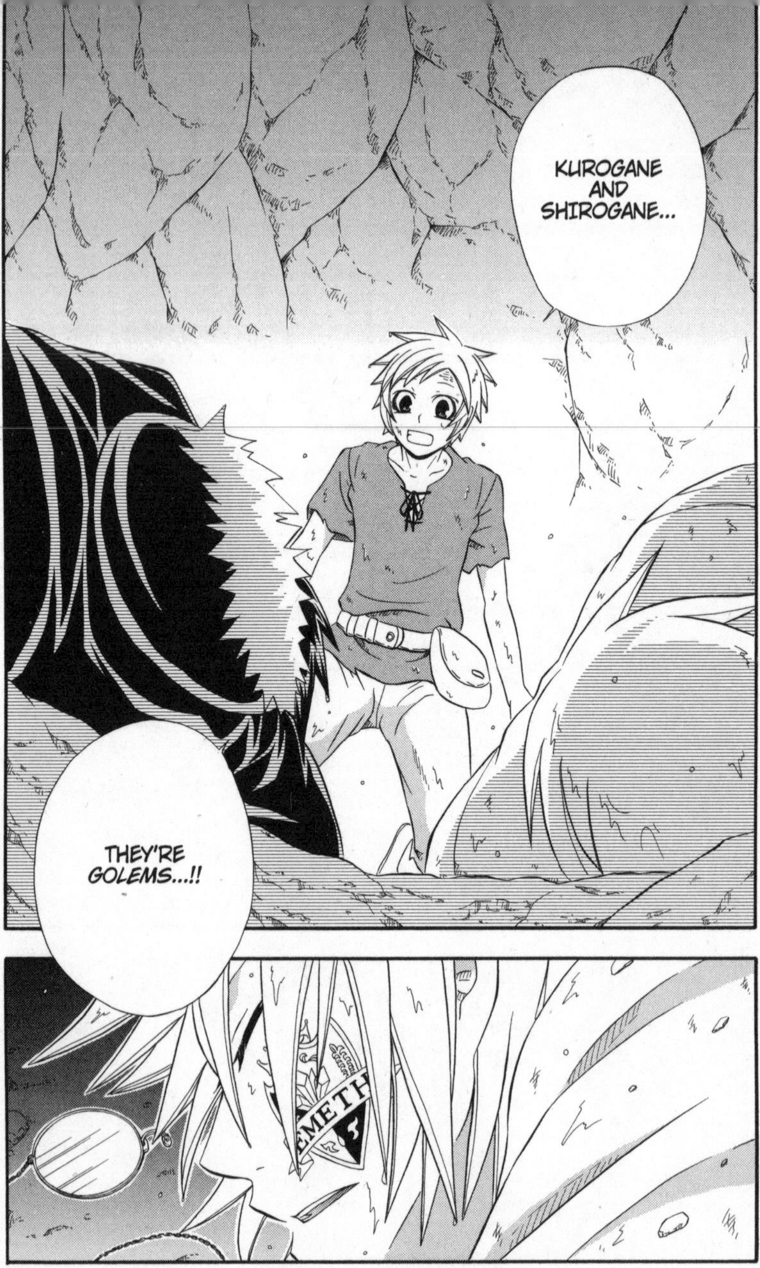
KUROGANE AND SHIROGANE...
THEY'RE GOLEMS...!!
EMETH

TO BE CONTINUED!

Afterword

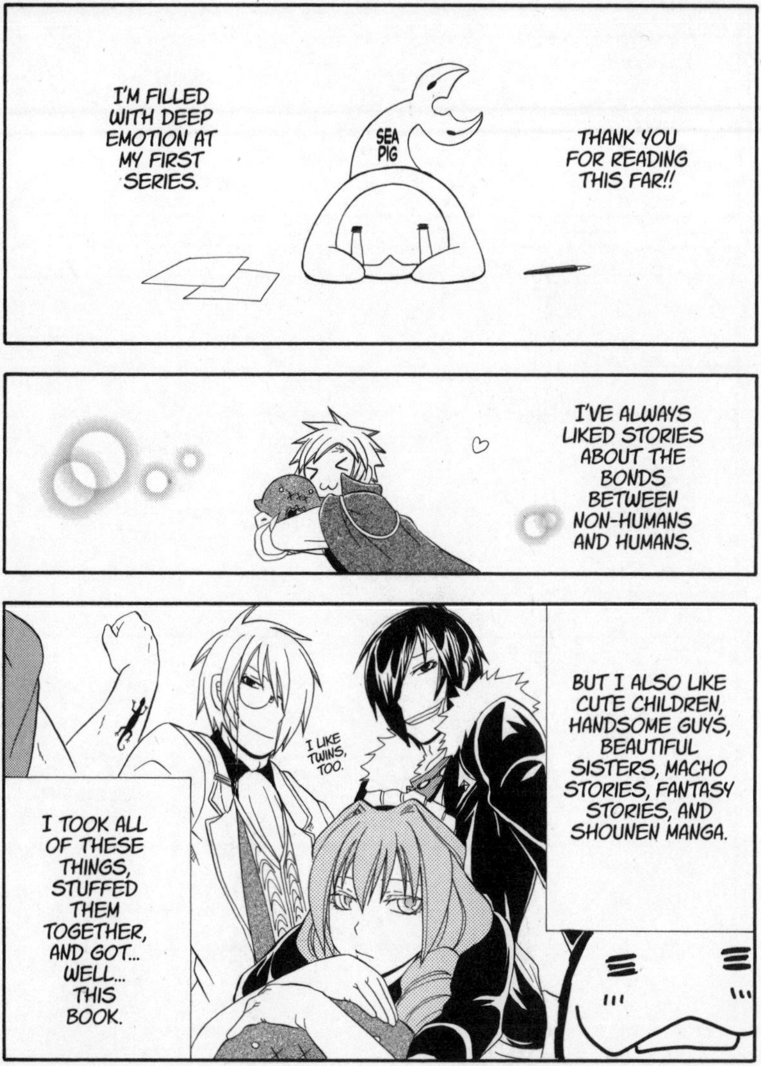
THANK YOU FOR READING THIS FAR!!
SEA PIG
I'M FILLED WITH DEEP EMOTION AT MY FIRST SERIES.
I'VE ALWAYS LIKED STORIES ABOUT THE BONDS BETWEEN NON-HUMANS AND HUMANS.
BUT I ALSO LIKE CUTE CHILDREN, HANDSOME GUYS, BEAUTIFUL SISTERS, MACHO STORIES, FANTASY STORIES, AND SHOUNEN MANGA.
I LIKE TWINS, TOO.
I TOOK ALL OF THESE THINGS, STUFFED THEM TOGETHER, AND GOT... WELL... THIS BOOK.

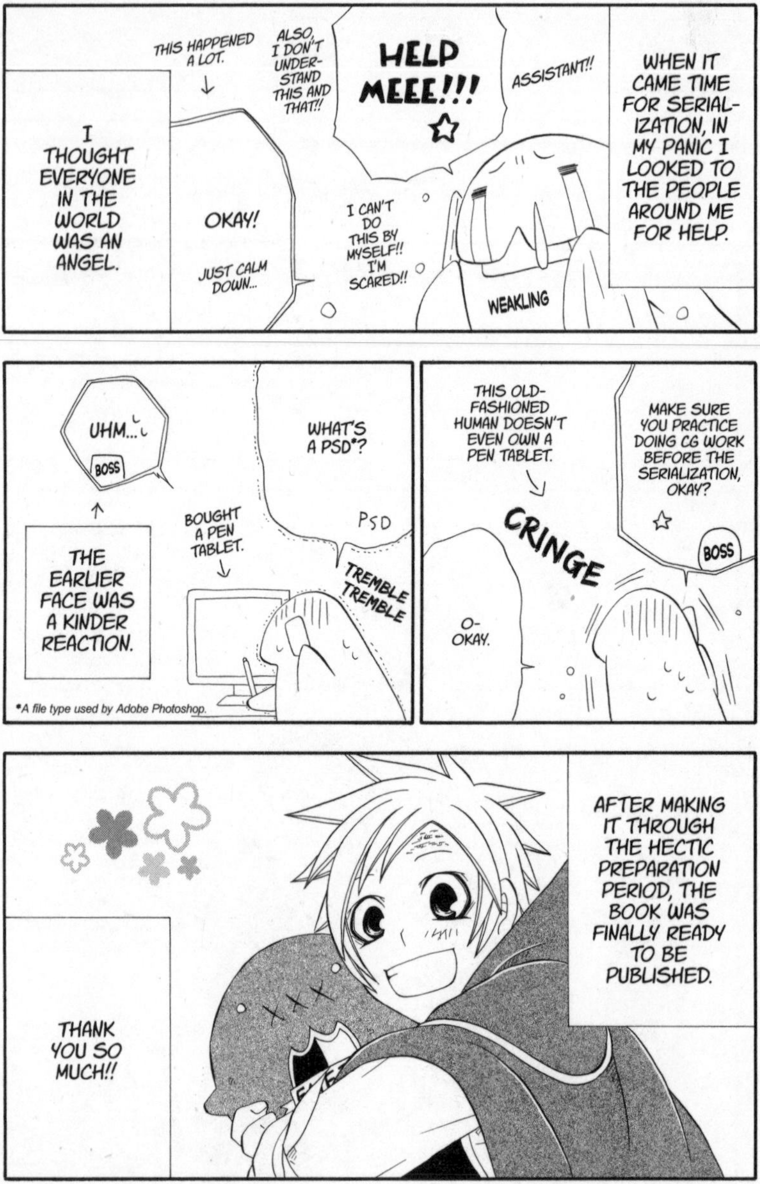
WHEN IT CAME TIME FOR SERIAL-IZATION, IN MY PANIC I LOOKED TO THE PEOPLE AROUND ME FOR HELP.
ASSISTANT!!
HELP MEEE!!! ☆
ALSO, I DON'T UNDER-STAND THIS AND THAT!!
THIS HAPPENED A LOT.
I CAN'T DO THIS BY MYSELF!! I'M SCARED!!
WEAKLING
OKAY!
JUST CALM DOWN...
I THOUGHT EVERYONE IN THE WORLD WAS AN ANGEL.
MAKE SURE YOU PRACTICE DOING CG WORK BEFORE THE SERIALIZATION, OKAY? ☆
BOSS
THIS OLD-FASHIONED HUMAN DOESN'T EVEN OWN A PEN TABLET.
CRINGE
O-OKAY.
WHAT'S A PSD*?
PSD
TREMBLE TREMBLE
BOUGHT A PEN TABLET.
UHM...
BOSS
THE EARLIER FACE WAS A KINDER REACTION.
AFTER MAKING IT THROUGH THE HECTIC PREPARATION PERIOD, THE BOOK WAS FINALLY READY TO BE PUBLISHED.
THANK YOU SO MUCH!!

*A file type used by Adobe Photoshop.

LASTLY, TO ALL OF THE PEOPLE WHO WORKED AND COLLABORATED ON THIS MANGA...
BOW
THANK YOU VERY VERY MUCH!!

Special ☆ Thanks

K. ABE-SAN

S. I-SAN

M. I-SAN

ITO-SAN

OKUYAMA-SAN

OYAMA-SAN

S. K-SAN

TOFU-SAN

SATO-SAN

SHISHIDO-SAN

MOMO-SAN

SUPERVISOR: AYAKO KIMIJIMA

AND YOU!!

Clay was alone with no memories and no family...

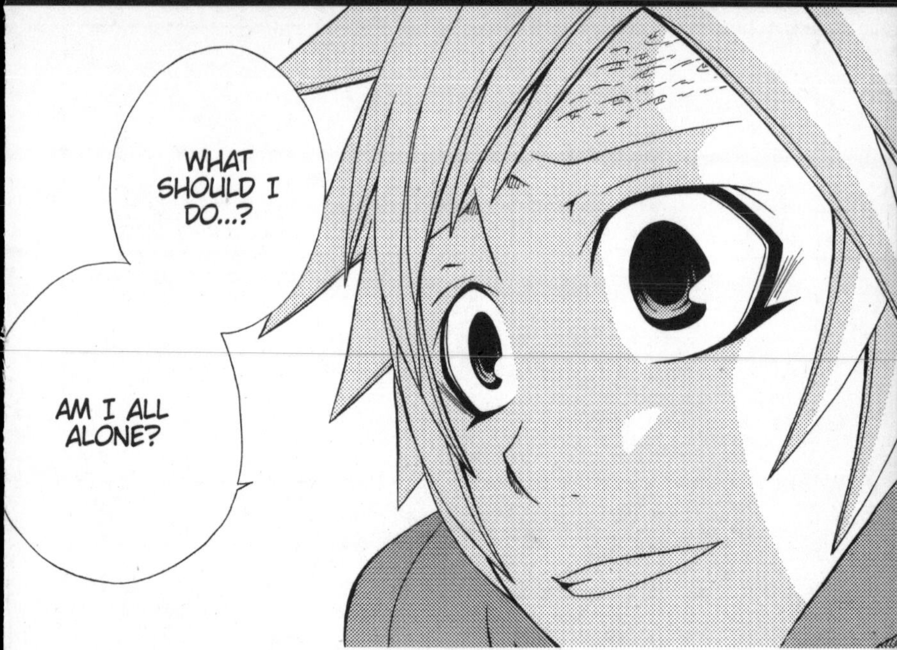
WHAT SHOULD I DO...?
AM I ALL ALONE?

but then, they appeared before him...

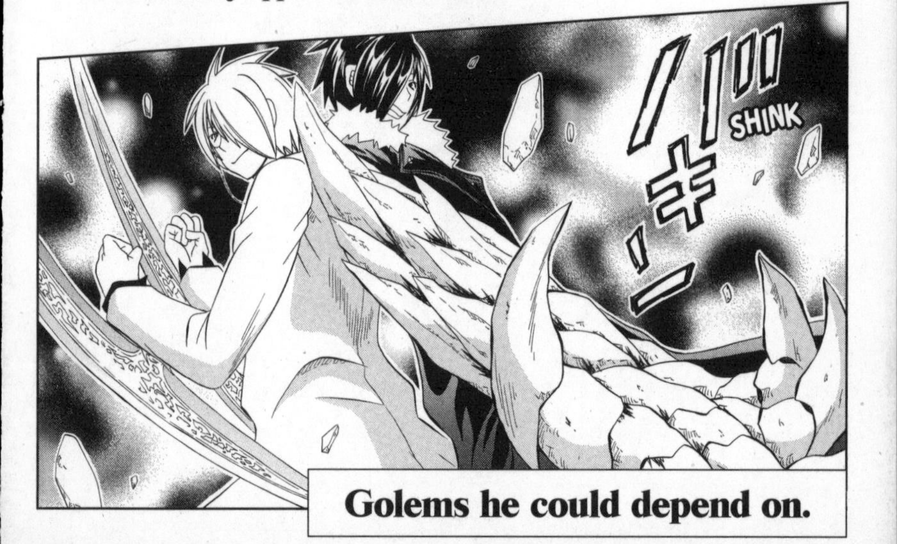
SHINK
Golems he could depend on.

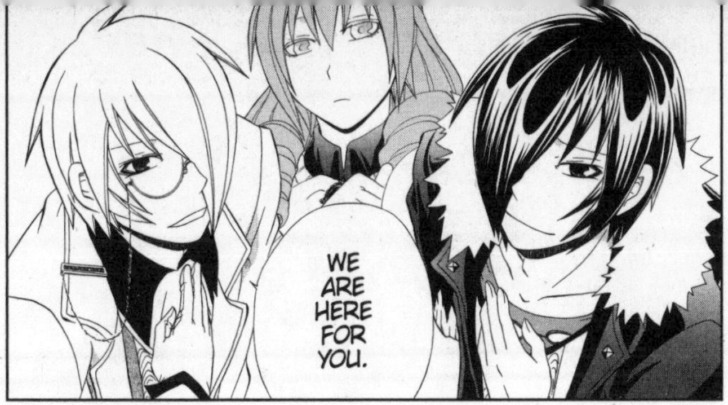
WE ARE HERE FOR YOU.

After joining a new family, Clay's happy memories begin.

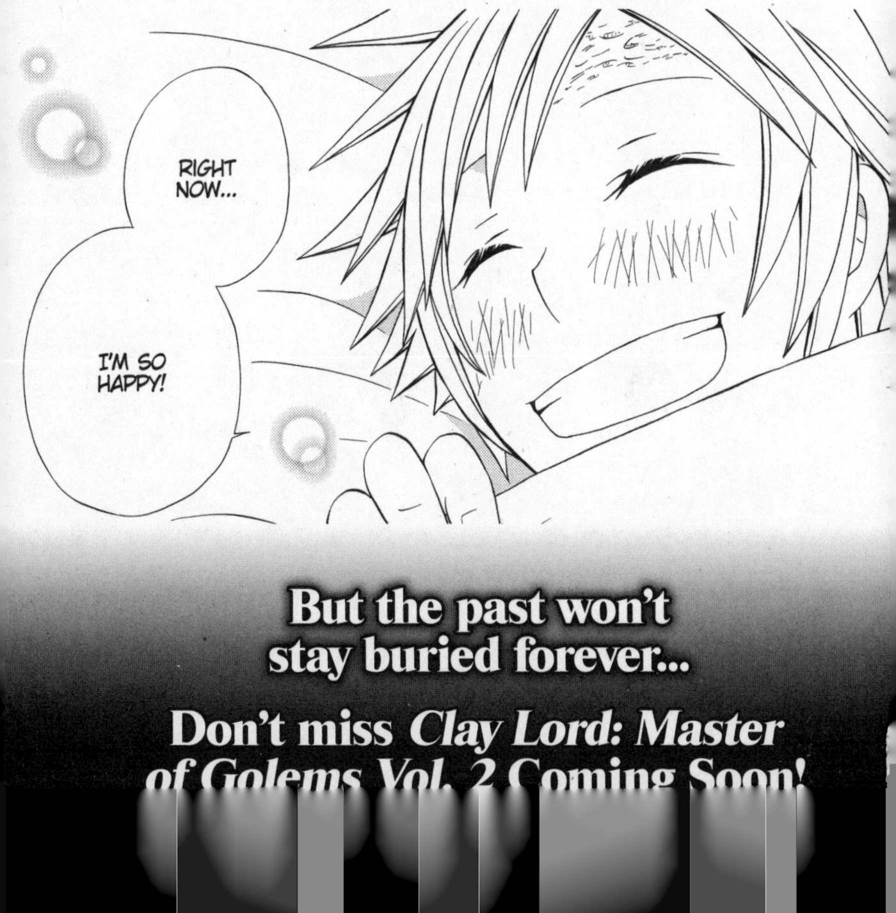
RIGHT NOW...
I'M SO HAPPY!

But the past won't stay buried forever...

Don't miss *Clay Lord: Master of Golems* Vol. 2 Coming Soon!